INTERVIEWING

INTERVIEWING

Principles and Practices

NINTH EDITION

Charles J. Stewart
Purdue University

William B. Cash, Jr.
National Louis University

Boston   Burr Ridge, IL   Dubuque, IA   Madison, WI   New York
San Francisco   St. Louis   Bangkok   Bogotá   Caracas   Lisbon   London   Madrid
Mexico City   Milan   New Delhi   Seoul   Singapore   Sydney   Taipei   Toronto

McGraw-Hill Higher Education

*A Division of The **McGraw-Hill** Companies*

1 2 3 4 5 6 7 8 9 0 DOC/DOC 9 0 9 8 7 6 5 4 3 2 1 0 9

ISBN 0-07-229718-2

Vice president/Editor-in-chief: *Thalia Dorwick*
Editorial director: *Phillip A. Butcher*
Sponsoring editor: *Marjorie Byers*
Developmental editor: *Jennie Katsaros*
Marketing manager: *Kelly May*
Project manager: *Christine A. Vaughan*
Senior production supervisor: *Lori Koetters*
Designer: *Kiera Cunningham*
Photo research coordinator: *Sharon Miller*
Supplement coordinator: *Matthew Perry*
Compositor: *GAC Indianapolis*
Typeface: *10/12 Times*
Printer: *R. R. Donnelley & Sons Company*

Library of Congress Cataloging-in-Publication Data
Stewart, Charles J.
    Interviewing: principles and practices / Charles J. Stewart,
  William B. Cash, Jr. — 9th ed.
        p. cm.
    Includes bibliographical references and index.
    ISBN 0-07-229718-2 (pbk.: alk. paper)
    1. Interviewing. 2. Employment interviewing. 3. Counseling.
  I. Cash, William B. II. Title.
  BF637.I5S75 1999
  158'.39—dc21   98-55406

http://www.mhhe.com

To Jane and Christine for their continuing patience and support.

PREFACE

This ninth edition of *Interviewing: Principles and Practices* continues to reflect the growing sophistication with which interviewing is being approached, the ever-expanding body of research in all types of interview settings, recent interpersonal communication theory, and the importance of equal opportunity laws on interviewing practices. We have made a concerted effort to include the latest research findings and developments throughout the text while continuing to maintain the emphasis on building interviewing skills for both interviewers and interviewees. The increasing diversification of the American workplace and the influences of the global village receive expanded treatment in several chapters. Each chapter includes new examples and illustrations, student activities, Internet exercises, and suggested resources. A new or revised interview at the end of each chapter gives students opportunities to apply theory and principles to a variety of realistic interviews. Chapters 5–11 are organized so they follow a natural sequence of stages in probing, survey, persuasive, employee selection, performance review, and counseling interviews.

A new Chapter 1 develops our definition of interviewing in more detail, identifies types of interviews, discusses the uses of interviewing, and addresses common criticisms of interviews. Students are introduced to the growing use of electronic interviews such as telephone interviews, conference calls, and video talk-back meetings. This chapter gives students a more thorough introduction to the nature, types, and uses of interviews to prepare them for the interviewing process discussed in Chapter 2.

Chapter 2 contains an expanded theoretical treatment of relationships in interviews, how perceptions affect relationships, the nature and development of relationships in other cultures and countries, and how women and men differ in their relationships. There is more emphasis on the importance of self-concept and self-esteem in interviews and how concepts such as self-image, self-esteem, and self-reliance differ in non-Western cultures that are collectivist rather than individualist. The discussion of the importance of self-disclosure in interviews incorporates politeness theory and notes how self-disclosure differs between sexes and among cultures. The nature and uses of verbal and nonverbal communication are expanded, and so are the discussions of language use and space according to age, sex, culture, and ethnicity. John Stewart's notion of dialogic listening is developed as listening for resolution and added to the traditional treatments of listening for comprehension, empathy, and evaluation. And the influence of outside forces on interview parties is discussed as an addition to the Cash-Stewart Model of Interviewing.

Chapter 3 emphasizes how verbal and nonverbal communication in openings and closings differs between males and females and how cultures other than Western ones regard handshaking, touching, and eye contact.

Chapter 4 discusses the apparent relevance of questions to interviewers and interviewees from other cultures. This chapter also addresses responses to questions that require personal disclosure and how men and women and those of differing cultures disclose information differently.

Chapter 5 on the probing interview focuses less on the journalistic interview to enhance the relevance of probing interviews to all students. It applies probing principles to interviews conducted by attorneys, police officers, recruiters, health care professionals, insurance claims investigators, teachers, and journalists.

Chapter 7 on the persuasive interview incorporates new discussions of several persuasion theories, including identification, balance or consistency, inoculation, forced or induced compliance, and psychological reactance. This chapter also addresses values differences in cultures and how cultures view time, bargaining, and relationship building. Cultures and genders differ with respect to socializing, small talk, and turn-taking during interviews.

Chapter 8 addresses the selection interview from the employer's perspective. It contains new discussions of the changing workplace and workforce, databases for locating skilled applicants, electronic systems for scanning resumes, quantitative tests to assess applicants, videotaping and video-conferencing, the behavior-based interview, nontraditional interviewing approaches, and on-the-job questions.

Chapter 9 addresses the selection interview from the applicant's perspective. It contains new discussions of the changing world of work, the reality of cultural diversity, organizational flattening, the 10 universal skills and attitudes essential for work in the twenty-first century, databases and Internet resources for searching for positions and learning about organizations, positions, and careers, and video- and teleconferencing for screening applicants. There are additional guidelines for preparing resumes and cover letters and new sample resumes, including a resume designed for electronic scanning.

Chapter 10 on performance review interviews introduces students to the 360-degree approach, which involves several observers of an employee's performance. Each evaluator is trained in behavioral observation, interviewing, and listening. This chapter also introduces students to the performance problem interview, which avoids the negative connotation and implication of guilt associated with the old discipline interview.

Chapter 12 on health care interviews discusses the effect of gender, age, ethnic group, and culture on the provider-patient relationship. It notes differences in information seeking, nonverbal interactions, and preference for verbal communication among differing cultures.

Some of the principles and guidelines presented in these 12 chapters may seem simple or obvious. However, in our experiences as professors, managers, practitioners, and consultants of interviewing in academic, professional, industrial, business, and social settings, we have found again and again that overlooking the simple and the obvious creates problems in real-life interviews.

We have included a sample interview at the end of each chapter, *not* as a perfect example of interviewing but to illustrate interviewing types, situations, approaches, and *mistakes* and to challenge students to distinguish between effective and ineffective interviewing practices. We believe that students can learn a great deal by applying the research and principles learned in a chapter to a realistic interview that allows them to detect when interview parties are right on target as well as when they miss the target completely. The role-playing cases at the ends of Chapters 5 through 12 provide students with opportunities to design and conduct practice interviews and to observe others' efforts to employ the principles discussed. Student activities at the end of each chapter provide ideas for in- and out-of-class exercises, experiences, and information gathering. The up-to-date resources at the end of each chapter will help students and instructors who are interested in delving more deeply into specific topics, theories, and types of interviews.

This book is designed for courses in such departments as speech, communication, journalism, business, supervision, education, political science, nursing, and social work. It is also useful in workshops in various fields. We believe this book is of value to beginning students as well as seasoned veterans because the principles, research, and techniques are changing rapidly in many fields. We have treated theory and research findings where applicable, but our primary concern is with principles and techniques that can be translated into immediate practice in and out of the classroom.

Resources for the Instructors

- A revised Instructor's Manual and Test Bank provides a wealth of sample interview assignments, a sample syllabus and optional units, critique forms, a field project assignment, and test items.

- A videotape, "Interviewing Practices," illustrates four types of interviews: probing, selection, persuasive, and performance. Students are challenged to answer questions posed by the narrator based on the concepts and principles in the text.

- A dedicated World Wide Web Site at http://www.mhhe.com/interview offers test review questions as well as up-to-date links to numerous sites with useful information and advice on job searches, a quick guide to conducting interviews, and journalistic, health-related, and sales interviewing.

We wish to express our gratitude to students at Purdue University and National Louis University–College of Management and to past and present colleagues and clients for their inspiration, suggestions, exercises, theories, criticism, and encouragement. We thank Fredric Jablin, Ralph Webb, Robert E. Smith, Suzanne Collins, Rebecca Parker, Mary Alice Baker, and Patrice Buzzanell for their resources, interest, and many suggestions. Special thanks are extended to Rebecca Parker of Western Illinois University for her valuable assistance with employment resumes; to Christina Holly, an undergraduate student at Purdue University, who provided valuable library research into the selection interview; and to Patti Jackson for her computer skills and support. We make a very special note of appreciation to the late W. Charles Redding for his assistance and encouragement since our first efforts to teach the principles and practices of interviewing.

CONTENTS

9 The Selection Interview: The Applicant   257

10 The Performance Interview   307

INTERVIEWING

An Introduction to Interviewing

By the time you decide to relax in the evening with a good book or to watch a favorite television program or video, you have taken part in a variety of interviews during the hours since the alarm awakened you too early in the morning. You probably did not interview for a new job, appear as a guest on the Oprah Winfrey show, or respond to questions from a reporter for the *Washington Post* or "60 Minutes." But think back over your day. Did you talk to a professor about an assignment? Did you ask a counselor for help with an academic problem? Did you sell your old computer? Did you give advice to a fellow worker about how to get along with a supervisor with an attitude? Did your roommate try to persuade you to attend a religious service next weekend? Each time you take part in interactions such as these, you are involved in an interview, perhaps the most common form of purposeful, planned communication. Unfortunately, in our everyday lives, we apply the word *interview* to a few formal settings in which we are only occasionally involved, usually the job interview.

Interviews range from formal to informal, highly structured to unstructured, sophisticated to simplistic, a few minutes to a few hours. Your purpose may be to give or get information, to counsel or receive counsel, to obtain a good position or recruit a good employee, to review or be reviewed, to persuade or be persuaded. You and the other party may be friends or antagonists, strangers or close acquaintances, superior or subordinate. But don't intimate interactions, conversations, speeches, small groups, and the mass media share many of these characteristics and purposes? Of course they do. What, then, is an interview, and how is it a unique form of communication? This chapter will provide a definition of the interview, explain each essential term in this definition, identify types of interviews, and discuss the uses of interviews.

The Interview Defined

An interview is an interactional communication process between two parties, at least one of whom has a predetermined and serious purpose, and usually involves the asking and answering of questions.

Interactional

The term *interactional* signifies an exchanging of roles, responsibilities, feelings, beliefs, motives, and information. If one party does all of the talking and the other does all of the listening, a *speech* to an audience of one, not an interview, is taking place.

Interactional does not mean equal, however. In some interviews, such as journalistic, counseling, and employee selection, an ideal ratio might be 70 percent to 30 percent, with the interviewee doing most of the talking. In others, such as information giving and sales, the ratio might be reversed. Interview parties often exchange roles of interviewer and interviewee as an interview progresses. For instance, if you ask questions about a new car or make a counteroffer, if you ask questions of a college recruiter, or if you ask a market survey taker to clarify a question or answer options, you assume the role of interviewer even though your primary role is interviewee. After the interviewer replies to your questions or counteroffer, he or she reassumes the role of interviewer.

Interactional also means a sharing of responsibilities during interviews. When we think of employment, informational, and health care interviews, we tend to focus on the responsibilities of one party—the applicant in the employment interview, the investigator or survey taker in the informational interview, and the physician or nurse in the health care interview. In reality, however, both parties are responsible for the success or failure of each interview. For example, the employer is responsible for studying the applicant's credentials, preparing insightful and challenging questions relevant for the position that is open, being up to date on information about the organization, and replying honestly and fully to the applicant's questions. On the other hand, the applicant is responsible for preparing thorough and honest credentials, researching the organization and position, responding honestly and fully to the employer's questions, and asking carefully phrased questions about the position and organization. One cannot expect assistance from a counselor or professor without disclosing information about a problem and both accepting and following up on the counsel received. It takes two to make an interview a success. This is why chapters in this book on specific types of interviews will address the roles of both interviewer and interviewee.

Interactional means a sharing of feelings (anger, pride, fear, sympathy), motives (security, popularity, belonging, ambition), and beliefs (social, political, religious, economic). Trenholm and Jensen define this process as "the act of creating and sharing meaning."[1] This creating and sharing comes from words and nonverbal signals—touches, hugs, punches on the arm, handshakes, and looks of concern—that express interest, concerns, and reactions. An interview is unlikely to be successful if either party withholds important feelings, motives, or beliefs. Imagine the outcome of an interview if I am afraid to tell you about my reasons for wanting a position, afraid to express my feelings about a proposal you are making that might affect my position in the company, or afraid to reveal religious beliefs that may be contrary to yours. Close interpersonal interchanges such as interviews involve risk that can be minimized but never eliminated, and if either party elects to "play it safe," the interview will fail.

Process

Process denotes a dynamic, ever-changing interaction, with many variables operating with and upon one another and a degree of system or structure. There is an energy in each interview that is generated by the parties and their desires to achieve goals. The interaction is never static, as changing roles, exchanging of information, and revelations of feelings and motives produce reactions and insights that lead into new and perhaps unexpected areas to explore. Although each interview is somewhat unique, all involve

photo by Bob Daemmrich/Stock Boston

■ *More than two people may be involved in an interview, but never more than two parties—an interviewer party and an interviewee party.*

basic communication ingredients such as perceptions, verbal and nonverbal messages, feedback, listening, motivation, expectations, and assumptions.

An abundance of recent research reveals how gender, age, and culture may affect the dynamics of the communication process and the outcome of an interview. An interview does not occur in isolation. It occurs at a specific time, in a specific place, and is preceded or followed by events that have impacts on it. Each participant brings a set of experiences, expectations, pressures, and personal limitations to the interview. As in many processes, once an interview begins, the participants "cannot not communicate."[2] They may communicate poorly during an interview and fail to get the help needed, select a poor employee, fail to give information correctly, or antagonize a client, but they will communicate something as long as they are in sight or sound of one another.

Two Parties

The term *two parties* signifies that interviews may involve two or more people (two recruiters interviewing an applicant, a reporter interviewing two students about their experiences with a sun-powered car, three friends discussing an apartment with a landlord, parents discussing their daughter with her teacher) but never more than *two parties*—an interviewer party and an interviewee party. If more than two parties are involved (a student, faculty member, and chair of the grade appeals committee discussing a possible grade change, or four members of a design team creating an advertising campaign), a small group interaction is occurring, not an interview.

Predetermined and Serious Purpose

The phrase *predetermined and serious purpose* means that at least one of the parties comes to an interview with a goal—other than mere enjoyment—and plans to focus on specific subject matter. The predetermined and serious purpose distinguishes the interview from social conversation, although conversation often plays important roles in interviews. And while conversations are rarely organized in advance, interviews must have a degree of advance planning and structure, even if you have little more than a purpose and topics jotted down on a piece of paper or a few questions in mind. Can you imagine going to a friend to borrow money or to a professor to discuss a grade without giving thought to how you will begin, the case you will present, the questions you will ask, how you will reply to answers, or what you will say if your request is rejected? On the other hand, can you imagine wanting to have lunch with a person who always plans conversations ahead of time, including topics, time allotted to each, and preferred outcomes? Most of us would avoid such a person like the proverbial plague.

Asking and Answering Questions

Asking and answering questions takes place in virtually all interviews. Some interviews, such as market surveys and journalistic interviews, consist entirely of questions and answers. Others, such as employment, counseling, and health care, include a mixture of questions and information giving. And still others, such as sales and training, involve occasional questions for strategic purposes. It is difficult to imagine an interview without questions because they are the tools interviewers and interviewees employ to obtain information, check the accuracy of messages sent and received, verify impressions and assumptions, and provoke feeling or thought. Most interviews are only as good as the questions asked and the answers received.

Types of Interviews
Now that you have an understanding of what an interview is and is not, let us examine a variety of interview types from a "situational schema" W. Charles Redding developed that arranges interviews according to their functions. Table 1.1 is an elaboration of Redding's schema. During the following discussion of interview types, it will become obvious that you are involved in interviews far more often than you believe.

Information Giving

Information giving interviews include those in which the primary function is giving information, data, direction, instruction, orientation, or clarification. You rely upon interviews to orient new employees, students, and members of organizations or to train, instruct, or coach people in specific behaviors necessary for performing work tasks, playing games, counseling others, or developing skills. For instance, you may explain to a new employee how working hours are determined in the restaurant where you work, residence hall policies to incoming students, procedures for appealing a grade, or how to develop an effective resume for internships. You may train a roommate to use a new computer, a student taking part in a phone-a-thon to avoid quick hang-ups, or a friend to play golf. Job-related instructions are critical daily interviews in organizations. For instance, outgoing shifts of nurses, police officers, and production crews must relay to incoming shifts accurate and complete information about the status of patients, criminal investigations, and products. Chapter 12 on the health care interview discusses the causes for loss and distortion of information and effective ways to exchange information through interviews.

Information Gathering

Information gathering interviews include those in which the primary function is to obtain facts, opinions, data, feelings, attitudes, beliefs, reactions, and feedback. For instance, organizations use surveys and polls to determine reasons for actions, trends in beliefs, attitudes toward political candidates and new products, the effects of advertising

Table 1.1   *Types of interviews*

1. Information giving
   a. Orientation
   b. Training, instruction, coaching
   c. Job-related instructions
   d. Briefings

2. Information gathering
   a. Surveys and polls
   b. Exit interviews
   c. Research interviews
   d. Investigations: insurance, police, etc.
   e. Medical, psychological, case history, diagnostic, caseworker, etc.
   f. Journalistic

3. Selection
   a. Screening
   b. Determinate
   c. Placement

4. Problems of interviewee's behavior
   a. Appraisal, evaluative, review
   b. Separation, firing
   c. Correction, discipline, reprimand
   d. Counseling

5. Problems of interviewer's behavior
   a. Receiving complaints
   b. Grievances
   c. Receiving suggestions

6. Problem solving
   a. Discussing mutually shared problems
   b. Receiving suggestions for solutions

7. Persuasion
   a. Selling products and services
   b. Recruiting members
   c. Fund-raising and development
   d. Changing the way a party feels, thinks, or acts

campaigns, habits of television viewers and radio listeners, and voting intentions. Employers use exit interviews to discover why employees are leaving positions for ones with other organizations and what steps might be taken to retain quality employees. College students, professors, and others use interviews in their research projects. As a student, you use interviews to obtain clarification of assignments or portions of readings, learn how best to prepare for examinations, and discover why a paper received a grade of C instead of A. Journalists, police officers, and insurance claims adjusters use investigative interviews to determine causes of crimes and accidents and who might be responsible. Counselors and health care providers use interviews to diagnose learning, psychological, and medical problems and to propose possible solutions. Historians use interviews with veterans, actors, former American presidents, survivors of disasters, baseball players, industrialists, and college alumni to create oral histories to aid future historians in their understanding of events, people, administrations, and organizations. Charter 5 on the probing interview, Chapter 6 on the survey interview, and Chapter 12 on the health care interview discuss ways to gather information effectively in a variety of interview settings.

Selection

Selection interviews include those in which the primary function of one party is to screen, select, and place job applicants, employees, and members of organizations and that of the other party is to screen and select positions or memberships. Recruiters for all types of organizations (companies, fraternities and sororities, the military, social organizations, religious groups) employ *screening interviews*. The typical campus interview at the placement center designed to reduce the number of applicants by weeding out those who do not meet basic qualifications is a screening interview. An Air Force recruiter, for instance, will talk to all interested applicants but select a small number for further interviews and testing. Applicants take part in screening interviews to determine which ones meet their basic criteria for joining. A person interested in a military career may interview recruiters from the Navy, Coast Guard, Marines, Army, and Air Force to decide which one or ones to pursue further. Organizations use *determinate interviews* (what you may call a "plant trip") to decide whether a select group of applicants, perhaps a single applicant, will be hired, admitted to membership, sent to officer candidate school, or baptized. Applicants take part in determinate interviews to decide whether or not to accept an offer of a position or membership.

Organizations use *transfer* or *placement interviews* to promote members, assign them to positions, or move them from one assignment or location to another. All selection interviews are designed to assess either the education, training, experiences, abilities, and personal characteristics of applicants or the organizational characteristics, nature of a position, location, benefits, and potential for advancement to determine if the position or applicant is the best fit. Chapter 8 addresses the employer in the selection interview, and Chapter 9 addresses the applicant in the selection interview.

Problems of Interviewee's Behavior

In interviews concerning problems of interviewee's behavior, the primary function is to perceive accurately a person's behavior, problem, or performance with the goal of helping this person to see its nature, causes, effects, and possible solutions. For instance, employers use performance review interviews primarily to motivate employees to continue excellent performance or to improve average or poor performance, and secondarily to assess training needs, enhance communication, strengthen staff relationships, and create a positive atmosphere and working environment. Interviewees hope to get feedback and guidance and have the opportunity to give input about their performances, future with the organization, and goals for the next review period. Schools, corporations, churches, and professional associations use interviews to reprimand and discipline, to correct behavior, and to fire or expel individuals if performance or behavior is severe or seems incorrectable.

Many professions such as medicine, law, and consulting have established ethical codes to govern the professional behavior of members. Violations of these codes may result in censure, penalties, or expulsion. Academic counselors, placement counselors, psychologists, psychiatrists, and lay counselors, such as parents, teachers, and colleagues, use interviews to help patients, clients, students, married couples, and friends understand and alleviate personal problems ranging from learning disabilities, substance abuse, and psychological phobias, to poor grades, spotty attendance, negative attitudes, and low self-esteem. Chapter 10 on the performance interview, Chapter 11 on the counseling interview, and Chapter 12 on the health care interview discuss interviewing principles that deal with problems of the interviewee's behavior.

Problems of the Interviewer's Behavior

In interviews concerning problems of the interviewer's behavior, the primary function is for the interviewer to receive complaints, grievances, or suggestions and to work out solutions acceptable to both parties. Interviews in this category are customer complaints (about service, products, or billing), student complaints (about grades, assignments, instructor comments made during class, and counseling), employee grievances (about unfair treatment, inadequate raises, poor working conditions, or harassment because of sex, age, race, and ethnicity), and patient complaints (about medical costs, type or result of treatment, poor communication with a provider, and insurance coverage).

Complaints may be informal customer or employee gripes or formal grievances filed through a grade appeals committee, labor union, or consumer protection agency. The complaint may be directly against an owner, professor, department head, or physician or against the person's manufacturing company, department, university, or medical center. In this second situation, the interviewer may act as the manufacturer's representative, manager of customer relations, dean, university public relations director, or medical center administrator who must attempt to resolve the complaint. Chapter 10 on the performance review interview and Chapter 12 on the health care interview address situations in which the interviewer's behavior is at issue.

Problem Solving

Problem-solving interviews are those designed to analyze and resolve a problem of concern to both interviewer and interviewee. In some instances, the roles of interviewer and interviewee are equally shared for most of the interview. The problems addressed are not personal problems of either party but genuinely shared concerns or problems both parties wish to explore and resolve. For instance, two members of an organization, often with one being a superior to the other, may meet to discuss campus housing, the loss of a client, a computer software need, a research project, the hiring of a new staff member, or a decline in sales. Success of the interview is determined by how the problem is solved, not by who came up with the best proposal or solution.

Persuasion

Persuasion interviews include those in which the primary function is to change the interviewee's ways of thinking, feeling, or acting. Too often we think of the persuasive interview as only a sales transaction, and we do use persuasive interviews to purchase or sell tickets, trucks, suits and dresses, houses, computer hardware and software, insurance, magazine subscriptions, and services ranging from painting houses for college expenses to investing in the stock market. But we also use persuasive interviews to *gain support* for teams, political candidates, proposed courses of action, and positions on issues. We may use a persuasive interview to *recruit* a person for our softball team, college, church, social movement, or investment club. We use persuasive interviews to *urge actions* such as voting, attending class, spending spring break in the Virgin Islands, going to a symphony, eating at a specific restaurant, or proposing marriage. We not only use persuasive interviews to bring about actions, but we use them to *alter or reinforce* political, social, religious, economic, and scientific beliefs and attitudes toward people, places, things, groups, and actions.

Many interviews that we do not place under persuasion include important persuasive elements. For instance, employers must convince ideal applicants to accept positions with their organizations, and applicants must convince employers that they are ideal for the openings being filled. Physicians must convince patients to take prescriptions, to have surgical procedures, or to change behaviors such as smoking or drinking. Counselors may have to persuade clients to follow through on solutions they have discussed. And journalists may have to convince persons to talk to them about accidents, scandals, crimes, lawsuits, or investigations. Chapter 7 discusses ways to prepare for and take part in a variety of persuasive interviews.

As Redding's situational schema reveals, there are many types of interviews with a wide variety of purposes and functions for both interviewer and interviewee. Some of us are ideally suited for one type of interview and poorly suited for another. For instance, an expert sales interviewer who is adept at controlling the situation might be a poor counselor because he or she is reluctant to turn the control of the interview over to the other party. An excellent investigative reporter who is highly skilled at probing into answers and getting respondents to reveal what they are reluctant to reveal may be a poor survey taker who cannot deviate a single word from the prepared interview form. And an experienced recruiter might be a poor applicant. A few years ago when large numbers of executives became victims of downsizing, many turned out to be inept at searching and interviewing for new positions.

Uses of Interviewing

Now that we have defined the interview and identified its many types, one last question remains for this chapter. When should you use an interview instead of e-mail, a questionnaire, written examination, letter, speech, or small group to inform, obtain information, select employees or a position, counsel or be counseled, review an employee's performance, diagnose a patient's medical problem, persuade, or purchase a product? The answer depends upon the situation, time constraints, availability of respondents or interviewers, purposes, subject matter, or importance of the endeavor. Here are some general guidelines to help you decide.

When to Use an Interview

First, use an interview to verify that an interviewer or interviewee is who he or she claims to be or when you must match interviewees with specific criteria such as age, sex, race, educational level, income range, political beliefs, membership, and so on. There is no guarantee, for example, that a returned questionnaire has been filled out by the person in a household or company you needed to respond.

Second, use an interview to control timing, presence of other people, questions and answers, and situation. It may be critical, for instance, that questions are answered in a specific order or that no other person (wife, roommate, fellow employee, supervisor) is present to influence answers. You may need reactions immediately before or after an event, but a mailed questionnaire may take days to be sent out and returned. Questionnaires typically continue to dribble in long after a survey is concluded.

Third, use an interview to motivate people to take part, listen, and respond freely, openly, and accurately. The face-to-face or ear-to-ear interview (a great many screening, fund-raising, sales, and opinion poll interviews are conducted over the telephone) in which you can give a party your personal and undivided attention, exhibit interest in *this* party, and discover the most relevant buttons to push is more effective in motivating people than speeches, form letters, and questionnaires. Nearly every college uses phone-a-thons to contact alumni by telephone each year to raise funds. A student who is highly motivated and personal makes an excellent fund-raiser. It is also easier to establish credibility with a respondent who can observe your appearance and credentials, hear vocal inflections, and observe eye contact, gestures, and movement.

Fourth, use an interview when you need to adapt to each interviewee. For example, you might not want to ask the same questions, provide the same answer options, or make the same arguments to every member of the football team, all staff members at your church, or all students at a residence hall. Several years ago, one of the authors and his family "won" a free stay at a residential resort in the Ozark mountains of Arkansas. It was a very pleasant vacation, and representatives of the resort visited briefly only one evening to make a low-pressure sales pitch. In the days that followed, the author and his wife talked to other "winners" and discovered that different demographic groups had received different persuasive efforts. Young parents with small children were told of the vacation benefits for families, including impressive facilities such as swimming pools, lakes for fishing and boating, and wooded trails. Middle-aged couples were told of the investment opportunities that would pay high dividends. And older couples were told of the retirement opportunities and benefits offered at the resort. The face-to-face interview allowed the resort to adapt to each couple's abilities, needs, and desires.

Fifth, use an interview when you need detailed and lengthy answers. People will not write lengthy, detailed answers on questionnaires or respond at length in front of audiences. Even during many interviews, probing or follow-up questions are essential because answers may be brief, vague, inaccurate, incomplete, or suggestible. You may need to ask several probing questions before an interviewee will disclose a single piece of information you need. Only the interview allows you to do this.

Sixth, use an interview when you need to examine personal backgrounds, actions, and experiences that reveal beliefs and attitudes and evoke emotions. Most people are reluctant to reveal personal information and feelings before audiences or in writing to unknown persons. An interview allows you to probe for true self-disclosure and to observe how a person reacts verbally and nonverbally.

Seventh, use an interview when you might need to explain, clarify, or justify questions or answers. It is frustrating when filling out questionnaires to be unable to ask about the phrasing of questions and to answer options that are unclear or do not include how you really feel. It is equally frustrating for interviewers to receive completed questionnaires only to discover that respondents have misinterpreted some questions, confused how they were to respond, left some critical questions unanswered, or checked more than one option when only one was requested.

Eighth, use an interview when it is important to observe the interviewer's or interviewee's appearance, dress, manner, and nonverbal communication. Such observations are impossible in written communications and inadequate in small groups.

Ninth, use an interview as a supplement or follow-up for questionnaires, application forms, and written responses. One technique is to follow a written questionnaire with a random individual or group interview. The interview may reveal why the results are as they are, serve as a validating method, discover problems with the survey questionnaire, or bind the hard data with oral expression.

Electronic Interviews

Telephone interviews, conference calls, and video talk-back meetings are becoming commonplace. If you doubt this, consider the numerous sales calls you receive each week that interrupt your dinners. Although some organizations continue to abuse the telephone interview by, for example, pretending to conduct research surveys when they are actually selling products or services, most use the telephone for legitimate purposes. It is increasingly common for organizations to conduct initial job screening interviews over the telephone. Telephone interviews save time, are less expensive than sending staff members to numerous locations or paying the expenses of applicants to travel to interview locations, and allow several members of an organization to ask questions and to hear replies from each applicant. The use of conference calls and video talk-back is increasing among organizations with multiple locations or clients scattered over a wide geographical area. The interviewer or interviewee can talk to several people at one time, answer or clarify questions directly, be

photo by Charles Gupton/Stock Boston

▧ *The Internet can provide important information on positions and organizations and background on interviewers and interviewees.*

O N   T H E   W E B

Learn more about the growing uses of electronic interviews in a variety of settings. Search at least three databases under headings such as telephone interviews, conference calls, and video talk-back. Try search engines such as ComAbstracts (http://www.cios.org), Yahoo (http://www.yahoo.com), Infoseek (http://www.infoseek.com), and ERIC (http://www.indiana.edu/~eric_rec).

Why are electronic interviews becoming commonplace? In which interview settings are they most common? What are the advantages and disadvantages of electronic interviews? What are suggested guidelines for taking part as interviewer and interviewee? How will new electronic developments affect interviews in the future?

seen or heard while responding, and receive immediate feedback. Time and money saved, problems resolved, agreements reached, and directness of communication will increase the use of electronic interviews in the future.

Criticisms of Interviewing

Interviewing is not without critics who question the validity of information given or received, decisions made, employees or positions selected, and counseling conducted in face-to-face interviews. It would be foolish to claim that all or perhaps most interviews are successful in attaining the goals for which they are conducted. To paraphrase Winston Churchill's comment about the failings of democracy, the interview is far from perfect but it is often the best means to give and get information, counsel, persuade, select employees and positions, and review performance.

Because we are involved in interviews every day, we too often assume that the process is simple and requires little, if any, formal training. What is so difficult about asking a few questions, providing a few answers, or exchanging a bit of information or advice? But if you think interviewing is simple and basic skills come naturally, recall some of your recent experiences: the inept recruiter who kept talking about her accomplishments or who was uninformed about the position; the applicant who confused your company with another or had no idea what he wanted in a position; the professor who got very defensive as soon as you started talking about a course requirement or grade; the political pollster who asked leading questions or who became agitated over your answers; or the computer salesperson who could not answer your questions about a system or who could talk only in computerese.

Most of us learn how to interview by observing others or taking part in interviews, thus perpetuating many poor interviewing practices handed down from one generation to another. We assume that practice makes perfect; but 20 years of experience may be 1 year of flawed experience repeated 20 times, sort of like our golf swing, reading skills, or cooking. There is a vast difference between skilled and unskilled interviewers and interviewees, and the skilled ones know that practice makes perfect only *if you know what you are practicing*. A study in England, for example, discovered that physicians who did not receive formal training in interviewing patients actually became less effective interviewers as the years went on, not more effective.[3]

Purposes of This Book

Our purposes in writing this book are twofold. First, we want to introduce you to the basic skills applicable for all interviews (Chapters 2 to 4) and specific skills needed in specialized settings (Chapters 5 to 12). Second, we want to help you improve your interviewing skills for a *lifetime*, not merely while you are a student or a recent graduate looking for your first position. Unless you are very unusual, you will be an applicant only a few times during your working life, but you will be an interviewer helping your employers locate and hire top-quality staff on a continual basis. Whether you become an engineer, teacher, biologist, attorney, journalist, physician, nurse, sales representative, industrialist, researcher, member of the clergy, or business owner, you must learn how to get and give information, select employees and be selected, review and be reviewed, persuade and be persuaded, counsel and be counseled. Students frequently ask us following reading and class discussions, "Isn't this just a bunch of common sense?" The answer is yes. But in our combined 65 years of experience in conducting interviews, teaching interviewing courses, lecturing on different types of interviews, and consulting with a wide variety of schools, government agencies, professional associations, and corporations, "common sense" is what a surprising percentage of interviewers and interviewees fail to exhibit. This book combines old-fashioned common sense with the most recent research and principles to assist you in learning what to practice, how, and when.

The first essential step in developing and improving interviewing skills is to understand the deceptively complex interviewing process and its many interacting variables. Successful interviewing requires you to understand both parties, the exchanging of roles, perceptions of self and other, communication interactions, feedback, situation, and the influence of outside forces. Chapter 2 explains and illustrates the interviewing process by developing a model step-by-step that contains all of the fundamental elements that interact in each interview.

Summary

The interview is an interactional communication process between two parties, at least one of whom has a predetermined and serious purpose, and usually involves the asking and answering of questions. This definition encompasses a wide variety of interview settings that require training, preparation, interpersonal skills, flexibility, and a willingness to face risks involved in intimate, person-to-person interactions.

An Interview for Review and Analysis

Kathy Gonzalez is a member of Quality Education for Our Children, an organization concerned with an upcoming school board decision on whether to renovate extensively and add an addition to the existing junior and senior high school in Westport or to build a new school at the north edge of town on property the school system owns. Either proposal will cost more than $45,000,000. The school board seems to be leaning toward an addition and renovation, while the community seems divided on the issue, with some opposed to any action that would raise taxes. Quality Education for Our Children is conducting a survey of residents to determine if there is a majority opinion. The interviewees, Jacob and Sarah Stein, are residents of a north-side neighborhood and have two children, one in elementary school and one in junior high. They are unacquainted with Kathy Gonzalez.

As you read this interview, think about answers to the following questions: When are roles and responsibilities exchanged during this interaction? What is the approximate ratio of listening and speaking, and how appropriate is it for this interaction? What are the most obvious elements of this process? How many parties are there in this interaction? What is the predetermined purpose of this interview? Do the interviewees reveal a purpose as the interview progresses? What roles do questions play? What type of interview is this? How is this interaction fundamentally different from a speech, small group discussion, and conversation?

1. **Kathy:** Hi, I'm Kathy Gonzalez, and I live about three streets over on Ashford.

2. **Sarah:** Hi Kathy, I'm Sarah Stein. You must live near the Markles; I teach with Bill at the Westport Middle School.

3. **Kathy:** Yes, they live just across the street from us. Sarah, I'm a member of Quality Education for Our Children, an organization of people in the community like you, that came about because of concerns with the proposals for renovating the current high school or building a new one close to this area. We're conducting a survey of families with children in the Westport school system to see which proposal, or perhaps a different one, is preferred by those who will be most directly affected by the board's decision.

4. **Jacob:** Who is it Sarah?

5. **Sarah:** It's a member of Quality Education for Our Children doing a survey on the high school.

6. **Jacob:** Hi, I'm Jacob Stein. I was just reading about your group in the paper. As I understand it, your organization is not supporting either proposal at this time.

7. **Kathy:** That's correct. We're trying to assure the input of the citizens of Westport, particularly those with children in the school system. Do you have a few minutes to answer some questions?

8. **Sarah:** Yes, I think so. We've just finished dinner.

9. **Kathy:** First, do you have children in the system?

10. **Sarah:** Yes, a daughter in elementary school and a son in junior high.

11. **Kathy:** Do you favor renovation of the current high school or building a new one on school property on the north edge of town?

12. **Jacob:** I assume the renovation proposal would include a new addition for science and computer labs and a junior high gym?

13. **Kathy:** Yes, it would.

14. **Sarah:** Jacob and I have somewhat different views. I tend to favor renovation.

15. **Kathy:** And why is this?

16. **Sarah:** I think it would be good for the community to retain the junior and senior high school in the center of town rather than on one edge. I'm afraid a school on one side of town might divide the community.

17. **Kathy:** Any other reasons for your preference?

18. **Sarah:** I think having an abandoned high school would seriously affect the property values of homes in that area.

19. **Kathy:** And, Jacob, why do you favor a new high school?

20. **Jacob:** Well, which proposal do you prefer?

21. **Kathy:** I would rather not state my personal position because we are trying not to influence how families respond to our questions. We want to remain objective.

22. **Jacob:** Well, I can appreciate that. I personally think it is a waste of money to spend more than $45,000,000 on renovation and a new addition to an old complex when the same money will provide a brand new, state-of-the-art facility.

23. **Kathy:** Are there other reasons?

24. **Jacob:** Yes. I believe the junior-senior high school should be built out in this area where most of the system's school children live. Why spend thousands of dollars to bus them to the center of town when they could walk to a new school? I wouldn't mind seeing the old high school used as a separate junior high. I have never supported the idea of mixing junior and senior high school students.

25. **Sarah:** Jacob and I disagree on this point. I believe the older students are a good influence on the younger ones. Also, some excellent teachers instruct both junior and senior high classes, so the combination makes sense.

26. **Kathy:** Thanks for taking part in our survey.

27. **Jacob:** I'm still curious about how you feel.

28. **Sarah:** Say hi to the Markles for us.

29. **Kathy:** I certainly will. Have a good evening.

Student Activities

1. Keep a log of interviews you take part in during a week. Classify them according to Redding's schema of interview types. Note their length, size of the parties involved, the roles you played, and the purpose of each interview party. What did you discover about your participation in interviews during a single week?

2. Select another person (roommate, friend, classmate, family member, someone you work with) who is willing to interview you and be interviewed by you. Each of you should take five minutes to discover everything you can about the other. When the two interviews are completed, think about these questions: What did you learn that was new? What assumptions proved faulty? What proportions of time did you spend speaking and listening? How were the interviews like and unlike social conversations?

3. First, make a list of what you consider to be characteristics of good and bad interviews. Second, observe several interviews on television and classify them as good or bad according to your criteria. Third, determine how your criteria need to be modified. What influences did television have on your classifications and criteria? What influences did interviewers and interviewees have? For instance, if you liked or disliked the interviewer (Sam Donaldson, Oprah Winfrey, Larry King, Barbara Walters) or the interviewee (Newt Gingrich, Hillary Clinton, Jesse Jackson, Harrison Ford), how did this affect your judgments?

4. Observe several different types of interviews (journalistic, sales, counseling, information giving) and note their characteristics. What were the similarities and differences among these types of interviews? Which similarities and differences were due more to the interviewer or interviewee than to interview type? Which personal characteristics were essential for interviewers in conducting these interviews effectively?

Notes

1. Sarah Trenholm and Arthur Jensen, *Interpersonal Communication* (Belmont, CA: Wadsworth, 1996), p. 25.

2. Michael T. Motley, "Communication as Interaction: A Reply to Beach and Bavelas," *Western Journal of Speech Communication* 54 (Fall 1990), pp. 613–23.

3. R. A. Barbee and S. A. Feldman, "Three Year Longitudinal Study of the Medical Interview and Its Relationship to Student Performance in Clinical Medicine," *Journal of Medical Education* 45 (1970), pp. 770–76.

Resources

Gorden, Raymond L. *Basic Interviewing Skills*. Prospect Heights, IL: Waveland Press, 1992.

Holstein, James A., and Robert L. Kahn. *The Active Interview*. Newbury Park, CA: Sage, 1995.

Kanter, Arnold B. *The Complete Book of Interviewing: Everything You Need to Know from Both Sides of the Table*. New York: Times Books, 1995.

Killenberg, George M., and Rob Anderson. *Before the Story: Interviewing and Communication Skills for Journalists*. New York: St. Martin's Press, 1989.

Roter, Debra, and Judith A. Hall. *Doctor Talking with Patients, Patients Talking with Doctors: Improving Communication in Medical Visits*. Westport, CT: Auburn House, 1992.

The Interviewing Process

2

I n Chapter 1, we defined the interview as an interactional communication process between two parties, at least one of whom has a predetermined and serious purpose,
and usually involves the asking and answering of questions. This chapter explains and
illustrates this interactional communication process through a step-by-step development
of the Cash-Stewart Model of Interviewing, which contains all of the fundamental elements of an interview. We will present each part of the model in detail and discuss the
relationships between the most fundamental element—the two parties—and the other
elements that make the interview a dynamic and sometimes perplexing process.

Two Parties in the Interview

The two circles in Figure 2.1 represent the two parties
present in interviews. Each party is a unique product
of culture, environment, education, training, and experiences. Each is an interesting mixture of personality
traits: optimistic-pessimistic, trusting-suspicious, flexible-inflexible, sociable-unsocia-
ble, sympathetic-censorious. Each adheres to specific beliefs, attitudes, and values. And
each is motivated by an ever-changing variety of expectations, desires, needs, and interests. In a very real sense, "the whole person speaks and the whole person listens" in
interactions we call interviews.[1] Though both parties consist of unique individuals, they
must act together if the interview is to be successful. As Stewart and Logan write, "No
one person can completely control a communication event, and no single person or action causes—or can be blamed for—a communication outcome."[2] You must perceive
the interview to be a collaborative process.

The circles overlap to portray the interview as a *relational* form of communication
in which interview parties are connected interpersonally and have varying degrees of interest in the relationship and the outcome of the interview. Littlejohn defines a relationship as "a set of expectations two people have for their behavior based on the pattern of
interaction between them."[3] These expectations come from how we act and what we say
during interactions with others. A relationship may commence at the start of the interview or have a history that began before this interview. For instance, you may encounter
a reporter or recruiter for the first and last time, or you may interview a supervisor, academic counselor, or associate with whom you have a long-standing and long-lasting relationship. Interviews between parties with no relational histories are often difficult

Figure 2.1   *The interview parties*

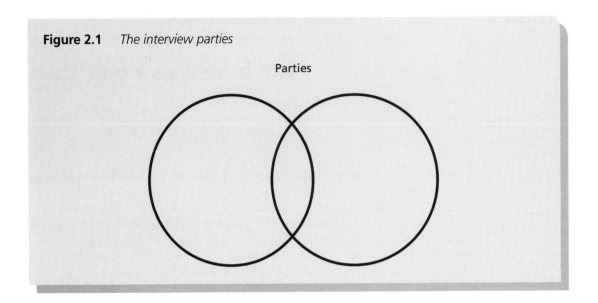

"precisely because we don't know the rules and so we don't know exactly how to coordinate our conversational moves."[4] Regardless of relational history, however, relationships never stay the same. They change over time and during interactions. Stewart and Logan write that "each time they communicate, relational partners construct and modify patterns that define who they are for and with each other."[5] And Littlejohn states that "people in a relationship are always creating a set of expectations, reinforcing old ones, or changing an existing pattern of interaction."[6]

Just as people and interactions change, so do situations. For instance, you may have a pleasant, supportive relationship with a superior or client until you file a complaint about the organization or the client makes demands that you perceive to be unwarranted. Some people can deal with simple and familiar situations but have difficulty adapting to unusual situations or unanticipated demands encountered during interviews. As Trenholm and Jensen note, "First of all, it takes experience and flexibility. A person who knows only one way to do things will have trouble confronting new approaches; the more we learn about alternative ways of organizing relationships, the more flexible we can become. Second, relational competence involves the ability to use feedback effectively."[7] The nature of interview relationships is determined by a number of critical dimensions. We will focus on five of particular relevance to the interview as a form of interpersonal communication: similarity, inclusion/involvement, affection/liking, control/dominance, and trust.

Similarity

Relationships are enhanced when interviewer and interviewee *share* cultural norms and values, environmental influences, training, experiences, personality traits, attitudes, and expectations. Both parties may come from the same city, share Hispanic heritage, be optimistic about their economic futures, attend the same church, adhere to certain social traditions, desire to be treated fairly, and want to attain or give accurate and adequate information. In some situations, you may find it easier to interview a person of the same sex, culture, or age. Do not be oblivious to differences between you and the other party, but recognize important characteristics you share. Awareness of similarities allows interview parties to understand one another, establish areas of common ground, and adapt to each other's needs, perceptions, desires, and customs.

You are more likely to communicate effectively if you can expand the area of *perceived similarities* (the area where the circles overlap) and reduce the areas of *perceived differences* (the areas of the circles that do not overlap). Be aware, however, of the danger of noting a few similarities between you and the other party—dress, age, attendance at the same university—and then assuming that you have a great deal more in common than you do. Membership in the same social club, religious organization, or political party, for instance, does not guarantee that both parties share critical beliefs, values, or attitudes. Many unethical people rely upon faulty assumptions.

Inclusion/Involvement

Relationships are enhanced when both parties desire to be included in the interview. Too often this is not the case. For instance, an applicant may be eager to meet with a recruiter from a major advertising firm, but the recruiter, having conducted interviews every half hour since early morning, may be tired of talking to applicants and long for a quiet dinner with family. You may welcome the publicity of newspaper and television coverage for your new business venture but not the reporter assigned to you. Words and actions are likely to communicate a lack of interest in the interview or attitudes toward the other party and affect the relationship.

Relationships are enhanced when both parties are actively involved. The more actively involved you are in an interview, the more satisfying you are likely to find the relationship. Few of us like to be "talked to," let alone "talked down to." Applicants find it frustrating, for instance, when recruiters do most of the talking and they are unable to "sell themselves." As consumers, we get irritated at salespersons who will not stop their sales pitches long enough for us to answer or ask questions. And, as patients, we do not appreciate being treated by health care professionals as if we are children.

Affection/Liking

Relationships are enhanced when both parties like and respect one another and when there is a high degree of warmth or friendship. Some people find it difficult, especially in formal settings, to get or give affection or to communicate how much they like the other party. Some fear closeness and prefer to keep others, acquaintances as well as strangers, at arm's length. Supervisors fear getting too close to persons they must direct, evaluate, and reward. You may want to approach a friend about giving to a fund-raising campaign but fear the request for money will have a negative impact on your relationship. You may come to an interview with a positive, ambivalent, or hostile attitude toward the other party, often due to compatible or incompatible needs, desires, demands, and perceptions of the likely outcome of the interview.

Ideal affection or liking occurs in an interview when the parties establish a "we" instead of a "me-you" or "we-they" feeling. You cannot establish great warmth and friendship during a five- or ten-minute interview with a client, customer, or interviewee, but you can try to communicate in such a way that the other party finds you pleasant, willing to listen, fair, and understanding—likable.

Control/Dominance

Relationships are enhanced when both parties share control and neither seeks to dominate the interview. Either party may have considerable control or potential dominance. As an interviewee, you may say no to a survey taker and close the door. If you do not wish to listen to a sales pitch, you may hang up the telephone. As an interviewer, you may dominate a performance interview, ask leading or loaded questions in a journalistic interview, or withhold information during a medical interview.

Control and dominance often pose problems in interviews because they tend to involve organizational or social hierarchy or chain of command: president over vice president, sales director over sales representative, dean over professor, professor over student, parent over child. This upward and downward communication may pose problems for both parties. One party often has the power to dictate if an interview will occur; when, where, and how it will be conducted; who the other party will be; the results of the interview; and how these results may be used. If you are in a subordinate position, try to attain or sustain a reasonable degree of control during the interview; if you are in a superior position, try to share a reasonable degree of control. See Chapter 10 for a discussion of defensive and supportive climates in interviews.

Trust

Relationships are enhanced if the parties trust one another and perceive each other as honest, sincere, dependable, truthful, reliable, and safe. This dimension is critical, for instance, in journalistic, persuasive, employee selection, performance reviews, counseling, and health care interviews in which an expected positive outcome may prove instead to be a public embarrassment, an unrewarding position or ineffective employee, poor advice, a loss of money, or endangered health. You will not take people into your confidence if you cannot trust them to keep their word or fear they will react negatively. Trust is essential in the intimate, one-on-one interview because both the interview and its outcome usually affect us directly and perhaps immediately.

The interview relationship is mutual because both parties must contribute to its development and sustenance if the interview is to be successful. Even in interviews at a mall, on the street, or over the telephone, interviewees perceive within seconds why they are being interviewed, what will happen to the information they share, and whether they want to participate. At the same time, interviewers perceive the suitability of the interviewee, the person's desire and willingness to cooperate, and whether the relationship is likely to be positive or negative. Once both parties agree to speak or listen, ask or answer questions, give or seek information, they become interdependent and assume degrees of control and responsibility for the outcome of the interview.

Global Relationships

Since our work and social worlds are now becoming global in nature, become aware of how relationships differ among countries and cultures. In the United States, we tend to

ON THE WEB

We have emphasized the importance of relationships in interviews. You have read about how perceptions, nature, and development of relationships are affected by each party's gender, culture, and age. As our world shrinks and our international interactions become more frequent, we will need to understand and appreciate cultural differences if we are to communicate effectively. The World Wide Web contains a wealth of multicultural resources. Expand your understanding of how culture may affect interviews by using resources such as Yahoo: Society and Culture (http://www.yahoo.com/society, http://www.yahoo.com/culture, and http://www.yahoo.com/cultures), Ernst & Young's Doing Business Around the World (http://www.eyi.com/tdbaw.htm), and Global Village Access Network (http://www.mwsolutions.com/gvan/index/Welcome.html).

have numerous relationships that are friendly and informal, sometimes developing them while we are waiting in lines or sitting together on airplanes.[8] Arabs also tend to begin and develop relationships quickly; but unlike Americans, who dislike taking advantage of relationships by asking for favors, Arabs feel that friends have a duty to help and provide favors to one another. Germans develop relationships slowly because they consider relationships to be very important. Employing first names before a relationship is firmly established is considered rude behavior. Japanese prefer not to interact with strangers or foreigners, prefer doing business with people they have known for some years, and take a great deal of time establishing relationships. And while Americans create and discard relationships frequently, Australians make deeper and longer-lasting commitments. As you will see later in this chapter, you must be cautious when using and interpreting nonverbal behavior as indicators of relationships.

Men and Women in Relationships

If relationships are determined by what we say and how we say it, then sex of participants is also critical in establishing and refining relationships. Research suggests that women use communication as a primary way to establish relationships, whereas men communicate "to exert control, preserve independence, and enhance status."[9] Thus, men's talk tends to be directive and goal oriented, employing statements that "tend to press compliance, agreement, or belief" on the other party. Women's talk, on the other hand, is more polite and expressive, containing less intense words, qualifiers (perhaps, maybe, sometimes), and disclaimers ("Maybe I'm wrong, but," "I may not fully understand the situation, but," "It may not be a good move, but").[10]

Interchanging Roles during Interviews

The small circles within the two large circles in Figure 2.2 signify that roles are frequently interchanged during interviews. Both parties speak and listen from time to time, are likely to ask and answer questions, and take on the roles and responsibilities of interview*er* and interview*ee*. (Note that in figures throughout the book, R = interviewer and E = interviewee.) Neither party should

Figure 2.2   *The switching of roles*

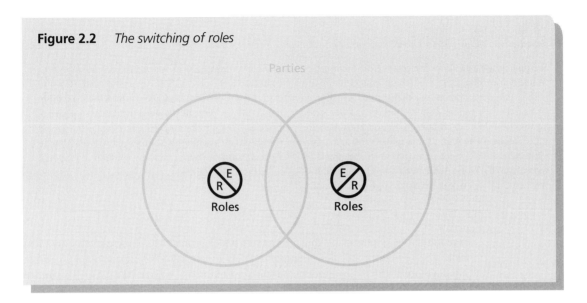

either sit back and expect the other to make the interview a success single-handedly or try to dominate the interaction.

The degree to which roles are interchanged and control is shared may be affected by the status or expertise of the parties who initiated the interview, type of interview, and the atmosphere of the interaction—supportive or defensive, friendly or hostile, warm or cool, formal or informal. Trenholm and Jensen claim that supervisors, because of their status, are freer to start and stop discussions, interrupt subordinates, use an informal mode of address, and disclose information.[11] Which of two fundamental approaches an interviewer selects—directive or nondirective—significantly affects the exchanging of interviewer and interviewee roles during interviews.

Directive Approach

In a directive approach, the interviewer establishes the purpose of the interview and attempts to control the pacing, climate, formality, and drift of the interview. Questions are likely to be closed and perhaps leading, with short, direct answers desired. Although an aggressive interviewee may take command as the interview progresses, the intent is for the interviewer to control the interview. Typical directive interviews include information giving, information gathering (surveys and opinion polls), employment selection, disciplinary, and persuasive interviews (particularly sales). The directive approach has a number of advantages and disadvantages.

Advantages

1. It is easy to learn.
2. It takes less time.
3. It is easy to maintain control.

Disadvantages

1. It is inflexible.
2. It may reduce motivation to take part.

4. It can provide quantifiable data.

5. It can supplement other methods of data collection such as questionnaires and observations.

6. It can be replicated by standardizing variables such as voice, facial expressions, and appearance.

3. It is limited in variety and depth of subject matter.

4. It limits the interviewer's range of techniques.

5. It often replaces more effective and efficient means of collecting data.

6. The validity of the information may be questioned because of variables such as voice, facial expressions, and appearance.

The following exchange illustrates a directive interviewing approach:

1. **Interviewer:** Do you plan to vote in the fall election?

2. **Interviewee:** Yes, I do.

3. **Interviewer:** Are you most likely to vote Democratic or Republican?

4. **Interviewee:** I usually split my ticket

5. **Interviewer:** When you split your ticket, do you tend to vote for more Democratic candidates or more Republican candidates?

6. **Interviewee:** More Republicans.

7. **Interviewer:** If the election were being help today, would you vote for Williams or Martinez for governor?

8. **Interviewee:** Martinez.

Nondirective Approach

In a nondirective approach, the interviewer may allow the interviewee to control the purpose, subject matter, tenor, climate, formality, and pacing. Questions are likely to be open-ended and neutral to give the interviewee maximum opportunity to respond as desired. Typical nondirective interviews are information getting (journalistic, oral history, investigations), counseling, performance review, and problem solving. The nondirective approach has a number of advantages and disadvantages:

Advantages

1. It can motivate the interviewee to take part.

2. It allows the interviewer greater flexibility.

3. It allows the interviewer to probe deeply into subject matter.

4. It gives the interviewee greater freedom to give lengthy answers and to volunteer information.

Disadvantages

1. It is time-consuming.

2. It requires acute psychological insight and sensitivity.

3. The interviewer may lose control of the interview.

4. It often generates unneeded or unwanted information.

5. It tends to generate excessive information.

5. It tends to generate more information.

6. It allows the interviewer to adapt to each interviewee.

6. Adaptation to each interviewee may reduce or complicate replicability.

The following is a nondirective interview exchange:

1. **Interviewer:** Why did you become a campus police officer?

2. **Interviewee:** I really like the university atmosphere and working with students. So when I completed my degree in criminology, I decided to apply for a position with a university police department.

3. **Interviewer:** Tell me about a typical day on the job.

4. **Interviewee:** I begin my shift at seven in the morning. Aside from the usual parking tickets and patrolling the campus area, I respond to emergency calls that range from pedestrian-car accidents to students with medical problems while they are in the classroom. And increasingly I am called to investigate thefts of books, computers, sound systems, and television sets.

5. **Interviewer:** Where do you hope to be career-wise five years from now?

Combination of Approaches

Interviewers often find it appropriate to use a combination of directive and nondirective approaches in the same interview. For instance, a counselor might use a nondirective approach while assessing a student's or family's problems and switch to a directive approach when explaining possible courses of action or regulations. A recruiter might use a nondirective approach in the early minutes of an interview to relax an applicant and establish feelings of trust, concern, and interest. Then the recruiter would switch to a directive approach when asking challenging questions and giving information about the organization and position. The recruiter would return to a nondirective approach by giving the applicant an opportunity to ask questions. Interviewers must be flexible enough to determine when a particular approach is most appropriate and when to switch from one approach to another. Chapter 11 on counseling interviewing and Chapter 12 on health care interviewing discuss further the nature and uses of directive and nondirective interviewing approaches.

Too often, perhaps, the selection of an interviewing approach may be governed by societal roles and expectations rather than by the interview parties. Stewart writes that we tend to behave as prescribed by the roles we play in life. For instance, an employee, applicant, or patient "enters an interview expecting that the interviewer will direct and influence one's conversational behaviors much more extensively than one will influence the interviewer's behavior. We both make it happen that way."[12] The predictability of such social roles "reduces the uncertainty of both parties and imbues our conversations with some guiding structure," including appropriate questioning, disclosure, language, and nonverbal communication. Adherence to societal roles and expectations, however, may not result in the most productive interview. Roles and expectations should guide but not dictate the choice of interviewing approach.

Perceptions of the Interviewer and Interviewee

The double-ended arrows in Figure 2.3 symbolize that each party comes to an interview with perceptions of self and the other party, and these perceptions may change positively or negatively as the interview progresses. Theorists claim that our relationships are largely due to our perceptions and that these relationships determine how we communicate. It is essential, then, that both interview parties are aware of their self-perceptions, how they perceive the other party, how the other party perceives self, and how the other party perceives them.

Self-Perception

The perception you have of yourself, self-concept, comes from physical, social, and psychological perceptions. You derive these perceptions from your experiences, activities, beliefs, attitudes, values, accomplishments, possessions, and interactions with others, particularly your superior and subordinate roles and relationships. Your self-concept is a dual creation of your interpretations and how you perceive others to have interpreted the many ingredients of who you have been, are, and hope to be. These "others" include groups to which you belong or desire to belong as well as "significant others" who influence you interpersonally. Self-concepts are often clouded by the variety of expectations we, family, society, professions, and organizations place upon us. We may have different self-concepts as we move from one situation or role to another. We may feel very self-confident when dealing with professional responsibilities where we are in charge but inept in social or family settings we cannot control.

Self-esteem, the "positive or negative feelings we associate with our self-images," is an important element of self-concept. Trenholm and Jensen claim that a person with

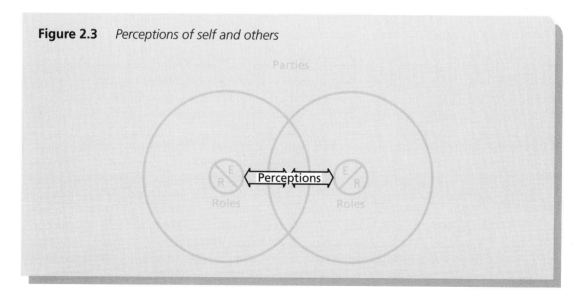

Figure 2.3 *Perceptions of self and others*

high self-esteem "is more perceptive, more confident, and more likely to express personal attitudes even if unpopular. . . . People with low self-esteem want the approval of others but are usually so pre-occupied with and down on themselves that they fail to interpret other people's behavior accurately."[13] It is important to understand how you perceive yourself and how the other party perceives himself or herself, because self-concept (particularly self-esteem) may determine whether an interview takes place and, if so, the success or failure of the interview. For example, you may be reluctant to take part in a performance review interview because you fear what your supervisor might say or you have had bad experiences with reviews in the past. You may succeed or fail in an interview because you are convinced you will—the self-fulfilling prophecy: I told you I could do it/I knew I couldn't do it; I just knew I would get the offer/I just knew I wouldn't get the offer; I thought I could handle the negotiation/I felt I wasn't ready for this level of negotiation. Self-perceptions influence messages sent and received, risks taken, confidence, and degree of self-disclosure.

While concepts such as self-image, self-esteem, self-reliance, self-awareness, and self-determination are central in American and Western culture because of our emphasis on the individual, they are not central in Eastern cultures and South American countries. Japanese, Chinese, and Indians, for example, are collectivist rather than individualist cultures and are more concerned with the image, esteem, and achievement of the group. Attributing the successful negotiations for a business venture to an individual in China would be considered egotistical, self-advancing, and disrespectful. Success is attributed to the group or team. Failure to appreciate cultural differences causes many communication problems for American interviewers and interviewees.

Perceptions of the Other Party

How each party perceives the other also affects how they approach the interview and how they react during the interview. For instance, you may be influenced by the other's reputation—a brilliant scientist, a stern supervisor, a reporter who asks embarrassing questions, an interviewee who is usually evasive, an attorney with allegedly high or low ethical standards. Previous encounters with a person may lead you to look forward to or dread an interview. Your perception of the other may be influenced by age, sex, race, ethnic group, physical size, attractiveness, and associations—particularly if they differ significantly from you. And endorsement of a person by someone you admire may alter the way you perceive the person.

If you are flexible and adaptable, perceptions of the other party may change as an interview progresses. Perceptions may be affected by the way the interview is opened, the other party's appearance, attitudes expressed, nonverbal communication, questions asked, answers received, information exchanged, arguments presented, structure followed, and the closing. Relationships and interactions are affected positively or negatively by the nature of exchanges: when questions are followed by information desired rather than refusals or evasiveness, when requests are followed by discussion or agreement rather than demands followed by compliance, or when constructive criticism is followed by understanding rather than by fear or resentment.

Figure 2.4 *Communication interactions*

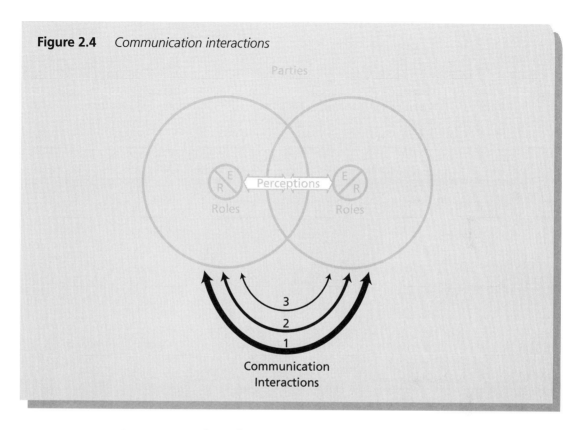

Communication
Interactions

Communication Interactions

The curved arrows in Figure 2.4 that link the two parties symbolize the communication levels of verbal and nonverbal interactions that occur during interviews. The three numbered levels differ in degree of self-disclosure, amount of risk encountered, perceived meanings, and both amount and type of content exchanged.

Levels of Interactions

Level 1 interactions deal with relatively safe, nonthreatening areas of inquiry such as hometown, profession, sports, courses you are taking, and products your company produces. These inquiries produce answers that are safe, socially acceptable, comfortable, and ambiguous, such as Wilmington, North Carolina; attorney practicing intellectual properties law; football games recently attended; courses being taken, such as English 305, Engineering 429, and Management 200; electronic parts for Ford. When you respond to inquiries about how things are going with phrases such as "Not bad, how about you," "Okay, I guess," or "Can't complain," you are fostering Level 1 interactions. Your answers do not reveal judgments, attitudes, or feelings.

Each level is like a metaphorical door, with the door being slightly ajar in Level 1 interactions. You may allow general ideas, surface feelings, and basic information to pass through, but you may close the door quickly and safely if the other party seems to move too quickly or into threatening territory. The thickness of the arrow indicates that Level 1 communication interchanges are most frequent in interviews, particularly during the early minutes when each party is sizing up the other and the situation. And the length of the arrow symbolizes relational distance. Level 1 interactions take place between total strangers, superiors and subordinates, persons who dislike each other, and those who perceive the other party as dissimilar, untrustworthy, or domineering.

The following interview segment illustrates Level 1 interactions.

1. **Interviewer:** Good morning Glenn. How are you today?
2. **Interviewee:** Fine thanks.
3. **Interviewer:** And how's your family?
4. **Interviewee:** They're doing real well in spite of the flu that's been going around.
5. **Interviewer:** And your father?
6. **Interviewee:** As well as can be expected, but thanks for asking.
7. **Interviewer:** Glad to hear that. Well, I just received the quarterly sales reports from accounting and would like to get your reactions.
8. **Interviewee:** I got them yesterday morning.
9. **Interviewer:** What are your reactions?
10. **Interviewee:** Mixed I guess.
11. **Interviewer:** Me too.

Notice how both parties are playing it safe during these interchanges. The first topics are not threatening, and neither party reveals how he or she feels about the quarterly reports.

Level 2 interactions deal with more personal and controversial areas of inquiry such as education, professional experiences, use of free time, and preferred products. They delve more into behaviors, thoughts, attitudes, beliefs, and feelings. Responses tend to be half-safe, half-revealing ones as the respondent seeks to cooperate without divulging too much. If a professor asks for your reactions to an interviewing field project, for instance, you might respond with such statements as "I found it interesting but very time-consuming," or "I enjoyed doing the interviews but not the written report."

The metaphorical door is half open (the optimist's view) or half closed (the pessimist's view) as more specific and revealing ideas, feelings, and information pass through. Though willing to take more risk, you retain the ability to close the door quickly when necessary. The thickness of the arrow signifies that Level 2 interactions are less frequent than Level 1, and the length of the arrow indicates that a closer relationship between parties is necessary to move from the superficial to the revealing.

The following interview segment illustrates Level 2 interactions.

1. **Interviewer:** I just received the quarterly sales reports from accounting and would like to get your reactions.

2. **Interviewee:** Well, I'm generally pleased with my sales, but I know there is always room for improvement.

3. **Interviewer:** Uh huh. What are you thinking of doing differently next quarter?

4. **Interviewee:** For one thing, I hope the new computer system will allow me to process inquiries more quickly.

5. **Interviewer:** Anything else?

6. **Interviewee:** Well, I want to consider some of the interpersonal techniques presented at the in-service seminar last week. The ones on nonverbal communication seemed to hit home.

Notice that the interviewer is pushing the interviewee toward revealing comments, and the interviewee, though cautious, is more specific and revealing in responses.

Level 3 interactions deal with highly intimate and controversial areas of inquiry such as family life, income, indebtedness, health, and relationships. They elicit responses that *fully* disclose a person's feelings, beliefs, attitudes, and perceptions. Little is held back, and you might get more than you bargained for.

The metaphorical door is wide open. The risk is great to both parties, but so are the potential benefits. The arrow is thin to indicate that Level 3 interactions are infrequent in interviews and may be unattainable until a second or third interview. And the arrow is short because the relationship between parties must be positive or close because of perceived similarities, desire to be included and involved, feelings of warmth or friendship, sharing of control, and a high level of trust.

The following interview segment illustrates Level 3 interactions.

1. **Interviewer:** Frank, according to the quarterly reports from accounting, your sales are down nearly 20 percent from last quarter.

2. **Interviewee:** Well, quite frankly I was disappointed with the figures, though not totally surprised. I knew this would not be a good quarter for me.

3. **Interviewer:** I see.

4. **Interviewee:** I don't think I've been following up my contacts as quickly and effectively as I usually do. I need to structure my time better, and I plan to set aside time each day just for follow-ups.

5. **Interviewer:** Is your drinking problem under control, Frank?

6. **Interviewee:** Yes. I mean there are occasions when I have fallen off the wagon, so to speak. I thought I could get along without the AA meetings, but I can't.

7. **Interviewer:** What can I do to help?

Notice these interactions deal with more personal, intimate matters and result in disclosure of personal matters and concerns. The interviewee is taking a considerable risk in admitting failure to follow up leads and that an old problem has resurfaced.

The unstructured nature of many interviews and the question-answer-question format of many interviews may make communication levels unpredictable and difficult to change. It is essential in all but the simplest of interactions to get beyond Level 1 to

Level 2 or Level 3 if you are to gain information, detect feelings, attain self-disclosure, discover insights, and obtain commitments necessary to achieve your purpose.

Relationships, perceptions, responses, and situation determine which levels are reached. *How* parties communicate may be as important as *what* they communicate. Stewart and Logan address the risks of self-disclosing:

> When you choose to make some of your personal self available to someone else, you give that person some options or choices that you cannot completely control. The person may dislike the you that he or she comes to know. You may be ridiculed for your thoughts and feelings. Or the other person may tell someone else something you don't want known. You may feel embarrassed, hurt, angry, or something even worse.[14]

Unlike small groups or audiences for speeches into which we can blend or hide, the intimate, interpersonal nature of the interview is often threatening because it places our egos and sometimes our social, financial, professional, psychological, or physical welfare on the line. An interview may deal with *your* behavior, *your* performance, *your* reputation, *your* decisions, *your* weaknesses, *your* feelings, *your* money, or *your* future—not those of others in a group or audience or some hypothetical being.

As interviewer and interviewee, you need to understand how and why interviews are threatening and what motivates people to take part at Levels 2 and 3 instead of at safe Level 1. Here are some guidelines for motivating people to communicate beyond Level 1 and disclose beliefs, attitudes, and feelings as well as facts.

1. Parties are likely to communicate beyond Level 1 if they understand what you expect. Avoid tricks, gimmicks, or deceptions; be straightforward and honest.
2. Parties are likely to communicate beyond Level 1 if they are interested in you, your organization, or the subject matter of the interview.
3. Parties are likely to communicate beyond Level 1 if you seem sincerely interested in them and their best interests.
4. Parties are likely to communicate beyond Level 1 if they feel they can trust you to react with understanding and tact, maintain confidences, use the information fairly, and report what they say accurately and completely.
5. Parties are likely to communicate beyond Level 1 if you offer them a tangible reward (money, products, services, position) or an intangible reward (appreciation, feeling of accomplishment, pride in a contribution, an opportunity to help).
6. Parties are likely to communicate beyond Level 1 if you do so.

Levels of communication and self-disclosure are influenced by *sex and culture*. Women, for instance, disclose more than men and, except for anger, are allowed to express emotions (fear, sadness, sympathy) more than men. Because women are perceived to be better listeners and more responsive than men, disclosure is highest between woman-to-woman parties, next highest between woman-to-man parties, and lowest among man-to-man parties.[15]

Culture may determine what is disclosed to whom and how. For example, Americans of European descent may disclose about a wider range of topics than Japanese and Chinese, disclose more about their careers and less about their families than Ghanians, and disclose to more different types of people than Asians. Asians tend to disclose more to those with expertise and ability to exhibit honest and positive attitudes than to those who like to talk and show more emotional feelings. Research suggests that people in a high-context culture, such as Japan and China, in which they are expected to know and follow cultural norms, disclose less than those in a low-context culture, such as the United States and Great Britain, where cultural norms are less well known and more flexible. Interpersonal conflict may result if you overdisclose, underdisclose, or disclose to the wrong person in differing cultures.

While cultures vary in how, when, and to whom self-disclosure is appropriate, some theorists claim that the notion of politeness is universal. According to "politeness theory," all humans desire to be appreciated and protected. Littlejohn writes:

> *Positive face* is the desire to be appreciated and approved, to be liked and honored, and *positive politeness* is designed to meet these desires. Showing concern, complimenting, and using respectful forms of address are examples. *Negative face* is the desire to be free from imposition or intrusion, and *negative politeness* is designed to protect the other person when negative face needs are threatened. Acknowledging the imposition when making a request is a common example.[16]

You encounter situations when politeness is essential not only when dealing with persons from other cultures but whenever you challenge a grade, complain about a product or service, submit to a performance review, take part in a disciplinary procedure, and meet with a counselor or client.

Regardless of level, communication interactions may be verbal or nonverbal and intentional or unintentional. It is usually impossible to separate the verbal from the nonverbal during interviews, but we will do so in this chapter for discussion purposes.

Verbal Interactions

Words are merely arbitrary connections of letters that serve as symbols for people, animals, things, events, ideas, beliefs, and feelings. That they are imperfect vehicles for communication with others is brought home to us nearly every day in misunderstandings, confusions, embarrassments, antagonisms, and hurt feelings over what we *assume* to be perfectly clear, common, and neutral words. In fact, some claim that *the greatest single problem with human communication is the assumption of it*. We sometimes exclaim in exasperation that if people would just learn to use words properly, we would have no communication problems, but the arbitrary nature of language, not improper use, is often the root cause of miscommunication during interviews.

Multiple meanings: Simple words have many meanings. "Cultivate" has meanings ranging from breaking up the soil and raising crops to enhancing culture, refining the mind, encouraging, and making friends. "Game" may connote a chess match, basketball game, wild animal, or willingness to try new things.

Ambiguities: Some words are so *ambiguous* that any two parties may assign very different meanings to them. What are a "nice" vacation, an "affordable" college education, a "simple" tax form, a "large" city, and a "living wage"? Who is not "middle class" in America? When is a person "young," "middle-aged," or "old"? How do we know that something is "one of the best" or "one of the finest"?

Sound-alike words: The oral nature of interviews may lead to confusion because of similar sounding words that have very different meanings. Examples include sail and sale, bowl and bull, bear and bare, hole and whole, and to, too, or two. Think of times when you were startled by a word only to realize later through context that you had misinterpreted what the other party meant. A banker in Los Angeles related an incident in which she was talking to a banking associate in Chicago and thought she heard the other say, "We're axing John." The associate had meant "asking John."

Connotations: Many words have *positive or negative connotations*. You can describe an interview suit as "inexpensive" or "cheap," your roommate as having "beliefs" or "prejudices," a supervisor who "leads" or "dictates," a transaction as a "cost" or an "investment." Few of us would admit to "manipulating" others during interviews, but the verb "to manipulate" has as many positive as negative meanings:

Negative Meanings	Positive Meanings
Cunning	Touch
Trick	Handle
Scheme	Use
Deceive	Exercise
Undermine	Set in motion

Jargon: Not only are many common words confusing, but we make communication difficult by altering or creating words for a variety of purposes. For instance, every profession and nearly every organization has its own specialized jargon. Politicians talk about "sound bites" or placing an appropriate "spin" on a problem. Computer enthusiasts speak of megabytes, RAM, and ROM. And a communication professor may want to discuss metacommunication, morphogenesis, the sociofugal-sociopetal axis, or homeostasis with you.

Slang: Each generation has a kind of unofficial jargon we call *slang*. Fast, powerful cars went from "keen" and "neat" in the 1940s and 1950s, to "hot," "cool," "groovy," and "far out" in the 1960s and 1970s, to "decent," "tough," and "mean" in the 1980s, to "awesome," "way cool," "outrageous," and "white hot" in the 1990s. As we approach the year 2000, these cars are "rockin'," "slammin'," "jammin'," "poppin'," and "kickin'." Using slang properly places us in the in-group, and we may get a "charge" or "rush" when others do not understand us or use the slang incorrectly.

Euphemisms: We often substitute better sounding words for common ones, what we call *euphemisms*. We are more likely to see a "life-like" Christmas tree advertised than an "artificial" one. A person may inquire about the location of the "powder room" rather than the "toilet." We deal with "sales associates" rather than "clerks." You will not find a "big and tall" area in a women's clothing department; but you will find areas reserved for "women's sizes," "queen sizes," "full sizes," or "plus sizes."

Naming: We *label* people, places, and things to make them not merely *sound better* but *appear* very different, to affect the way we view reality. A scientific document on the dangers of smoking may become a "political" document. Do not expect to hear a political leader refer to a terrible economic mess as a "depression"; such events since the "big one" in the 1930s have become "recessions," "downturns," or "market adjustments." When we substitute woman for girl, flight attendant for stewardess, supervisor for foreman, or anchor for anchorman, we are not being "politically correct" but are attempting to affect perceptions of reality. "Girls" and "boys" do not work as engineers, physicians, teachers, and managers; women and men do.

Ordering words: How we order words in a sentence can communicate different messages, lead to confusion, or provoke laughter. Strange headlines or statements may embarrass one party and provide humor for another. Here are a few examples:

> Warden says inmates may have three guns.
> This being Easter Sunday, we will ask Mrs. Brown to come forward and lay an
>   egg on the altar.
> Slain man filling in for colleague.
> Death causes change.

Power words: Some writers distinguish between *power* speech forms and *powerless* speech forms.[17] Words expressing certainty, challenges, orders, verbal aggression, leading questions, and metaphors are power forms. Celebrated phrases of the past few years include "Read my lips!" "Make my day!" "Take your best shot!" "Learn to live with it!" and "Get a life!" Powerless speech forms include apologies, disclaimers, excuses, indirect questions, and nonfluencies such as "Uh," "And uh," Umm," and "You know." Few people are impressed with opening phrases such as "I didn't mean to . . . ," "It's not my fault that . . . ," and "Do you think maybe . . . ?"

Although we assume all Americans speak the same language, there are regional, age, and role differences. People in New Jersey go to the "shore," while those in Florida go to the "beach." A person in New England is likely to ask if you would like a "soda," while a person in the Midwest is likely to ask if you would like a "Coke." A government "entitlement" program, such as Social Security or Medicare, is likely to have very different meanings for 24-year-old and 84-year-old interviewees. Baseball batters and hitters have always perceived the word "strike" quite differently, but the prolonged major league baseball strike in 1994 and 1995 gave a new and shared meaning to both.

Studies of gender and communication during the past decade have noted a variety of differences in language use among men and women. For example, men tend to be socialized into developing and using power speech forms and to dominate interactions; women tend to be socialized into developing powerless speech forms and to foster relationships and exchanges during interactions. Research indicates that women's talk is more polite and expressive, contains more qualifiers and disclaimers, makes more color distinctions, includes fewer mechanical and technical terms, and is more tentative than men's talk.[18] Men not only can use more intense language than women, but they are often expected to do so because it is considered masculine. If a woman uses the same language, she may be termed "bitchy," "pushy," or "opinionated" or accused of trying to be a man. Speaking styles, ingrained in many of us since childhood, help to explain why many women find it difficult to operate equally and effectively in a male-dominated society such as the United States. We must be cautious, however, when stereotyping language differences among genders. Julia Wood writes, "Despite jokes about women's talkativeness, research indicates that in most contexts, men not only hold their own but dominate the conversation."[19] In addition, men tend to interrupt women more than they do other men and do so to state opinions; women tend to interrupt to ask questions. Recent studies also indicate, however, that both men and women use tentative forms of speech in specific contexts and with a variety of people to facilitate communication.

If American men and women differ in use of words, such differences are magnified in the global village even when parties are speaking the same language. North Americans, according to researchers, tend to value precision, directness, explicit words, power speech forms, and use of "I" to begin sentences. We value tough or straight talk.[20] On the other hand, other cultures value the group or collective rather than the individual and rarely begin with "I" or call attention to themselves. Chinese children are taught to downplay self-expression. Japanese tend to be implicit rather than explicit and employ ambiguous words and qualifiers. Koreans prefer not to give negative or "no" responses; rather, they tend to imply disagreements in order to maintain group harmony. And Arabic-speaking peoples tend to employ what is referred to as "sweet talk," or accommodating language with elaborate metaphors and similes.

It is little wonder that, as famous linguist Irving Lee stated years ago, we often "talk past" one another instead of with one another.[21] Here are a few guidelines to enhance effective use of language during interviews. Choose words and phrases carefully and be aware of how the other party may interpret or misinterpret them. Expand your vocabulary. Be aware of slight changes in words that alter meanings considerably, such as revocable or irrevocable clauses in your apartment lease. Listen to the context in which words are used to distinguish the specific way similar sounding words are being used. Before an interview occurs, learn the jargon of professions and groups, while being aware of your own. Detect euphemisms and renaming as they occur, including your own. Keep up to date with changing uses of language and slang so you can share language and meanings with other parties. Know how the meanings and connotations of words may be affected by sex, age, race, culture, ethnic group, and situation. Be sensitive to and avoid words and labels that might antagonize, embarrass, or offend another person. Be as precise as possible by giving an age range instead of saying "middle age," a population figure instead of saying "medium-sized city," a salary figure instead of "competitive salary," or a ranking of a college or program instead of "one of the top schools." Never *assume* effective communication is taking place.

Nonverbal Interactions

The oral, face-to-face nature of the interview means that successful communication relies upon both words and nonverbal signals such as physical appearance, dress, eye contact, voice, touches, handshakes, winks, punches on the arm, posture, and proximity of the two parties. Some writers claim that 65 to 93 percent of communication is carried through nonverbal acts and appearances that reveal emotions, personality traits, attitudes, reactions, certainty, interest, happiness, status, role-playing, and time availability. The intimate nature of the interview (with parties often a mere arm's length apart) magnifies the importance of nonverbal communication because both parties are likely to detect everything the other does and does not do, assigning meanings to the simplest behavioral acts such as head nods, pauses, inflections of voice, glances at watches, and silence. Your facial expressions are likely to be your most effective nonverbal channel. The interactive nature of the interview depends upon nonverbal signals to regulate the flow of communication and turn-taking. Research shows that we rely on nonverbal cues to express ourselves and interpret the expressions of others, but it also shows that these cues can mislead or be misread.[22]

Sometimes *a single behavioral act* conveys a message. Poor eye contact may "tell" the other party that you have something to hide, a limp handshake that you are timid, a serious facial expression that you are sincere, touching a hand or arm that you are sympathetic or understanding, or a puzzled expression that you are confused. Your rate of speaking and conducting an interview may communicate urgency (fast speed), the gravity of the situation (slow speed), lack of interest (fast speed), lack of preparation (slow speed), nervousness (fast speed and breathless voice), or indecision (halting voice). Silence may encourage the other to talk, signal that you are not in a hurry, express agreement with what is being said, and keep a party talking.

More often you send and receive a message with *a combination of behavioral acts* that enhance the impact of the message. For instance, you may show you are interested in what a person is saying by leaning forward, maintaining good eye contact, nodding your head, and having a serious facial expression. Fidgeting, crossing and uncrossing your arms and legs, sitting rigid, looking down, furrowing your brow, and speaking in a high-pitched voice may reveal a high level of anxiety, fear, or agitation. A drooping body, frowning, and slow speaking rate may reveal sadness or resignation to anticipated failure or discipline. Leaning backward, staring at the other party, raising an eyebrow, and shaking your head may signal disagreement, anger, or disgust. The way you shake hands and look the other in the eye may signal a degree of trust and trustworthiness. Body movements, gestures, and posture may show dynamism or lack of it. *Remember that any behavioral act may be interpreted in a meaningful way by the person receiving.* The message may be intentional or unintentional, accurate or inaccurate. You may not intend to communicate boredom with a yawn or looking at a clock, but the other party may read it that way.

Physical appearance and dress are particularly important during the first few minutes of interviews as the interview parties get to know and respect one another. This critical first impression often begins before words are exchanged. Whether we want to admit it or not, we tend to respond more favorably to attractive persons who are neither too fat nor too thin, tall rather than short, shapely rather than unshapely, pretty and handsome rather than plain or ugly. We perceive attractive persons to be more poised, outgoing, interesting, and sociable. You may not be able to do much about your height, weight, shape, or handsomeness, but you can be neat and clean with well-groomed hair. Wear neat, clean, pressed, well-fitting clothing that is appropriate for the interview situation. Keep accessories such as earrings, bracelets, necklaces, rings, and watches to a minimum.

Makeup and cologne should enhance appearance rather than call attention to themselves. Remember, how you dress and prepare yourself physically for an interview reveals how you feel about yourself, the other party, the situation, and the nature and importance of the interview. Dress and physical appearance can affect your self-concept, determine credibility with the other party, reveal status within an organization, and gain appropriate attention.

Many studies reveal that *nonverbal communication is more important than verbal communication*. Some research indicates that nonverbal actions exchange feelings and emotions more accurately; convey meanings and intentions relatively free of deception, distortion, and confusion; are more efficient; are more suitable for suggesting or imparting ideas and emotions indirectly; and are critical for high-quality communication. Nonverbal behaviors are assumed to be more truthful than words, and if verbal and nonverbal messages conflict—sending mixed messages—we are likely to believe the nonverbal. *How* you say something tends to dominate *what* you say.

Some theorists argue, however, that it is nearly impossible to isolate the verbal from the nonverbal because they are so intertwined during interviews that they are "completely interdependent."[23] For example, the nonverbal may *complement* the verbal. Vocal stress may call attention to an important word (like underlining or italicizing in print): "I am *not* in the market for a new car" or "My *interest* income last year was $8,365." Vocal inflection may give specific meanings to words, such as complementing the verbal with a sincere tone of voice and deliberate speaking rate. A serious facial expression and direct eye contact may help your words communicate sympathy and understanding. The nonverbal accentuates and verifies your words. Nonverbal actions may *reinforce* verbal messages: a head nod while saying yes, a head shake while saying no, or an extended arm with the hand up while saying stop. "Give us two hamburgers" may be reinforced with two raised fingers. A nonverbal action may act as a *substitute* for words. You may point to a chair without saying, "Sit here please," or shrug your shoulders to express "I don't care," and the interviewee will translate your actions into words. Nonverbal substitutes, a kind of everyday sign language, may be more effective and less disruptive than words. You may remain silent to communicate "Go on," "I agree," "I am interested in what you have to say," or "I don't understand."

Nonverbal actions can be confusing and interpreted in a variety of ways. The nature of your *relationship* (degree of liking, trust, similarity, involvement, control) may determine how you interpret nonverbal behavior. For example, you may (depending on your relationship with a person) see a yawn as a sign of boredom or disinterest in what you are saying or as a sign of lack of sleep or time of day. You may note poor posture and interpret it as a sloppy habit or as being at ease. You may interpret a soft voice as a sign of weakness or as a measure of self-control. You may note rumpled or out-of-style clothing and see the party as unprofessional or creative.

Gender differences between interview parties may affect interviews because women seem to be more skilled at and rely more on nonverbal communication than men. For instance, research indicates that facial expressions, pauses, and bodily gestures are more important in women's interactions than men's, perhaps because women are more expressive than men. Women tend to gaze more and are less uncomfortable when eye contact is broken. Men's lower-pitched voices are viewed as more credible, more

Be aware of cultural differences in nonverbal communication.

photo by Bob Daemmrich/The Image Works

dynamic than women's higher-pitched voices. Female parties stand or sit closer than opposite-sex parties, and males maintain more distance than opposite-sex or female parties.

Cultures share many nonverbal signals. Around the world a person is likely to nod the head in agreement, shake the head in disagreement, give a thumbs down for disapproval, shake a fist in anger, and clap hands for approval. In spite of similarities, nonverbal communication differs among cultures, including between black and white Americans. Black participants tend to maintain eye contact more when speaking than listening and give more nonverbal feedback when listening than whites. In general, black Americans are more animated and personal, whereas white Americans are more subdued. Black Americans tend to avoid eye contact with superiors out of respect, a trait that white superiors often misinterpret as a sign of disinterest, lack of confidence, or dishonesty. And black Americans tend to touch more and stand closer together when communicating than do white Americans.[24]

On the *global scene,* Americans are taught to look others in the eye when speaking to them, whereas Africans are taught to avoid eye contact when listening to others. An honest "look me in the eye" for a Westerner may express a lack of respect to an Asian. An American widens his or her eyes to show wonder or surprise; the Chinese do so to express anger, the French to express disbelief, and Hispanics to show lack of understanding. Americans are taught to smile in response to a smile, but this is not so in Israel. Japanese are taught to mask negative feelings with smiles and laughter. Americans are taught to have little direct physical contact with others while communicating, but Mediterranean and Latin countries encourage direct contact. On a loudness scale of 1 to 10, with 10 being high, Arabs would be near 10, Americans would be near the middle, and Europeans would be near 1. Arabs perceive loudness as signs of strength and sincerity and softness as signs of weakness and deviousness. Not surprisingly, many Americans and Europeans see Arabs as pushy and rude. A firm handshake is important in American society but signals nothing in Japan. Common gestures have a wide variety of meanings. A circular motion of a finger around an ear means crazy in many countries, but it signals "You have a telephone call" in the Netherlands. Fingers in a circle means okay in the United States but is an obscene gesture in Brazil. Thumbs up is a rude gesture in Australia and a simple okay or all's well in other countries. As intercultural contacts become increasingly common in the United States and throughout the world, it will

Figure 2.5 *Feedback*

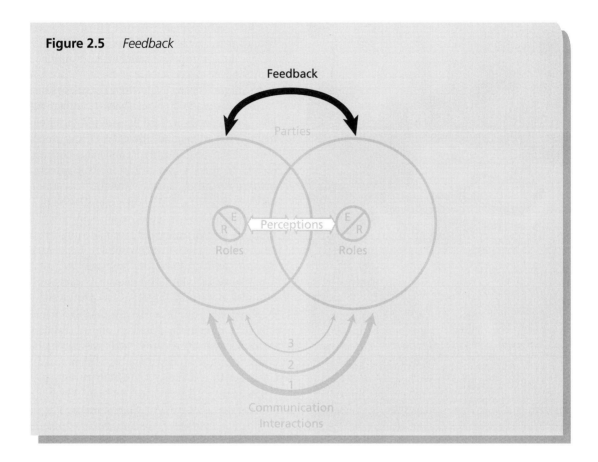

become ever more critical for you to understand the interconnections between words and nonverbal actions and how these are interpreted by diverse people and cultures.

Feedback

The large, double-ended arrow that links the top of the party circles (see Figure 2.5) symbolizes the heavy stream of feedback between interview parties. Feedback is both verbal (questions and answers, arguments and counterarguments, agreements and disagreements, challenges and compliances) and nonverbal (facial expressions, gestures, raised eyebrows, eye contact, vocal utterances, and posture). It is more immediate and pervasive during interviews than in any other form of planned, purposeful communication. And meaningful feedback, sent and received, is essential if you are to verify what is being communicated and how well it is being communicated.

Feedback is detected through *observing* and *listening* carefully and insightfully. Observe everything that does and does not take place during an interview, including the tone of the interaction, seating arrangement, and proximity of the parties. Be particularly observant of changes in eye contact, posture, attentiveness, voice, and manner. For example, does the other party move closer or farther away; does the opening conversational tone become more formal as you get into controversial areas; does eye contact lessen as the interview progresses; does the other party seem to be more or less willing to disclose information? Be careful of reading too much into small nonverbal actions and changes. A person may be fidgeting not because of your questions or responses but because the chair is hard or uncomfortable. A person may be paying less attention not because of boredom but because the room is hot or because of fatigue from jet lag. A person may speak softly because he or she always speaks softly, not because of who you are or the interview purpose. A person who seems to be hiding something because of poor eye contact, soft voice, and hesitancy may simply be shy. Strive to be perceptive, sensitive, and receptive.

Listening skills are essential to obtaining information, detecting feedback cues, and motivating the other party to respond beyond Level 1. You cannot hear and assess the steady stream of feedback in interviews if you have your mouth open and your ears closed. Even though we often listen more than we talk during interviews, few of us listen well. Surveys of hundreds of corporations in the United States have revealed that poor listening skills are a major barrier in nearly all positions from accountants to supervisors; good listening skills are considered critical to entry-level positions, effective performance, high productivity, managerial competency, and promotion within most organizations.

When we are the interviewer, we often do not listen carefully to either the questions we ask or the answers we receive. And when we are the interviewee, we often do not listen carefully to the questions we are asked or the answers we give. Occasionally a friendly critic will remark, "Did you hear what you just said (asked)?" "You should hear yourself." Or "Let me ask that question again." We may not listen because we are not interested in the interview or what the other party is asking or saying. We may be so concerned about our primary role in the interview, questioner or respondent, that we do not listen. We may be too easily distracted by the other party's appearance or status, the physical surroundings, or interruptions and noise such as ringing telephones, traffic outside, or people walking through the area. And most of our schooling and training has prepared us for talking, not listening.

There are four approaches to listening: for comprehension, for empathy, for evaluation, and for resolution. Each approach is designed to play a specific role in helping you give, receive, and process information during interviews, and any one of the approaches may dominate all or part of an interview. Physicians, sales representatives, journalists, and counselors, for example, may use all four in a single interview.

Listening for Comprehension

Listening for comprehension is primarily a method of receiving, understanding, and remembering a message "as close as possible to that which the sender intended."[25] The purpose is to concentrate on a question, answer, or reaction to understand and remain objective, not to inspect critically or make judgments. This listening approach is critical for giving and getting information in many types of interviews and during the first minutes of interviews when you are determining how to react. Here are some guidelines for listening for comprehension:

1. Listen attentively and insightfully to an answer before phrasing your question.
2. Be patient, particularly when information seems irrelevant or uninteresting.
3. Listen for content and ideas, no matter how difficult they are to understand.
4. Take notes to retain information accurately and to show that you are listening.
5. Clarify information through repetitions and reflective questions.

> Are you saying you don't want to make a change at this time?
>
> Was that at 9:15 on Wednesday the 19th?
>
> Why, again, do we need legal counsel?

6. Probe for additional information that will clarify a situation.

> What do you know about . . . ?
>
> Tell me more about . . . .
>
> Why do you think this program is too difficult for high school students?

7. Ask for specific information when a message is vague or unclear.

> What do you mean by limited warranty?
>
> What were your responsibilities as assistant manager?
>
> When do you plan to graduate?

8. Identify beliefs, attitudes, and feelings.

> Why do you feel that way?
>
> What is your attitude toward IRAs?
>
> How do you feel about transferring these operations to Mexico?

Listening for Empathy

Listening for empathy is a method of responding beyond merely receiving and comprehending messages. You communicate to the other party an attitude of genuine concern, understanding, and involvement. Listen with sensitivity and provide verbal and nonverbal feedback. Strive to put yourself in the other's place to understand and appreciate what the other person is experiencing and feeling. Empathic listening is total response. You reassure, comfort, express warmth, and show unconditional positive regard for the other party. Highly personal and emotional issues, such as performance in a course, illness, family problems, financial problems, and career changes, require empathic listening. The genuineness of empathic listening is a measure of its success. Empathic listening points the way to possible actions. Listening for empathy is not synonymous with expressing sympathy. Sympathy implies feeling sorry for someone; empathy is the ability to place yourself in another's situation. You say verbally and nonverbally, "As much as I can, I am trying to understand your thoughts, feelings, and limitations." Here are some guidelines for listening with empathy:

1. Show you are listening and interested.
2. Do not interrupt.
3. Do not react too quickly to controversial or antagonistic comments and questions.

   Let a person talk out apparent hostilities toward you and others.

   Do not become defensive without listening to everything said and implied.

4. Strive to be comfortable with strong displays of emotion.

   If a person cries, remain silent and give the person time to become composed.

   Avoid unhelpful comments such as "I know" or "It'll be okay."

   If a person launches into a morbid account, hear it out without showing discomfort or impatience.

5. Remain nonevaluative unless you have no choice.

   You must realize that my situation is not exactly like yours, but if I were in your situation . . . .

   I can understand your anger over the time it has taken your insurance company to react to the flood, but . . . .

6. Listen with an eye toward giving options and directions.

   That's one option, of course. Others are . . . .

   Many clients are confused by the new tax laws. You might consider . . . .

7. Respond with candor.

   No, I cannot place myself in your situation, because I have never experienced such a loss.

   Yes, your e-mail did make me angry for a while.

Listening for Evaluation

Listening for evaluation (sometimes called *critical listening*) goes beyond comprehension and empathy to making judgments about what you hear and observe. Usually evaluative listening should follow comprehension and empathy because you are not ready to judge a message until you understand the sender and comprehend the verbal and nonverbal signals and the substance of the message. Evaluative listening is critical in many interviews, but openly expressing your criticism may seriously diminish cooperation and level of disclosure. Here are some guidelines for evaluative listening:

1. Listen carefully to an entire question or answer before making judgments.
2. Pay close attention to both words and how they are communicated nonverbally.
3. Listen to the content, including reasoning, evidence, and rank ordering of points.
4. If you are unsure of what is being said or asked, ask for clarification.
5. Do not become defensive, and refuse to be baited into overreacting because of leading questions or emotion-laden words.
6. Often it is wise to withhold final evaluations until an interview is concluded and you have time to understand and judge appropriately.

Listening for Resolution

John Stewart has developed a fourth type of listening that he calls "dialogic listening."[26] He writes that dialogic listening focuses on "ours" rather than "mine" or "yours" and believes the agenda for resolving a problem or task supersedes the individual. This type of listening is most appropriate for problem-solving interviews when the goal is the resolution of a problem or task, not the solving of a problem for one party, giving information to another, getting information from another, selecting a new member, or reviewing performance. Stewart likens dialogic listening to adding clay to a mold; the idea is to see how the other person will react, what the person will add, how this will affect the shape and content of the product. Here are some guidelines:

1. Remain modest and humble.
2. Trust the other party to make significant contributions.
3. Be open-ended in your questions and responses.
4. Focus on the communication not the psychology of the interview.
5. Focus on the present rather than past or future.
6. Encourage the other party to say more.
7. Encourage the other party to respond to what you have offered.
8. Run with metaphors either party introduces.
9. Paraphrase and add to the other party's responses and ideas.
10. Use questions to encourage moving forward.

> What's next?
>
> Now what?
>
> Where do we go from here?

Although insightful listening is critical to both interviewer and interviewee, we find it difficult to listen, let alone to choose the appropriate listening approach. Listening is an invisible skill, so it is difficult to emulate by observing. And we learn to be passive listeners as children, students, employees, and subordinates. We are not encouraged to react verbally and nonverbally but merely to sit and accept (or appear to accept) what is presented to us. We all have had experiences with persons (parents, peers, teachers, physicians, police officers, employers) who would not listen to us, regardless of what we had to say. A few months ago, a fund-raiser for a charity called the home of one of the authors. He was interested in giving to the charity but wanted written information on the organization and the opportunity to send a donation through the mail. The fund-raiser was determined to get an immediate commitment of a specific dollar donation over the telephone that evening. The effort ended with no commitment and no donation.

You can become a more effective listener by working at it.[27] First, strive to be a listener as much as you want to be a talker. Be as satisfied when listening to others as you are when listening to yourself. Second, overcome the "entertainment syndrome," the expectation that you must be entertained in all settings and the attitude that anything "boring" can be ignored. Little in this world, either in or out of the classroom, is continually exciting and entertaining, but most is important to listen to. Third, be an active listener by attending carefully and critically to words, arguments, and evidence and by observing nonverbal clues such as voice, face, gestures, eye contact, and movements. Fourth, concentrate on listening despite distractions such as physical surroundings, interruptions, mannerisms, appearance, and dress. And fifth, use the most appropriate listening approach or approaches for each interview. Be flexible.

The Interview Situation

All interviews come about because of an *exigency*—a need marked by a degree of urgency. You may *need* a part-time job to help pay college expenses, counseling to improve your grade in a class, a new computer, information for a term paper or newspaper story, or medical attention for a persistent headache. The *degree of urgency* in each of these situations depends upon the seriousness of your financial status, whether a low grade will keep you from graduating or merely having a higher GPA, the state of your computer, the deadline for your paper or story, or the severity of your headache. Need determines the *type of interview* in which you will take part: information getting, information giving, persuasive, employment selection, performance review, performance problem, counseling, health care, and so on. Need, urgency, and type help shape the interview atmosphere. For instance, the atmosphere in a selection interview is very different from that in a reprimand interview, and the atmosphere in a market survey is very different from that in a mental or physical health care interview. Need, urgency, type, and *organizational policies* place specific restraints on the initiation of the interview, the parties, perceptions, roles being played, levels of interactions, degree of self-disclosure, nature of messages, feedback, and whether the appropriate interviewing approach is directive, nondirective, or a combination of the two. Organizational policies often prescribe how staff members will structure and conduct survey, selection, performance review or problem, discipline, counseling, and health care interviews.

No interview takes place in a vacuum. Each interview occurs at a given time and in a given place. A variety of situational variables, symbolized by the imploding arrows in Figure 2.6, affect each interview positively and negatively. These include location, architecture, temperature, seating arrangement, furniture, objects, physical distance between parties, territoriality, noise, interruptions, privacy, time of day and week, and events that precede and follow the interview.

Time of Day, Week, and Year

Each of us tends to communicate best at different times of the day, week, and year. For instance, you might be a morning, afternoon, or evening person, meaning this is the optimum time for your performance, production, communication, thinking, creativity, handling of conflicts, and dealing with highly important, intricate, or delicate matters. It is usually unwise to attempt to handle difficult issues or exchange important and extensive information just before lunch when parties are hungry and late in the day or work shift when they are tired mentally and physically. Monday mornings and Friday afternoons are times when moods tend to be dark and motivation low. Holidays such as Christmas, Memorial Day, Thanksgiving, and Yom Kippur are good for some types of

Figure 2.6 *Situational variables*

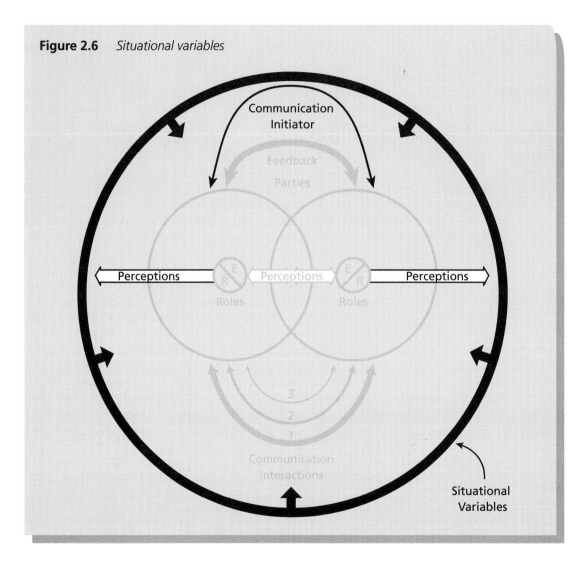

interviews (sales, employment selection, journalistic) but bad times for others (dismissals, reprimands, investigations, health care). Counselors note marked increases in crisis interviews with lonely people during family-oriented and happy seasons such as Thanksgiving, Christmas, and Passover. Many police officers claim that full moons bring out strange behaviors in people.

Be aware of events that precede or follow an interview. Tuesday afternoons may ordinarily be good times for a manager or professor, but not *this* Tuesday because of a poor quarterly production report just delivered or a nasty confrontation with another student minutes before you arrive. A student facing a major examination after an interview for an internship may find it difficult to concentrate and answer questions. Traffic accidents, layoffs, personal problems, happy or sad news, and intraorganizational squabbles may affect your mood, expectations, concentration, and communication.

Initiating the Interview

The arrows that emerge from the top of the situational circle and touch each party (see Figure 2.6) signify that either party may initiate an interview. For example, you may walk into a professor's office to talk about a test grade, or a professor may call you in to talk about the test grade. A car salesperson who sold you a car two years ago might contact you about purchasing a different vehicle, or you might call the salesperson about possible end-of-the-year deals. In the first scenario, you are likely to feel more in control when you initiate the interview than when the professor, a person in authority, does so. And in the second, the salesperson would prefer a situation in which you show interest by initiating the contact to the situation in which he or she must make a cold call to a person who may neither need nor want a different car.

The situation often determines who initiates an interview and who must be interviewed. A police officer must interview those involved in a traffic accident; a reporter must interview members of the school board proposing a new drug-testing policy for student athletes; and a college senior must interview for positions relevant to areas of study. Conversely, the person who initiates affects the situation by determining how the contact is initiated and where and when the interview will take place. You can affect the climate of the interview by initiating the interview directly rather than through a secretary or staff member, by telling the other party what the interview will be about, and by initiating the interview in a warm and friendly manner. Except in unusual circumstances, it is important to alleviate fears, anxieties, and uncertainties the other party may have by initiating the interview in a positive and informative manner.

Perceptions of the Situation

Perceptions of the situation are symbolized in the interviewing model (Figure 2.6) by the arrows that run from each party to the situational circle. Remember that each person comes to an interview with somewhat unique perceptions of the situation (purpose, need, urgency, timing, setting). The interviewer may see the interview as merely a routine, everyday activity, nothing special or exciting, while the interviewee may see the interview as an extraordinary, once-in-a-lifetime event likely to affect career, advancement, marriage, financial plans, health, or social status. A recruiter, for example, may interview a dozen college seniors a day and perceive each interview as merely business as usual. Each senior, however, may perceive the interview as the opportunity of a lifetime, an event anticipated and planned for months or years. A fire may be a routine event for firefighters and reporters but not for victims. Medical examinations may be routine for physicians but not for patients who fear they have mono, AIDS, cancer, or heart problems.

The setting may be perceived quite differently by interview parties. A supervisor may view the conference room as a neutral setting, while an employee may see it as a hostile environment, particularly if workers get fired there. A professor may feel very relaxed sitting behind a desk, but a student may feel threatened when sitting in front of the desk. A salesperson may want to call people at their homes around dinnertime because that is when they are most likely to be home, while customers may see such calls as rude because they interrupt dinner and important family time. Both parties have vested interests in the nature and outcome of interviews, but their goals may be quite different. A sales representative wants to sell you a set of encyclopedias, and you want to spend your money on a new sound system. While you are doing research for a term paper on the Vietnam War, you may see a combat veteran of that conflict as a source of important insights, but the veteran may want his experiences and thoughts to remain private. A political pollster wants you to respond to questions about the upcoming primary election, and you want to watch the Masters golf tournament on television.

Interview parties are most likely to communicate beyond Level 1 interchanges if they perceive the situation to be familiar rather than strange, informal rather than formal, warm rather than cold, private rather than open to others, and close rather than distant physically, socially, and psychologically. Organizations attempt to enhance concentration and motivation with well-lighted, pleasantly painted, moderate-sized rooms with comfortable furniture, temperature, and ventilation. Some attempt to create business and professional settings that resemble living rooms, dining rooms, family rooms, and studies to make interviewees feel more at home and thus more willing and able to communicate at Levels 2 and 3.

Territoriality

All of us are territorial. We stake out our physical and psychological space and resent those who invade it with their possessions, eyes, voices, or bodies. Think of how you have reacted to invasions of territory: to persons who walked into a professor's office while you were interacting with the professor about a class problem, to persons at another table listening to your conversation during lunch with a prospective employer or employee, to persons talking loudly at the next workstation when you were attempting to give information to a supervisor, to persons who took a seat at the same small table while you were talking about a personal problem with a friend. You are likely to feel uncomfortable with a person who insists on talking nose-to-nose and may react by backing up, placing furniture between the two of you, or terminating the interview as quickly as possible. Two to four feet—approximately an arm's length or on opposite sides of a table or desk—seems to be an optimum distance. The next time you are in a library or airport, notice how people stake out

photo by Bob Daemmrich/The Image Works

■ *A corner seating arrangement is preferred by many interviewers and interviewees.*

their territory with coats, books, purses, and briefcases so others cannot get too close. You are less likely to react negatively to territorial incursions by friends, peers, superiors, high-status persons, or people who explain why they are encroaching. You may extend an invitation by removing coats from chairs and moving books or briefcases.

Research suggests that status, relationship, situation, and feelings of parties toward one another affect the size of the protective bubble with which we are comfortable. High-status people stand or sit closer to low-status people, whereas low-status people prefer greater distances when dealing with superiors. We are likely to maintain a greater distance with a stranger than with a close associate. Some people when angry want to "get in your face," whereas others may widen the space because their anger is translated into distancing themselves from you physically and socially.

Age, sex, and culture also determine our space preferences. For instance, people of the same age stand or sit closer together than those of mixed ages, particularly when the age difference is great. All-male parties tend to arrange themselves farther apart than all-female or mixed-sex parties. We, as North Americans, prefer to maintain a greater personal distance with other parties than do Middle Eastern and Latin American peoples. Many Arabs and Latin Americans see us as distant and cold, while we see them as intruding into our space. Northern Europeans tend to prefer greater personal distance than southern Europeans.

Seating arrangement may help or hinder an interview. Status, gender, furnishings, cultural norms, relationship between parties, and personal preferences may influence seating arrangement. For example, a superior and a subordinate may sit across a desk from one another (arrangement A in Figure 2.7), providing appropriate distance in a formal setting when one party desires to maintain a superior position. Two chairs at right angles near the corner of a desk or table (arrangement B) create a less formal atmosphere and a greater feeling of equality between parties. Many students and staff have remarked to the authors that they prefer this arrangement with college professors and department heads or supervisors. You may remove physical obstacles and reduce the superior-subordinate atmosphere further by placing chairs at opposite sides of a small coffee table or by omitting the table altogether (arrangements C and D). A circular table (arrangement E) is growing in popularity, especially in counseling interviews or interviews involving more than two people, because it avoids a head-of-the-table position, allows participants to pass around materials, and provides a surface on which to write, review materials, or place refreshments. The circular table or chairs around a small table works well for panel or group interviews. Arrangement F is most suitable when one or both parties consist of several persons.

Take into consideration whose turf you are on during an interview. For instance, you are likely to feel more comfortable, more relaxed, and less threatened in your home, room, office, or place of business than on another's turf, particularly that of a stranger, supervisor, or high-status person such as president of your college or owner of the company. When one of the authors was chairperson of the editorial board of his university's press, a professor appeared in his office one afternoon and asked if he would mind coming to the professor's office to discuss a book manuscript. The author assumed the professor had a manuscript laid out for him to see, but there was no manuscript to see.

Figure 2.7   *Seating arrangements*

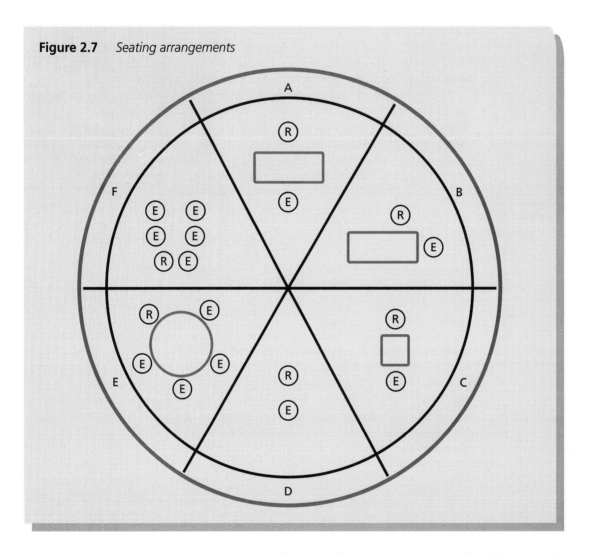

The professor was comfortable discussing his book project only in his office where he felt more in control. We tend to protect our turf. Think of your reactions when you walked into your room or office and found another person in your chair or at your desk or noticed that someone had moved items around on your worktable.

When there is a choice, select the location most conducive to effective communication. The setting might be your place so you can feel more relaxed and in charge or because you have designed it with effective communication in mind or to show you have a highly professional and successful career or profession. The setting might be neutral, such as a restaurant or conference room, to avoid turf problems. Or it might be the other's residence because you want to talk about family concerns, the campus because you want a recruit to see its beauty and friendliness, or the other's place of business because you want to talk about business computers.

Objects and Decorations

Do not underestimate the importance of objects and decorations in creating an appropriate atmosphere and interview climate. Trophies, awards, degrees, and licenses suitably displayed and framed communicate your achievements, professional credibility, and stature in your field. Pictures, statues, and busts of organizational leaders or famous persons, particularly those who have used your services or given you special recognition, communicate organizational and personal history, success, recognition, endorsement, and contacts. Models or samples of products both display and advertise your products and their quality. Colors of walls, types of carpeting, wall hangings, wallpaper, and curtains can provide the climate most appropriate for you and your organization and most conducive to effective communication.

Noise

Noise in an interview refers to anything that interferes with the communication process. For instance, it may be background noise such as machinery, doors opening and closing, squeaking chairs, music, others talking, objects being dropped or unloaded from trucks, footsteps outside the room, and traffic or aircraft. The interview may be interrupted by a ringing telephone, the arrival of a faxed letter, or an e-mail message. Other frequent distractions include people coming in and out of the room, walking by an open door, or asking the other party or you for answers, directions, or assistance. The authors are surprised by the number of students who will walk into an office and interrupt an interview between a professor and student.

You may generate noise by coming to an interview fatigued, angry about an incident unrelated to the interview, overwhelmed with personal problems, or thinking about the next interview. You may be easily distracted by a headache, upset stomach, or hangover. Additionally, you may succumb to looking out a window at traffic, building construction, flowers, or scenery. Or you may concentrate on pictures, objects, furniture in the room, or the other party's note taking, dress, appearance, or mannerisms.

You can limit the negative influences of noise by selecting locations free of background noise. Sometimes noise can be reduced by closing a door, window, or curtain; taking the phone off the hook; turning off your computer, television, or CD player; and informing others you do not wish to be disturbed. Limit self-generated noise by coming to an interview physically and psychologically ready to concentrate. Chapter 5 offers suggestions for note taking that avoids distracting others.

Outside Forces

Although our primary concern should be with the two parties in a specific situation, we must be aware of possible outside forces that may influence one or both parties during and after the interview (see Figure 2.8). Common outside forces are family, associates, friends, employers, government agencies, and professional associations. Many of these forces have input before the interview by providing guidelines for taking part in the interview, topics to cover, structure to follow, questions to ask, demands to make, or attitude to take. Some union contracts, for example, prescribe what questions can be asked and how they are to be phrased during employment interviews. No deviations or probing questions are permitted.

Outside forces may impact the interview when parties try to follow advice and guidelines or think about postinterview reactions of outside forces to how they will report what took place, particularly questions, answers, topics covered, and demands. For example, an interviewer may take a hard line in a negotiation or ask pressure questions during a selection interview because that is what the company demands and what he or she needs to report following the interview. An interviewee may respond as outside forces have suggested or say what he or she wants to tell them later. A person who fears that IRS or superiors will discover what was said during an interview may be very reluctant to reply openly to your questions. It seems that we can be sued, reprimanded, or fired for almost anything we say today on controversial issues.

Be aware of how outside forces may affect your role in the interview. Which advice is wise to take; which is appropriate for you; which must you take? How might your inclination to satisfy the group following the interview negatively affect the interview? And be aware of outside forces impinging on the other party. This awareness will help

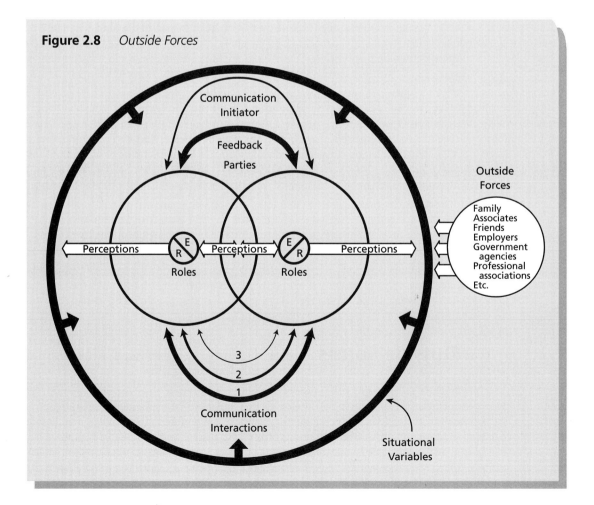

Figure 2.8   *Outside Forces*

you understand attitudes, responses, and behavior and avoid questions and topics off-limits to the interviewee. For instance, we often make demands and let off steam to product representatives on the telephone who have no authority to grant our wishes and who are not responsible for the problem. As bearers of bad news, they become the company's scapegoats and our targets.

Summary

In this chapter, we developed a summary model of the interviewing process that contains the many interacting variables present in each interview: two parties, exchanging of roles, perceptions, verbal and nonverbal messages, feedback, situation, and outside forces. Interviewing is a dynamic, complicated process between two complex parties operating with imperfect verbal and nonverbal symbols guided and controlled by perceptions and the situation. The ability to listen (for comprehension, empathy, evaluation, and resolution) and to employ silence strategically are often more important than what we have to say.

A thorough understanding of the process and the multidimensional relationship that exists between parties is a prerequisite for successful interviewing. Both parties must be aware that *perceptions* of self, the other party, how the other party sees us, and the situation are critical in determining how interviews progress and desired outcomes are achieved. We must acknowledge and adapt to the influence of outside forces.

Interviewer and interviewee must be *flexible* and *adaptable* not only because each party is somewhat unique, but also because each is molded and affected by demographics such as age, sex, race, and culture. This chapter has tried to make you aware of how demographics and culture affect relationships, self-esteem, disclosure, levels of communication, language, nonverbal communication, and territoriality. In the increasingly small global village of the twenty-first century, you must be aware of how different people and different cultures communicate.

An Interview for Review and Analysis

This interview is designed to incorporate all of the principles and theories presented in this chapter and to provide you with an opportunity to analyze them and determine how they affect the interview and the relationship between the two parties.[28] Begin by reading carefully the description of the two parties and the situation. Note the goal of this interview. Then, as you read carefully each interaction, think about the questions posed for review and analysis. Finally, what suggestions would you offer to the manager and Joe for handling such situations and for improving interviewing skills?

Joe is a production supervisor with 20 years of experience and a good record. The plant manager is considering him for promotion, and, as a first step in that process, this interview is exploratory rather than decision making. Company policy stipulates that employees are *not* to be informed when being actively considered for promotion, so Joe is unaware that a promotion may be in the offing. Company policy does allow mentioning, in general terms, overall considerations related to the current workforce situation and to established company criteria for promotions. Two hours prior to the interview, Joe receives a call from the manager's secretary asking him to report to the manager. No reason is given. Joe enters the manager's office at 4:30 P.M. (his shift ends at 5:00 P.M.) and is seated across the desk from the manager.

What perceptions do Joe and the manager have of themselves, one another, and the situation? When do the parties exchange the roles of interviewer and interviewee? Using such dimensions as similarity, inclusion/involvement, affection/liking, control/dominance, and trust, assess the relationship between Joe and the manager. How does this relationship seem to affect the interview. At which communication levels are most interactions, and why is this so? How do words influence the interview? How does nonverbal behavior affect the interview? Which listening approaches do Joe and the manager employ most often, and how appropriate are these? Which interviewing approach (directive, nondirective, or combination) does the manager employ, and how does this approach affect interactions? How do situational variables influence this interview? What roles, if any, do outside forces play in this interview?

1. **Manager:** Well Joe, come on in. (*smiling*) Sit down. It's been quite a while since we've had time for a real chat.

2. **Joe:** (*sitting facing the manager*) Thank you sir. (*soft voice*)

3. **Manager:** (*very serious facial expression and tone of voice*) How are things moving along these days, Joe? *Everything* under control in your section?

4. **Joe:** Oh, yeah, fine, I guess. No complaints. (*fast speaking rate*)

5. **Manager:** I'm *glad* to hear that there are no *complaints*. (*pause*) You think, then, you're doing a pretty good job?

6. **Joe:** As good a job as I know how, sir. (*shifts weight in chair*)

7. **Manager:** Good. (*pause; looks Joe directly in the eyes*) By the way, have you ever thought of . . . uh, doing *something else*?

8. **Joe:** (*pause; speaks slowly*) Well . . . uh, yes and no, I guess. However, I do like this job very much. (*rapidly*) It's a job I know very thoroughly.

9. **Manager:** Hmmm, I see. You mean you would not like to change your job, then?

10. **Joe:** Uh . . . no . . . no . . . I really don't think I would.

11. **Manager:** (*looking closely at Joe; measuring his words*) I see. Just why do you want to stay on your present job?

12. **Joe:** Well, I know the work real well. And everybody seems to like me.

13. **Manager:** *Seems* to like you? (*looks Joe directly in the eyes*)

14. **Joe:** Oh . . . now and then there may be one or two people who don't like one of my decisions. But we always manage to get along.

15. **Manager:** Some people don't like you, then? (*sounds accusatory*)

16. **Joe:** Well, I wouldn't exactly say *that*. I've had a couple of people who have been sore because I didn't give them some overtime.

17. **Manager:** That's the *only* reason some people haven't been too fond of you?

18. **Joe:** Really, sir, that's the only thing of importance I can think of. They goof off too much. (*firm voice, direct eye contact*)

19. **Manager:** You don't like people who loaf on the job?

20. **Joe:** No, absolutely not! Everyone should pitch in and do their share.

21. **Manager:** I assume, of course, that you do yours!

22. **Joe:** Of course!

23. **Manager:** (*pause*) Uh . . . Joe, did you ever think of . . . uh, *bettering* yourself?

24. **Joe:** I guess anyone who has any brains or ambition wants to try to do better.

25. **Manager:** Just what do you mean by *that*?

26. **Joe:** Well, I mean that almost anyone can find ways to improve. (*looks down*)

27. **Manager:** You think, then, you handle your job well right now?

28. **Joe:** Oh, I'm sure there's always room for improvement. Do you have anything *specific* in mind, sir?

29. **Manager:** Joe, have you ever thought of bettering yourself on . . . *another* job?

30. **Joe:** Oh I really do like this job and company very much, sir! This is a job I feel I know very well. The company has been very good to me.

31. **Manager:** I'm not sure you were listening *carefully* to my question, Joe. Let me ask it again. Have you ever thought of bettering yourself on *another* job?

32. **Joe:** Well, that's hard to answer, sir, because I really like my job.

33. **Manager:** You haven't considered the *possibility* of another job?

34. **Joe:** Well, everybody daydreams a little about how things might be at another company or your own business. But I haven't given it much serious thought.

35. **Manager:** I take it, then, that you prefer definitely to stay on your present job.

36. **Joe:** Oh, yes. As I've said, I'm happy in my job at this company. Do you have something in mind for another job *here*, sir? (*rapid speaking voice*)

37. **Manager:** Oh, don't worry about that, Joe. It's been good to have a little chat with you, Joe. We'll have to get together again before too long. Lots of luck. See you later. (*shakes Joe's hand firmly without meeting his eyes*)

Student Activities

1. Identify a person with whom you have had a positive and long-standing relationship. Assess this relationship by considering the relational dimensions discussed in this chapter: similarity, inclusion/involvement, affection/liking, control/dominance, and trust. Which dimension is most important for your relationship? When the relationship was threatened or changed in the past, positively or negatively, what were the nature of these threats or changes? How did you and the other party adapt to and resolve threats and changes?

2. Observe three interviews: one between two men, one between two women, and one between a man and a woman. Focus on the similarities and differences in word selection and nonverbal communication. Which characteristics of the parties do you think influenced these similarities and differences the most: sex, age, race, or culture?

3. Visit several professional offices and observe the physical surroundings. How are they designed for the types of interviews that take place there? Which seem most comfortable and conducive to communication and why? Which do you find least comfortable and conducive to communication and why? What do the surroundings tell you about the people who created them or work in them? How would you change them, and what does this say about you?

4. Watch an interview on television that lasts at least 15 minutes. Note the levels of communication between the interviewer and interviewee. Which levels did you detect in this interview? Which level dominated and when? How can you account for the levels and the one that dominated? Consider such factors as relationship, climate of the interview, motivation, topics, trust, rewards, questions, culture, and demographic characteristics of the parties in your accounting.

Notes

1. Robert S. Goyer, W. Charles Redding, and John T. Rickey, *Interviewing Principles and Techniques: A Project Text* (Dubuque, IA: Wm. C. Brown, 1968), p. 23.

2. John Stewart and Carole Logan, *Together: Communicating Interpersonally* (New York: McGraw-Hill, 1998), pp. 22 and 85.

3. Stephen W. Littlejohn, *Theories of Human Communication* (Belmont, CA: Wadsworth, 1996), p. 250.

4. Sarah Trenholm and Arthur Jensen, *Interpersonal Communication* (Belmont, CA: Wadsworth, 1996), p. 107.

5. Stewart and Logan, p. 277.

6. Littlejohn, p. 251.

7. Trenholm and Jensen, p. 44.

8. Donald W. Klopf, *Intercultural Encounters* (Englewood, CO: Morton, 1998), pp. 176–93; and Carley H. Dodd, *Dynamics of Intercultural Communication* (New York: McGraw-Hill, 1995), pp. 21–24.

9. Stewart and Logan, p. 84.

10. Trenholm and Jensen, pp. 103–4.

11. Trenholm and Jensen, p. 358.

12. John Stewart, ed., *Bridges Not Walls: A Book about Interpersonal Communication* (New York: McGraw-Hill, 1995), p. 278.

13. Trenholm and Jensen, p. 219.

14. Stewart and Logan, p. 257.

15. Diana K. Ivy and Phil Backlund, *Exploring Gender Speak: Personal Effectiveness in Gender Communication* (New York: McGraw-Hill, 1994), p. 219.

16. Littlejohn, p. 262.

17. Sik Hung Ng and James J. Bradac, *Power in Language: Verbal Communication and Social Influence* (Newbury Park, CA: Sage, 1993), pp. 45–51.

18. Trenholm and Jensen, pp. 103–4; and Ivy and Backlund, pp. 163–65.

19. Julia T. Wood, "Gendered Interaction: Masculine and Feminine Styles of Verbal Communication," in Kathleen S. Verderber, ed., *Voices: A Selection of Multicultural Readings* (Belmont, CA: Wadsworth, 1995), p. 24.

20. William B. Gudykunst, *Bridging Differences: Effective Intergroup Communication* (Newbury Park, CA: Sage, 1991), pp. 42–59.

21. Irving J. Lee, *How to Talk with People* (New York: Harper & Row, 1952), pp. 11–26.

22. Judee K. Burgoon, David B. Buller, and W. Gill Woodall, *Nonverbal Communication: The Unspoken Dialogue* (New York: Harper & Row, 1989), pp. 4–7.

23. Stewart, p. 52.

24. Trenholm and Jensen, pp. 68 and 391–92; and Klopf, pp. 232–33.

25. Andrew Wolvin and Carolyn Gwynn Coakley, *Listening* (Dubuque, IA: Wm. C. Brown, 1992), p. 223.

26. Stewart, pp. 188–99; and Stewart and Logan, pp. 200–4.

27. James J. Floyd, *Listening: A Practical Approach* (Glenview, IL: Scott, Foresman, 1985), pp. 20–28.

28. Adapted from Benjamin Balinsky and Ruth Burger, *The Executive Interview,* pp. 24–25. Copyright 1959 by Benjamin Balinsky and Ruth Burger. It is reprinted by permission of HarperCollins and W. Charles Redding.

Resources

Klopf, Donald W. *Intercultural Encounters*. Englewood, CO: Morton, 1998.

Samovar, Larry A., and Richard E. Porter. *Communication between Cultures*. Belmont, CA: Wadsworth, 1995.

Stewart, John, ed. *Bridges Not Walls: A Book about Interpersonal Communication*. New York: McGraw-Hill, 1995.

Trenholm, Sarah, and Arthur Jensen. *Interpersonal Communication*. Belmont, CA: Wadsworth, 1996.

Wood, Julia T. *But I Thought You Meant . . . Misunderstandings in Human Communication*. Mountain View, CA: Mayfield, 1998.

Structuring the Interview

3

As noted in Chapter 1, every interview must have a degree of structure, a characteristic that sets it apart from conversation. The degree and nature of structure are determined by type, purpose, length, and complexity. And while each type of interview (survey, probing, persuasive, employment, performance review, counseling, health care) may require a somewhat different structure, a number of principles and techniques are applicable to all. This chapter focuses on these principles and techniques and three major interview parts: (1) opening, (2) body, and (3) closing.

The Opening

The few seconds or minutes you spend in the opening are often the most important portion of the interview. What you do and say, or fail to do and say—as either interviewer or interviewee—influences how the other party perceives you and the situation. It sets the tone for the interview and affects your willingness or ability to go beyond Level 1 interactions. These seconds often determine whether the interview will continue at all. The tone set, for instance, may be serious or lighthearted, optimistic or pessimistic, professional or nonprofessional, formal or informal, threatening or nonthreatening, relaxed or tense. Be sure the tone is the one you *intended* to set and is most *appropriate* for your purpose and the situation. The primary function of the opening is to motivate both parties to participate willingly and to communicate freely and accurately. A poor opening may lead to a defensive climate with superficial, vague, and inaccurate responses or to no interview at all. If dissatisfied with your initial approach, a person may say no, walk away, close the door, or hang up the phone.

The Two-Step Process

A two-step process of establishing rapport and orienting the other party encourages active participation in the opening and willingness to continue into the body of the interview. Which step comes first, what is included in each step, and how content is communicated depends upon the situation, relationship between the parties, and interviewer preference.

Rapport is a process of maintaining or establishing the relationship between interviewer and interviewee by creating feelings of goodwill and trust. You may begin with a self-introduction ("Good morning, I'm Debra Shank with Motorola") or a greeting ("Good morning Bob") accompanied by appropriate nonverbal actions such as a firm

photo by S. Agricola/The Image Works

■ *What you do and say in the opening seconds sets the tone for the remainder of the interview.*

handshake, eye contact, a smile, a nod, and a pleasant, friendly voice.[1] The rapport step may then proceed to personal inquiries ("How are the new pagers doing?" "How are you?"). Small talk about the weather, mutual acquaintances, families, sports, or current events is common and often expected. You may flavor the personal inquiry and small talk with tasteful humor. Be aware that customs of a geographical area, organizational traditions or policies, culture, status differences, relationship, formality of the occasion, interview type, and situation help determine the appropriate verbal and nonverbal rapport-building techniques of each interview. It is usually unwise to refer to strangers, superiors in your organization, or high-status persons by first name. They may perceive this as being too informal or familiar. Humor or small talk may be inappropriate if an interviewee is busy or the situation is highly formal or serious. Overdoing "sweet talk," congratulation, praise, and admiration, can turn off an interviewee, particularly if you appear to be insincere. Be flexible and adaptive.

Orientation is usually the second step in the opening. You may explain the purpose, length, and nature of the interview. You may introduce the organization you represent and explain how the information will be used. You may explain why and how this party was selected. Analyze each situation carefully to determine how much orientation is essential. Do not assume that because you and the other party appear to be similar in obvious ways, such as sex, appearance, language, educational background, or culture, that you are similar in ways critical to the success of the interview. LaRay Barna writes that "the aura of similarity is a serious stumbling block to successful intercultural communication. A look-alike facade is deceiving when representatives from contrasting cultures meet, each wearing Western dress, speaking English, and using similar greeting rituals."[2] You may be lulled into assuming that you also share similar nonverbal codes, beliefs, attitudes, and values; as Barna notes, "Unless there is overt reporting of assumptions made by each party, which seldom happens, there is no chance of comparing impressions and correcting misinterpretations." These same problems occur within cultures when we make faulty assumptions. Be sure orientation includes both parties so each knows the other and what to expect during the interview.

Rapport and orientation are often intermixed and serve the essential function of reducing relational uncertainty. By the end of the opening, both parties should be aware of important similarities between them, the desire of each to take part and be involved in the process, degree of warmth or friendliness that will pervade the interview, how control will be shared, and levels of trust. An inadequate opening may mislead one or both parties and create problems during or following the interview. Recall how angry you became when you discovered a telephone call you thought was a survey or a call from a friend was actually a clever ruse for a sales pitch.

The rapport and orientation steps are illustrated in the following opening.

1. **Interviewer:** Good evening Mrs. Bowers. I'm Jacob Myers from Transcom Cable. You received a flyer last week about the cable update in Briertown.

2. **Interviewee:** Yes, we received it just yesterday. Aren't you Sean's father?

3. **Interviewer:** That's right. I think he and your son Kyle are on the track team together. Your landscaping looks beautiful.

4. **Interviewee:** Thanks. We had Nature's Habitat redo the yard this spring.

5. **Interviewer:** Well, as our flyer explained, we are interested in discovering which channels currently included in the basic offering are most and least watched by our subscribers. Could I have about 10 minutes of your time this evening?

6. **Interviewee:** If that's all the time it will take, sure.

Common Opening Techniques

Be creative and imaginative in the way you open interviews, but always adapt each opening to the interviewee and the situation. The following common opening techniques, designed to get your creative juices flowing, may serve as entire openings, aid in building rapport, or orient the interviewee.

1. *State the purpose*. This technique makes it clear why you are conducting the interview. There are occasions, however, when stating a detailed purpose would make its achievement impossible. This is the case in some research, survey, and persuasive interviews. You may need to withhold some of your purpose until later in the interview or disguise it to get honest, unguarded answers, to get the interviewee to take part in the interview, or to avoid or reduce defensiveness.

    I'm trying to discover our computer hardware and software needs for the next fiscal year.

2. *Summarize the problem*. This technique is useful when an interviewee is unaware of a problem, vaguely aware of it, or unaware of important details. Be sure your summary is complete enough to inform the interviewee but not so extensive that it goes beyond the opening to what should be discussed in the body of the interview.

    It's now been two years since we adopted a flexible work schedule for our customer relations staff. A survey shows the staff really likes flextime. However, during this time, customer complaints about the length of time it takes to reach someone in customer relations have increased by 27 percent. I want to discuss customer concerns and ways we can maintain flextime while making sure adequate staff are available at all times.

3. *Explain how the problem was discovered.* This technique explains how you discovered a problem exists. Be honest and specific in revealing sources of information, and try not to place the interviewee on the defensive.

> Two students from your 8:30 class were waiting for me when I came in this morning. They are concerned about the field project you just added to the course requirements with only three weeks remaining in the semester.

4. *Mention an incentive or reward for taking part.* This technique can be effective if the incentive is appealing to the interviewee. It must be significant enough to make a difference. Be careful of using this opening in informational interviews because many salespersons use a gift to motivate people to listen to their pitches. It may become difficult to convince the respondent that you only want to get or give information after using this technique.

> Hi Alice. A few months ago, after your Hawaiian cruise, you said you might be interested in an Alaskan tour and cruise next summer. I just received materials from American Alaskan Cruise Lines about discounted fares for the first two weeks of September.

5. *Request advice or assistance.* This is a common interview opening because assistance is often what an interviewer needs. Be sure your need is clear, precise, and one your selected interviewee can meet. Be sincere in asking for advice. Do not use this as merely an opening technique for another purpose.

> Dr. Asante, I'm having difficulty distinguishing balance theories from forced compliance theories.

6. *Refer to the known position of the interviewee.* This technique identifies the interviewee's position on an issue or problem. Be cautious because a tactless or seemingly hostile reference to a known position may create a defensive attitude or antagonize the interviewee. A common problem is an inaccurate interpretation of the interviewee's position.

> Kathy, do you have a few minutes before the meeting to discuss the sale of the property on Elm? I understand you are proposing that it be leased rather than sold to the McMadden Foundation.

7. *Refer to the person who sent you to the interviewee.* Never use a person's name without his or her permission to do so, and be sure the person you name did send you to the interviewee. Try to discover if the interviewee knows, respects, and likes the person you intend to name. It can be embarrassing or disastrous to discover, only after using a name, that the interviewee does not recall or intensely dislikes your reference.

> I'm writing an article for the *Racing Times* on some of the early raceways in this state. Jack Shanklan, who raced a lot in the Midwest in the 1930s, said you were involved in the operation of Jungle Park outside Rockville and could give me some important details on this popular raceway.

8. *Refer to the organization you represent.* In this opening, you refer to an organization rather than a person. The hope is that this reference will orient and motivate, not antagonize, the interviewee. You will face many situations in which

you must name your organization because your position with this organization dictates whom you will interview, when, where, and why. Some interview parties will not be fans of your organization. Be prepared to handle negative reactions.

> Hi, I'm Jessica Kim from Kagle, Isaacs, and O'Leary. We're representing your neighbor Washington Post in his negligence case against Great Northern Gas and Power Company.

9. *Request a specific amount of time.* Ask for or state a realistic time. By the end of this period, either complete your task or begin to close the interview. Give the interviewee an opportunity to continue the interview or to terminate it, perhaps arranging for another meeting. "Got a second?" is probably the most overused and misused interview opening. You can hardly give your name in one second, let alone conduct your business. If you tell a person you need 45 minutes, the person may say no; but if you do not reveal the time needed, the person may end the interview because of another commitment or become angry because of the impression you needed only a few minutes. The best solution is to make an appointment for interviews that require more than 5 or 10 minutes.

> Jack, I've had an opportunity to look through the resumes of the candidates for the accounting position. Do you have 10 minutes to discuss these with me?

10. *Ask a question.* Open-ended, easy-to-answer questions may enhance trust and begin to orient the interviewee. Common opening questions include

> What are you looking for in a computer?
>
> How may I be of assistance?
>
> What do you think of the candidate pool?

Be careful of employing closed questions that can be answered with a quick no. Common closed questions that often go nowhere include

> Can I help you?
>
> Do you need assistance?
>
> Are you being taken care of?

Many interviewees find questions with a single, obvious answer insulting.

> Do you want your children to have a good education?
>
> Are you concerned about your company's future?
>
> Would you like to save money?

These 10 common opening techniques should give you hints about forming effective openings in interviews. Realize, of course, that most openings include a strategic combination of techniques to meet the needs and desires of both interview parties. Create an opening that is most appropriate for each interview and situation. Avoid the temptation to use a standard opening for each type of interview. Pay particular attention to the relationship you have with the interviewee. And, above all, involve the interviewee in the opening. As an interviewee, you should insist on playing an active role from the beginning. Too many interviewers make the opening a monologue in which the interviewee is merely a bystander.

Nonverbal Communication in Openings

The verbal opening techniques discussed above must be accompanied by appropriate nonverbal communication. An effective opening depends upon how you look, act, and say what you say. Nonverbal communication is critical in creating that all-important, favorable first impression. It signals sincerity, trust and trustworthiness, warmth, interest in the interview and the other party, the seriousness of the interview, and the emotions being experienced.

You should always knock before entering a room, even if the door is open and you are a superior or in your own home, building, or organization. You are entering someone else's space, and any perceived violation of this territory is likely to begin the interview poorly. Wait until the other party gives you a signal to enter, such as a smile, head nod, wave, or pointing to a chair. Maintain good eye contact, but do not stare. Eye contact shows trust and allows you to pick up signals such as "come in," "be seated," "sit there," and "I'm interested/willing to talk to you."

As noted in Chapter 2, your appearance and dress contribute a great deal to first impressions. Both should communicate attractiveness, neatness, maturity, professionalism, and knowledge of what is appropriate dress for *this* interview and setting. Your voice and facial expression should communicate the gravity of the situation and your relationship with the other party: stranger, acquaintance, colleague, business contact, friend. Do not let your appearance signal catastrophe when the interview will deal with routine matters, friendliness when you are about to discipline a person, warmth when you are angry, happiness when a major problem needs urgent attention, or closeness when you have never met the other person or you are lower in the organizational hierarchy. If you shake hands, give a firm but not crushing handshake. Be careful of overdoing hand-shaking with acquaintances and colleagues you work with everyday and during very informal interviews. Touching another on the hand, arm, or shoulder is generally appropriate only when both parties have an established and close relationship and the situation warrants it.

It is difficult to overestimate the importance of verbal and nonverbal communication in openings, but be careful of reading too much into simple words and nonverbal acts or trying to read everyone the same. Even people of apparently similar backgrounds may differ significantly in communicative behavior. For example, Lillian Glass has catalogued 105 "talk differences" between American men and women in basic areas of communication: body language, facial language, speech and voice patterns, language content, and behavioral patterns. She has found, for instance, that men (when compared to women) touch others more often, tend to avoid eye contact and not look directly at the other person, sound more abrupt and less approachable, make direct accusations, and give fewer compliments.[3]

Recall the discussions of cultural differences in Chapter 2. While Americans tend to share rules for greeting others, these rules are not always shared with other cultures. Remember, shaking hands is a Western custom, particularly in the United States. While we expect, if not demand, that a person look us in the eyes to exhibit trust, openness, and sincerity, other cultures consider such eye contact to be impolite and insulting. The United States is not a touching society, but you should not be shocked if a party from Italy or Latin America touches you during an opening.

Quiz 1—Interview Openings

How satisfactory is each of the following openings? Consider the interviewing situation and type, the techniques used, and what is omitted. How might each be improved? Do not *assume* that each opening is unsatisfactory.

1. This is an interview taking place in a professor's office. The student, one of 250 in a large lecture course, has not made an appointment.

   > Are we going to do anything important in class on Friday?

2. This is a survey interview taking place at the front door of an apartment. The parties do not know one another.

   > Good evening Robert. (*smiling, shakes hands vigorously*) Got a minute? I would like to ask you a few questions about the city's plans to toughen the inspection of rental properties for possible code violations.

3. This is an interview for an internship taking place in a marketing division.

   > Hi. (*shaking hands*) I'm Sarah Giovanni from Microsoft. Won't you be seated. A beautiful day, isn't it? How is your semester going?

4. This interview is taking place between a sales manager and representative.

   > I got a curious call last night from Percy Taylor at Taylor Designs. (*serious tone of voice, frowning*) He said you basically told him we did not want his business anymore. What's going on?

5. This interview is taking place in the hallway near the U.S. Senate chamber between ABC reporter Sam Donaldson and a senator. The senator is heading toward a committee meeting

   > Senator Marlboro! (*waving and shouting*) Would you comment on your vote to table the tobacco bill?

The Body

In a brief, informal interview, you may prepare little more than a few questions or topic areas and operate from memory or a piece of notepaper. In a longer, more formal interview, you may prepare a detailed outline of topics or carefully phrased questions. And in the most formal of interviews, such as surveys, you may prepare a virtual script for the interview containing all questions to be asked and answer options for each. We urge you to prepare no less than an interview guide.

The Interview Guide

An interview guide is a carefully structured outline of topics and subtopics to be covered during an interview. A guide helps you develop specific areas of inquiry relevant to your purpose rather than a list of questions. This degree of structure will ensure that you cover all important topics and prevent you from forgetting to ask about some topics. It may suggest follow-up questions to ask and aid you in distinguishing relevant from irrelevant information. It will assist you in recording answers and help you recall information later.

Since the interview guide is an outline, review the fundamentals of outlining you have learned over the years so you can impose a clear, systematic structure on each interview. Standard outline patterns or sequences are quite useful for interviews.

A *topical sequence* follows natural divisions of a topic or issue. For example, an interview on a departmental budget might be divided into salaries, supplies and expenses, capital purchases, repairs, and travel. An interview during a search for a graduate school might include admissions criteria, areas of study, degree requirements, funding sources, and information on the department. Journalists frequently employ single-word, topic guides: what, when, where, who, how, and why.

A *time sequence* treats topics or parts in chronological order. For instance, an interviewer explaining how to make prints might move from stage one to stage two to stage three. A recruiter probing into a student's educational background might move from high school, to community college, to the university or probe into the student's employment record by beginning with the current position and going backward in time.

A *space sequence* arranges topics according to spatial divisions: left to right, top to bottom, north to south, or neighborhood to neighborhood. An architect explaining the physical arrangement of a new home might move from the entryway to the living room, dining room, kitchen, family room, master bedroom, and other bedrooms. A pro at a golf course might introduce you to a new course hole by hole, beginning with number one and proceeding hole by hole to eighteen.

A *cause-to-effect sequence* deals with causes and effects. For instance, what caused a rise or decline in the stock market, an increase or decrease in church attendance, low or high income, sales loss or gain, rise or decline in on-campus job interviews? An interviewer might begin with a cause or causes and then proceed to effect, or discuss an apparent effect and then move to possible causes.

A *problem-solution sequence* consists of a problem phase and a solution phase. A campus safety officer and the dean of students might first discuss an increase in auto-pedestrian accidents on campus and then solutions to make campus streets safer. A farmer might discuss a drainage problem with a contractor to determine what might be done to eliminate flooding of fields and loss of crops.

Assume that you are entering your last semester in college, and you have decided to tour Europe before entering graduate school in the fall. You have scheduled an interview with a travel agent in your hometown. First, decide on the major areas of information you want, such as the following topical sequence:

    I.   Air transportation to Europe
   II.   Cost of the tour
  III.   Countries included in the tour
  IV.   Side tours available

Second, place possible subtopics under each major area, such as the following:

    I.   Air transportation to Europe
       A.   Cost
       B.   Airlines
       C.   Destinations

    II.   Cost of the tour
        A.   Hotel
        B.   Meals
        C.   Transportation
    III.   Countries included in the tour
        A.   Great Britain
        B.   Scandinavia
        C.   France
        D.   Germany
        E.   Spain
    IV.   Side tours available
        A.   Cost
        B.   Length
        C.   Transportation
        D.   Activities

Third, determine if each subtopic contains important subtopics to cover. For instance, you might want to ask about specific countries in Scandinavia or areas of Spain. You might want information on side tour activities such as mountain climbing, white-water rafting, historic sights, and skiing. Some areas, such as cost of air transportation to Europe or meals, may need no additional subtopics to ensure free and open responses. You may not know enough to develop subdivisions under some headings, or they may allow you to discover subtopics as the interview progresses.

You may employ more than one sequence in an interview. The sample outline is a topical sequence of major divisions, but a spatial sequence would be most appropriate for subdivisions under Eastern Europe. You may develop the problem part of a problem-solution sequence from cause to effect.

Interview Schedules

After completing an interview guide, decide if additional structuring and preparation are needed. The guide may be sufficient, or you may need to turn all or part of it into questions. If you settle on a guide, you will conduct a *nonscheduled interview*. The nonscheduled interview is most appropriate when the information area is extremely broad, interviewees and their information levels differ significantly, interviewees are reluctant to respond or have poor memories, or you have little preparation time. The two *major advantages* of the nonscheduled interview evolve around the unlimited freedom to (1) probe into answers and (2) adapt to different situations and people. It is the most flexible of interview schedules. The *major disadvantages* are that nonscheduled interviews require more skill, are difficult to replicate, provide no easy means of recording answers, present problems in controlling for time limits, and allow interviewer bias to creep into unplanned questions. *Interviewer bias* occurs when interviewees respond in ways they think you want them to respond (usually because of verbal and nonverbal signals you send, who you are, or whom you represent) rather than express true feelings, attitudes, and beliefs.

The *moderately scheduled interview* contains all major questions with possible probing questions under each. You change the phrases in your guide to questions. The

moderate schedule, like the nonscheduled interview, allows freedom to probe into answers and adapt to different interviewees and situations. In addition, it imposes a greater
degree of structure on the interview, forces a higher level of preparation, aids in recording answers, and is easier to conduct and replicate. You need not create every question
on the spot but have them thought out and carefully worded in advance. This lessens
pressures on you during the interview. And since interview parties tend to wander during unstructured interviews, listing questions makes it easier to keep on track and return
to your structure when desired. Journalists, broadcasters, medical personnel, recruiters,
counselors, lawyers, police officers, and insurance investigators, to name a few, rely primarily on nonscheduled and moderately scheduled interviews. A moderately scheduled
interview would look like this:

    I.   As a recent college graduate, what bothers you most these days?
        A.   What about the stock market?
        B.   What about the economy?
        C.   What about crime?

    II.   Why did you choose the position with Andersen Consulting?
        A.   How important was the nature of the position?
        B.   How important was the salary?
        C.   How important was the company?
        D.   How important was geographical location?
        E.   How important was potential for advancement?

    III.   What are your long-range career plans?
        A.   What do you hope to be doing 10 years from now?
        B.   How important is it that you earn a substantial amount of money?
        C.   What effect is family likely have on your long-range career plans?
        D.   What might lead you to a career change?

    A *highly scheduled interview* includes all of your questions and the exact wording
to be used with each interviewee. It permits no unplanned probing, word changes, or de-
viation from the schedule. Questions are usually closed in nature so respondents can
give brief, specific answers. Highly scheduled interviews are easy to replicate and conduct. They take less time than either nonscheduled or moderately scheduled interviews
because they do not allow either party to stray into irrelevant, even if interesting, areas
or get carried away with long discussions in one or a few areas. However, flexibility and
adaptation are not possible. Probing questions, if any, must be planned. Researchers and
survey takers use highly scheduled interviews.

    I.   Which issue facing your family today concerns you most?
        A.   Which is the most important reason why this issue concerns your
           family the most?
        B.   When did this issue begin to concern your family the most?
        C.   How does your family plan to address this issue during the year?

    II.   Do you think economic conditions will be better or worse for your family
        next year?

    A. *(If the answer is better)*: Why do you think economic conditions will be better for your family next year?

    B. *(If the answer is worse)*: Why do you think economic conditions will be worse for your family next year?

III. Families seem to be returning to organized religion.

    A. Which is the most important reason for this trend?

    B. Do you predict this trend will continue or fall off?

    C. Have members of your family returned to organized religion in the past two years?

The *highly scheduled standardized interview* is the most thoroughly planned and structured. All questions and answer options are stated in identical words to each interviewee, who then picks answers from those provided. There is no straying from the schedule by either party. Highly scheduled standardized interviews are the easiest to conduct, record, tabulate, and replicate, so even novice interviewers can handle them. However, the breadth of information is restricted, and probing into answers, explaining questions, and adapting to different interviewees are not permitted. Built-in interviewer bias may be worse than accidental bias encountered in nonscheduled and moderately scheduled interviews. Respondents have no chance to explain, amplify, qualify, or question answer options. Researchers and survey takers interested in precise information, replicability, and reliability use highly scheduled standardized interviews because their procedures must produce the same results in repeated interviews by several interviewers. The following is a highly scheduled standardized interview.

I. Which one of the following problems do you feel is most critical for the new president of the university to address?

    A. Computers for students

    B. Student housing

    C. The library

    D. Security

    E. Class size

II. How likely is it that the president will address this problem effectively?

    A. Highly likely

    B. Likely

    C. Unsure

    D. Unlikely

    E. Highly unlikely

III. Who do you think should determine the priorities of the new president?

    A. Student body

    B. Faculty

    C. Deans of the schools

    D. The president

    E. Board of trustees

IV. Rank order the following sacrifices you would be willing to make to solve the university's pressing problems.

A. Pay higher tuition
B. Pay higher residence hall fees
C. Pay special fees for lab classes
D. Take part in fund-raising activities
E. Provide own computer hardware and software

Each interviewing schedule has unique advantages and disadvantages. Your task is to choose the schedule best suited to your needs, skills, type or types of information desired, and situation. Do not fall into the trap of trying to apply a favorite schedule to all interviews. A schedule designed for a survey would be a terrible schedule for an employment interview. Be aware of the options you have and which one or ones seem most appropriate for a specific interview. Figure 3.1 summarizes the major advantages and disadvantages of each schedule.

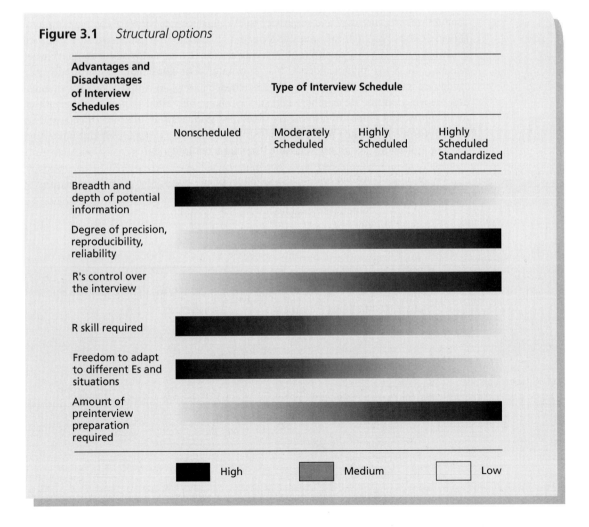

Figure 3.1   *Structural options*

Consider combining schedules, such as using a nonscheduled approach during the opening minutes, a moderately scheduled approach when you need to probe and adapt to a specific interviewee, and a highly scheduled standardized approach for easily quantifiable information such as demographic data on age, gender, religion, formal education, marital status, and organizational memberships. Although schedules are usually lists of questions, they may range from a topic outline to a manuscript. For example, you might write out major arguments for a persuasive interview, instructions for an information giving interview, and the opening and closing for a survey interview.

The Closing

Closings are usually brief, but they are very important to the success of each interview. Once you have asked or answered the last question, made your last point, or come to some sort of agreement with the other party, it is tempting to relax and feel the interview is done. But an abrupt or tactless closing may undo the relationship established during the interview and agreements reached by making the other party feel like a discarded container—important only as long as you need what is inside. Each interview forms or revises the relationship between the two parties and creates positive or negative expectations about future interactions. Effective closings enhance relationships and interview results; ineffective closings diminish both.

Functions and Guidelines for Closings

Closings have three primary functions.[4] First, the closing may signal the termination of the interview but not the relationship. We continue business, professional, and casual relationships with other parties for years, and each interview adds something positive or negative to this association. Many tasks require more than one interview to complete, so a common element of closings is an agreement about when and where the next interview will take place:

> Let's meet in the conference room next Wednesday at the same time.
> Why don't we meet in the Union at 2:00?
> I'll e-mail you when I return from my vacation to set up another meeting.

Simple phrases may communicate the likely interval between interviews. Phrases such as "See you" or "Until next time" tend to signal short intervals. "Goodbye" and "So long" tend to signal lengthy or forever intervals. "Let's stay in touch" and "Don't be a stranger" tend to signal moderate intervals. "We'll be in touch" and "We'll call you" may signal the traditional brush-off that means never. Be aware of cultural differences and expectations between you and the other party that may lead to confusion about these common closing phrases. People in other cultures may not understand that "We'll call you" is a brush-off and wait expectedly for our call.

Second, the closing may express supportiveness to enhance the relationship and bring the interview to a positive close. One or both parties may express appreciation or pleasure and hope for or intention of future contacts.

> I really appreciate your support and look forward to our next meeting.

photo by Bob Daemmrich/Stock Boston

■ *Remember that the interview is not completed until the interviewer and interviewee are out of sight and sound of one another.*

Thanks for your help. You've given me information I could not get from any other source. I'll let you know when my study is finished.

I hope we can work together again next semester. This has been very helpful.

Third, the closing may summarize the interview. Even when there is no systematic summary, either party or both may use the closing to bring the interview to an orderly ending and pull together the issues, concerns, agreements, and information shared. Be sure your summarizing comments are accurate and address major areas of information, analysis, or agreement.

Here are some guidelines for closing interviews. First, be sincere and honest. Make no promises you cannot or will not keep. Second, do not rush the closing. The "law of recency" suggests that people recall the last thing said or done during an interview, so being rushed or dismissed with an ill-chosen phrase may place the interview results, your relationship, and future contacts in jeopardy. Remember that the closing is an integral part of the interview, not something tacked onto the end. Third, do not introduce new topics or ideas when the interview has *in fact* or *psychologically* come to a close. Fourth, remember that the interview is "not over until it's over." The other party is likely to be observing and interpreting everything you say and do, and everything you do *not* say and do *not* do, until you are out of sight and sound. A slip of the lip or an inappropriate nonverbal act may negate all that you have accomplished from the opening to the closing. Fifth, avoid *false closings*. False closings occur when our verbal and nonverbal messages signal that the interview is coming to a close when it is not. Sixth, leave the door open and perhaps set the groundwork for future contacts. If additional contact is planned, explain what will happen, where it will happen, when it will happen, and why it will happen. If appropriate, make an appointment before leaving. And seventh, avoid what Erving Goffman has called *failed departures*.[5] All of us have experienced these unpleasant departures. A failed departure occurs when you have brought an interview to a successful close and taken leave from the other party. Then an hour or so later you run into this party in the hall, parking lot, or restaurant. The result is often awkward because both of you have said your goodbyes (after interviewing for or quitting a job, talking to a counselor, recruiting a person for an organization, purchasing a product), and now you must think of something appropriate to say when there is really nothing to say. Practice situations to determine what you might say when this happens so you can avoid awkward and embarrassing moments.

Closing Techniques

As with openings, be creative and imaginative in the way you close interviews. Adapt each closing to the interviewee and the situation. The following techniques may serve as entire closings, begin the closing process, or complete the closing.

1. *Offer to answer questions.* Be sincere in your desire to answer questions and give the other party adequate time to ask. Do not give a brief answer to one question and then end the interview.

    Any questions at this time?

    Do you have any questions about these arrangements?

    Now, I'm anxious to hear your questions.

2. *Use clearinghouse questions.* A clearinghouse question allows you to determine if you have covered all topics, answered all questions, or resolved all concerns. Be sure your request is communicated as an honest and sincere effort to ferret out unaddressed questions, information, or areas of concern, not as a formality.

    Anything else before I leave?

    Are there any questions I have not addressed?

    Can you think of anything we haven't accounted for?

3. *Declare the completion of your purpose.* Simply state that your task is completed. The word "well" probably signals more closings than any other word or phrase. When we hear it, we automatically assume that leave-taking is commencing and begin to wind things up.

    Well, that's all the questions I have.

    Well, that's everything I wanted to talk about.

    Okay, that should get me ready for the exam.

4. *Make personal inquiries.* Personal inquiries are pleasant ways to end interviews, but they must be sincere. Give the interviewee adequate time to address an inquiry or concern. Do not make them if you do not mean them.

    I hear your son made the all-star team.

    I understand that you are engaged.

    I hope the exam goes well for you.

5. *Make professional inquiries.* Professional inquiries tend to be formal, but like personal ones, they must be sincere and show genuine interest. Most of us appreciate persons who show interest in our careers or career preparation.

    How is your co-op program with Lilly?

    Are you going to attend the national meeting in Detroit?

    When does your semester start?

6. *Signal that time is up.* This technique is most effective when a time limit is announced or agreed to in the opening. Be tactful in calling time, and avoid the impression that you are running an interview assembly line.

> Our time is up for this week. We can begin next week where we left off.
>
> That's all the time we have for today.
>
> Our scheduled time is up, so let's . . . .

7. *Explain the reason for the closing.* Say honestly why you must close the interview. A phony-sounding reason can do irreparable harm to the interview and relationship.

> I have another appointment waiting at 1:30; maybe we can . . . .
>
> I'm sorry, but I have a class in five minutes.
>
> I must leave now to catch my ride.

8. *Express appreciation or satisfaction.* A note of appreciation or satisfaction is a common closing technique because we have usually received something—information, assistance, evaluation, a story, a sale, a position, a recruit. Be sincere and avoid any hint of sarcasm.

> I've really enjoyed talking with you. Thanks for your help.
>
> Thanks for taking the time to meet with me.
>
> Thanks for your feedback. I'll try what you suggested.

9. *Arrange for the next meeting.* If appropriate, set up the next meeting or reveal what will happen next, including date, time, place, topic, content, or purpose.

> Let's get together again on July 1 at 1:00 P.M.
>
> Could you come to Salt Lake City during the week of November 8?
>
> Check your calendar to see if May 24 is free for another session.

10. *Summarize the interview.* A summary closing is common for informational, performance, counseling, and sales interviews. It may repeat important information, stages, and agreements or verify accuracy and agreement.

> Okay, I think we're set. You want a Gateway Solo with a Pentium processor, Microsoft Word, a mini-dock, an EV700 monitor, and a black keyboard and mouse. Is this correct?

Nonverbal Closing Actions

In their classic study of leave-taking, Mark Knapp and his colleagues discovered that people employed a number of nonverbal actions to signal when closings were commencing.[6] When we want to close an interaction, researchers found that we employ such nonverbal signals as straightening up in our seat, leaning forward, standing up, moving away from the other party, uncrossing our legs, placing our hands on our knees as if preparing to rise, breaking eye contact, offering to shake hands, making various hand movements, smiling, and looking at the clock. Be aware of these nonverbal actions so you can signal correctly when you want to close an interview, detect when another wants to close, and avoid sending unintentional closing signals. Remember that any behavioral act may be interpreted in a meaningful way by the other party. You may be unaware that you looked at your watch or leaned forward, but the other party may take these as leave-taking activities. Or you may look at a clock to be sure you have adequate time remaining, not to begin the closing.

Be constantly aware of what your words and actions are "saying" to the other party. Decide before or during an interview which closing techniques are most suitable. Your role in the interview and your relationship with the other party may dictate some techniques, rule out others, and determine who will initiate the closing and when. Most often you will combine several verbal and nonverbal techniques into effective closings.

> Well (*glancing at your watch*), I see it's almost time to leave for the airport. (*leaning forward and smiling*) We seem to be in general agreement about the merger with Rising Star Oil; (*rising from your chair*) and we're aware of potential regulatory problems. (*handing a copy of notes to the other party*) Thanks for meeting after hours; I know it's been a long day. Have a good vacation in Maine (*a waving hand motion*).

Quiz 2—Interview Closings

How satisfactory is each of the following closings? Consider the interviewing situation and type, the techniques used, nonverbal communication, and what is omitted. How might each be improved? Do not *assume* each closing is unsatisfactory.

1. This is a marriage counseling interview. A couple who have been married for seven years and have a three-year-old daughter are experiencing difficulties in their marriage. This is the second session with this counselor.

   > Well, (*straightening up*) our time's up. I think you've accomplished a great deal this morning. You're making some important headway. (*sitting back*) How do you both feel about today's session?

2. This is an employment interview in the personnel office of Champion Sportwear. Margaret Walters is a senior in retail management with average grades and no retail or management experience.

   > (*standing up*) I see it's time for my next appointment. It's been a pleasure meeting you Ms. Walters. (*shakes hands*) We'll call you. (*vocal stress*)

3. This is a persuasive interview at an appliance store. Josh and Jim are roommates and are shopping for a large-screen television set and entertainment center for their apartment.

   > Thanks for coming in. I think you'd like this Toshiba 3000.

4. This is a market survey taking place in the walkway at a shopping mall by Market Research Incorporated. Sara and Mike are shopping with their young children.

   > (*looking through the interview form*) That's all the questions I have. Really a nice day isn't it?

ON THE WEB

This chapter has presented structural principles and types appropriate for a wide variety of interviews. Use the Internet to locate sample interviews on issues such as education, the economy, foreign affairs, and technology. Study and analyze the openings, schedules, and closings used in these interviews. Use the questions provided in your text to analyze the interview in this chapter. Two useful Internet resources for locating interviews are CNN (http://cnn.com) and C-SPAN (http://indycable.com/cabletv/comastindy upgrade/ch24.htm).

5. This is a health care interview taking place at Spelterville Clinic. Dave is having his annual checkup.

Interviewer: I think you're in great shape. (*looking at a wall clock*) How's your golf game going?

Interviewee: I broke 90 for the first time last Saturday.

Interviewer: (*moving toward the door, smiling*) See you soon.

Summary

All three parts of each interview—opening, body, and closing—are vital to its success. Do not underestimate the importance of words and nonverbal actions and reactions during all three stages of interviews. Be conscious of cultural differences in the importance and meaning of handshaking, eye contact, voice, touch, and gestures.

The opening influences how both parties perceive themselves and one another. It sets the tone for the remainder of the interview, orients the interviewee, affects the willingness of both parties to communicate beyond Level 1. It often determines whether the interview will continue or end prematurely. Select opening techniques most appropriate for each interview.

The body of the interview must be carefully structured with an appropriate sequence that guides the interviewer's questions, areas of information, or points systematically and allows the interviewee to understand where the interview is going and why. A nonscheduled interview is simply an interview guide with topics and subtopics an interviewer wants to cover during the interview. A moderately scheduled interview contains all major questions and possible probing questions under each. A highly scheduled interview includes all questions to be asked during an interview. A highly scheduled standardized interview contains all questions to be asked with prescribed answer options under each.

The closing not only brings the interview to an end, but it may summarize information, verify agreements, arrange future contacts, and enhance your relationship with the other party. A good closing should make both parties glad they took part and leave them feeling pleased with the results. Be sincere and honest. Do not rush the closing.

An Interview for Review and Analysis

This interview is taking place between a reporter for the student daily newspaper and a professor of biology. The University Senate has been discussing a set of recommendations for mandatory course-instructor evaluations in all courses with more than five students. Professor Osaka has been an outspoken critic of course-instructor evaluations. The location is Professor Osaka's office.

How satisfactory is the opening? How might it be improved? Which type or types of sequences does the student employ? Which type of schedule does the student employ? How appropriate are the sequences and schedule for this interview? How satisfactory is the closing? How might it be improved? How might nonverbal communication have influenced the opening, body, and closing?

1. **Student:** Good afternoon Professor . . . Osaka. (*shakes Professor Osaka's hand and glances around the office*) This is a really nice office.

2. **Professor:** It comes with my administrative position. (*serious facial expression*) Are you Dale McBride with the student newspaper?

3. **Student:** Yeah, I'm Dale. (*nervous grin*) I called you on the phone.

4. **Professor:** Have a seat. How can I help you?

5. **Student:** Well, as you probably know, we're doing a series on the Senate's consideration of mandatory course-instructor evaluations for all courses. (*rapid rate of speaking*) I'll only take a couple minutes . . . (*opens notebook and peruses the survey questions*) I understand you are opposed to evaluations.

6. **Professor:** Yes, I am.

7. **Student:** (*looking at his notes*) Why?

8. **Professor:** (*shrugs shoulders*) I think they're a waste of time because students don't know how to evaluate courses. They become popularity contests.

9. **Student:** What do you think about the proposed system?

10. **Professor:** It's no better and no worse than ones we've tried in the past.

11. **Student:** What problems do you see in the proposal?

12. **Professor:** Well, first, it assumes students understand what constitutes good and bad teaching. I don't think they do. And second, no single system will fit all courses that range in size from a handful of students to several hundred.

13. **Student:** I see. Are there other problems?

14. **Professor:** Yes. I think mandatory evaluations violate my academic freedom.

15. **Student:** How might the Senate meet your concerns?

16. **Professor:** It could scrap the whole thing.

17. **Student:** President Stiles, Vice President Totten, and the board of trustees have mandated that the Senate come up with a course-instructor evaluation program.

18. **Professor:** (*frowns*) I'm aware of the pressure on the Senate.

19. **Student:** What, then, will you propose at the next Senate meeting?

20. **Professor:** Well, to be quite frank, I think course-instructor evaluations are a waste of time, but I suppose they're going to come in some form.

21. **Student:** (*smiles*) Yes, so . . . ?

22. **Professor:** First, they should be department-specific.

23. **Student:** How will this solve the problem?

24. **Professor:** Faculties in each department should have a say as to the evaluation in their courses.

25. **Student:** And?

26. **Professor:** Different criteria and procedures should be developed to address class size and the way courses are taught.

27. **Student:** Well (*looks over notes, closes the notebook, and then looks at the professor*), that's all I need. Do you have any final reactions?

28. **Professor:** No. (*looks at his watch*) I guess not. Just don't place too much faith in paper-and-pencil evaluations of courses and instructors.

29. **Student:** (*stands up*) Okay, thanks; I'll make note of that. (*leaves the office*)

Student Activities

1. During a 24-hour period, keep a record of the openings of interviews in which you take part or observe. Which techniques were most common? How were these techniques related to relationships, interview types, situations, and length of interviews? Which nonverbal actions did you observe, and how did these affect the openings? How effective were rapport building and orientation?

2. During a 24-hour period, keep a record of the closings of interviews in which you take part. Which techniques were most common? How were these techniques related to relationships, interview types, situations, and length of interviews. Which nonverbal actions did you observe, and how did these affect the closings? Did you detect any false closings, and if so, how did the parties handle them and bring interviews to a close?

3. Videotape a televised interview and try to construct an interview guide from it. Which sequences did you discover? Which schedule did you discover? How did the interview type, situation, parties, relationships, and issue seem to affect selection of sequences and schedule?

4. Conduct one interview over the telephone and one face-to-face in which you focus on interview structure. Compare the methods you used to open and close the different interview types. Which factors determine the techniques employed or avoided? Which interview schedules did you employ? In addition to getting

information on structure, note the differences in opening, body, and closing in the two interviews you conducted. How did the telephone affect your interview structure, particularly the opening and closing?

Notes

1. Paul D. Krivonos and Mark L. Knapp, "Initiating Communication: What Do You Say When You Say Hello?" *Central States Speech Journal* 26 (1975), pp. 115–25.

2. LaRay M. Barna, "Stumbling Blocks in Intercultural Communication," in Larry A. Samovar and Richard E. Porter, eds., *Intercultural Communication: A Reader* (Belmont, CA: Wadsworth, 1988), pp. 323–24.

3. Lillian Glass, *He Says, She Says: Closing the Communication Gap between the Sexes* (New York: Putnam, 1993), pp. 45–59.

4. Mark L. Knapp, Roderick P. Hart, Gustav W. Friedrich, and Gary M. Shulman, "The Rhetoric of Goodbye: Verbal and Nonverbal Correlates of Human Leave-Taking," *Speech Monographs* 40 (1973), pp. 182–98.

5. Erving Goffman, *Relations in Public* (New York: Basic Books, 1971), p. 88.

6. Knapp et al., pp. 182–98.

Resources

Barone, Jeanne Tessier, and Jo Young Switzer. *Interviewing Art and Skill.* Boston: Allyn and Bacon, 1995.

Killenberg, George M., and Rob Anderson. *Before the Story: Interviewing and Communication Skills for Journalists.* New York: St. Martin's Press, 1989.

Metzler, Ken. *Creative Interviewing.* Englewood Cliffs, NJ: Prentice Hall, 1989.

Wilson, Gerald L., and H. Lloyd Goodall, Jr. *Interviewing in Context.* New York: McGraw-Hill, 1991.

Zunin, Leonard, and Natalie Zunin. *The First Four Minutes.* Los Angeles: Nash, 1986.

Questions and Their Uses

A s we noted in Chapter 1 when we defined interviewing, it is difficult to imagine an interview that does not include questions and answers. A knowledge of both types and uses of questions is crucial whether you are talking to a professor, being recruited for a position, responding to a survey, acting as a counselor, getting information from an accident victim, taking part in a performance review, selling or purchasing a product or service, or persuading a friend to join your sorority or fraternity. Even when giving information, you are likely to use questions to check on facts, assess the accuracy of opinions, clarify what you have heard, and verify that the other party is receiving and comprehending what you are saying. Virtually no interview takes place without questions, and a great many interviews consist entirely of questions and answers. A question is *any statement or nonverbal act that invites an answer*; it need not be an interrogative sentence followed by a question mark.

This chapter focuses on the tools of the trade for interviewers and interviewees: types of questions, phrasing questions, common question pitfalls, and question sequences. As we introduce you to what may seem like an endless array of questions, it is natural to ask why you need to learn all of these types of questions and their names. After all, isn't a question merely a question? Yes, but in the same sense that a screwdriver is a screwdriver, a wrench is a wrench, and a saw is a saw. Like questions, all of these tools come in various shapes and sizes and each is designed to accomplish specific tasks efficiently and effectively.

Screwdrivers, for example, include slot, Phillips head, Torx, and square. Recall the frustration you experienced when you had a slot screwdriver when a Phillips head screw needed loosening or tightening. Remember when a screw came out of your sunglasses and all you had in the car toolbox was a set of screwdrivers far too large for the tiny screw from your glasses? Or perhaps you were trying to hang draperies in your new apartment and had plenty of Torx head (star-shaped) screwdrivers when a small, square head was needed to install the pulley mechanism for the draw cord. After much exasperation and words we cannot print here, you may have managed to get the job done, or perhaps you failed and went out to buy the proper tool. Such is the case with questions. You need to know the types of question tools available and their uses so you can select the most appropriate one without wasting time, experiencing frustration, shocking the other party, or delaying the completion of a simple task.

If you are aware of the many types of questions available and their unique capabilities, then you can conduct and take part in interviews more effectively and efficiently and enjoy the process. For example, you will not ask a question designed to obtain a one-word answer when you want a detailed answer, ask a question that introduces a new topic when the previous topic remains largely unexplored, or ask a question that leads the interviewee to give the answer he or she thinks you want to hear rather than one that reveals correct information or feelings. Although a listing of types and subtypes of questions may seem endless, each question has three characteristics: (1) open or closed, (2) primary or secondary, and (3) neutral or leading.[1]

Open and Closed Questions

Open and closed questions differ in the amount of information they invite respondents to provide and the degree of control the interviewer desires to maintain. The amount of information may range from a single word to hundreds of words.

Open Questions

Open questions are broad, often specifying only a topic, and allow the respondent considerable freedom in determining the amount and kind of information to give. Some questions are *highly open* with virtually no restrictions, such as

> Tell me about yourself.
> What do you know about our agency?
> How do you feel about campaign finance reform?

Other questions are *moderately open*. They contain some restrictions on answers but give respondents considerable leeway, such as the following:

> Tell me about your family.
> What do you know about our agency's clientele?
> How do you feel about Senator Tout's campaign finance reform bill?

Public opinion pollsters may hand a statement, picture, or product offer to a person or ask a person to review a series of potential advertisements. Then they might ask,

> How would you respond to this statement?
> What comes to mind when you look at this picture?
> Pick the advertisement you find most appealing and explain why.

Open questions have several advantages. For instance, they invite respondents to do the talking and determine the nature and amount of information to give. In giving lengthy answers, respondents may reveal what they think is important and volunteer important information you might not think to ask for. Open questions communicate interest and trust in the respondent's judgment. They are usually easier to answer and pose less threat to respondents, and the longer answers they generate are more likely to reveal respondent uncertainty, intensity of feelings, perceptions, prejudices, and stereotypes than are answers to closed questions.

photo by Michael Newman/Photo Edit

Open questions let the respondent do the talking and allow the interviewer to listen and observe.

Open questions also have several disadvantages. A single answer may consume a significant portion of interview time because the respondent determines the length and nature of each answer. On the one hand, respondents may dwell on unimportant or irrelevant information; on the other hand, they may withhold important information they feel is irrelevant or too obvious, well known, sensitive, or dangerous. You must be skilled in keeping respondents on track and maintaining control by tactfully intervening to move to your next question. Lengthy, sometimes rambling answers are difficult to record, replicate from one interview to another, and code.

Closed Questions

Closed questions are restrictive in nature and may supply answer options. Some are *moderately closed*, asking for a specific piece of information, such as

> Which chemistry courses have you had?
> When did you move from San Diego to Milwaukee?
> How long have you collected baseball cards?

Other questions are *highly closed*, and respondents must select appropriate answers from lists, just like multiple choice tests. Questions such as the following are common in surveys, employment questionnaires, and medical admissions forms:

Which of these brands of root beer have you purchased during the past year?

____ Dog n Suds	____ Barq's
____ Stewart	____ A & W
____ IBC	____ Other _____

What is the highest educational level you have achieved?

____ Some high school
____ High school graduate
____ Some college or technical school
____ College or technical school graduate
____ Some graduate school
____ Master's degree

I would like you to rate the following breakfast cereals on a scale of one to five. If you strongly like the cereal, give it a five. If you like the cereal, give it a four. If you neither like nor dislike the cereal, give it a three. If you dislike the cereal, give it a two. If you strongly dislike the cereal, give it a one.

Shredded Wheat	1	2	3	4	5
Frosted Flakes	1	2	3	4	5
Grape-nuts	1	2	3	4	5
Cheerios	1	2	3	4	5
Total	1	2	3	4	5

Many closed questions are *bipolar* in that they limit respondents to one of two polar choices, for example,

Do you usually purchase coffee with or without caffeine?
Do you usually purchase regular or diet colas?
Do you usually purchase brand name or generic brand soups?

Other bipolar questions ask for an evaluation or attitude, for example,

Do you agree or disagree with the court's decision?
Do you approve or disapprove of random drug tests for professional athletes?
Do you like or dislike the new registration procedures?

Perhaps the most common bipolar questions ask for yes or no responses, for example,

Have you signed up for the trip to Washington?
Do you use the campus bus system?
Are you aware of my attendance policy?

Regardless of their specific nature, bipolar questions assume that there are only two possible answers and that the answers are poles apart: like/dislike, approve/disapprove, agree/disagree, high/low, yes/no. They do not allow for "undecided," "no opinion," or "don't know" answers or for variations in degrees of liking, feeling, or using.

Closed questions have several advantages. For instance, you can control the length of answers and guide respondents to specific information you need. Closed questions require little effort from either party and allow you to ask more questions, in more areas, in less time. And answers are easy to replicate, code, tabulate, and analyze from one interview to another.

Closed questions also have disadvantages. Answers to closed questions often contain too little information, requiring you to ask additional questions. And they do not reveal *why* a person has a particular attitude or typically makes certain choices. For instance, an interviewee may not know which soups are brand name and which are generic, or the person may purchase approximately the same number of each. Interviewers tend to talk more than interviewees when asking closed questions, and interviewees have little or no opportunity to volunteer or explain information. And it is possible for respondents to rate, rank, select an answer, or say yes or no without knowing anything about the topic.

Figure 4.1 illustrates the major advantages and disadvantages of open and closed questions. As the interviewer applies more constraint to a question, the amount of data decreases. As the amount of data decreases, the interviewer's control increases, less time and skill are required, and the degree of precision, reliability, and reproducibility increases. On the other hand, as the interviewer lessens constraint, the amount of data increases, and interviewees reveal knowledge level, understanding, reasons for feeling or acting, and hidden motives. Many interviews include open and closed questions with varying degrees of constraint to get the information desired. For instance, an interviewer might follow up a two-choice question such as "Do you prefer Coke or Pepsi?" with a more open-ended question such as "Why do you prefer Pepsi?"

Figure 4.1   *Question options*

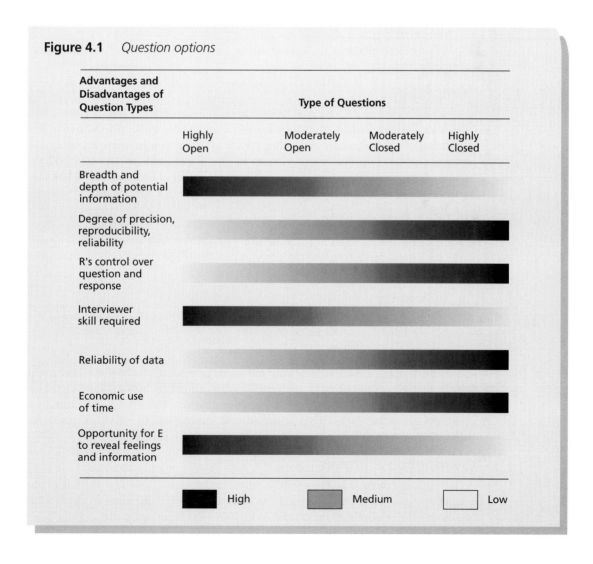

Primary and Secondary Questions

Questions may be primary or secondary. *Primary questions* introduce topics or new areas within a topic and can stand alone even when taken out of context.

> Where were you on the night of December 20?
> What is your favorite vegetable?
> Tell me about your internship with Sears.

All examples of open and closed questions presented earlier are primary questions.

Secondary questions attempt to elicit further information following a primary or another secondary question, so they are often called *probing* or *follow-up* questions. They may be open or closed. Secondary questions are essential when a respondent does not respond to your question or the answer appears to be incomplete, superficial, vague, suggestible, irrelevant, or inaccurate.

Silent Probes

You may use a silent probe when you feel an answer is incomplete or the respondent seems hesitant to continue. Remain silent for a few moments and use appropriate nonverbal signals such as eye contact, a head nod, sitting back in your seat, or a gesture to encourage the person to continue. Silence also shows interest in what is being said and respect for both the answer and the respondent. Silence may communicate belief or disbelief and understanding or confusion more tactfully than words and may avoid a defensive climate.

Nudging Probes

Use a nudging probe if a silent probe fails or you feel you must employ verbal signals to get at what you need. It nudges the interviewee to reply or to continue with an answer. The nudging probe is usually simple and brief, such as,

> I see.   And?
> Go on.   So?
> And then?   Please continue.
> Yes?   Uh-huh?

A common mistake of both interviewers and interviewees is the belief that all questions must be multiple-word sentences, not verbal nudges. Too often, instead of urging the respondent to continue, a lengthy probing question stifles the interchange or is actually a primary question that opens up a new area or topic, the opposite of what the situation requires. Further information is lost and feelings may remain undetected.

Clearinghouse Probes

A clearinghouse probe is an essential tool when you are unsure you have elicited all important or available information and have no further specific questions in mind. Such questions give respondents opportunities to volunteer information that did not seem warranted by your original questions. A clearinghouse probe "clears out" an area or topic, such as the following:

Did you see anything else when you saw the car leave the garage?
What have I not asked for that might be important?
Have I missed anything that you can think of?
Before we move on to another issue, is there anything we have not covered?

If you ask a good clearinghouse probe, you can go on to your next topic reasonably confident that you mined all that was worth mining in the previous topic. You did not fail to learn something because you did not ask for it specifically.

Informational Probes

Informational probing questions are important tools to get additional information or explanations. For example, if an answer appears to be *superficial*, you might begin a probing or follow-up question with phrases such as,

Tell me more about . . . .   How did Chad feel about . . . ?
What happened after . . . ?   Explain further the criteria that . . . .
How did you react to . . . ?   What did you say when . . . ?

Many answers seem *vague* or *ambiguous*, perhaps inviting a number of interpretations. You might ask an informational probe such as,

I'm not sure I understand your point.
What do you have in mind when you say "a decent salary"?
Please define "multiple family dwelling" for me.

Some answers seem to *suggest* feelings or attitudes in addition to factual material. You might ask an informational probe such as,

Why do you feel that way?
What is your attitude toward pesticides now?
How strongly do you feel about that?

Restatement Probes

A respondent may not answer a primary question you have posed or answer only part of it. Or a person may give information that has little or nothing to do with what you asked. Rather than create a new secondary question, it may be more effective to restate your original question, perhaps using vocal emphasis to draw attention to your original concern, or rephrase the original question slightly. Be tactful. You do not want to embarrass or antagonize the interviewee. The following are restatement probes:

Case 1

1. **Interviewer:** What do you think of the proposed state park near Oak Bluff?

2. **Interviewee:** Well, I'll tell you one thing. It's about time that we put some brakes on government in this country. The little guy doesn't count for much anymore.

3. **Interviewer:** What about the *park proposal*?

Case 2

1. **Interviewer:** Tell me about your background.
2. **Interviewee:** We had a very large family. I'm one of five boys and two girls. We had some great times together and still keep in touch. All of us have gone to college, and one brother is an attorney and one sister is a surgeon.
3. **Interviewer:** And what about your background beyond your brothers and sisters?

If a person seems hesitant to answer your question or answers only part of it, you may be guilty of asking an unclear question or one that seems to demand what is not easy to provide. Restate your question in a clearer, easier to answer fashion. For example,

1. **Interviewer:** Please define responsibility for me.
2. **Interviewee:** Well . . . uh . . . .
3. **Interviewer:** In your own words, what does it mean to be responsible?

If you are guilty of asking a multiple question and the respondent answers only part of it, restate the part left unanswered. Do not go to your next primary question as if you received all you asked for. For instance,

1. **Interviewer:** What are some of your hobbies and nonprofessional activities?
2. **Interviewee:** I like to do woodworking, mainly furniture, and I do a lot of gardening during the summer months. I don't do vegetables, just flowers.
3. **Interviewer:** And what are some of your nonprofessional activities?

Reflective Probes

A reflective probing question *reflects* the answer received to verify its accuracy or to clarify it so you are certain you have interpreted it as the respondent intended. Be sure the respondent understands that you are seeking verification and clarification, not attempting to lead or trap the person into giving the answer you want to hear or to challenge the person's honesty or intelligence. Be tactful verbally and nonverbally. If you think an answer is inaccurate (wrong date or figure, inaccurate quotation, mix-up in words), you might ask a reflective question such as the following:

> You mean the *twenty-first,* don't you?
> Was that *net* or *gross* income?
> Are you sure you left the message on *Jane's* desk?

If you are unsure about what the respondent has said or implied, ask a reflective question to resolve your uncertainty, such as the following:

> You feel, then, that the apartment will be ready for fall?
> Are you saying you were cheated?
> Am I correct in assuming that the majority of the team will be in summer classes?

Mirror Probes

The mirror question is an essential tool when you want to be certain you have understood a series of answers or have retained information accurately. The mirror question is closely related to the reflective question; but the mirror question, rather than reflecting an answer just received, *summarizes* a series of answers or interchanges to ensure accurate understanding and retention. It may mirror an entire interview. If asked properly, both reflective and mirror questions can help you avoid errors caused by faulty assumptions, poor memory, or misinterpretations. For example, a person may ask a mirror question to be certain of instructions, such as the following:

> Okay, we have an agreement. I will swap you lots 12, 17, and 23 for lots 13, 16, and 22. I will provide lots 26 and 27 so you can extend Bluebird Lane from Webster to Calhoun. I will take care of all street sign changes, and you will construct a new subdivision sign. Are these your understandings?

An applicant for a position might use a mirror question to be certain he or she understands the elements of an employment offer, such as,

> If I understand what you have said, the position you are offering me is a field engineer in the Princeton office. I would begin work on June 15 in the Princeton office and remain there for at least six weeks of orientation and training. Then I would be assigned to a construction project in central New Jersey. My starting salary would be $35,000 with a 2.5 percent increase after the training period.

The use of secondary or probing questions separates skilled from unskilled interviewers and interviewees. The unskilled person thinks ahead to the next question on the schedule, anticipates questions prematurely, or is in a hurry to move on. The skilled person listens carefully to each response to determine if the answer is satisfactory. If it is not, the questioner determines the probable cause within seconds and phrases an appropriate secondary question to elicit more relevant, accurate, and complete information. Skillful probing can heighten the other party's motivation because the questioner is obviously interested and paying close attention to what is being said.

Secondary questions may cause problems, however. Sometimes if a person does not respond immediately to one of our questions, we jump in with a probing question when none would be needed if we were *patient*. Also, we must phrase probing questions carefully and be aware of vocal emphasis. Stanley Payne illustrates how the meaning of a simple "why" question can be altered by stressing different words:[2]

Why do you say that?

Why *do* you say that?

Why do *you* say that?

Why do you *say* that?

Why do you say *that*?

The "simple" why question may unintentionally communicate disapproval, disbelief, or mistrust, or put the other party on the defensive by *appearing* to demand justifications, explanations, and rationales. A poorly phrased secondary question may alter the meaning of the primary question or bias the reply. When using reflective or mirror questions, do not misquote a person or put words into the person's mouth. The respondent may feel you have not listened or are playing games. Avoid curious probing for information you do not need, especially if this information may be embarrassing.

Quiz 1—Supply the Secondary Question

Supply an appropriate secondary (probing) question for each of the following interactions. Be sure your question probes into an answer and is not a primary question introducing a new facet of the topic. Watch your assumptions about answers. And phrase your questions tactfully.

1. **Interviewer:** Why would you like to work for us?

   Interviewee: I've always enjoyed working outdoors, even in really cold winters and really hot summers. And Minnesota has thousands of lakes.

   Interviewer:

2. **Interviewer:** How much candy do you eat in a week?

   Interviewee: A lot.

   Interviewer:

3. **Interviewer:** How did you like your last job?

   Interviewee: It was fine.

   Interviewer:

4. **Interviewer:** Tell me about your supervisor at Star Bioanalytics?

   Interviewee: She was a good supervisor with a lot of experience.

   Interviewer:

5. **Interviewer:** What did you think of Reverend Vancel's sermon?

   Interviewee: It wasn't bad.

   Interviewer:

6. **Interviewer:** How do you feel about paperwork?

   Interviewee: It's part of the job.

   Interviewer:

7. **Interviewer:** Define cooperation for me.

   Interviewee: (*no response*)

   Interviewee:

8. **Interviewer:** Are you going to the national conference?

   Interviewee: I'm going to the regional conference in May.

   Interviewer:

9. **Interviewer:** Who do you think is the greatest baseball player of all time?

   Interviewee: Michael Jordan, without a doubt.

   Interviewer:

10. **Interviewer:** Which medical plan do you plan to select?

    Interviewee: Oh, I don't know.

    Interviewer:

Neutral and Leading Questions

All questions discussed and illustrated so far have been *neutral* questions. The respondent could decide upon an answer without any overt direction or pressure from the questioner. In bipolar questions, for instance, a respondent may choose between two equal choices: yes/no, approve/disapprove, agree/disagree.

Questions that suggest implicitly or explicitly the answer expected or desired are called *leading* questions because the questioner leads the respondent toward a particular answer by making "it easier or more tempting for the respondent to give one answer than another."[3] A person merely agrees with the interviewer. Leading questions may be intentional or unintentional, implicit or explicit, verbal or nonverbal.

The varying degrees of leading and the distinction between neutral and leading questions are illustrated in the following questions.

Neutral Questions	Leading Questions
1. Do you like shellfish?	1. I assume you like shellfish?
2. Are you going to graduation?	2. You're going to graduation, aren't you?
3. How do you feel about residence hall food?	3. Do you dislike residence hall food like most students?
4. How did this sequel compare to the original?	4. Didn't you like the original better than the sequel?
5. How do you feel about the new work rules?	5. How do you feel about the stupid new work rules?
6. Tell me about your drinking habits.	6. When was the last time you got drunk?
7. Have you ever cheated on exams?	7. Have you stopped cheating on exams?
8. Would you classify yourself as liberal or conservative?	8. Would you classify yourself as conservative or radical?
9. How do you feel about affirmative action?	9. Don't you think affirmative action is unfair to white males like me?

All nine leading questions make it easier for a person to reply in a particular way. The potential for interviewer bias is obvious. The situation, tone of the interview, manner in which the question is asked, and relationship with the interviewer would determine the respondent's ability or willingness to ignore the direction provided. For instance, if you were in a nonthreatening, informal, pleasant situation with a friend or equal in the organizational or social hierarchy, you might ignore or even object to the obvious leading questions. However, if you were in a threatening, formal situation with a superior, you might feel obligated to answer as the interviewer desires. At other times, you might go along with the interviewer because you want to be cooperative; if that's the answer the person wants to hear, you give it.

The first four leading questions are mild in direction. Each appears to be bipolar, to ask for a yes or no, agree or disagree response. However, the phrasing of each guides the respondent toward one pole; they are actually *unipolar* questions. You may ask a leading question unintentionally by accidentally phrasing a bipolar question in a leading manner, so you may avoid many leading questions by limiting your use of bipolar questions, by opening up your questions. Respondents could ignore the direction of questions 1, 2, and 4 if their relationship did not seem to depend on yes answers. Question 3 uses a bandwagon (follow-the-crowd) technique, and a respondent's answer might depend upon past experiences with this interviewer and whether the respondent wants to go along with the majority. A person with ambivalent or apathetic feelings might just go along with the answer the interviewer seems to want.

Loaded Questions

The last five questions provide strong direction and virtual dictation of the "correct" answer; these are called *loaded* questions. Loaded questions are the most extreme form of leading questions. Questions 5 and 8 are loaded because of *name calling* and *emotionally charged words*. In response to question 8, a person is likely to choose the least onerous of the choices provided, conservative, because few of us see ourselves as radical. Questions 6 and 7 *entrap* the respondent. Question 6 implies that the respondent has been drunk at least once. Question 7 charges the person with cheating in the past. Either a yes or a no may get the person in trouble. And question 9 places social pressure on the respondent to say yes.

Since leading questions have potential for severe interviewer bias, avoid them *unless you know what you are doing*. Introductory phrases such as "According to the law," "As we all know," "As witnesses have testified," "As stated by the CEO" may lead respondents to give "acceptable" responses rather than their true feelings or beliefs. Be aware that you can turn a neutral question into a leading question by the nonverbal manner in which you ask it. For example, you might appear to demand a certain answer by leaning toward the respondent or looking the person directly in the eyes. You might place vocal emphasis on a key word:

> Do you *like* that suit?
> *When* did you *show up* for work this morning?
> Are you going to vote *for* the new contract?

Regardless of their potential for mischief, leading questions have valuable uses. Employment interviewers may want to see how interviewees respond under stress. Persuasive interviewers use leading questions to obtain agreements, such as "Do you see why it is imperative to buy *now*?" Reporters ask leading questions to provoke

Figure 4.2   *Types of questions*

	Neutral		Leading	
	Open	**Closed**	**Open**	**Closed**
Primary	How do you feel about the new labor contract?	Do you approve or disapprove of the new labor contract?	Most highly skilled workers favor the new labor contract; how do you feel about it?	Do you favor the new labor contract like most skilled workers I have talked to?
Secondary	Why do you feel that way?	Is your approval moderate or strong?	If you favor the contract, why did you speak against it?	Do you favor the new contract, then, merely because other skilled workers favor it?

unguarded replies or to prod reluctant interviewees into responding. Counselors have discovered that questions such as "When was the last time you used marijuana?" show that a whole range of answers is acceptable and will not shock the interviewer.

Do not confuse neutral mirror and reflective probing questions with leading questions. Mirrors and reflectives may appear to direct respondents toward particular answers, but their purposes are clarification and verification, not leading or direction. If they lead by accident, they are failures.

Figure 4.2 compares types of questions available to interviewers and interviewees. Types include open and closed, primary and secondary, and neutral and leading questions.

Quiz 2—Identification of Questions

We have now introduced you to the question tools available for conducting and taking part in interviews efficiently and effectively. As a check to see if you know and understand these tools, identify each of the following questions in four ways: (1) open or closed, (2) primary or secondary, (3) neutral or leading, and (4) whether it is a special type of question tool—bipolar, loaded, nudging probe, clearinghouse probe, informational probe, restatement probe, reflective probe, or mirror probe.

1. Don't you find her irritating?
2. Tell me about your new puppy.
3. So?
4. By "25 percent off marked price," then, you are referring to the printed price rather than one written in red ink?
5. What is your favorite soft drink?

6. Let me check to be sure I have my class schedule correct. On Monday, Wednesday, and Friday, I have English 450 at 8:30, Management 382 at 9:30, and CE 412 at 11:30. On Tuesday and Thursday, I have the design project lab from 9:30 to 11:30 and Physics 321 from 2:15 to 4:15. Right?

7. Do you eat out at least once a week?

8. Anything else I need to know about Dirk?

9. Should we continue our overly generous contribution to the athletic program?

10. How do you *explain* that?

Phrasing Questions

Careful wording of questions is essential to obtaining free, accurate, honest, and thorough answers. Phrasing questions, particularly when creating probing questions on the spot, is not an easy task. Keep five factors in mind: language, relevance, information level, complexity, and accessibility.

Language

In Chapter 2 we discussed a variety of language problems and uses and how they may affect interactions with others. Review this discussion carefully because how you phrase questions will affect the answers you receive and whether answers go beyond superficial Level 1 to more revealing Levels 2 and 3. Kahn and Cannell advise interview parties to use "language that communicates successfully to the least sophisticated respondents and at the same time avoids the appearance of oversimplification."[4] Never "talk down" to another party. Do not mimic respondents' slang or jargon by inserting "you know," "cool," or "virtual" into questions, but use common words instead of uncommon words: "going to college" instead of "matriculating," "toilet" instead of "commode," and "careless" rather than "improvident."

Do not assume the other party will share your language. Remember that many words have multiple meanings, are ambiguous, sound alike, and have both positive and negative meanings. The following interaction between a patient and a physician illustrates professional jargon and sound-alike word problems:[5]

1. **Physician:** How about varicose veins?

2. **Patient:** Well, I have veins, but I don't know if they are close or not.

photo by J. Pickerell/The Image Works

How you ask a question may bias the answer you receive.

And the interaction below between an attorney and a physician shows how the wording of a question may lead to an angry response rather than effective exchange of information:[6]

1. **Attorney:** Do you recall the time that you examined the body?
2. **Physician:** The autopsy started around 8:30 P.M.
3. **Attorney:** And Mr. Dennington was dead at that time?
4. **Physician:** No, he was sitting on the table wondering why I was doing an autopsy.

We are all guilty of employing words with vague meanings as if they had commonly accepted reference points: much, many, most, average, fair, hot, cold, a lot, or small. What would yes answers to each of the following questions really tell us?

> Do you eat red meat often?
> Are you a light sleeper?
> Are you familiar with the iMAC computer?

If, for instance, a person said yes to the first question, how would you interpret the answer? That he or she eats red meat several times a week? Or everyday? Or two or three times a day? What do "light" and "familiar" mean in the last two questions?

An *oxymoron* occurs when we combine seemingly contradictory words. The results are often strange and humorous at the expense of the party using them. Common oxymorons are

Genuine imitation cowhide	Exact estimate
Almost exactly	Plastic glasses
Small crowd	

Depending upon attitudes and experiences, an interview party might see the following as oxymorons: dorm food, army intelligence, government organization, rap music. Our point is simple. Be precise in language selection and explain any word that may be unknown, unclear, or mistaken for a similar-sounding word.

The way we select words and string them together can also create communication problems. Poorly phrased newspaper headlines such as the following may provide us with comic relief, but not for the editor or the subject:

> Prosecution ends in baby beating.
> Gas chamber executions may be a health hazzard.
> Cause of AIDS found, scientists.

In a survey of children and television, interviewers first asked parents, "Do you control your children's viewing of television?" A majority said no. But when asked later, "Do you allow your children to watch any television program they desire to watch?" a majority also said no. The second question apparently sounded too lenient to respondents; and even if they did not "control" their children's television viewing, they were reluctant to say they imposed no control. In a religious survey, interviewers asked one set of respondents, "Is it okay to smoke while praying?" Over 90 percent said no. When they asked another set of respondents, "Is it okay to pray while smoking?" over 90 percent said yes. Although these would appear to be rephrased versions of the same question, respondents clearly interpreted them differently. The first sounded sacrilegious, lighting up while praying; but the second sounded good, praying while you are smoking. Some might say you'd better start praying if you smoke!

Relevance

If there is a possibility that a respondent might not see the relevance of a question (either primary or secondary), be sure to explain its relation to your purpose and needs to motivate the person to respond freely and accurately. Phrase your questions carefully to avoid obtrusive language. The order or placing of questions may affect perceived relevance. For example, ask for demographic data such as age, salary, educational level, geographic location, political party, or religious preference at the beginning or end of the interview, not somewhere in the middle. The end of the interview is usually preferable because by then you should have established trust and have asked a number of clearly relevant questions. If during a political survey or public opinion poll on medical costs, your first question is "How old are you?" or "What is your income," an interviewee has a right to wonder what this has to do with the election or an issue such as medical costs. If there can be any doubt about relevance, explain why you need to ask for this information.

Be aware that what might appear to be irrelevant to us might be highly relevant to a person from another culture. For instance, Japanese often ask many personal questions early in interactions so they can learn important characteristics about the person they are interacting with, including personality, knowledge, skills, and background. A Japanese party might ask you where you were born, where you went to school, how you feel about Japanese food, what Japanese you speak, and about your hobbies. You might think of these questions as irrelevant or too personal.

Information Level

Respondents must have a store of knowledge that enables them to respond comfortably and intelligently. Questions beyond the respondent's information may cause embarrassment or resentment because none of us want to appear uninformed, ill informed, uneducated, or unintelligent, in private or before strangers. Our motivation to cooperate will dwindle quickly. Ask for information in common categories or frames of reference, such as pounds rather than ounces of sugar, cups rather than pots of coffee, water bills in dollars rather than gallons, or a number of hours of television viewing per day rather than month or year. Beware that respondents may fake answers or give vague, ambiguous responses rather than admit ignorance. Recall how you have provided long, rambling answers to essay test questions when you knew little or nothing. If you ask people if they know Mary Walters, a fictitious person, you are likely to get answers such as "The name sounds familiar," "I think I've heard of her," or "I'm not sure" rather than "no" answers. This is particularly so if respondents think they should know Mary.

Questions beneath respondents' information levels may insult their intelligence, wisdom, or experiences. This occurs when you use overly simple words, request elementary information from an expert, or provide too much explanation. Determine if a respondent is a lay person, a novice, or an expert on the subject matter and whether public opinion or authoritative knowledge is needed. For instance, the following questions might be acceptable for the general public but not for gun collectors, hunters, target shooters, or members: "How do you feel about the NRA's (the National Rifle Association) lobbying efforts against the ban on assault rifles?" Or "Are you familiar with the NRA's lobbying efforts against gun control?"

Do not assume that respondents will have the information you want. Many us of are narrow specialists in our professional fields or know little about other academic departments within our colleges. Large percentages of people cannot name the U.S. senators from their states, their U.S. representatives, the governor of their states, or the vice president of the United States. Many do not know the population of their cities, annual incomes, or wedding dates. Current trends, world events, new books, and the status of the economy are known by surprisingly few people. Abbreviations may cause trouble because we know the reference only by its full name. For instance, we may know what an occupational therapist does but not what an OT does. On the other hand, we may know a procedure, organization, or place by its initials but not by its formal name: EKG, TVA, or DC. Many organizations have the same initials. If a person attended ISU, was that Idaho State University, Iowa State University, or Indiana State University?

Complexity

Questions should be simple, clear requests for limited amounts of information. Avoid complex questions that challenge respondents to figure out what you want or contain no obvious parameters. If you must ask a complicated question such as the following telephone marketing survey question, use sample answers to explain the scale or provide a small card containing the scale and a sample or two.

> I would like your opinion on brands of toothpaste. I would like you to rate these brands by using the numbers from plus five to minus five. If you like the brand, give it a number from plus one to plus five. The more you like it, the bigger the plus number you should give it. If you dislike the brand, give it a number from minus one to minus five. The more you dislike it, the bigger the minus number you should give it. If you neither like nor dislike the brand, give it a zero.

Some questions are unnecessarily complex because of poor wording. The following question was used in a research project on marriage relationships:

> Pick the most appropriate response. You feel that you understand each other, but you have never told them this.
> 1. You have never felt this way, or you have felt this way and told them this.
> 2. You occasionally have felt this way, but you have never told them this.
> 3. You frequently have felt this way, but you have never told them this.

Be cautious when asking global questions such as "Tell me about yourself" or "Tell me about your profession." Where is the respondent to begin and end? Are you as interviewer interested in certain topics, happenings, or issues? Many respondents find such wide open questions difficult to respond to without some guidelines or hints about what is needed or appropriate.

Accessibility

Accessibility refers to the respondent's capability of answering a question because of social, psychological, or situational constraints. As we grow up, many of us learn that it is more socially acceptable to be humble than boastful, so if an interviewer suggests we are beautiful, intelligent, creative, or generous, we are likely to pose an "Aw shucks, it was nothing attitude" or say "Yes" with a theatrical flourish and treat our answer as if it were a joke. To do otherwise, we have learned, could lead to ridicule or ostracism. Be aware of gender and cultural differences among respondents that might affect social and psychological accessibility. For example, research indicates that women when compared to men disclose more information about themselves, use more psychological or emotional verbs, discuss their personal lives more in business interactions, have less difficulty in expressing intimate feelings, talk more about other people's accomplishments and minimize their own, and appear to be more comfortable when hearing accolades about themselves.[7] Cultures also differ in accessibility, though caution is wise until you know an interviewer or interviewee.

When you pose questions in taboo areas—sex, personal income, religious convictions, health—you are asking for answers not easily accessible to many. If, as a health care professional, for example, you must investigate such topics, understand your relationship with the interviewee and pay attention to how you ask such questions verbally and nonverbally. Consider situational variables such as privacy, seating arrangement, and location. Embarrassing fertility situations with questions shouted in crowded waiting rooms have served as fodder for some recent hilarious television sit-coms, but few of us would trade places with one of these mythical patients. We may be psychologically unable to relate true feelings about a supervisor, teacher, friend, or parent to or in the presence of this person. And often we cannot discuss or express our feelings about a traumatic illness, accident, or loss of a loved one. If you must ask questions that pose accessibility problems, phrase them to lessen social and psychological constraints and avoid offending the respondent. Delay asking them until you have established a comfortable climate and good relationship with the respondent.

Quiz 3—What's Wrong with These Questions?

After reviewing the five factors of question phrasing—language, relevance, information level, complexity, and accessibility—identify the problem or problems with each question below and then rewrite it to make it a good question.

1. (First question in a political survey) Is your age 18–35, 36–50, 51–65, over 65?
2. When were you last inebriated?
3. Would you say Congress is doing a good job or that it could do better?
4. How beautiful do you think you are?
5. What effects would a flat tax have on different age and economic groups?
6. What are your reactions to the Johnson killing in Omaha?
7. Do you consider yourself to be of low intelligence, average intelligence, above-average intelligence, or high intelligence?
8. When did you last have an MRI?

9. Do you obey the drinking laws most of the time or when convenient?

10. (First two questions) Do you approve or disapprove of bioengineered food? What is bioengineered food?

Common Question Pitfalls

Because we often have to create questions on the spot, particularly secondary questions, we are prone to fall into common question pitfalls. These include the bipolar trap, the open-to-closed switch, the double-barreled inquisition, the leading push, the guessing game, and the yes (no) response.

The Bipolar Trap

You fall into the bipolar trap when you ask a bipolar question designed to elicit a yes or no answer when you really want specific information or an open-ended answer. This happens when you ask "Do you know what happened next?" instead of "What happened next?" "Are you familiar with our company?" instead of "What do you know about our company?" "Can you tell me the names of the students in your study group?" instead of "What are the names of the students in your study group?" You can avoid most bipolar traps by beginning questions with words and phrases such as what, why, how, explain, and tell me about in place of do, can, would, and will.

The Open-to-Closed Switch

The open-to-closed switch occurs when you ask an open question but, before the interviewee can respond, you rephrase the question into a closed or bipolar question. This trap is readily apparent in many interviews, such as,

> What were your first reactions when you were told you were selected? Did you believe the call?
> Tell me about your training in engineering? Did it include courses in management?
> Why did you move from California to Utah? Was it because of cost of living in California?

The open-to-closed switch seems to occur when questioners are still phrasing questions in their minds and, unfortunately, alter a perfectly good open question into a narrow, closed question. Notice how restricted the rephrased questions are in each of the sample questions. The respondent is likely to address only the second question and often with a simple yes or no. Imagine the amount and types of information the initial questions might have generated. Watch interviews on television news and talk shows to detect how often interviewers fall into this trap. Avoid the open-to-closed switch by preparing questions prior to the interview, listening to yourself as you ask a question, waiting silently after asking a question, and giving the respondent ample time to reply.

The Double-Barreled Inquisition

The double-barreled inquisition or multiple question occurs when you ask two or more questions at the same time instead of a single, precise question. Listen to your questions in everyday conversations, let alone formal interviews, and you will soon become aware of how often you ask double-barreled questions such as,

> When and how did you first get interested in playing the drums?
> What type of irons, driver, and putter do you have?
> What do you hope to be doing five years and ten years from now?

Respondents are unlikely to remember or address all parts of your question and will respond to what they remember, often the last part they heard. Some will select the portion they want to answer and ignore the rest. Respondents often feel they are being subjected to a third-degree inquisition when subjected to questions such as "Tell me the name, model, and year of your car, your license plate number, and when your driver's license expires." At the very least, you, as interviewer, are likely to find it necessary to repeat portions of your initial question to get all of the information you need. At worst, you may go to your next primary question and fail to obtain important information. Ask one question at a time. As an interviewee, you are likely to find it necessary to ask the interviewer to repeat parts of double-barreled questions. This can be frustrating and embarrassing. Be tactful.

The Leading Push

The leading push occurs when you ask an *unintentional* leading question that suggests how a person ought to respond. It is easy to interject your feelings or attitudes in questions, such as the following:

> You play video games *everyday*?
> I love to browse the Internet; how about you?
> Don't you think you were partly to blame for this scam?

Phrase your questions neutrally if you want honest answers and accurate information. Many people will go along with whatever answers you seem to desire or seem to be in their best interests. Use leading questions for specific purposes, and know what you are doing. If you do not hear yourself asking a leading question, you may get erroneous information and be unaware that you have fallen into a common question pitfall.

The Guessing Game

The guessing game occurs when interview parties attempt to guess information instead of ask for it. We often fall into this trap.

> Could the fire have been caused by a discarded cigarette?
> Did you attend college so you could get a better-paying job?
> Are you from Boston?

Interviewers such as journalists, health care professionals, recruiters, and investigators often ask strings of closed, guessing questions to obtain needed information when a single open-ended question could do the job more efficiently and effectively. And sometimes they never guess the correct answer because they do not ask for it. Follow a simple rule: Don't guess, ask.

The Yes (No) Response

The yes (no) response pitfall occurs when interviewers and interviewees mistakenly ask questions that have only one obvious answer, a yes or a no. Each of the following questions is likely to get an easily predictable response:

> Do you want to graduate?
> Are you a progressive bank?
> Do you want to get lung cancer?

You can avoid the yes (no) question pitfall if you *think* while phrasing questions. Do not ask the obvious unless you are doing so for motivational or disciplinary reasons, and even then their effectiveness is doubtful, as most parents and supervisors know. If you want to ask a bipolar question, be sure to include two poles; and if you do not want a bipolar answer, open up your question.

You can avoid common question pitfalls by planning most questions prior to the interview so you do not have to create them on the spot in the give-and-take of the interaction. When phrasing a question during an interview, think through it before uttering it, stop when you have asked a good open question instead of rephrasing it, and use bipolar questions sparingly. Above all, know the common question pitfalls well enough that you can catch yourself before you tumble into one.

Quiz 4—What Are the Pitfalls in These Questions?

Each of the following questions illustrates one or more of the common question pitfalls: bipolar trap, open-to-closed switch, double-barreled, leading push, guessing game, and yes (no) response. Identify the pitfall(s) of each question and rephrase it to make it a good question. Avoid a new pitfall in your revised question.

1. Tell me about your internship. When does it start?
2. (Asked by a member of the band) Did you enjoy the concert?
3. How was your vacation? Did you go to the beach like last year?
4. Do you want to miss the plane?
5. Tell me about your new job and your apartment.

6. Don't you think you should get a Jeep?

7. Do you think your back pain is from the new exercise machine?

8. How are the job and your family?

9. You're going to vote, aren't you?

10. Did you select this major because you thought it would be easy?

Question Sequences
So far we have been addressing individual question tools you can employ in different interview settings, but questions are often interconnected into strategic series or sequences. For example, you may arrange primary with primary questions and primary with secondary questions within a topic or to form a sequence for an entire interview. Common question sequences are the funnel, inverted funnel, tunnel, and quintamensional design.

Funnel Sequence

A funnel sequence begins with a broad, open-ended question and proceeds with more restricted questions, such as the following:

1. Tell me about the new career-path options in your department.

2. How do students feel about the new options?

3. Which options do you think will attract most students?

4. What are anticipated staff needs?

5. Do you think these options will aid student retention?

A funnel sequence beginning with an open-ended question is most appropriate when respondents are familiar with a topic, feel free to talk about it, want to express their feelings, and are willing to reveal and explain their attitudes. There is no need to warm them up or overcome barriers to disclosing information. Open questions are easier to answer, pose less threat to respondents, and get people talking, so the funnel sequence is a good way to begin the body of interviews. And the funnel sequence avoids possible conditioning or biasing of later responses. For instance, if you begin an interview with a closed question such as "Do you think we should legalize same-sex marriages?" you force the respondent to take a polar position that may affect the remainder of the interview and place the person on the defensive. An open question such as "How do you feel about legalizing same-sex marriages?" does not force a person to take a polarized position and allows for explanations and qualifications.

Inverted Funnel Sequence

The inverted funnel sequence begins with a closed question and proceeds toward open questions, such as the following:

1. When did you institute your current computer-training program?

2. What kinds of training are included?

3. Which kinds of training are selected most by employees?

4. How have you assessed the program's effectiveness?

5. As one who has taken advantage of the program, how do you feel about it?

The inverted funnel sequence is most useful when you need to motivate interviewees to respond. They may not want to talk about an unpleasant event. They may feel they do not know enough about a topic. Interviewees may be reluctant to talk to *you*. A respondent's memory or thought processes may need a bit of assistance, and a few closed questions may serve as warm-ups. Closed questions may work when open-ended ones might overwhelm a person. An inverted funnel sequence may progress toward a final clearinghouse probing question such as "Is there anything else you would like to add?"

Tunnel Sequence

The tunnel question sequence, sometimes called a "string of beads," is a series of similar questions, either open or closed, which may allow for little probing. Each question may cover a different topic, ask for a specific piece of information, or measure a different attitude. The following is a typical tunnel sequence:

1. Do you approve or disapprove of special prosecutors.

2. Do you think special prosecutors have too much power?

3. Do you think special prosecutors should have limits placed on their funds?

4. Do you think special prosecutors are too partisan?

5. Do you think special prosecutors will make it difficult to attract good candidates?

The tunnel sequence is common in polls, surveys, and admissions interviews designed to elicit reactions, attitudes, intentions, or bits of educational, medical, or demographic information. Data are easy to record and quantify. This sequence is unlikely to obtain in-depth information on a single topic and may be a series of bipolar questions.

Quintamensional Design Sequence

George Gallup developed the quintamensional design sequence to determine the intensity of opinions and attitudes.[8] This five-step approach proceeds from an interviewee's awareness of the issue to attitudes uninfluenced by the interviewer, specific attitudes, reasons for these attitudes, and intensity of attitude. For example,

1. *Awareness*: Tell me what you know about the proposed contract.

2. *Uninfluenced attitudes*: How, if at all, might these plans affect your career?

3. *Specific attitude*: Do you approve or disapprove of this contract?

4. *Reason*: Why do you feel this way?

5. *Intensity of attitude*: How strongly do you feel about this—strongly, very strongly, not something you will ever change your mind on?

The quintamensional design sequence has been an effective questioning tool for the Gallup organization in thousands of public opinion polls. You can use this sequence, modify it, or create one that works best for your purposes. Use your ingenuity to select and develop effective question sequences.

Quiz 5—Question Sequences

Which question sequence or combination would you employ in each of the situations described below? Why would you use this sequence or combination?

1. You are interviewing residents of your apartment complex about a proposed city ordinance that would limit the number of students who could share an apartment.

2. You are interviewing third-year law students for possible positions in your firm.

3. You are conducting a market survey for your company to assess the marketability of a new laser flashlight.

4. You are interviewing a college basketball coach about the influence of basketball summer camps on junior high school students.

5. You are a newspaper reporter and must interview a police officer about an altercation that occurred between three off-duty police officers and two fans after a recent baseball game.

Summary

Interview parties have a limitless variety of question tools to choose from, and each tool has unique characteristics, capabilities, and pitfalls. Knowing which question to select and how to use it is essential for interviewing effectiveness and efficiency. Each question has three characteristics: (1) open or closed, (2) primary or secondary, and (3) neutral or leading. Open questions are designed to elicit large amounts of information; closed questions are designed to elicit specific bits of information. Primary questions open up topics and subtopics; secondary questions probe into answers for more information, explanations, clarifications, and verifications. And neutral questions give respondents freedom to answer as they wish; leading questions nudge respondents toward answers interviewers want to hear.

Phrasing questions carefully is essential to get the information you need. Keep five factors in mind: language, relevance, information level, complexity, and accessibility. If you phrase questions carefully and think before asking, then you can avoid common question pitfalls such as the bipolar trap, the open-to-closed switch, the double-barreled inquisition, the leading push, the guessing game, and the yes (no) response.

And as you are developing your question tools, select a sequence that is most appropriate for your purpose and objectives. A funnel sequence begins with an open-ended question and moves gradually to more specific and closed questions. An inverted funnel sequence begins with a closed question and gradually opens up questions as the interviewee becomes ready to respond at length and in detail. The tunnel sequence consists of a string of similar questions (open or closed) that probe into a variety of topics. And the quintamensional design sequence allows you to assess attitudes and opinions and their intensity.

Remember that questions and question sequences are the tools of the trade for both interviewers and interviewees. If you know question types, unique uses, and both advantages and disadvantages, you can develop considerable interviewing skill and enjoy the experiences.

An Interview for Review and Analysis

These are portions of testimony by Mathilda Westberry during the Oklahoma City bombing trial on June 5, 1997. She is being cross-examined by a government prosecutor. Identify each question as open or closed, primary or secondary, neutral or leading, and whether it is a special question such as bipolar, loaded, silent probe, nudging probe, clearinghouse probe, informational probe, restatement probe, reflective probe, or mirror probe. How do questions meet the criteria of language, relevance, information level, complexity, and accessibility? Does the interviewer stumble into common question pitfalls that affect the interview negatively? Which question sequence or sequences are used? Can you detect question strategies of the prosecutor?

This is the opening series of questions by the prosecutor.

1. **Interviewer:** Where did you grow up?

2. **Interviewee:** Enid, Oklahoma.

3. **Interviewer:** And did you go to high school in that area?

4. **Interviewee:** Yes, I went to Kremlin High School, which is about eight miles north of Enid.

5. **Interviewer:** And after you finished high school, did you go on to college?

6. **Interviewee:** Yes, I went to nursing school at Enid General School of Nursing, and then went up to St. Paul Bible College in Minnesota.

7. **Interviewer:** When you were at St. Paul Bible College, did you meet somebody special there?

8. **Interviewee:** Yes, I met Bob Westberry.

9. **Interviewer:** Did you marry him.

10. **Interviewee:** Yes.

11 **Interviewer:** How long were you married to him?

12 **Interviewee:** Thirty-six and a half years.

13. **Interviewer:** Tell us what happened to him.

14. **Interviewee:** On the morning of April 19, it was a usual morning, and we got up and were preparing to go to work and at breakfast had spoken about the fact that the next day would be the anniversary date of our daughter's death on the 20th. And I went to—well, it was my practice to follow him to the door when he left for work. And on that particular morning, for some reason, I gave him a wack on the seat of the pants and told him an extra I love you, and then I went back to the cabinet, was fixing my lunch for the day. And I knew how long it would take for him to back out, and then I quick ran to the front door and watched him back off.

15. **Interviewer:** Did you ever see him again?

16. **Interviewee:** No. No.

This excerpt deals with the Westberry family, including Bob Westberry's relationship with his grandchildren.

1. **Interviewer:** And your youngest child is Glen, right?

2. **Interviewee:** Yes.

3. **Interviewer:** Your baby boy?

4. **Interviewee:** Yes.

5. **Interviewer:** And does Glen have a child?

6. **Interviewee:** Yes, David.

7. **Interviewer:** How old is David right now?

8. **Interviewee:** He's six and a half.

9. **Interviewer:** Now, as you and your husband—during your married years, did you have an opportunity to live close to any of your children?

10. **Interviewee:** We lived closest to Glen and Bev and David.

11. **Interviewer:** And that was after all your kids left the house, obviously; right?

12. **Interviewee:** Yeah.

13. **Interviewer:** And when were you living close to Glen and his wife and his child?

14. **Interviewee:** When we lived the first seven years in Hollywood, Florida, from 85 to 92, and then for a short time they relocated to Oklahoma when we moved to Oklahoma City in 92, November of 92.

15. **Interviewer:** And did your husband develop a relationship with David, your grandson?

16. **Interviewee:** Very close. Very close relationship between the two of them.

17. **Interviewer:** Describe that briefly for us, could you?

18. **Interviewee:** Well, he was—Bob was known as "papa" to all the grandchildren. And David had always been at our house a lot and of course preferred Bob much—you know, which I didn't mind.

This next excerpt deals with Bob Westberry's position with the Defense Investigative Services and how Mathilda Westberry learned of her husband's death.

1. **Interviewee:** And then in 1972, when DIS or Defense Investigative Services was started, and he was a charter member until he died.

2. **Interviewer:** So he was employed by the Defense Investigative Service in April of 1995?

3. **Interviewee:** Yes, yes, he was.

4. **Interviewer:** How long had he been an employee with them?

5. **Interviewee:** Since 1992.

6. **Interviewer:** 1992?

7. **Interviewee:** 72, I'm sorry.

8. **Interviewer:** And what was his assignment at the time of the bombing?

9. **Interviewee:** He was the senior agent in charge of SAC. They called them SACs.

10. **Interviewer:** So he ran the office there in Oklahoma City?

11. **Interviewee:** Yes, he was a supervisor, uh-huh.

12. **Interviewer:** Now, after the bombing, did you find out immediately what had happened to your husband?

13. **Interviewee:** No, I didn't. I didn't know for about 45 minutes.

14. **Interviewer:** And what did you learn?

15. **Interviewee:** Well, I was at work at Aetna, and there had been a lot of confusion in the office about the explosion and a fire downtown, and I tried to call him twice and with no response. And I was—continued to do my job, and then one of the fellows walked in that worked for Aetna and said it—you know, there was some thought it might have been the courthouse. And he said it wasn't the courthouse, it was the federal building, and that's when—the first time that I knew that anything could have possibly have happened to him.

Student Activities

1. Watch a "Booknotes" program on C-SPAN between Brian Lamb and an author. Identify the types of questions Brian Lamb asks. Which types of questions dominate? Which types of secondary questions does he use? Can you detect leading questions? Does he fall into any common pitfalls? Does he use one or more sequences?

2. Prepare two sets of questions—one with neutral questions and one with some of the questions reworded into leading questions. Interview six people, three with each schedule of questions. How did the answers vary to the neutral and leading questions? How did different people (age, gender, education, occupation) react to your different schedules of questions?

3. Create a schedule of closed questions, including a number of bipolar questions, on a controversial issue. Interview three people, a friend or family member, an acquaintance, and a stranger. Which ones gave you closed, bipolar answers and which elaborated regardless of question types used? How can you explain the differences in the responses? What does this tell you about asking closed questions?

4. Tape-record a series of investigative interviews during a program such as "20/20," "60 Minutes," or "Dateline" and see if you can detect common question pitfalls. Were these intentional or unintentional? How did these affect the answers received? How did they affect the climate of the interview?

Notes

1. See Stanley L. Payne, *The Art of Asking Questions* (Princeton, NJ: Princeton University Press, 1980), for an excellent discussion of types and uses of questions and difficulties in phrasing questions.

2. Payne, p. 204.

3. Robert L. Kahn and Charles F. Cannell, *The Dynamics of Interviewing* (New York: John Wiley & Sons, 1964), p. 205.

4. Kahn and Cannell, p. 112.

5. Roger W. Shuy, "The Medical Interview: Problems in Communication," *Primary Care* 3 (1976), pp. 376–77.

6. William T.G. Litant, "And Were You Present When Your Picture Was Taken?" *Lawyer's Journal* (Massachusetts Bar Association), May 1996.

7. Lillian Glass, *He Says, She Says: Closing the Communication Gap between the Sexes* (New York: Putnam, 1993), pp. 45–59.

8. George Gallup, "The Quintamensional Plan of Question Design," *Public Opinion Quarterly* 11 (1947), p. 385.

Resources

Barone, Jeanne Tessier, and Jo Young Switzer. *Interviewing Art and Skill*. Boston: Allyn and Bacon, 1995.

Kahn, Robert L., and Charles F. Cannell. *The Dynamics of Interviewing*. New York: John Wiley & Sons, 1982.

Long, Lynette; Louis V. Paradise; and Thomas J. Long. *Questioning: Skills for the Helping Process*. Monterey, CA: Brooks/Cole, 1981.

Payne, Stanley L. *The Art of Asking Questions*. Princeton, NJ: Princeton University Press, 1980.

Wood, Julia T. *But I Thought You Meant . . . Misunderstandings in Human Communication*. Mountain View, CA: Mayfield, 1998.

The Probing Interview

The probing interview is the most common type because journalists, attorneys, police officers, recruiters, health care professionals, insurance claims investigators, counselors, supervisors, teachers, students, parents, and children, to name a few, are involved in them every day. The interview may be as brief and informal as a person calling for technical assistance with a computer, a broadcast journalist checking with a source before airtime, or a student asking a librarian about the location of reference materials. Or it may be as lengthy and formal as an hour-long interview between a journalist and a world leader, an attorney and a client, or a researcher and a subject.

Regardless of length, formality, or setting, the *purpose* of the interview is to get relevant and timely information as accurately and completely as possible in the shortest amount of time. The *method* of gathering this information consists of careful questioning, insightful listening and observing, and *skillful probing* into answers to dig beneath surface information for specifics, explanations, feelings, attitudes, positions, and information an interviewee would rather not divulge. Successful probing interviews are neither easy nor accidental but thoroughly planned, sometimes rehearsed, and skillfully executed. There is no typical probing interview to serve as a model to follow because, as Eric Nalder the Pulitzer Prize–winning chief investigative reporter for the *Seattle Times* has stated, they are as varied as the conversations we have and the people we talk to.[1] Figure 5.1 illustrates the seven-stage process—not a simple formula—essential for most successful probing interviews.

1. Determining the Purpose

Before you begin to research a topic, develop an interview guide, or phrase questions, first determine *why* you are going to conduct one or more interviews instead of discovering the information through other means. Why conduct an interview if the information you need is readily available from the course syllabus, the Internet, the library, a company's annual reports, court documents, or other sources? Second, think carefully about the *end product* you envision. Will the interview provide a footnote to an environmental impact study for a proposed cattle operation, material for a term paper, evidence central to an investigation of a fire, or a transcript that constitutes most of a story in a magazine? You may not be as concerned about question

Figure 5.1   *Stages in probing interviews*

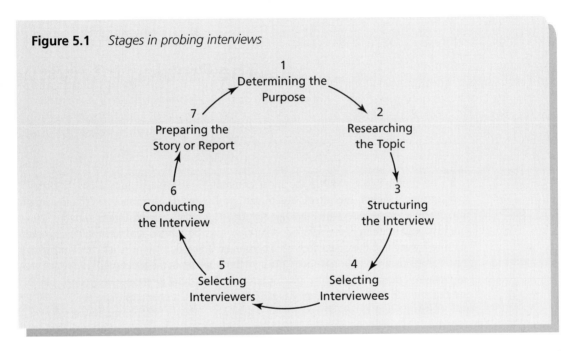

wording and note taking if the end product will be a class report as you would if the end product will be a key factor in a lawsuit, or one that might lead to a lawsuit.

Inevitably your twofold purpose will both affect and be affected by the situation. For instance, if your end product is to be a news feature story or a research report, this use of information may determine the length and number of interviews, how interviewees are selected, when and where the interviews will take place, and when your story or report must be completed. On the other hand, if you attend a news conference or briefing, this situation may dictate the types and numbers of questions you can ask, information available to you, whether some information will be off the record, and when you may report certain facts or intentions of a source. If you want to see how workers in your factory feel about issues such as affirmative action, job security, or medical benefits, your purpose will determine both situation and product. If your purpose is to diagnose an illness, get firsthand accounts of an accident, or investigate rumors of a student threatening to shoot another student or a teacher, situational factors such as apparent seriousness of the disease or availability of expert diagnosticians, broadcast or press deadlines, or recent violent incidents at other schools will determine the urgency of interviews, how long you can conduct interviews, and what you can ask ethically and legally.

2. Researching the Topic

Be thoroughly briefed on the interview topic so you can develop a detailed interview guide and ask intelligent and insightful questions that are free of errors. This will help you avoid requests for information readily available from other sources. Do not make false assumptions about

O N   T H E   W E B

Use the Internet to research your college or one that you might select as a graduate or professional school. For example, you can access the School of Liberal Arts and its 11 departments at Purdue University through a single Web address (http://www.sla.purdue.edu). Focus first on the college or university, then on the school or college within this larger structure, and finally on the department. What kinds of information are readily available? How up to date is the information? What kinds of information are not included that you would have to discover through interviews with faculty or students? What questions are raised by the information contained on the university, school, and department Web sites?

causes and effects, who knows what, the willingness of a source to give important information, or the ability of a source to give information accurately and without bias. The amount and kinds of information you need are determined by your goal and end product: production decision, news story, investigative report, diagnosis of a problem, or recommended course of action.

Search through your personal and organization's records, archives, and clipping files. Talk to colleagues and fellow students who have had occasion to study this topic. Search through corporate, church, school, and courthouse records, publications, and documents. Visit your local or college library for reference works, atlases, almanacs, organizational and city directories, government documents, books, encyclopedias, professional journals, newspapers, periodicals, and biographical dictionaries. Some topics will take you to specialized libraries devoted to law, medicine, former presidents, history, or technology. And this is the electronic age, so do not overlook information on the World Wide Web, CD/ROMs, and computer databases that are increasingly available with a few keystrokes on your office or home computer.

A show of ignorance or failure to do your homework may anger an interviewee, destroy your credibility with a source, and embarrass you and the organization you represent. Few events are more pathetic, for example, than an interviewer attempting to discuss a book with its author, query a member of Congress about a piece of legislation, or recruit a member for an organization without having read beyond the title page or abstract of the book, the first few paragraphs of a complicated bill, or the recruit's resume or application materials. These interviewers rarely learn anything new, gain insights, or ask about the respondents' experiences or opinions.

Proof that you have done your homework will impress the interviewee, show you cannot be easily fooled, and motivate the person to respond more readily and in depth. All of us are flattered when others take the time to learn about us and our interests, fields, accomplishments, and opinions because we have pride in what we do. Know appropriate jargon and technical terms, and use and pronounce them correctly. Know the respondent's name (and how it is pronounced), correct title, and organization. For instance, you should know if a person is a professor or an instructor, an editor or a reporter, a doctor (Ph.D., M.D., D.V.M., D.D.S.) or one without a degree. The rule is simple: Show sincere interest in me, and I will return the favor.

3. Structuring the Interview

While looking for information on your topic, pay attention to what is not included in available materials, such as explanations, interpretations of data, both sides of an issue, attitudes, and feelings. How dated is available information? What has happened in the interim that might alter attitudes, preliminary data, or cherished dogma? What anecdotes and quotations might be important for your report or story?

Interview Guide

As you research a topic, jot down areas and subareas that you might develop into an interview guide. The guide you construct may be an elaborate outline, major aspects of a topic, key words in your notebook, or the traditional journalistic interview guide: *who* was involved, *what* happened, *when* it happened, *where* it happened, *how* it happened, and *why* it happened. Chronological sequences are effective in moving through stories or happenings because they have occurred in time sequences. Or look for a logical sequence such as cause-to-effect or problem-to-solution. Remain flexible because few probing interviews will go exactly as planned.

The Opening

Plan an opening that will establish an atmosphere of mutual trust and respect and begin to establish a positive relationship between you and the interviewee. Avoid being too familiar with the interviewee by calling the person by first name or nickname when you are barely acquainted or beneath the person in the social, organizational, or professional hierarchy. In the opening minutes, you may identify yourself, your position, and the organization you represent; explain what you wish to discuss and why; reveal how the information will be used; and how long the interview will take.

Review the opening techniques discussed in Chapter 3 to determine which one or combination is best for this interview. For example, a tactful reference to the interviewee's position on an issue can get an interview underway: "I understand you support the city's purchase of the old Sears building and property. Why are you in favor of this action?" Or you may use an icebreaker question about a person's hobby, accomplishment, or activity of years ago in college or military service. Observe the surroundings when you arrive for an interview because a picture, award, model, furniture, or view out a window may provide an ideal means of initiating a friendly conversation with the interviewee. We find that icebreaker questions or comments get people talking and ready to discuss more substantive questions a few minutes later. Do not rely on a standard opening; design one to fit each occasion and interviewee. A casual compliment, friendly remark about a topic or mutual friend, or a bit of small talk might create a friendly, relaxed atmosphere with one person and produce the opposite effect with a busy, hassled interviewee who neither likes nor has time for small talk.

Be sure you and the interviewee have a mutual understanding of any ground rules governing the interaction before proceeding past the opening. This is particularly important in investigative interviews conducted by police officers, journalists, and supervisors. If everything of any importance is going to be off the record, why conduct the interview? Make it clear you will not agree to any retroactive off-the-record demands.

Be sure both of you understand what "off the record" means—not naming the source or using information only as background, for instance. If a person does not want to be quoted, try to get agreement that you may attribute the quotation to an "unnamed source" or work it into the text of your report without attribution.

The Body

If the interview will be brief or you are highly skilled and experienced in conducting probing interviews and phrasing questions, you may complete your planning with an interview guide and prepare to conduct a nonscheduled interview. If not, develop a moderate schedule that turns topic and subtopic areas into primary questions and provides possible secondary questions under each. The moderate schedule eliminates the necessity of creating every question at the moment of utterance and allows you to plan your wording carefully while not in the heat of the interview. At the same time, the moderate schedule gives you flexibility to delete questions and create new ones as the need or opportunity arises during the interview. For instance, you may inadvertently discover a highly important area not detected during your research or planning that warrants a detour and extensive questioning. Grasp the opportunity! Some interviewers fear such digressions because they might lose their train of thought or control of the interview. These are risks worth taking and are minimized by a moderate schedule. You can return to your schedule at any time and pick up where you left off. The freedom to *adapt* and *improvise* as the interviewee, situation, and response warrant make the moderate schedule ideal for probing interviews.

The Closing

The interview usually ends when you have the information you need or time runs out. If an interviewee has limited you to 15 minutes, complete your task in this time or prepare to close. Do not ignore the time limit or badger the person into continuing. The interviewee may grant additional time if you acknowledge that time is up and you need only a few more minutes; if not, close the interview positively and try to arrange for another one. Respect for the other's time constraints enhances the relationships.

Review the closing guidelines and techniques in Chapter 3, particularly the use of clearinghouse probes. Always show your appreciation for the interviewee's assistance. And remember that the interview is not over until both parties are out of sight and sound of one another. Look and listen for important information or insights during the closing moments when the interviewee's guard may be down.

4. Selecting Interviewees

In many instances, the situation or your purpose will determine the person or persons you must interview: an accident victim, a witness to a fire, a patient in need of assistance, a home owner who has been robbed, a technician who has information on a new phone system, a CEO who calls a press conference. At other times, you must select one or more interviewees from among several students, survivors, city council members, witnesses, or members of a soccer team. The interviewees may need to be experts on an issue or merely persons with differing points of view. Use four criteria.

Does the Interviewee Have the Information Desired?

The first criterion is whether a person has the information you need. What is the person's level of expertise through experiences, education, training, or positions? Was the person in a position to have observed the decision, proceedings, discovery, accident, or robbery? How was the person involved in determining a policy or course of action? Do you need to interview any adult, voter, or student or an authority or expert on the topic or issue? Is part of your purpose to assess a person's level of expertise?

For instance, as an oral historian, you may want to interview a person who was intimately involved in the moon landings, not merely a person who has written or read about them. As a journalist, you might interview a candidate to determine the person's knowledge of foreign affairs or tax laws. As a student, you might want to talk to the vice president for development to discuss fund-raising techniques or a professor about career opportunities in your major.

Be aware that interviewees may answer questions whether or not they have accurate understanding or knowledge. Listen to any call-in program to hear people make incredible claims, accusations, and observations from ignorance. Gorden writes about "key informants" who can supply information on local situations, assist in selecting and contacting knowledgeable interviewees, and aid in securing their cooperation.[2] Discover who these people are and how they might assist you in selecting respondents. A key informant might be a family member, friend, fellow member of a student organization, employer, professor, or person you are currently interviewing.

Is the Interviewee Available?

An ideal source might be too far away, available only for a few minutes when you need an in-depth interview, or unavailable until after your deadline. Consider the telephone or e-mail before giving up on a source. And never *assume* the person is *unavailable*. You may think a famous or high-status person such as a company president, sports star, senator, surgeon, or general is inaccessible, but stories abound among journalists and researchers about famous interviews that occurred merely because interviewers asked for interviews or were persistent in asking. Others took no for an answer before asking the question. Do not talk yourself out of an interview by being certain the person will not talk to you—a self-fulfilling prophecy:

> You don't have time to talk, do you?
> I know you're too busy to talk.
> I'm sure you don't want to talk to the press at this time.

Contact a possible go-between (Gorden's key informant) such as a mutual friend or associate, talk to an aide, follow a chain of command, or work through the public relations department to reach a person with your request for an interview. Go to where a person works, lives, or plays rather than expect the person to come to you. You may need to be explicit about who you are, whom you represent, what you want to talk about, how you will use the information you receive, how long the interview will take, and when and where it might take place. You may have to supply some or all of your questions in advance. Be careful of excessive demands about topics, questions, off-limit subjects, and off-the-record comments that may make the person not worth interviewing.

Is the Interviewee Willing to Give the Information Needed?

Respondents may be reluctant to meet with you for several reasons. They may mistrust you, your organization, your profession, or your position. They may be afraid of revealing information potentially harmful to themselves, their organizations, or significant others. Lawsuits seem to materialize today over almost anything a person might say about a person, organization, product, action, or another lawsuit. Organizations are particularly fearful of lawsuits and try to control persons who can speak for them. Potential interviewees may feel the information you desire is no one else's business. They may feel there is nothing in the interview for them that warrants the time and risks involved. Respondents who have dealt with the press and investigators can relate (and often do) times when they were misquoted, taken out of context, had information reported erroneously, or ended up being *the* focus of a report they thought was a study of many people. You may have to convince interviewees that you can be trusted for confidentiality, accuracy, thoroughness, and fair reporting.

People will cooperate if they have an interest in you, the topic, or the outcome of the interview. Point out why their interests will be better served if information and attitudes are known. Sometimes you may have to employ a bit of arm-twisting.

> If you don't tell your side of the story, we will have to rely on . . . .
> We cannot process your claim until we have your statement.
> The other party has already given their side of the incident.
> I can't do anything to stop the harassment if you're not willing to . . . .

Be careful of threats that can ruin an interview, damage your relationship, or preclude future contacts. Few of us take threats lightly. Also be equally wary of persons who seem too eager to be interviewed. What are their motivations and reputations?

Is the Interviewee Able to Transmit Information Freely and Accurately?

Any of several problems may make a person unacceptable as an information source: faulty memory, poor health, state of shock, inability to express or communicate ideas, proneness to exaggeration or oversimplification, unconscious repression or distortion of information, biases or prejudices, deliberate lying. A person may make so many demands for control of topics, questions, and off-the-record areas that an interview is a waste of time or compromises your ability to gain accurate and complete information. Elderly veterans may remember events very differently than they really were. A father or mother grieving over the loss of a child (and confronted with tape recorders, investigators, lights, and cameras) cannot be treated the same as a person commenting on production quotas or Christmas decorations. Journalists, attorneys, and police detectives often demand that persons relate minute details and exact timing of events that took place months or years before, but most of us have trouble recalling what we did yesterday and when. Add to these memory problems situations such as devastating tornados, fires, accidents, and scandals and you can understand why many interviewees are not lying but struggling to remember with any degree of accuracy.

If time permits, get to know interviewees ahead of time by researching their work and accomplishments, personalities, reputations, and levels of information. Learn about their biases, values, idiosyncrasies, vested interests, hobbies, and interviewing traits. How skilled are they at responding to (and perhaps evading) questions? Many persons are interviewed daily (police chiefs, political leaders, candidates, corporate officers, attorneys, college presidents), and a growing number have taken intensive courses in which they have learned how to confront interviewers of all types. Attorneys, prosecutors, and public relations officers rehearse witnesses and persons so they know exactly what to say to a litany of questions and when to say nothing at all. Thorough preparation will reveal how interviewees are likely to act and react when you contact and interview them. Webb and Salancik write that the interviewer "in time, should know [a] source well enough to be able to know when a distortion is occurring, from a facial expression that doesn't correspond to a certain reply."[3]

5. Selecting Interviewers

Eric Nalder claims that the number one trait of an ideal journalist, or any probing interviewer, is *curiosity* about everyone and everything. Along with curiosity, the interviewer should also be friendly, courteous, organized, a keen observer, and a good listener. The interviewer must be patient, persistent, and skillful at asking secondary questions. And when the interview ends, the interviewer must be able to write a coherent, organized, and interesting report after asking dozens of questions. A specific situation or interviewee may require the interviewer to be of a certain age, gender, race, ethnic group, religion, political party (or independent), or educational level. A 22-year-old interviewer might find it difficult to understand and probe effectively into the perceptions and expectations of an 80-year-old respondent. A woman might confide more readily in a female interviewer rather than a male interviewer. An interviewer of Chinese ancestry might be more effective because he or she understands the culture, traditions, and communication customs of Chinese businesspeople and political leaders.

Similarity or difference in status between interviewer (R) and interviewee (E) may offer unique advantages for the interviewer. These are shown in Figure 5.2. Some interviewees will not grant interviews to organizations or people they perceive to be of low status. As a result, organizations give important-sounding titles to their representatives: chief correspondent rather than correspondent, vice president instead of sales representative, editor rather than reporter, research director rather than poll taker, executive rather than supervisor. But other interviewees might feel good about being able to help someone just starting out. In a recent PBS interview, famous ABC news correspondent, anchor, and host David Brinkley remarked that he welcomed the opportunity to meet with journalism students and young reporters in his office, to show them around the studio, and to discuss the academic background they needed to be effective reporters. A senior partner at a law firm might feel the same way about a summer intern or a new associate.

Figure 5.2 *The advantages of status differences between interviewers and interviewees in probing interviews*

R Superior to E	R Equal to E	R Subordinate to E
1. R can easily control the interview.	1. Rapport is easily established.	1. E will not feel threatened.
2. E may feel motivated to please R.	2. Fewer communication barriers.	2. E may feel freer to speak.
3. R can observe E under pressure	3. Fewer social pressures.	3. R does not have to be an expert.
4. R can arrange the interview easily.	4. High degree of empathy possible.	4. E might feel sorry for R and want to help.
5. E might feel honored.	5. R and E will be at ease.	
6. R can reward E.		

In each of the following situations, who would be the ideal interviewer? Should the interviewer be superior to, equal to, or subordinate to the interviewee? Or would there be an ideal combination of role relationships?

Situation 1

A school superintendent wants to discover how the recent shooting of a star athlete is affecting fellow students at Woodrow Wilson High School.

> The interviewer must be a superior to these students in training, skills, and experiences and understand the effects of tragic accidents on young people. At the same time, the interviewer must be skilled at interviewing young people, have a good relationship with students, and be able to adapt to students on their communication and experience levels.

Situation 2

A developer wants to talk to someone at a large construction management firm about a hotel and golf resort he is planning to build.

> The interviewer and interviewee roles should be equally shared in this interview. Both parties would be asking and answering important questions, and both are experts in their areas—development and construction management. The other party must be a senior project manager with the construction firm because a developer with millions of dollars on the line does not want to discuss the matter with an inexperienced or low-ranking engineer.

Situation 3

A biology student wants to talk to someone about medical school, application procedures, and qualifications needed to get into a major school.

> The interviewer should be subordinate to the interviewee because the need is for an expert who has far more information and experience than the interviewer and can offer information and advice not available in other sources. A superior interviewee (professor, physician, medical school student) would not feel threatened by the student interviewer and might be motivated to help a student preparing for and making an important career decision. This poses an opportunity to influence directly a young person about to enter the interviewee's field.

Situation 4

The president of a Fortune 500 chemical manufacturing firm needs legal assistance in a pending lawsuit claiming one of its plants caused a large fish kill.

> The ideal relationship would be one between equals. The attorney would need to be a senior and highly successful member of the law firm because the president would not want to talk to a young associate. The expectation would be that one high-status person would deal directly with another high-status person. Later they might arrange interviews between associates from the chemical firm and the law firm, equals once again.

Situation 5

A professor wants to learn how students feel about recent changes he or she has made in lecture format, application quizzes, and testing methods.

> The professor's role as authority figure with powers to reward and punish through grading and his or her role in creating and implementing the course changes eliminates this person as the interviewer. Students would be reluctant to communicate beyond Level 1 because of the risks involved. The professor might create a survey instrument and then select an interviewer, perhaps a student, students respect and trust. This interviewer could establish rapport with fellow students, help them relax, pose less threat, and experience fewer communication barriers.

By the time you have researched and selected interviewees and interviewers, you should have an accurate picture of the relationship that will exist during the interview. Robert Ogles and other journalism professors note, for example, that journalistic interviews rely on "secondary relationships" that are nonintimate and limited to one or very few relational dimensions.[4] These dimensions tend to be more functional than emotional and rely on surface cues such as obvious similarities, appearance, and nonverbal behavior. But many interviews, including some journalistic interviews, involve all of the relational dimensions discussed in Chapter 2. Be aware of perceived *similarities and differences* of both parties. To what extent do you and the interviewee want to be *included and involved* in this interview? How much do you *like and respect* one another? How much *control and dominance* is each party likely to exert or try to exert during the interview? And what level of *trust* is each party likely to grant? A positive relationship is critical to the success of even the simplest probing interviews because they tend to delve into beliefs, attitudes, values, feelings, and inner secrets. Learn everything you can about the interviewee, including your past dealings with this person or organization, so you can establish rapport and motivate the interviewee to take part and communicate beyond safe and superficial Level 1 interactions.

6. Conducting the Interview

Interviewers tend to ask too many questions. This limits their opportunities to listen, observe, and think, essential activities in a probing interview that is nonscheduled or moderately scheduled. Here are guidelines for more effective use of questions.

Types and Uses of Questions

Most questions in probing interviews should be open-ended to motivate and encourage respondents to communicate. This is particularly true of opening questions.

> What do you know about the sinking of the *Titanic*?
> What were your first reactions when you heard the news?
> How do you feel about the new computer requirement for all majors?

Sometimes it is wise to begin with questions that do not sound like questions because they seem less demanding. For instance, you might begin with,

> Tell me what you saw just before the explosion.
> Describe your Black Cultural Center.
> Tell me about the assignment in History 320.

Thorough answers to open-ended questions give you an opportunity to listen appropriately (for comprehension, empathy, evaluation, resolution) and observe the interviewee's mannerisms, appearance, and nonverbal communication. Listening and observing help you determine the accuracy and relevance of answers and how the interviewee feels about you, the interview, the situation, and the topic. A raised eyebrow or a slight hesitancy of a respondent from another culture, for instance, may signal that you used a slang phrase, colloquialism, or oxymoron with which this person is unfamiliar or that sounds strange. Make the respondent the star of the interview.

Closed questions result in the interviewer talking more while listening and observing less. If you find yourself asking question after question and doing most of the work in an interview, you are undoubtedly asking too many closed questions and trying to guess information rather than ask for it. Be patient and persistent. Do not interrupt a respondent unless the person is obviously off target, is trying to evade your question, or seems likely to continue answering forever.

The flexible, adaptive nature of the probing interview requires you to use the full range of secondary questions. Review secondary questions in Chapter 4. Be an active listener, not a passive sponge. Use *silent probes* and *nudging probes* to prod inter-viewees to continue answering. Many people (particularly those with little education or information) tend to give the first opinion that comes to mind or to give a bit of infor-mation and wait to see if you want them to continue. So give them a nudge:

> And?   Go on.
> So?   Then what happened?

Informational probes detect cues in answers and ask for additional information or ex-planation. They help you avoid surface or superficial answers.

> How do you discover the cause of a fire?
> Who will be chairing the self-study committee?
> What do you mean by *good* possibility?

Restatement probes insist on the answer you did not receive to your primary question.

1. **Interviewer:** Do you serve alcohol at fraternity events?
2. **Interviewee:** That's against university policy.
3. **Interviewer:** I know, but do you serve alcohol at any fraternity events?

Reflective and *mirror probes* verify and clarify answers to check accuracy and under-standing, notes, memory, and interpretations. They are essential to accurate understand-ing and interpreting. For instance,

1. **Interviewer:** You think, then, the remodeling of the garage will be completed before classes resume in August? (*reflective probe*)
2. **Interviewee:** Yes; that's our current plan.
3. **Interviewer:** Okay. Here's what I hear you saying? The garage will be closed immediately after commencement in May. During the first four weeks, you will be repairing the deteriorated concrete on the upper ramps. During the second four weeks, you will be repairing the lower ramps. And in the final four weeks, you will be relining parking places, painting the guardrails, and replacing lighting for better security. Correct? (*mirror probe*)

Do not forget the *clearinghouse probe* that can reveal if you have obtained all available and important information on a topic before going to your next topic or closing.

> What else do you think I need to know before I make a decision?
> Did Jake say anything else?
> Is there anything else you can remember about that evening?

As you ask questions and probe into answers, be courteous, friendly, tactful, and nonargumentative. Do not get into a debate with the respondent. Be understanding when delving into sensitive or personal areas. Be prepared to back off if an interviewee be-comes emotionally upset or angry. Plowing ahead with probing questions could damage the interview and your future relationship with this person. There are times when you will need to pry into potentially embarrassing areas such as the nature of the illness of a student who is missing class frequently, family problems, personal or organizational finances, a person's employment history. Eric Nalder claims, "There are no embarrassing questions, only embarrassing answers."

Because you will create many questions on the spot in probing interviews, you are likely to fall into the common question pitfalls discussed in Chapter 4: the bipolar trap, the open-to-closed switch, the double-barreled inquisition, the leading push, the yes (no) response, and the guessing game. Review these carefully, and remember the rules: Think through questions before asking them; stop when you have asked a good, open-ended question; and avoid bipolar, leading, and guessing questions unless you are using them for specific reasons, not by accident. Know the pitfalls well enough so you can catch yourself before you tumble into one. The following good and bad examples will help you sharpen your question skills.

1. The bipolar trap:
   Bad: Do you like the new registration system?
   Good: How do you feel about the new registration system?
2. The open-to-closed switch:
   Bad: How do you think the football team will do this fall? Do you think it will go to a bowl game?
   Good: How do you think the football team will do this fall?
3. The double-barreled inquisition:
   Bad: What are your short-range and long-range travel plans?
   Good: What are your short-range travel plans?
4. The leading push:
   Bad: You're going to church regularly, aren't you?
   Good: How regular is your church attendance?
5. The guessing game:
   Bad: Did you come to Saint Mary-of-the-Woods College because your mother is an alum?
   Good: Why did you come to Saint Mary-of-the-Woods College?
6. The yes (no) response:
   Bad: Do you want this position?
   Good: How important is it that you get this position?

Sometimes you will need to break the rules to get information you want. It may be necessary to ask an obvious question even when you know the answer in advance:

I see you are into rollerblading?
What does a cornerback do?
Why are you considering a transfer to Denver?

Such simple and obvious questions can relax the respondent by getting the person talking about something that is well known and easy to talk about and show your interest in a topic important to the interviewee. A leading push such as "Come on, surely you didn't do that?" or "Don't you think it's time to tell the truth about your relationship with . . . ?" can provoke a respondent into an exciting interchange or revealing information far more interesting and valuable than a neutral question might elicit. You might have to ask a double-barreled question at a press conference to get two or three answers because it may be the only question you get to ask. And you may ask a bipolar or a yes (no) re-sponse question because you need to have a yes or no for the record. Above all, *know what you are doing and why.*

   Phrase your questions carefully to obtain the information you need by reviewing the criteria for phrasing questions discussed in Chapter 4: language, relevance, infor-mation level, accessibility, and complexity. Not only will well-phrased questions get more information and pry open reluctant interviewees, but they will help you avoid games some respondents play with interviewers who phrase questions poorly. The fol-lowing exchange took place during a recent election campaign in New Hampshire and was broadcast throughout the country, to the embarrassment of the interviewer:

1. **Reporter:** How are you going to vote on Tuesday?

2. **Resident:** How am I going to vote? Oh, the usual way. I'm going to take the form they hand me and put x's in the appropriate boxes. (*laughing*)

3. **Reporter:** (*pause*) Who are you going to vote for on Tuesday?

Open-to-closed switch questions often allow interviewees to escape by responding to an easier-to-answer second question. Some may wait to reply until you rephrase a question because you did not get an immediate reply. The rephrased question may be less threat-ening or difficult, perhaps requiring a simple yes or no.

Note Taking and Tape Recording

Whether you should take notes, use an audio or video tape recorder, or avoid both dur-ing probing interviews is a matter of opinion. Some expert interviewers say you should never take notes; others warn against too few or selective notes. Some find the tape recorder the best way to record information; others say you should never use such in-trusive and unreliable contraptions. The best advice seems to be to select the means best suited to your objectives, the situation, the interviewee, and the interview schedule. Ex-tensive note taking or tape recording may be necessary during lengthy nonscheduled or moderately scheduled interviews to help you recall exact figures, names, and statements and *how* answers were given. However, always ask permission before taking notes or using a tape recorder, explain why you want to or must do so, and how the notes or recording will be used. Some interviewers such as police officers and insurance claims investigators are required to tape interviews.

Note Taking

A major advantage of note taking is that it increases your *attention* to what is being said and how. And this increased attention not only shows respondents you are interested in what they are saying and concerned about accuracy, but it improves your ability to com-prehend and retain information. If you take notes, you do not have to worry about a ma-chine breaking down, running out of tape, or batteries going dead at a critical moment. Listening to entire interviews to pick out important bits of information is time-consuming,

photo by Robert Brenner/Photo Edit

■ *Effective note taking entails maintaining eye contact as much as possible.*

and transcriptions are costly in time and money.

But there are disadvantages to note taking. You can rarely take notes fast enough to record exactly what was said, especially if a respondent speaks rapidly. It is difficult to concentrate on questions and answers while writing notes, and you may fail to hear or probe into an answer because you are busy writing rather than listening. Note taking may hamper the flow of information because interviewees become fearful of what you are writing, are reluctant to talk while you are writing and not looking at them, or want to help you catch up with their answers. In an in-depth interview with a newspaper publisher, one of our students discovered that whenever she began to write, the interviewee would stop answering until she stopped writing, apparently to let her catch up. Before long, he arranged his chair so he could see what she was writing.

Here are a few guidelines for note taking. First, preserve effective communication with the interviewee by being as inconspicuous as possible with your note taking. Maintain eye contact while writing notes, and continue to listen closely to what is being said and how. You can preserve communication by using abbreviations or a form of professional or personal shorthand to speed up note taking and by writing down only important information. Second, avoid communicating to the interviewee what you think is important by not taking notes frantically during an answer. You might wait until the interviewee is answering another question before writing anything down. Some reporters, for example, ask a less important follow-up question, perhaps a throwaway question, immediately after a bombshell quote or revelation so they have time to write this down and not signal their reaction to the initial question. A simple solution is to develop the habit of taking some notes throughout interviews. Third, reduce interviewee curiosity or concern by asking permission before taking notes, by explaining why notes are necessary and helpful to both parties, and by showing the interviewee your notes occasionally to check accuracy. Nalder says that reviewing your notes with respondents not only satisfies curiosity and reduces anxiety but allows them to fill in the blanks and volunteer information. Fourth, avoid interviewee concern by agreeing to follow ground rules for the interview, explaining how you will use the information, or agreeing to let the person see your report prior to submitting or publishing it. And fifth, ensure accurate reporting by reviewing your notes immediately after the interview so you can fill in the gaps, complete abbreviations, and translate your shorthand.

Wolvin and Coakley discuss four methods of note taking.[5] First, *outline* the information you receive in answers. This method works best when you are interviewing from a carefully developed guide or schedule of questions that provides a ready-made outline to follow. Outlining can be very difficult if your interview is unstructured or it takes strange and unanticipated twists and turns. Second, record answers in *précis* form from what you have heard during several minutes of an interview. Instead of taking notes during or after each answer, write a summary of information from a number of questions and answers. Third, employ a *fact versus principle* method by writing main ideas on one side of a note page and important facts on the other. This method of note taking helps you retain both ideas and facts and their interrelationships. Fourth, employ a *mapping* method in which you (1) write and encircle main ideas, (2) write significant details or facts and connect them with lines to appropriate main ideas, and (3) write minor details or facts and connect them with lines to significant details or facts. This map of information is particularly effective when you obtain details, facts, and names of many people involved relevant to main ideas but widely spaced during an interview. The map shows how they are connected and interconnected.

Tape Recording

By using a tape recorder, you can relax and concentrate on questions and answers and probe more effectively into what is said and not said but implied. You can hear and watch *what* was said and *how* it was said hours or days afterward instead of relying on faulty memories. For example, we began to tape-record student interviews in class and grade them from both what we heard and observed in class and listened to later when we discovered we too often had missed important questions and answers while taking notes and filling out critique forms during classroom interviews. The critiques and grades became more accurate when we combined note taking and tape recording. A tape recorder may record unwanted discussions and noise in a crowd, but it can also pick up answers that might be inaudible at the time.

Unfortunately, tape recorders can malfunction or prove tricky to use. Batteries, even new ones, can go dead at the wrong time, and tapes can break or become entangled. A number of our students have used tape recorders during lengthy interviews for class projects only to discover the tapes were blank and they had to rely on memories not prepared for detailed reconstructions of answers or probing questions. Realize also that some people fear tape recorders and view them as intruders in intimate interviewing situations. Tapes provide permanent, undeniable records that threaten many people with unknown future consequences.

Here are a few guidelines for using tape recorders. First, reduce mechanical difficulties by knowing and testing a recorder thoroughly before the interview. Do not assume that it is in perfect working order. Take extra cassettes and batteries with you and a patch electric cord as a backup. Second, be sure you are thoroughly familiar with the tape recorder prior to the interview. It is not impressive to begin an interview with comments such as "This is a new tape recorder and I'm still trying to learn how to use it" or "I borrowed this tape recorder from my roommate, and I'm not sure how it works." There is no excuse for making such excuses. Practice using the recorder well before the interview is to begin. Third, reduce fears and objections by asking permission to use a recorder prior to the interview, explaining why the recorder is advantageous to both parties, placing the recorder in an inconspicuous location, and relying on either the built-in microphone or a small one that need not be stuck in the interviewee's face. And fourth, reduce problems with an interviewee who fears being recorded too accurately and potential negative consequences by offering to turn off the recorder when desired, revealing how the recorder will be used, and volunteering to let the interviewee check and edit statements before you use them. It is common to see faces blanked out and voices disguised in televised, investigative reports to protect sources.

There is considerable controversy over the permissibility of hidden microphones and secretly taped telephone interviews. Every week we can view reports on popular television shows such as "60 Minutes," "20/20," and "Dateline" that rely on concealed microphones and television cameras. Some interviewers and organizations consider hidden or unknown tape recording to be unethical and plainly dishonest and forbid it. Others allow it under special circumstances and with high-level organizational approval. And still others see it as little different from taking notes while conducting a telephone interview. We believe you should always tell an interviewee, whether on the telephone or face to face, that the conversation is being taped and why. All of us have the right to know when our interactions are recorded.

Handling Difficult Situations

You will encounter many difficult interviewing situations in the years ahead. You will manage them more effectively if you plan for them in advance and understand how to handle them when they occur unexpectedly. Here are a few difficult situations.

The Sanitized Setting versus the Real Setting

It is undoubtedly easier to interview persons in pleasant surroundings such as offices, homes, parks, and restaurants rather than in field settings of real-life action. However, experienced reporters and researchers recognize that field interviews are helpful in understanding an event, problem, or person and creating insightful questions. Most memorable interviews take place at the scenes of hurricanes, terrorist bombings, fires, plant accidents, building sites, and labor strikes. Researchers, investigators, and social workers go into prisons, hospitals, nursing homes, preschools, factories, and neighborhoods for the same reasons. Nalder claims that it is essential to interview people "at the place where they are doing the thing that you are writing about." It is important not only to *hear* answers but to *see* and get the *feel* of things. When Nalder was doing a book on oil tankers, for instance, a member of a crew told him he could not understand crews and oil tankers unless he was on board in the Gulf of Alaska during the violent seas of January "puking your guts out." He took this advice to see what oil tanker life was really like and got the most insightful interviews and feelings for his book because of his experiences and relationships with the crew.

In unsanitized settings, prepare yourself for unbelievable human suffering, unimaginable destruction, filthy conditions, and threats to your health and safety. Prepare for flexibility in structure and questions. Be sensitive in questions and actions. Too often we see reporters, insurance investigators, and representatives of government agencies intruding into medical emergencies and people's lives. Know where your rights as an interviewer end and another's right to privacy and dignity begins. Good sense and ethical judgment are key ingredients in probing interviews.

The Press Conference or Group Interview

The press conference or group interview severely limits your control over the situation and interviewee. The interviewee or a staff member may announce when and where the interview will take place and impose ground rules such as length and topics allowed. Protocol may enable the interviewer or staff members to end the interview without warning, perhaps to avoid or escape a difficult exchange. You may or may not get to ask the questions you have prepared, and you are unlikely to have an opportunity to probe deeply into answers. Listen carefully to answers other interviewers receive because they might provide valuable information and suggest questions you should ask, such as a secondary question to another reporter's primary question.

Your relationship with the interviewee at a press conference is critical. If the interviewee likes, respects, and trusts you, you may be picked from among several interviewers to ask questions. Interviewees call on interviewers they like and feel they can trust. If a relationship is hostile, they may refuse to recognize a person or give vague, superficial, or hostile answers and turn quickly to another interviewer to evade follow-up questions. You might ask a double-barreled question at a press conference if this is likely to be your only question.

The Broadcast Interview

The radio or television interview presents unique problems. Being on real or figurative stages may cause one or both parties to be extremely nervous or to engage in playacting because of audiences, cameras, microphones, and lights. Become familiar with the physical setting, including possible seating for you and the interviewee, audio and video equipment, technicians, and perhaps program format and purpose. Pay close attention to the briefing you receive concerning time limits, beginning and closing signals, and microphone use, levels, and locations. Adequate preparation reduces nervousness and enhances your efficiency and performance. A purpose of most broadcast interviews is to obtain answers or statements that can be replayed over the air or pictures that can be shown. Thus, recording equipment, recordings, appearance of both parties, and the setting are critical to end products.

Deadlines and extreme time limitations require questions that are direct, to the point, and moderately open. You may normally have an hour or two to discuss a problem with a client, customer, or employee, but a broadcast interaction may last no longer than a few seconds or minutes. Know your questions well enough to ask them from memory or from a few small cards because forms or lists of questions

photo by Robert Brenner/Photo Edit

■ *The broadcast interview presents unique problems for both parties.*

may make noise or cause you to appear awkward, amateurish, or unprepared. If you want the interview to appear to be spontaneous, do not provide questions to the interviewee prior to the broadcast. Spontaneous questions get spontaneous answers.

Some utterances or actions cannot be broadcast or may be embarrassing, such as profanities, obscene gestures, poor grammar, too many "uhs," "ahs," and "you knows," and excessive "blood and gore." Protesters may write profanities on their foreheads when they do not want to be on television. Some newspaper reporters, when being crowded out by cameras and microphones, shout obscenities to shut down their electronic counterparts and get closer to the action. A state legislator told one of the authors that he would purposely insert profanities into certain answers to prevent reporters from using them on the air.

Handling Difficult Interviewees

Probing interviews delve into feelings, attitudes, and reasons for actions, so they may hit raw nerves and evoke reactions ranging from tears and hostility to an interviewee stopping an interview instantly. The settings of disasters, crimes, election defeats, memorial ceremonies, deaths, and scandals are often tense, emotional, or embarrassing. Be prepared to handle difficult interviewees in difficult situations.

Emotional Interviewees

Respondents may burst into tears during interviews. And the problem is not helped when friends, associates, or family exclaim, "Oh, God!" or "Now stop that Jack!" or when interviewers blurt out, "I know just how you feel" or "Want a Kleenex?" Reactions such as the following may help if they are used *tactfully* and *sincerely*.

> It's okay to cry.
> Take your time.
> Want to stop for a few minutes?

You need not employ words, just silence, until the person regains composure and is ready to continue. If you have a close relationship with the interviewee, you might hold the person's hand or place your arm across his or her shoulders as a comforting gesture.

Above all, be sensitive to people who have experienced tragedies and do not invade their privacy merely for a few pictures, tearful comments for the six o'clock news, or curiosity. Almost any evening of the week, you can find at least one instance on the evening news in which a reporter will walk up to a parent who, only minutes before, has lost a child to a tragic accident or violent incident and ask, "How do you feel about your child's death?" or "Is the family devastated by this tragedy?" Practice common decency and use good sense. John and Denise Bittner suggest that you ask only direct and necessary questions at such times. "Remember, people in crisis situations are under a great deal of stress," they write. "A prolonged interview won't provide additional information; it will only upset people."[6]

Hostile Interviewees

If you detect hostility in an interviewee, try to determine if it is real or merely perceived on your part. If it is real, try to discover why. A person may feel angry, depressed, helpless, or frightened because of circumstances beyond his or her control, and you become a convenient target for releasing feelings. Hostility may be toward you, your organization, your position or profession, or the way information is likely to be used. Bad experiences with similar interviewers or ones from your organization may lead an interviewee to expect the worst from *you*. The person may simply be having a bad day because of a number of small things—late for work, difficulty finding a parking place, a computer problem, a no-show appointment—that lead to a hostile reaction.

A person may become hostile because of a question's timing, wording, or nonverbal components. For instance, you might substitute a better-sounding word such as "aides" for "handlers," "subsidy" for "welfare," "misled" for "lie," or "damage control" for "spin control." Do your questions sound like demands and threats? Have you invaded a person's territory and personal space? Do your physical presence and manner seem threatening? Large interviewers often appear threatening, particularly to much smaller or female interviewees. Be careful of unwarranted pressure tactics. Allow a hostile interviewee to blow off steam. Sometimes you can reduce hostility by going to another topic, remaining silent, or asking open-ended questions that give the interviewee a great deal of latitude. Do not reply in kind. A nondirective strategy such as the following might reveal the source of hostility and reduce it:

> You appear to be very angry at the moment.
> You seem very upset; would you like to talk about it?
> Do I detect a note of frustration in your answers?

Ault and Emery offer a simple rule: "Treat the average person with respect, and he [she] will do the same."[7]

Reticent Interviewees

If a person seems unwilling or unable to talk, try to discover why. The person may be inhibited by you or your position, the situation, the topic, the surroundings, or other people nearby. Lack of privacy will inhibit communication. Think of a time when you went to a professor or supervisor with a personal problem and the setting was in a small cubicle or open area in which other persons could overhear. Do not underestimate how inhibited many people become around authority figures, supervisors, investigators, and journalists. Reticence may be a family or personal trait that has nothing to do with you or the interview and cannot be altered during the interview. Some people simply do not talk much, what we call the "silent types."

You can work more effectively with a reticent person by changing your style from formal to informal, cool professional to warm associate, disapproving to approving. You can alter your question strategies (from open to closed questions or from nondirective to directive) until the interviewee is warmed up and ready to give longer answers. You can change topics and search for ones less threatening and easier for the interviewee to talk about. A careful self-introduction and orientation about the nature of the interview will open up some reticent interviewees. Discuss easy, nonthreatening topics during early minutes so interviewees can respond easily and openly. Some interviewers make it a habit to look around a person's room, office, or place of work for pictures, objects, awards, or views outside windows as conversation starters. Use silence to encourage persons to talk, but some people will "out-silence" the most patient interviewer and silence can become very awkward in a short time. Employ nudging probes to keep respondents talking and good listening techniques to show you are interested.

Talkative Interviewees

The talkative person shows the opposite tendencies of reticent persons. Some people love to talk to anyone at any time and will give lengthy answers to highly closed questions. Responding in interviews makes them feel important, and they become too helpful. You may have difficulty shutting them off and keeping them on track.

One tactic is to use highly targeted, closed questions that give talkative interviewees less verbal maneuverability and more direction. Look for natural openings or slight pauses for a chance to insert a question or redirect the interview, such as,

Talking about large contracts, did you . . . .   I'm glad to hear that, now . . . .

That brings up an important point.   Good, now . . . .

That's very interesting, now let's discuss . . . .

Use obvious interruptions only as a last resort.

Nonverbal actions may signal that you wish to go to another question or topic. Use eye contact, lean forward, or gesture with your hand to signal you want to move on or to ask another question. You might nod your head as if to say "I've got it; that's enough." Look at your schedule of questions to suggest you are ready to ask your next question. Stop taking notes to suggest you have all needed information from the previous question. Glance at your watch or a clock to signal that time is important and is fleeting. Be tactful and sensitive in whatever nonverbal signals you use. Telephone interviews pose problems because you have few nonverbal signals to halt answers, so interviewees tend to give long, rambling answers when responding over the telephone.

Evasive Interviewees

Interviewees may try to evade questions that force them to reveal feelings or prejudices, make them take stands or give specific information, or may incriminate them in some way. Evasive strategies include humor, fake hostility, counterquestions, and ambiguous language. President Reagan was famous for his stories, some of which were made up or from his old movies. President Bush was famous for long answers that were nearly unintelligible. President Clinton earned the nickname "Slick Willie" because of his ability to slip and slide past tough questions. This ability helped and hindered him during his stormy years in the White House. President John Kennedy was adept at using humor to evade questions he did not want to answer during press conferences. He dodged one question this way:[8]

1. **Reporter:** There have been published reports that some high-placed Republican people have been making overtures to your secretary of defense for him to be their 1968 candidate for president. If you thought that Mr. McNamara were seriously considering these overtures, would you continue him in your cabinet?

2. **President:** I have too high a regard for him to launch his candidacy yet.

On another occasion, President Kennedy took advantage of a poorly phrased question to evade answering it.

1. **Reporter:** Mr. President, Senator Margaret Chase Smith has proposed a watchdog committee be created. What is your reaction?
2. **President:** To watch congressmen and senators? Well, that will be fine if they feel they should be watched.

The people attending these press conferences laughed, and Kennedy recognized another reporter, avoiding answers to either question. Another common tactic is to ask a counterquestion, revolving the question onto you:

> Well, how would *you* answer that?
> What do *you* think we should do?
> Tell me about *your* financial affairs, and I will tell you about mine.

Other respondents merely answer another question, one you have not asked but one they want to address. Others give long, impressive-sounding answers that say nothing.

Be persistent in your questioning, perhaps by merely repeating or slightly rephrasing a question. Laugh with the interviewee, for instance, and then go right back to the topic or issue. You might go to other questions and come back to this one later. Remind the respondent tactfully, if possible, that your job is to ask the questions or that you are not the one in the position of responsibility or authority to make decisions or take actions. It is irrelevant what you think. At times you may have to resort to leading or loaded questions such as the following to evoke meaningful responses:

> When you became Chairman of the Board you said you would . . . .
> The public (voters, consumers, students, residents) has a right to know . . . .
> Isn't this a watered-down version of your earlier agreement?
> Are you saying that you would rather have a terrorist blow up the courthouse
> than spend the tax money necessary for appropriate security?

Use leading and loaded questions as a last resort because you can easily turn an evasive interviewee into a hostile one.

Embarrassing Interviewees

Interviewees may intentionally or unintentionally embarrass themselves or you. "Bloopers" are particularly difficult to handle when others are witnessing an interview in person or through the broadcast media. Sometimes an embarrassing exchange occurs because an interviewer pushes too far and the interviewee wants to end it. This exchange occurred between an attorney and a physician:[9]

1. **Attorney:** Doctor, before you performed the autopsy, did you check for a pulse?
2. **Physician:** No.

3. **Attorney:** Did you check for blood pressure?

4. **Physician:** No.

5. **Attorney:** Did you check for breathing?

6. **Physician:** No.

7. **Attorney:** So, then it is possible that the patient was alive when you began the autopsy?

8. **Physician:** No.

9. **Attorney:** How can you be so sure Doctor?

10. **Physician:** Because his brain was sitting on my desk in a jar.

11. **Attorney:** But could the patient have still been alive nevertheless?

12. **Physician:** It is possible that he could have been alive practicing law somewhere.

Know when to stop. The best approach to embarrassing situations is to drop the subject and, if necessary, come back to it later. Some interviewees will purposely try to embarrass you. Keep your cool. Do not become defensive or antagonistic, because either will make you look bad and prevent you from thinking clearly about your next question. Never purposely try to embarrass an interviewee.

Confused Interviewees

Respondents may become confused by a topic or question. Be prepared to handle confused persons without embarrassing them or creating hostility. You may restate your question tactfully or rephrase it in a slightly different way. Or you may come back to the question later in the interview. Be conscious of jargon and words with multiple meanings. This exchange took place between an attorney and a witness:[10]

1. **Attorney:** Is your appearance here this morning pursuant to a deposition notice which I sent to your attorney?

2. **Witness:** No, this is how I dress when I go to work.

Watch how you react nonverbally. Broadcast journalists who get strange responses rarely exhibit a hint of a smile or shock. They go on to the next question or topic as if nothing embarrassing happened.

Dissimilar Interviewees

Interviewees may be dissimilar to one another and to you, and these dissimilarities may pose considerable problems if you do not adapt to them. In previous chapters, we have identified important communicative characteristics unique to males and females and different cultures. Gender differences are important in probing interviews. For example, compared with women, men tend to talk more, monopolize conversations, make more direct statements (beat around the bush less often), answer questions with declarations (women tend to answer questions with questions), get to the point sooner in answers, and respond to questions with minimal responses (yep, nope, fine, okay, sure). Many elderly respondents tend to be less trusting because of experiences and insecurity. However, they are often communication starved and may be *very* talkative in interviews.

We tend to stereotype ethnic groups such as Asian-Americans, African-Americans, and Mexican-Americans and expect them to act in certain ways during interviews. They in turn have often developed solidarity through in-group codes, symbols, expectations, and enemies that those of us outside the group neither share nor understand. Some research indicates that African-Americans prefer indirect questions, consider extensive probing to be intrusive, and prefer more frequent and equal turn-taking. Mexican-American respondents may rely more on emotion, intuition, and feeling than midwestern European-Americans. Persons of rural backgrounds value personal know-how, skills, practicality, simplicity, and self-sufficiency more than those of urban backgrounds. As an interviewer, then, adapt your questioning and structure to different interviewees and be aware of gender and cultural differences so you can motivate interviewees and truly understand the answers you receive.

7. Preparing the Story or Report

You are now ready to review the information and observations obtained through one or more interviews to see if you have obtained the information necessary to satisfy your purpose. Jog your memory, read through your notes, and listen or view tape recordings. You may have to sift through hundreds or thousands of words, statements, facts, opinions, and impressions to locate what is most important to include in your report or story. Check answers with other sources, especially if there is reason to suspect that an interviewee lied or gave inaccurate information.

Once you know what you have obtained from the interview stage, perform essential editing chores. If you are preparing a verbatim interview for publication or dissemination, determine whether you should include grammatical errors, mispronounced words, expletives, slang, and vocalized pauses such as "uh," "and uh," "ummm," and "you know." What about repetitious statements, long and rambling explanations, and simple errors made by interviewees who do or do not know differently? Readers and listeners may enjoy the account with all of the warts showing, but both interview parties may be embarrassed and lose credibility. You might never get another interview with this person or organization.

Determine if it is necessary to preface answers and questions so readers and listeners will have a clear understanding of each. You might edit some of your questions to make answers more pointed and meaningful. When quoting from notes or memory, strive for accuracy. Do not put words into an interviewee's mouth. Be sure proper qualifiers are included. Do not understate or overstate an interviewee's opinions, attitudes, intentions, or commitments. Be sure both questions and answers are reported in proper context. The rule is simple: Be honest and fair.

The technical steps of report or story preparation are beyond the scope of this book (see the resources at the end of this chapter), but we want to close with a few precautions. Remember the ground rules agreed to and what information is off the record.

Violations of agreements will harm you and future interviewers. Be patient. Be careful of assumptions. Carefully check sources and reports. A few years ago Ted Mann, the former sports publicist for Duke University, picked up the morning paper and discovered to his surprise that he was dead. It had all started when a friend of a reporter who worked for a rescue squad told him Mann was dead. The reporter called the Mann home to verify the report, and the woman who answered the phone said, "Mr. Mann's not here. He's gone." The reporter assumed this phrase was a euphemism for dead and that the woman had verified Mann's death. He wrote an obituary on this false assumption.[11] Ted Mann was appreciative of all the eulogies and wonderful things people said about him and, most of all, for the inaccuracy of the report. Strive for accuracy and fairness in every fact and interpretation. And be cautious.

The Respondent in the Probing Interview

Most attention in books on interviewing is naturally focused on the *interviewer* because most readers and students are concerned with learning how to conduct interviews effectively. But all of us are *interviewees* at least as often, and probably more often, than we are interviewers. Let's turn our attention, then, to how you can be a more effective respondent in interviews. Figure 5.3 illustrates the six-stage process the interviewee should follow in preparing for and responding during probing interviews.

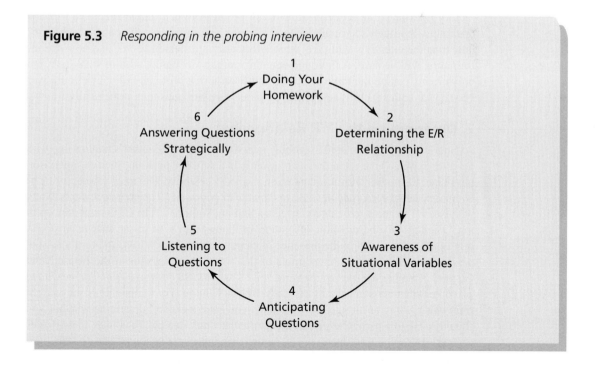

Figure 5.3 *Responding in the probing interview*

1 Doing Your Homework

2 Determining the E/R Relationship

3 Awareness of Situational Variables

4 Anticipating Questions

5 Listening to Questions

6 Answering Questions Strategically

1. Doing Your Homework

Do your homework before taking part in probing interviews. Be thoroughly briefed on topics that might come up, including recent events, accidents, controversies, innovations, decisions, and administrative actions. What roles have you played in any of these? Contact members of your organization to be sure you understand organizational policies, positions, and involvements and what authority you have to speak for the organization or a subunit of that organization. Is there a more knowledgeable or authoritative person than you who should be the interviewee?

Learn everything you can about the person who will interview you, including such characteristics as age, gender, ethnic group, education and training, special interests, and experiences. What are the interviewer's attitudes toward you, your organization, and the topic: friendly/hostile, trusting/suspicious, formal/informal, interested/disinterested. Do not assume the person has little background in your area of expertise. Some reporters, for instance, have engineering, management, or science degrees or have developed a high level of expertise on topics, such as the environment, Lyme disease, or foreign affairs. A mother of a hyperactive child may have become an expert on hyperactivity. A member of the clergy may have been an Air Force fighter pilot before attending theology school. A chemist may be a highly regarded member of a jazz group. What is the interviewer's reputation for fairness and honesty? What questioning techniques does the interviewer usually employ?

Interviews often take place without warning. A person may call you on the phone; stop by your office or home; appear at your front door; or approach you on the street or factory floor or at the scene of an event or accident. When this happens, be sure the opening is thorough so you understand who the person is, who the person represents, how long the interview will take, what information the person wants, and how this information will be used. A thorough opening, perhaps including a bit of small talk, not only orients you on the topic, purpose, and relationship with the interviewer but gives you time to collect your thoughts and prepare to answer questions strategically.

2. Determining the E/R Relationship

A major problem encountered in probing interviews is the interviewer's relationship with the interviewee. Quite often the interviewer is in a superior position, such as supervisor, physician, instructor, attorney, counselor, or media celebrity. The interviewee, trying to communicate upward, may be overawed by the interviewer: "The president wants to talk with *me*!" "I'm going to be interviewed by Barbara Walters." "The CEO wants my opinion." Feelings of subordination, obligation, or flattery may lead you to answer any question asked, particularly in the presence of cameras and microphones, and turn a normal person into "Silly Putty." An example of this was former Speaker of the House Newt Gingrich's mother whispering the word "bitch" when CBS correspondent Connie Chung asked her what her son called First Lady Hillary Clinton. Try to maintain your equilibrium when acting as an interviewee, and if you have a choice, determine whether you should speak to a particular person at a particular time. Realize, of course, that refusals of interviews often lead interviewers, particularly investigative journalists, to state ominously that the party in question "was unavailable for comment." Such statements imply guilt but are preferable to foolish comments that become headlines and lead to major difficulties for you or your organization.

Just as interviewers should assess relationships between parties, so should interviewees. What is your relational history with the interviewer? How similar and dissimilar in important and relevant ways are you? How willing and eager are both parties to take part in this interview? An interviewer may dread an interview as much as you. What is the degree of warmth and friendship that exists between you and the interviewer at the time of the interview? How much control will you have? Does the interviewer have a reputation for dominating interactions? To what degree will you and the other party perceive one another as trustworthy, reliable, and safe?

3. Awareness of Situational Variables

Be aware of variables that are likely to affect the situation. When will the interview take place? How might events prior to and afterward affect the interview? Defer some interviews until you are well informed and ready to cope with difficult questions. Why should the interviewer be thoroughly prepared and you unprepared? Where will the interview take place, and how advantageous is this to you? What will be the physical setting? Will an audience be present? If the interview will be broadcast, review the discussion of such interviews presented earlier in this chapter. What outside influences do you need to take into account?

You may wish to establish some ground rules for an interview such as time, place, length, which topics are off-limits or off-the-record, and who the interviewer(s) will be. Occasionally you may require that questions be submitted in advance so you can prepare well-thought-out answers with accurate and substantial data. Be realistic in your demands. If Larry King wants to interview you on his show, you cannot demand a different interviewer. If you demand that all interesting topics be off-limits, there is no need to interview you. And if you demand extensive control over questions, quotations, and reports, most interviewers will go to someone else. How much control you have depends upon your importance as a source, your relationship with the interviewer, the situation, and how eager you are to get your side or point of view reported.

4. Anticipating Questions

Your homework should allow you to anticipate most questions that may be asked. Think about how you might respond to specific questions. What might be the most important thing to say or to avoid saying? How should you qualify answers? What words should you avoid? How can you support the assertions and claims you make? Are there organizational policies on how you can respond, if at all, to specific questions? How might you respond to questions you cannot answer because of lack of information, need for secrecy, protection of sources, organizational decisions, legal consequences, or self-incrimination? It may be wise to rehearse some answers to meet special circumstances. In the constant news stories concerning Monica Lewinsky's relationship with President Clinton throughout 1998, sources often referred to how Lewinsky's attorney was preparing her and President Clinton's lawyers and staff were preparing him for their answers before the grand jury.

5. Listening to Questions

What should you do while an interviewer is asking a question? First, *listen* and *think* before answering. Persons on television and radio newscasts make statements at scenes of accidents, crimes, or controversies that they will regret the next day. Americans of Middle Eastern descent will not soon forget reports after the horrible bombing of the federal building in Oklahoma City in 1995 that claimed three "Middle Eastern looking" men were being sought in connection with the bombing. African-Americans are often accused of crimes they did not commit because interviewees claimed to see a black man in the area or commiting the crime. False statements and reports not only insult millions of Americans but lead to death threats and discrimination. Some interviewees responsible for making such unsubstantiated statements will be fired, and others will be sued, arrested, investigated, reprimanded, or embarrassed. Listen carefully to what is being asked. Listen for words you may not know or may misinterpret. Listen for verbal and nonverbal cues that reveal feelings as well as facts.

Second, be *patient*. Do not assume you know what a question is before it is completed. React to a question only after fully hearing and understanding it. And do not interrupt an interviewer; not only is it impolite, but what the interviewer is saying may help you understand the question and determine your answer.

Third, *focus your attention* on the question being asked at the moment. Do not continue to replay a previous answer that is now history. Also, do not anticipate future questions to the point where you end up not hearing the current question.

Fourth, *focus on both the interviewer and the question*. Watch for nonverbal signals that complement the verbal and reveal the interviewer's feelings, attitudes, and beliefs. Listen with your eyes and ears. Do not focus on other persons or the surroundings. This is particularly important during broadcast interviews that involve several persons, studios, cameras, monitors, and microphones and during interviews in the field that involve spectators, noise, traffic, and distracting objects.

Fifth, *do not dismiss a question too quickly* as irrelevant or stupid. The interviewer may have a very good reason for asking the question, and it may be one in a series leading up to a highly important question. An icebreaker question, for instance, may not add much to the content of the interview but a great deal to the interaction between parties. An interviewer may be using an inverted funnel sequence, which would explain a series of closed questions to which you would rather respond at length. You will get your opportunity. An interviewer may have a very good reason for asking questions such as "If you could be a wild animal, which would you choose?" or "If you were to win 50 million dollars today, what would you do?"

And sixth, *avoid becoming defensive*. You cannot think clearly when angry, and you may blurt out words, claims, or accusations you will regret. And remember that becoming hostile reduces you to the level of the interviewer. The old saying "killing a person with kindness" can be applied to probing interviews in which conflict becomes the norm. Maintain the moral and ethical high ground during probing interviews.

6. Answering Questions Strategically

Design answers carefully. A good answer is concise, precise, carefully organized, clearly worded, logical, well supported, and to the point. Avoid overkill or underkill in answers.

Give answers, not sermons or lectures. Do not make excuses; give reasons and explanations. Be pleasant, polite, and tactful. Do not underestimate the interviewer's knowledge or intelligence. When you give a personal opinion, be sure the interviewer understands you are speaking for yourself and not your organization. If you do not know an answer, say so. You may promise to get the information.

Insist upon adequate time to think through and present your answers, particularly when answering tough, thought-provoking, or tricky questions. If an interviewer cuts you off in mid-answer or apparently wants a brief answer, cooperate as long as it suits *your* purpose. If brief answers may compromise you or your organization, refuse to continue until given adequate time. If the interviewer still tries to plow ahead, terminate the interview. You need not participate in a third-degree inquisition. And do not allow the interviewer to put words into your mouth with statements such as "What you're really saying is . . . ." or "That sounds like lying to me." Think and speak for yourself.

Learn how to use the many strategies for responding to questions. One strategy is to ask the interviewer to repeat, rephrase, or explain long, complicated, or unclear questions. Do not try to answer a question you cannot remember or understand. A second strategy is to preface answers carefully and tactfully. Note why a question is bad, tough, or tricky; do not merely say that it is so. Preface a long answer by explaining why it must be so. Provide a substantial explanation of why you must refuse to answer, or simply say "No comment." A third strategy is to rephrase a question for the interviewer or the audience that may be listening or observing: "If what you're asking is . . . ," "You're trying to get me to . . . ," or "She is asking . . . ." A fourth strategy is to challenge the content of questions. Challenge unsupported assertions, assumptions, inferential leaps, causal fallacies, and inaccurate "facts" and quotations. And a fifth strategy is to answer a question with a question. Use this strategy sparingly because it can create hostility between interview parties if you employ it too often.

Respond to specific types of questions to your benefit. If a question is *double-barreled*, reply to the part you can recall and can answer most effectively. Let the interviewer worry about the remaining parts. If a question is *bipolar* or *multiple choice*, be sure the choices are fair and the only ones possible. If they are not, explain or qualify your answer or insist upon additional options. For example, the question "Do you think Japanese or German cars are the best made?" does not allow for American, South Korean, Italian, or Swedish cars. If one of these is your preferred answer, comment, "Of the two choices you have given, I think German-made cars are better. However, I believe American-made cars are as good as and, in some cases, better than either German or Japanese cars." Answer a yes or no bipolar question with a simple yes or no when it is to your advantage, and elaborate when it is not. Take full advantage of *clearinghouse* questions to present information you would like the interviewer to hear. Search *reflective* and *mirror* questions for accuracy and completeness because they may provide you with the best opportunities to detect misinterpretations, gaps, and inaccuracies in the interviewer's memory and notes. And do not be pushed into giving an answer you do not agree with because the question is *leading* or *loaded*. If a question is designed to entrap you, a classical "Are you still beating your wife" question, refuse to answer until it is unloaded.

Organize long answers like minispeeches with an introduction, body, and conclusion. Use signaling phrases such as "First . . . , second . . . , third . . . " so interviewers can understand what you are saying and remember information accurately. Be careful of abbreviations because not everyone knows, for example, what OT (occupational therapist), FCC (Federal Communications Commission), and ATF (Alcohol, Tobacco, and Firearms) refer to. Use humor carefully. Good humor in answers is tasteful, tactful, spontaneous, appropriate (for you, the interviewer, and the situation), fresh, and satirical rather than sarcastic. Use examples to illustrate points: "It looks a lot like a Chrysler minivan" or "She will remind you of Maud." We all like good stories, whether fictional or nonfictional, and they maintain an interviewer's attention, illustrate points, and are easy to recall. Use analogies and metaphors to compare unknown or complicated things, procedures, and concepts to ones with which the interviewer is familiar.

Summary

The probing interview is the most common type because it is used daily by persons ranging from journalists, police officers, and health care professionals to students, teachers, and parents. Length and formality vary, but the purpose and method are the same: to get needed information as accurately and completely as possible in the shortest amount of time. The means are careful questioning, listening, observing, and probing. Although preparation of an interview guide or schedule is important, the interviewer must remain flexible and adapt to each interviewee, situation, and response. This chapter has presented a series of stages for a structured approach to the probing interview that calls for thorough preparation and flexibility.

Interviewees need not be passive participants in probing interviews. When given advance notice, interviewees should prepare thoroughly. They should share control with the interviewer and not submit meekly to whatever is asked or demanded. And they should know the principles and strategies of effective answers. Good listening is essential. The result will be a better interview for both parties. This chapter has presented a series of stages to guide the interviewee's preparation for and participation in probing interviews. The nature of each stage will depend upon the situation and the relationship between the interviewer and interviewee.

A Probing Interview for Review and Analysis

The interviewer is an investigator for the University Security Department. There have been several incidents on campus in which electronic equipment has been stolen from laboratories and classrooms, including computers, printers, video projectors, and remote controls. She is interviewing a student who was working late in Swartz Hall the night several video projectors were stolen from classrooms and three laptop computers were stolen from a writing lab.

As you review this probing interview, ask such questions as: How satisfactory is the opening? Do primary questions avoid common question pitfalls? How effective are the secondary or probing questions? How well does the interviewer listen and detect clues in answers? What areas of potentially valuable information does the interviewer discover and fail to discover? How satisfactory is the closing? Focus also on the interviewee. How sufficient are his answers? Which answer strategies does he employ? How well does he play his role as interviewee in this situation?

1. **Interviewer:** Good evening. I'm Susan Night from the University Security Department. You're Pete Payton?

2. **Interviewee:** Yes, I am.

3. **Interviewer:** I called you early this morning.

4. **Interviewee:** Yes, I recognized you from the *Daily Student.* Have a seat.

5. **Interviewer:** I'd like to talk to you about the thefts in Swartz Hall three nights ago. (*placing a tape recorder on a table in front of Pete and turning it on*)

6. **Interviewee:** Oh . . . okay. I've talked to the campus cops already.

7. **Interviewer:** That's okay. I'm working on a fairly long investigation of thefts of electronic equipment on campus. Why don't you tell me about this recent incident from the time you entered Swartz Hall that evening.

8. **Interviewee:** Well . . . I didn't know anything had happened until the cops stopped me when I left the building about midnight.

9. **Interviewer:** That's fine, but begin at the beginning.

10. **Interviewee:** I went to Swartz Hall about seven for a Young Democrats meeting that lasted until about 8:30 or so.

11. **Interviewer:** Um-hmm?

12. **Interviewee:** I hung around there for a while waiting for Jane Francis to join me. We're working on the same project together. She showed up about 9:15 and we went to the Political Science Computer Lab to work on our project. We had a lot of data to crunch.

13. **Interviewer:** I'm sure. And you didn't leave Swartz Hall until midnight?

14. **Interviewee:** Well, yeah, we went down the street to the Grill for Cokes about 10:30, but we were gone only a few minutes.

15. **Interviewer:** Okay. And then what did you do?

16. **Interviewee:** We worked in the lab until we left about midnight.

17. **Interviewer:** Were other students in the lab?

18. **Interviewee:** Uh huh, four or five students and some maintenance people.

19. **Interviewer:** Anybody else come or go?

20. **Interviewee:** An occasional student would come in for a while and leave.

21. **Interviewer:** Anybody else?

22. **Interviewee:** Well . . . yeah. A couple of other maintenance people would come in once in a while and report to the others in the lab.

23. **Interviewer:** You did make sure the outside door was locked when you came and went for your Coke, didn't you?

24. **Interviewee:** That's standard procedure for using the lab late at night.

25. **Interviewer:** And then?

26. **Interviewee:** Jane and I were stopped by the cops when we left the building about midnight. We told them everything we saw and did.

27. **Interviewer:** And you didn't see or hear anything unusual that night?

28. **Interviewee:** No . . . just the maintenance people installing some new equipment.

29. **Interviewer:** Tell me about that.

30. **Interviewee:** Well, the maintenance people, you know, were working that night and coming and going.

31. **Interviewer:** How do you know they were maintenance people?

32. **Interviewee:** They had coveralls on with a university logo over the right pocket.

33. **Interviewer:** I see.

34. **Interviewee:** It's great that we're getting so much new equipment.

35. **Interviewer:** What new equipment?

36. **Interviewee:** The equipment I saw being unloaded from a van when Jane and I went for Cokes.

37. **Interviewer:** You're sure this was new equipment?

38. **Interviewee:** Sure. They had them in boxes with company names on them.

39. **Interviewer:** You didn't think it was a funny time for maintenance people to be installing equipment?

40. **Interviewee:** No. They have to wait until evening classes are over, and lots of maintenance work is done on campus at night.

41. **Interviewer:** So you arrived in Swartz Hall at around 7:00, attended a meeting until about 8:30, and waited for another student until about 9:00. The two of you worked in the lab until midnight and left only one time for five to ten minutes. You saw maintenance people working and unloading equipment.

42. **Interviewee:** That's about it.

43. **Interviewer:** Is there anything else you can recall about that night?

44. **Interviewee:** No. Well . . . it did seem rather quiet that evening in the labs.

45. **Interviewer:** If you can think of anything else, please call me.

Probing Role-Playing Cases

A New Product Case

You are a recent graduate in computer technology and have just been hired by a small medical instrument manufacturing company. The company would like to replace its desktop computers with laptops and docking stations. Your assignment is to research the available laptops and docking stations to determine which would be best and most cost-effective for your company's staff. Your interviewee is a technical sales representative for Dell Computer. This interview will take place over the telephone.

A Missing Child

A few years ago, five-month-old Steven Dye disappeared from a supermarket in Cottonville, Texas, while being taken care of by Maeva Tonus, a frequent babysitter for the Dyes. Steven has never been found. The interviewer is an investigator for a national organization that searches for missing children. He has made an appointment with Maeva, now 21 years old, who has become very reluctant to speak with investigators of any type because inevitably they look on to her as a suspect.

A Case of Prejudice

The interviewer is a reporter for the daily *Star-Times* published in Chambers, Indiana, in the heart of a tomato-growing area. The area for many years saw the arrival each summer of hundreds of migrant workers from the Southwest hired by farmers to pick tomatoes. As machinery began to replace the workers, many workers decided to settle permanently in the area and work in auto factories and canneries. During the past three months, there have been a number of violent and hateful acts aimed at this predominantly Spanish-speaking population. The interviewer has arranged an interview with Maria Espinoza, a spokesperson for the former migrants, who are becoming increasingly frightened by the atmosphere in Chambers.

Closing a School

The public school system in Gaines, Georgia, has been experiencing a decline in enrollments and, with the decline, the likelihood of a million-dollar deficit in school funding. The elected school board has decided to close one elementary school, combine the junior and senior high schools, and eliminate 20 teaching positions. The interviewer has three children in the Gaines system and is seriously considering a run for the school board in the next election. She has arranged an interview with Dave Morton, who served for many years as a very popular principal at a Gaines elementary school and served on the school board for one term when he retired. Dave Morton and the interviewer have been friendly neighbors for nearly 25 years.

Student Activities

1. Compare and contrast the sample attitude survey in Chapter 6 with the probing interview in this chapter. How are the openings similar and different? How are questions similar and different? What are the apparent question sequences? What schedules are used? How are the closings similar and different? What interviewing skills are required for the participants of each interview?

2. Interview a newspaper journalist and a broadcast journalist about their interviewing experiences and techniques. How does the nature of the medium affect interviewers and interviewees? How does the medium affect interview structure, questioning

techniques, and note taking? What advice do they give about note taking and tape recording of interviews? How do the end products differ? What constraints does each medium place on interviewers?

3. Attend a press conference in which one person is answering questions from several interviewers. How is this situation similar to and different from one-on-one interviews? What stated or implied rules governed this interview? What skills are required of interviewers and interviewee? How did the interviewee recognize interviewers? What answering strategies did the interviewee use? What questioning strategies did interviewers use?

4. Interview a police or insurance investigator about the skills and techniques required for conducting investigative or interrogation interviews. How do they prepare for these interviews? How do they structure them? Which types of questions do they use most often? When is it necessary to violate question rules for achieving specific effects? How often do they use the "good guy–bad guy" technique, and how well does it work? How do they determine when they receive a truthful or untruthful answer to neutral, leading, and stress questions?

Notes

1. Eric Nalder, *Newspaper Interviewing Techniques*, Regional Reporters Association meeting at the National Press Club, March 28, 1994, The C-SPAN Networks (West Lafayette, IN: Public Affairs Video Archives, 1994).

2. Raymond L. Gorden, *Interviewing: Strategy, Techniques, and Tactics* (Homewood, IL: Dorsey Press, 1980), p. 135.

3. Eugene C. Webb and Jerry R. Salancik, "The Interview or the Only Wheel in Town," *Journalism Monographs* 2 (1966), p. 18.

4. Robert Ogles is a professor of communication at Purdue University.

5. Andrew D. Wolvin and Carolyn Gwynn Coakley, *Listening* (Dubuque, IA: William C. Brown, 1992), pp. 251–58.

6. John R. Bittner and Denise A. Bittner, *Radio Journalism* (Englewood Cliffs, NJ: Prentice Hall, 1977), p. 53.

7. Phillip H. Ault and Edwin Emery, *Reporting the News* (New York: Dodd, Mead, & Co., 1959), p. 125.

8. Bill Adler, ed., *The Kennedy Wit* (New York: Citadel Press, 1964), p. 81.

9. Originally cited in "The Point of View," a publication of the Alameda district attorney's office.

10. William T. G. Litant, "And, Were You Present When Your Picture Was Taken?" *Lawyer's Journal* (Massachusetts Bar Association), May 1996.

11. "Man Reads His Obituary in Paper," *Journal and Courier*, Lafayette–West Lafayette, Indiana, June 13, 1985, p. D4.

Resources

Chirban, John T. *Interviewing in Depth*. Thousand Oaks, CA: Sage, 1996.

Greaney, Thomas M. "Five Keys to a Successful Media Interview." *Communication World*, April–May 1997, pp. 35–37.

Kessler, Lauren, and Duncan McDonald. *The Search: Information Gathering for the Mass Media*. Belmont, CA: Wadsworth, 1992.

Killenberg, George M., and Rob Anderson. *Before the Story: Interviewing and Communication Skills for Journalists*. New York: St. Martin's Press, 1989.

Metzler, Ken. *Creative Interviewing: The Writer's Guide to Gathering Information by Asking Questions*. Englewood Cliffs, NJ: Prentice Hall, 1989.

The Survey Interview

I t is estimated that 30 million survey interviews are conducted in the United States every year by some 2,000 research firms, the federal government, companies, universities, medical centers, political candidates, and others too numerous to mention. Most of us are involved in either taking or conducting surveys on a regular basis.

Manufacturers use surveys to gauge consumer desires, intents, trends, and satisfaction and to discover how consumers feel about their products and competing products. Advertisers use market research surveys to predict and judge the effectiveness of advertising campaigns and methods. Politicians rely upon polls to determine voter concerns, beliefs, and attitudes and to assess their identification and popularity among potential voters. Reliance upon polls has become so pervasive that many politicians are accused of basing all of their opinions and voting decisions upon which way the polls are going. Survey research organizations such as Gallup and Harris use survey methods to measure public opinion about current issues and give us weekly reports on the ratings of presidents. The television networks conducted surveys within minutes after President Clinton completed his brief and historic speech concerning his grand jury testimony in 1998. Journalists employ survey techniques to get solid facts on which to base news reports and interpretations, so-called precision journalism. Colleges and universities conduct surveys to determine how students feel about the education they are receiving and proposed changes in curriculum, housing projects, and school calendars. And students conduct surveys to determine which music groups to bring to campus, which courses are most popular, and which issues are most important to students. As one team of researchers put it, "Surveys reach out and touch everyone."[1]

The survey is the most meticulously planned and executed of interviews because its purpose is to establish a solid base of fact from which to draw conclusions, make interpretations, and determine future courses of action. Whereas flexibility and adaptability describe the probing interview, reliability (assurance that the same information was collected each time in repeated interviews) and replicability (the ability to duplicate interviews regardless of interviewer, interviewees, and situation) describe the survey interview.

Sloppy preparation and informal interview techniques will not do for surveys. Too often we hear someone at a meeting call for a survey as if surveys are simple to create and conduct. A systematic approach that begins with determining a purpose and conducting background research and ends with analysis of data is essential for a successful survey. Figure 6.1 illustrates the seven-stage process for survey interviews.

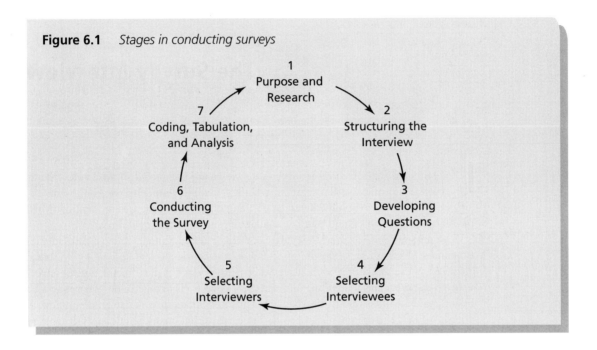

Figure 6.1   *Stages in conducting surveys*

1. Determining the Purpose and Conducting Research

Begin preparation for a survey by deciding what you need to discover about a topic and why: housing needs of college students, voters' images of presidential candidates, attitudes of investors toward mutual funds, recruiter preferences for resume formats. Your purpose and research will determine the topic areas, structure, questions, interviewers, and degree of precision most appropriate for your survey.

Determining Purpose

Babbie writes that surveys have one or more of three purposes.[2] You may *explore* a topic to become more familiar with it. The topic can be as persistent as taxes or crime, as new as high-definition television, or as shocking as the bombing of American embassies in Africa and mass shooting of students at schools in small towns and cities. You may want to *describe* a situation or event such as reactions of fans to a realignment of baseball teams in the major leagues, voter apathy in primary elections, or banking customer reactions to a bank merger. Or you may want to *explain* a phenomenon such as why people voted for a resolution requiring all instruction in school to be in English or why students protested the adequacy of the college library.

You may have multiple purposes for a survey if you want to explore and explain or describe and explain. Regardless, however, you must decide what you want to do and why. Consider several factors when delineating the purpose of your survey.

First, how soon must you complete the survey and compile the results? A professor may have months to devote to a research project, but a market researcher may have weeks, and a political pollster or journalist only days or hours.

Second, how much time will you have for each interview? Shoppers or people on their lunch hours will not submit to 15- or 20-minute interviews. But what can you accomplish well in four or five minutes? Research indicates that longer interviews not only cover more areas but tend to be more reliable than short interviews.

Third, how will you use the information you obtain? For example, do you want to determine general feelings or attitudes of students or residents or to generate precise statistics for forecasts, decision making, or determining causes of effects such as market share or teen sex? Uses of results dictate how accurate and reliable your data must be. Accuracy and reliability determine question schedule, types and uses of questions, and the number and types of people surveyed.

Fourth, what are your short- and long-range goals? Do you need to assess opinions or attitudes at a specific time: the end of a sales campaign, immediately after a speech or announcement, following a serious decline in the stock market? If so, a *cross-sectional* study in which you take a slice of what is known, thought, or felt during a narrow time span is warranted. But if your purpose is to determine trends over time, such as throughout an antismoking campaign, during a model year for a truck, or as students progress from first to last year in college, then a *longitudinal* study is called for.

And fifth, what are your resources? A national cross-sectional study or a 10-year, longitudinal study of children from preschool to high school will be costly in time, funds, interviewers, and data analysis. Will funds and researchers be available and interested in this study over eight or nine years? Even simple surveys are costly in time and money. What is your level of expertise? Are you capable of creating and conducting a complex, scientific survey?

Conducting Research

Once you know your purpose, investigate all aspects of the problem or issue. Do not *assume* you have enough knowledge of or familiarity with a topic to begin structuring a survey and writing questions. Read about the topic or issue, exploring its past, present, and future and both proposed and attempted solutions. Check every potentially valuable resource such as organizational files and archives, correspondence and interviews with knowledgeable people, government documents, professional journals, books, previous surveys on this topic, the Internet, newsmagazines, and newspapers. Talk to people who have explored this topic or are or have been involved. Victims of violent crime or those who have climbed Mount McKinley may give you unique insights into crime and mountain climbing unavailable in any printed resource.

Your research should reveal information already available in other sources that need not be gathered in your survey. Become a miniexpert on the topic so you are familiar with unique terminology and technical concepts. If you are going to be dealing with such concepts as "religious fundamentalism," "feminism," or "conservative political views," you must be able to specify the meaning of these terms to the satisfaction of interviewees as well as future readers and users of your survey results. Your research should reveal past attitudes and opinions and speculations about current attitudes and opinions. Your research should enable you to detect the weaknesses of previous surveys. And a thorough knowledge of the topic should give you insights into the nature and size of the population you must sample, the complexities of the issue, and potential intentional and unintentional inaccuracies in answers during your interviews.

2. Structuring the Interview

Once you have determined your purpose, assessed your resources, and conducted research, develop an interview guide with major topics and subtopics. The survey interview tends to be the most thoroughly structured interview you will conduct.

Interview Guide

An interview guide, as a preliminary step, will help you structure the interview clearly and be certain you cover all areas of information needed. The following outline might serve as a guide for a survey of students to determine what affects their choice of housing.

  I.   Housing preferences
        A.   Type of residence
              1.   Residence hall
              2.   Apartment
              3.   Sorority or fraternity
              4.   Cooperative
        B.   Rooms
              1.   Number
              2.   Size
              3.   Type
        C.   Number of persons in the household
        D.   Appliances
              1.   Refrigerator
              2.   Range
              3.   Microwave
              4.   Dishwasher
              5.   Clothes washer and dryer
        E.   Facilities
              1.   Equipped fitness and exercise room
              2.   Swimming pool
              3.   Club room
  II.   Cost of housing
        A.   Rent

        B.   Deposit
        C.   Facilities charges
        D.   Food
        E.   Maintenance
III.   Transportation
        A.   Means of transportation
            1.   Personal auto
            2.   City bus system
            3.   Bicycle
            4.   Motorcycle
            5.   Other
        B.   Transportation needs
            1.   To classes
            2.   To library and computer labs in evening
            3.   To medical appointments
            4.   To shop
            5.   To attend entertainment
            6.   Other
        C.   Parking

The traditional journalistic interview guide (who, what, when, where, how, and why) may be sufficient for the simplest of surveys, but most require the transformation of the guide into a highly scheduled standardized format.

The Opening

Structure your survey so that respondents go through identical interviews. Write out your opening and recite it verbatim. The following opening includes a greeting, statement of purpose, a simple request, and qualifier questions. It is the beginning of a highly scheduled standardized interview.

> Hello, my name is _____, from Market Associates, a national research firm. We are conducting a survey here at Whitewater Mall to see how you feel about the mix of stores currently in the mall and what stores you would like to see added. The survey takes only about five minutes and will give valuable shopper feedback to the mall owners and management. (*Go to first question.*)
>
> 1. Are you from this area? (*If yes, place an X by the answer and go to q. 2. If no, terminate the interview.*)
>
>   Yes _____ 1-1
>   No _____ 1-2
>
> 2. Do you shop at Whitewater Mall at least once a month? (*If yes, place an X by the answer and go to q. 3. If no, terminate the interview.*)
>
>   Yes _____ 2-1
>   No _____ 2-2

This opening identifies the interviewer and organization and states a general purpose. Notice that the interviewee is not asked to respond. The interviewer moves smoothly and quickly from orientation to the first question without giving the respondent an opportunity to refuse to take part. There are no icebreaker questions or small talk, which are important in probing interviews. The first two questions are employed to determine the interviewee's qualifications: a resident of the area and a fairly frequent shopper at the mall. Notice the survey provides instructions on the schedule for each interviewer to follow and has precoded each question for ease of tabulating results when the survey is completed.

In some surveys, the opening does not identify the group that is paying for the poll (the Democratic or Republican party for instance) or the specific purpose (to determine which strategies to employ during the remainder of the campaign) because such information might influence how interviewees respond. When a newspaper such as the *New York Times* or the *St. Louis Post Dispatch,* a cable or television network such as ABC or CNN, or a well-known polling group such as Harris or Gallup conducts a survey, the organization's name is used to enhance the prestige of the poll and the interviewer, to reduce suspicion that a candidate or corporation is behind the survey, and to motivate respondents to cooperate.

If your survey is dealing with sensitive matters and information, you must provide effective assurances of confidentiality in the opening to improve your chances of accurate and complete responses. A recent study also indicated a simple prepaid, nonmonetary incentive, such as a ballpoint pen, made during the opening can increase response rates and result in greater completeness in answers during the early portion of survey interviews.[3]

The Closing

The closing of surveys is usually brief and expresses appreciation for the time and effort expended to aid the survey. For example,

> That's all of the questions I have. Thank you very much for your help.

If the survey organizer wants a respondent's telephone number to verify that a valid interview took place, the closing might resemble the following:

> That's all the questions I have. May I have your telephone number so my employer can check to see if this interview was conducted in the prescribed manner? *(gets the number)* Thank you very much for your help.

If you can provide respondents with results of the survey, a common practice in research interviews, your closing might be:

> That's all the questions I have. I want to thank you for your help, and if you'll give me your address, I'll be sure that you receive a copy of the results of this study. *(gets the address)* Thanks again for your help.

Expect some interviewees to be very reluctant about giving strangers their telephone numbers or addresses. Be prepared to back off from either request if the interviewee appears anxious, suspicious, or very reluctant. Do not sacrifice the rapport and goodwill you have created during the interview. When one of the authors was conducting polls in his neighborhood for a political party, he discovered that many respondents were reluctant to give their telephone numbers for fear they would be targeted for calls from candidates during the campaign. With permission from the party, he stopped asking for telephone numbers, and closings went much smoother.

Respondents may be curious about your survey or very interested in your topic and want to discuss it with you. You may do so if time allows, if the respondent will have no opportunity to discuss the survey with future interviewees, and if the survey organization or group has no objections. Do not get defensive about the survey or bad-mouth it: "Hey, I'm just doing my job!" or "I know some of these questions are worded poorly, but . . . ." Do not try to enhance your credibility at the expense of the survey.

3. Developing Questions

Phrase each question with great care; interviewers cannot rephrase, explain, or expand on questions during interviews without risking the ability to replicate interviews, an essential element of surveys. All interviewees must hear the same question asked in the same manner. A slight change in wording or vocal emphasis on a particular word can generate different answers.

Phrasing Questions

Be sure each question is clearly worded, relevant to your survey, appropriate to the respondent's level of knowledge, neither too complex nor too simple, and socially and psychologically accessible. This is not a simple task when respondents may be of both sexes and differ widely in age, income level, education, intelligence, occupation, geographical area, and experiences. The increasing diversity of the American population may result in respondents being from several continents and cultures.

Be aware that a single word might alter significantly how people respond to a question, thereby altering the results of your survey. Several years ago researchers asked the following question to one group of respondents: "Do you think the United States should allow public speeches against democracy?" The results were "should allow" 21 percent and "should not allow" 62 percent. Then these researchers substituted a single word and asked respondents: "Do you think the United States should forbid public speeches against democracy?" The results were "should not forbid" 39 percent and "should forbid" 46 percent.[4] Respondents obviously viewed the word "forbid" as a much stronger and more dangerous action than "not allow"—perhaps un-American—even though the effect of the governmental policy would be the same. Imagine how people responded to the following item in a survey by a member of Congress in his home district: "Should we continue our overly generous support of the United Nations?" Who would be in favor of donating "over generously" to any organization? And the following interaction took place over the telephone.

1. **Interviewer:** Good evening, I'm calling preferred customers of Antonio's Pizza [the name is changed to protect the guilty party] about our Preferred Customer Card. Have you ever tried Antonio's pizza?

2. **Interviewee:** How could I be a preferred customer if I have never eaten Antonio's pizza?

3. **Interviewer:** *(long pause)* Gee, no one ever asked me that before. The manager just gave me a list of people to call.

Survey researchers warn against phrasing questions negatively because they can be misleading and confusing. For instance, Edwards and Thomas note that "a negative answer to a negatively worded statement may not be equivalent to the positive answer to a positively worded statement."[5] Even the explanation sounds confusing, does it *not?* They help by giving this example: "Disagreeing with the statement 'My work is not meaningful' does not necessarily mean that the same individual would have agreed with the statement 'My work is meaningful.' " They also note that forcing a respondent to disagree with a negative statement can be confusing. Think of the difficulties you have had with negatively phrased multiple-choice questions in examinations. Babbie warns that many respondents will read over the word "not" in a questionnaire or fail to hear it during an interview, so many of those in favor of a statement such as "The U.S. should not recognize Cuba" and many of those who disagree will answer the same way. "And" adds Babbie, "you may never know which is which."[6]

Sample Question Development

Many questions will evolve as you develop your schedule. Consider, for example, how you might develop what appears to be a simple question on highway safety. The first version may be,

> How do you feel about the state-imposed seat-belt law?

This question seems innocuous until you take a closer look. "State-*imposed*" is both unnecessary and is likely to bias the results because it sounds evil and oppressive. Government is telling us what to do! The openness of the question may elicit a wide range of responses from "Angry," "Frustrated," "It's another step toward socialism," and "I think it's a (choice four-letter word) dumb law" to "It saves lives," "It's okay for highway driving," "It will reduce our insurance costs," "It's great," and "I don't know." Some interviewees may give long speeches on the pros or cons of the seat-belt law or government interference in our lives. The variety, length, and ambiguity of such responses would create a recording nightmare for you and require secondary questions that would be difficult to plan for and to code.

Try a second version. Close the question up, perhaps something like this:

> Are you for, against, or have no feelings about the state's seat-belt law?
>
> For   _____
> Against   _____
> No feelings   _____

This question eliminates the bias of the first question and resolves potential problems with recording answers, but it may be too closed. A respondent may not be simply for or against the seat-belt law, feeling, for instance, that the law is unacceptable for in-town driving but acceptable for highways where speed limits range from 55 to 70 mph or more. And this same person might feel that the law is fine for cars but not for trucks that are safer. The "no feelings" option may generate a large percentage of "undecided" or "don't know" answers.

Try a third version that allows for degrees of feeling and clarifies types of vehicles and highways.

> Do you strongly agree, agree, disagree, or strongly disagree with this statement: The seat-belt law in this state should apply to all cars and trucks, except tractor trailers, on all roads.
>
> Strongly agree   ____
> Agree   ____
> Disagree   ____
> Strongly disagree   ____
> Undecided   ____
> Why?   _____
> *(Ask only of respondents choosing strongly agree or strongly disagree.)*

This third version assesses intensity of feelings, is easy to record, and specifies cars and types of trucks on all roads. A built-in secondary "why" question may discover reasons for strong feelings, such as concerns about safety, conservation of gasoline, delays in reaching distant cities, and being out of step with other states. We suggest that you limit the probing "why" question to those expressing strong feelings because our experience indicates that those with moderate responses tend not to have ready explanations for agreeing/disagreeing or liking/disliking. They just do. Other questions may delve into the law on different types of roads and for different types of vehicles, including school and commercial buses.

Work with each of your questions until they satisfy phrasing criteria and are designed to obtain the information you need. This is how you avoid embarrassment, confusion, and inaccurate results. Later we will address the pretesting of surveys to detect potential problems with phrasing of questions.

Question Strategies

Survey interviewers have developed a number of question strategies to assess knowledge level, honesty, and consistency, reduce undecided answers, prevent order bias, and incorporate probing questions.

Filter Strategy

The filter strategy enables the interviewer to determine the interviewee's knowledge of a topic. For example,

1. **Interviewer:** Are you familiar with the new telemarketing code of ethics?
2. **Interviewee:** Yes, I am.
3. **Interviewer:** What do you know about the code?

If the interviewee says no, then the interviewer will go to the next topic area. If the interviewee says yes, then the interviewer asks the interviewee to reveal the extent and accuracy of this knowledge. Through this follow-up question the interviewer may discover that the respondent has this code of ethics confused with another or may be highly misinformed about the new code. Many interviewees will say yes to bipolar questions even when they have no idea what the interviewer is talking about, because they do not want to appear ignorant or uninformed. The filter strategy ferrets out this tendency.

Repeat Strategy

The repeat strategy enables the interviewer to determine if an interviewee is consistent in responses on a topic, particularly a controversial one. The interviewer may ask the same question several minutes apart and later compare answers for consistency. A variation of this strategy is to disguise the question by rephrasing it.

6. Are you in favor of the antismoking bill before Congress?

14. Do you think the antismoking bill should be approved?

Another example of a repeat strategy is to go from a moderately closed to a highly closed question, such as,

21. How often do you have a physical checkup?

31. I am going to read a number of frequencies for physical checkups. Stop me when I read the frequency that includes yours.

6 months   _____
12 months   _____
18 months   _____
24 months   _____
More than 24 months _____

If the repetition is too obvious, the interviewee might object to answering the same question twice. Be sure rewording does not change the meaning of the original question. It must be essentially the same to determine consistency.

Leaning Strategy

Many respondents are reluctant to take stands or make decisions, some because they do not want to reveal their feelings or future actions. Interviewers employ leaning questions, not to be confused with leading questions, to reduce the number of "undecided" and "don't know" answers.

7a. If the presidential election were being held today, who would you vote for?
(*If undecided, ask q. 7b.*)

Bush   ____
Gore   ____
Undecided ____

7b. Well, do you lean more toward Bush or Gore at this time?

Bush ____
Gore ____
Undecided ____

The "undecided" option must remain in question 7b because an interviewee may be truly undecided at the moment. A variation of the leaning question is, "Well, if you had to vote today, would you vote for Bush or Gore?" Clearly stated "undecided" and "don't know" options tend to invite large percentages of these answers, particularly when a question asks for censure of people, organizations, or products. This is why many survey interviewers will not provide such options when asking the original question. The intent is to make the respondent take a stand or make a decision.

Shuffle Strategy

The last choices in a question tend to get negative or superficial evaluations because respondents become bored or tired. Sometimes an option is selected because it is the first mentioned or the last heard. The shuffle strategy varies the order of questions or answer options from one interview to the next to prevent *order bias*. The method of rotation would be carefully explained when training interviewers to conduct the survey. Notice the instructions to interviewers in the following example:

Now I'm going to read a list of major airlines, and I want you to tell me if you have a highly favorable, favorable, neutral, unfavorable, or highly unfavorable opinion of each. (*Rotate order of airlines from interview to interview. Encircle answers received.*)

	Highly favorable	Favorable	Neutral	Unfavorable	Highly unfavorable
Delta	5	4	3	2	1
American	5	4	3	2	1
Northwest	5	4	3	2	1
United	5	4	3	2	1
Southwest	5	4	3	2	1
U.S. Airways	5	4	3	2	1
TWA	5	4	3	2	1

The fact and myth of order bias has led to some strange events in politics, "persuasive" surveys by reform and lobbying groups, and advertising. A few years ago a political candidate in Indiana had his name changed legally so it would begin with A and thus would be at the top of ballots on election day, the belief being that voters select the top names in lists of candidates for city council seats and other offices. He lost, but his and similar actions have led many states to shuffle names so they are not in alphabetical order. Be aware that the shuffle strategy may eliminate order bias but cause confusion and errors in recording answers unless interviewers are well trained in shuffling options and the coding system is easy for them to use.

Chain or Contingency Strategy

The highly scheduled standardized format of surveys allows for *planned* secondary questions that enable interviewers to probe into initial answers. This is called a *chain* or *contingency strategy* and is illustrated in the following series from a market survey. Notice the built-in instructions for ease of recording answers and tabulating data.

1a.   During the past month, have you received any samples of cereal?
      (Place an X by the answer received.)

      Yes _____ *(Ask q.1b.)*
      No _____ *(Skip to q. 2a.)*

1b.   Which brands of cereal did you receive? *(Do not read the list.)*

      Frosted Flakes   _____
      Post Raisin Brand   _____
      Cheerios   _____
      Grape Nuts   _____
      Shredded Wheat   _____
      Other   _____ *(Please specify.)*

1c.   *(Ask only if Grape Nuts is not mentioned in q.1b., otherwise skip to q.1d.)*
      Did you receive a free sample of Grape Nuts?

      Yes _____ *(Ask q.1d.)*
      No _____ *(Skip to q. 2a.)*

1d.   Did you eat the free sample?

      Yes _____ *(Skip to q. 2a.)*
      No _____ *(Ask q. 1e.)*

1e.   Why didn't you eat the free sample?
      _____   _____

The chain or contingency strategy allows interviewers to probe into answers while maintaining control of the process and ensuring replicability.

Question Scales

Survey interviewers have developed a variety of scale or multiple-choice questions that delve more deeply into topics and feelings than bipolar questions but still allow for ease of recording and tabulation of data.

Interval Scales

Interval scales provide distances between measures. For example, *evaluative interval scales* (often called *Likert scales*) ask respondents to make judgments about persons, places, things, or ideas. The scale may range from five to nine answer options (five is most common) with opposite poles such as "strongly like . . . strongly dislike," "strongly agree . . . strongly disagree," or "very important . . . not important at all." Here are two examples of evaluative interval scales:

Do you strongly agree, agree, have no opinion, disagree, or strongly disagree with the recent gun control legislation?

Strongly agree   ____
Agree   ____
Neutral   ____
Disagree   ____
Strongly disagree   ____

Please use the phrases on this card to tell how the video you just viewed on Olean will affect your purchase of potato chips that are prepared with Olean instead of vegetable oils.

Increases my interest a lot   ____
Increases my interest a little   ____
Will not affect my interest   ____
Decreases my interest a little   ____
Decreases my interest a lot   ____

Interviewers will often provide respondents with cards (color-coded to tell them apart) for complex questions or ones with many choices or options to remember. A card eliminates the faulty-recall problem that many respondents experience, because they can study the answers or objects they are evaluating, rating, or ranking in some way.

Frequency interval scales ask respondents to select a number that most accurately reflects how often they do something or use something. For example,

How frequently do you watch network evening news programs?

6–7 days a week   ____
4–5 days a week   ____
2–3 days a week   ____
1 day a week   ____
Less than once a week   ____
Never   ____

Numerical interval scales ask respondents to select a range or level that accurately reflects their age, income, educational level, or rank in an organization.

I am going to read several age groupings. Please stop me when I read the one in which you belong.

18–24   ____
25–34   ____
35–49   ____
50–64   ____
65 and over   ____

Nominal Scales

Nominal scales provide mutually exclusive variables and ask respondents to pick the most accurate variable. These are often "self-reports" and do not ask respondents to rate or rank choices or to pick a choice along an evaluative, numerical, or frequency continuum as interval scales do. Choices may be in any order. For example, you might ask,

Do you currently live in a

Residence hall	____
Coop	____
Sorority/fraternity	____
Apartment	____
Other	_____

When you last purchased sneakers, which brand did you buy:

Nike	____
Adidas	____
Reebok	____
Vans	____
Converse	____
None of the above	_____

In nominal questions, the options are mutually exclusive and include most likely or all options from which to choose. This is why "other" or "none of the above" is the final option in the examples. The respondent must be able to choose one of the options.

Ordinal Scales

All ordinal questions ask respondents to *rate* or *rank* the options provided in their *relationship* to one another, not to choose the most accurate option as in interval and nominal scales. A rating ordinal scale might look like the following:

You have now experienced four American presidents in your lifetime. Please rate each as excellent, above average, average, below average, or poor.

Carter	Excellent	Above Average	Average	Below Average	Poor
Reagan	Excellent	Above Average	Average	Below Average	Poor
Bush	Excellent	Above Average	Average	Below Average	Poor
Clinton	Excellent	Above Average	Average	Below Average	Poor

Notice that, unlike the other scales that ask for a single response, this rating scale generates four answers, and respondents will consciously compare the four presidents to one another in developing their answers. You might ask respondents to rank order options. For instance,

On this card are the names of 10 past presidents. Rank order them in terms of greatness or contribution to the country.

President	Rank	President	Rank
George Washington	____	Woodrow Wilson	____
Thomas Jefferson	____	Franklin Roosevelt	____
Andrew Jackson	____	Harry Truman	____
Abraham Lincoln	____	Dwight Eisenhower	____
Theodore Roosevelt	____	Ronald Reagan	____

The ordinal question below asks respondents to select among and rank order options.

On this card are several reasons cited frequently for support of a flat income tax to replace the current graduated income tax. Pick the three you think are most important and rank them in order of importance to you.

____	Fairness	____	Reduction of power of the IRS
____	Ease of reporting	____	Decrease in taxes
____	Cost-effective in collecting	____	Reduction of government bureaucracy

Bogardus Social Distance Scale

The Bogardus Social Distance Scale is employed to determine how people feel about social relationships and distances. Does a person's attitude or feeling change as the issue comes closer to home? This scale usually moves progressively from remote to close relationships and distances to detect changes as proximity narrows. For example, you might use the following Bogardus Social Distance Scale to determine how students feel about international graduate students teaching university courses.

1. Do you favor international graduate students teaching in American universities?
2. Do you favor international graduate students teaching at your university?
3. Do you favor international graduate students teaching in your school or college?
4. Do you favor international graduate students teaching in your major?
5. Do you favor international graduate students teaching the courses you are taking?

In many question scales, respondents are somewhat safely removed from the attitude or feeling they are expressing about a product, issue, or person. The Bogardus Social Distance Scale brings an issue ever closer to home so it is no longer something impersonal or that only affects others "over there."

Answer scales are designed to obtain a range of results, but many respondents try to "psyche out" survey takers, somewhat as many students do when taking multiple-choice tests. For instance, respondents may try to pick "normal" answers in nominal and ordinal scales and safe, moderate, or middle options in interval scales. Rather than admit they do not know the correct answer, even when there is no correct answer, respondents may pick the option that stands out, such as the second in a list that includes 10 percent, 15 percent, 20 percent, 30 percent, and 40 percent. Respondents who first agree that a certain activity would make most people uneasy are less likely then to admit ever engaging in that activity and may attempt to change the subject.[7] Phrase scale-type questions carefully and observe reactions during interviews to detect patterns of responses and interviewee comprehension. For instance, long scales or complicated ratings or rankings may confuse respondents without either party realizing it.

Question Sequences

The question sequences discussed earlier are suitable for survey interviews. The tunnel sequence is common in surveys when no strategic lineup of questions is needed. Gallup's Quintamensional Design Sequence, or a variation of it, is appropriate when you want to explore intensity of attitudes and opinions. Because funnel and inverted funnel sequences include open-ended questions, answers are often difficult to record and may pose coding and tabulation problems. The wealth of information you are likely to get from moderately open questions may be worth the problems involved. A study of the effects of question order suggests that general questions should come first and more specific questions should follow—a funnel sequence.[8]

4. Selecting Interviewees

Select interviewees carefully because they are your sources of your data. The best schedule of questions will be of little help if you talk to the wrong people.

Defining the Population

The first step in selecting interviewees is to define the *population* or *target group* you wish to study. The population may be as small and similar as members of a singles group at a church or as large and diverse as all adults in the United States. Often you may be interested in only a subset of a larger population, such as all women in a singles group or all registered voters in Ohio or Clark County. If, for instance, you want to determine how residents of a neighborhood feel about its safety, your population might include all adult residents (those over 18) or the head or heads of households in the neighborhood. Your final population should include all persons who are able and qualified to respond to your questions and about whom you want to draw conclusions.

If your target population is small (members of a tennis team, sales associates at a department store, or the design staff in your company), interview all of them. Most surveys are concerned, however, with populations that far exceed your time, financial, and personal limitations—the 35,000 students at your university, all adult residents of a city of 125,000, all people who own PCs. Dozens of interviewers could not interview all of these people even if they had unlimited time and money because it would be impossible to locate each member of the population. Since you cannot interview all students or residents, for example, you interview *some* of them and extend your findings to *all* of them. You claim that this sample accurately *represents* the whole.

Sampling Principles

The fundamental principle of all sampling is that your sample accurately represents the population or target group you are studying. It is a miniature version of the whole. The old-time watermelon seller practiced this principle when he or she would take a large knife and carefully cut out a triangular plug from a watermelon. This plug was to show us what the *entire* watermelon was like.

Each potential respondent from a defined population must have an equal chance of being selected. You must determine, then, the probability that each person might be selected to decide upon an acceptable *margin of error.* The precision of your survey is the "degree of similarity between sample results and the results from a 100 percent count obtained in an identical manner."[9] Most surveys are designed to attain a 95 percent *level of confidence,* or the mathematical probability that 95 times out of 100 interviewees would give results within 5 percentage points (your margin of error) either way of the figures that would have been obtained if you had interviewed your entire selected population. If you listen to a network news program this evening, you are likely to hear the results of a survey by NBC–Associated Press, CBS–*New York Times,* or ABC–*Washington Post,* or Harris. The reporter will note that the survey has a margin of error of 4 percent either way. This means that if 42 percent of respondents approve of the way Congress is doing its job, the real figure might be as low as 38 percent or as high as 46 percent because of the built-in margin of error.

The tolerable margin of error depends upon the use of the survey results. If you hope to predict the outcome of an election or the effects of a new medical treatment, then you must strive for a small margin of error. If you are conducting a survey to determine how people feel about the corporation for which they work or the church they attend, you may tolerate a higher margin of error because statistical precision is less critical. The size of your sample—the actual number of people you will interview—is determined, then, by the size of the population and the acceptable margin of error.

There is no magical formula for determining number of interviewees. The Gallup organization produces accurate national surveys with a margin of error in the 3 percent range from a sample of 1,500. Size of sample is less important than how you take the sample. Standard formulas reveal that as a population increases in size, the percentage of the population necessary for a sample declines rapidly. In other words, you would have to interview a larger percentage of 5,000 people than of 50,000 people to attain equally accurate results. Formulas also reveal that you must increase greatly the size of your sample to reduce the margin of error from 5 percent to 4 percent to 3 percent. The small reduction in the margin of error may not be worth the added cost of significantly more interviews. Meyer offers the following table that shows the sample sizes of various populations necessary for a 5 percent margin of error and a 95 percent level of confidence.[10]

Population Size	Sample Size	Population Size	Sample Size
Infinity	384	5,000	357
500,000	384	3,000	341
100,000	383	2,000	322
50,000	381	1,000	278
10,000	370		

Sampling Techniques

The simplest method of selecting a representative sampling of your population is to do a *simple random sampling*. If you have a complete roster of all persons in your population, place all names in the legendary hat, shake the hat so they are thoroughly mixed, and draw out one name at a time until you have your sample. If your state has a lottery, you see a random selection each evening when Ping-Pong balls containing numbers are sent flying about in a glass enclosure and one ball pops out at a time.

Another random sample method is to assign a number to each potential respondent and create or purchase a *table of random numbers*. With eyes closed, place a finger on a number and read a combination up, down, across to left or right, or diagonally. Select this number as part of your sample or decide to read the last digit of the number touched (46) and the first digit of the numeral to the right (29) and thus contact respondent number 62. Repeat this process until the sample is completed.

A third method of sampling is called *skip interval* or *random digit*. In this method, for example, you may choose every tenth number in the telephone book, every twentieth name in a roster of students, or every other person who walks into a department store. This common sampling technique may have some built-in flaws. For instance, 15 percent or more of the population may have unlisted phone numbers, and some groups (students, the poor, migrant workers, persons in the process of moving) may not have telephones or names in directories. A voter, customer, or membership roster might not be up to date or might be divided according to majors, seniority, job classification, or membership category and thus produce a nonrepresentative sample of the whole. Time of day, day of the week, location of a strip mall, and stores in the mall may determine the types of persons most likely to shop there: homemakers, professionals, self-employed, unemployed, retired, late-shift factory workers, teenagers.

Simple random sampling procedures often do not provide adequate representation of subgroups within your population, even when drawn from a hat. If your population has clearly definable groups (males and females; education levels; income levels; and diverse cultural groups), you would be wise to employ a *stratified random sampling*. This method allows you to include a minimum number of respondents from each group, typically the percentage of the group in your target population. For instance, if you know that your targeted population consists of 52 percent women and 48 percent men, 88 percent white Americans and 12 percent black Americans, and 55 percent registered Republicans and 45 percent registered Democrats, your sample would reflect these percentages. If most of your respondents turn out to be white male Democrats, you cannot generalize to the whole population with any degree of accuracy. The same would be the case if most of your respondents were juniors and seniors but you were trying to survey all college students.

Some survey organizations give *sample points* to interviewers. Each sample point represents a geographical area (a square block or mile, for instance) that contains specific types of persons (grain farmers or retired persons, for instance). Instructions may tell interviewers to skip corner houses (corner houses are often more expensive) and then try every other house on the outside of the four-block area until they have obtained two interviews with males and two with females. This sample point or *block sampling* method gives the survey designer control over selection of interviewees without resorting to lists of names, random digits, or telephone numbers. Points or blocks are carefully chosen to represent the diverse elements within your population.

A common and inaccurate method of sampling is *self-selection.* We see this method used every day in radio and television talk shows, on local evening newscasts, and reports of mail arriving in congressional offices on such volatile issues as gun control, abortion, welfare reform, and affirmative action. Who is likely to call C-SPAN, Rush Limbaugh, Larry King, or the local television station? You guessed it—those most opposed or most in favor of an action, the extremes. Moderates do not call or write, but those in opposition do. In the issues above, it is a foregone conclusion that the majority of self-selected respondents would be anti–gun control, antiabortion, pro-welfare reform, and anti–affirmative action. Randomness and representation of diverse elements of your population disappear in self-selected samples.

5. Selecting Interviewers   Select interviewers with three questions in mind.

Number Needed

If you plan to interview a small number of persons and the interviews will be brief, one interviewer may be sufficient. But most often you will need several interviewers. This is particularly so if the interviews will be lengthy, the sample is large, the time allotted for the survey is short, and the interviewees are scattered around the state or country. Large and difficult interviewing assignments result in serious interviewer fatigue and decline in motivation.[11] You cannot overburden interviewers without damaging the quality of interviews and the data received.

photo by Alan Oddie/Photo Edit

■ *The first step in selecting interviewees is to define the population or target group you wish to study.*

Qualifications

What special qualifications are required? A highly scheduled or highly scheduled standardized interview does not require an interviewer to be an expert on the topic or skilled in phrasing questions and probing into answers. It does require a person who can learn and follow the guidelines presented and the schedule as developed. The person must be able to read the questions verbatim and effectively and record answers quickly and accurately. The person must be interested in the topic, able to listen, and able to remain neutral. College students and middle-aged homemakers tend to be excellent survey interviewers because they have the necessary qualifications, are inexpensive to employ, and enjoy meeting and talking with people. If a survey requires probing and adaptation to different interviewees, professionally trained interviewers tend to be more efficient and to produce more accurate results.[12]

Personal Characteristics

What personal characteristics are optimal? Interviewers who are older, are nonthreatening, and have an optimistic outlook get better response rates and cooperation, regardless of their experiences. Apparently age generates credibility and self-confidence, and optimism motivates interviewees to cooperate.[13] One study discovered that personality and attitude of the interviewer are by far the most important elements in shaping interviewee attitudes toward surveys.[14] The interviewer must be pleasant, friendly, warm, and relaxed in demeanor and appear honest and trustworthy.

Recent studies also report that nearly one-third of respondents believe that answering survey questions will neither benefit them nor influence decisions, that there are too many surveys, that surveys are too long, and that interviewers ask too many personal questions. Some 36 percent of respondents in one study said they had been asked to take part in "false surveys," sales interviews disguised as informational surveys.[15] Clearly, survey interviewers must be aware of relational dimensions such as warmth, involvement, dominance, and trust, and make every effort to establish a positive relationship with each respondent. They must be able to determine quickly whether an interviewee wants a friendly, chatty interviewer or a more impersonal, professional interviewer.

Similarity is an important relational dimension in survey interviews. The interviewer should dress similar to interviewees; if you look like me, I am more likely to cooperate and answer appropriately. An in-group relationship with the interviewee (black to black, senior citizen to senior citizen, Cuban to Cuban, or female to female) may avoid cultural and communication barriers and enhance trust because the interviewer is more likely to be perceived as safe and capable of understanding and being sympathetic. An out-group relationship (white to black, young citizen to senior citizen, European-American to Cuban-American, male to female) may pose less ego threat, and the interview may be perceived as a new experience and a means of recognition.

6. Conducting the Survey

Poor execution of interviews can undo the most thorough preparation. Provide training sessions and carefully written instructions for interviewers.

Training Interviewers

Training results in greater use of appropriate probing questions, feedback, and giving instructions.[16] Discuss common interviewee criticisms, and stress the importance of following the question schedule exactly as printed. Explain complex questions and recording methods. Be sure interviewers understand the sampling techniques employed. Emphasize the need to replicate interviews to enhance reliability and attain an acceptable margin of error and level of confidence. The following is a typical list of instructions provided to interviewers.

1. Study the question schedule thoroughly so you can "ask" rather than "read" questions and record answers quickly and accurately.

2. Dress appropriately; be neat and well groomed; and do not wear any buttons or insignia that may identify you with a particular group or position on the issue being surveyed and thus bias the survey results by encouraging interviewees to respond in particular ways.

3. Be on time for all appointments.

4. Do not conduct interviews too early in the morning or too late at night.

5. Be friendly, businesslike, and sincerely interested in the interview.

6. Speak clearly and loudly enough to be heard easily; maintain good eye contact without staring; and do not rush through the interview.

7. If persons say they do not have time, use statements such as, "This will only take a few minutes" or "I can ask you questions while you are working (shopping)." Do not pressure an interviewee to take part.

8. Ask all questions on the schedule and exactly as worded.

9. Do not change the order of questions, and change the order of answer options only when instructions on the schedule tell you to do so.

10. If a person does not answer a question as asked, repeat the question but do not rephrase it because rephrasing may alter the response received.

11. Do not define terms.

12. Record answers as prescribed on the schedule. Write or print answers to open questions carefully and clearly.

13. Give respondents adequate time to think and respond; do not fidget or look at your watch.

14. Do not become defensive at interviewee reactions or debate responses.

15. When you have obtained the answer to the last question, thank the interviewee for cooperating and excuse yourself.

16. Do not discuss the survey with the interviewee.

Pretesting the Interview

Pretest the interview schedule and procedures on a small sample of interviewees in your target population to detect potential problems. The best-laid plans on paper may not work during real interviews. Conduct complete interviews, not merely specific questions, including the opening and closing, all questions, and recording of answers. Do not leave anything to chance. For instance, in a political poll conducted by one of our classes, students deleted the question "What do you like or dislike about living in Indiana?" because it took too much time, generated little useful data, and posed a coding nightmare because of diverse replies. When interviewees were handed a list of political candidates and asked, "What do you like or dislike about . . . ?" many became embarrassed or gave vague answers because they did not know some of the candidates. This question was replaced with a Likert scale from "strongly like" to "strongly dislike," including a "don't know" option, and interviewers probed into reasons for liking or disliking only for candidates ranked in the extreme positions on the scale. Respondents tended to know something about candidates they strongly liked or strongly disliked. Interviewers also discovered that scale questions tended to confuse elderly respondents, so they added special explanations to complex questions.

Here are typical questions you ask when pretesting a survey:

1. How well did interviewees seem to understand what you wanted and why?
2. Which questions required explanations?
3. How effectively did questions elicit the kind and amount of information desired?
4. Did you have any problems recording answers to open questions?
5. Did any questions elicit information already obtained in prior or later questions?
6. Did respondents react hesitantly or negatively to any questions?
7. How adequate were answer options?
8. Was interviewer or order bias apparent at any time during the interview?
9. Were instructions on the schedule clear?
10. How easily and meaningfully can answers be tabulated for analysis?

Once you have analyzed the pretest results and made alterations in procedures, questions, and answer options, you should be ready to conduct the survey.

Interviewing by Telephone

A growing number of interviewers are turning to the telephone for an easier, faster, and less expensive means of conducting surveys. You can interview people around the world without moving from your office or home, flying or driving long distances, or contracting with people far removed from the control of your presence.

Some studies comparing telephone and face-to-face interviews suggest that the two methods produce similar results, with respondents giving fewer "socially acceptable" answers over the telephone and preferring the anonymity it provides (particularly in certain neighborhoods).[17] However, other studies have urged caution in turning too quickly to the telephone for surveys. One study discovered that many interviewers do not like telephone interviews, and this attitude may affect responses. Another study found that fewer interviewees (particularly older ones) prefer the telephone, and there is a lower degree of cooperation in telephone interviews.[18] Many people feel uneasy about discussing sensitive issues with strangers they cannot see, and it is difficult for interviewers to make convincing confidentiality guarantees when they are not face-to-face with respondents.[19] Add to these problems the growing number of persons with unlisted telephone numbers and those who are using answering machines and call identifiers to filter out unwanted calls, including surveys. And, as we noted earlier, a great many people have experienced bogus or fake telephone surveys.

photo by Laura Dwight/Photo Edit

■ *A growing number of interviewers are turning to the telephone for easier and less expensive means of conducting surveys and polls.*

Regardless of the potential problems with telephone surveys, they are becoming more frequent. A single face-to-face or personal interview may cost more than $100. Locating respondents at home is more difficult because fewer and fewer traditional homemakers exist and flexible working hours make it difficult to predict when a person will be home. Fewer than 50 percent of large city contacts consent to interview, but organizations want to interview persons over a wide geographical area.

The opening of the telephone interview is critical to cooperation because the great majority of refusals occur prior to your first question: one-third in the opening seconds, one-third during the orientation, and one-third at the point of listing household members. Speaking skills (pitch, vocal variety, loudness, rate, and distinct enunciation), particularly during the opening, seem to be more important than content. As one study concluded, "Respondents react to cues communicated by the interviewer's voice and may grant or refuse an interview on that basis."[20] Telephone interviewers apparently must establish trust through vocal and verbal analogs to the personal appearance, credentials, and survey materials that enhance trust in face-to-face interviews.

The literature on surveys contains important advice for would-be telephone interviewers. Develop an informal but professional style that is courteous and friendly, avoiding pressure or defensiveness. People will hang up if you try to "make" them participate. Get the respondent involved as quickly as possible in answering questions because active involvement will motivate a person to take part and reply effectively. Try not to give a person a reason or opportunity to hang up on you. Pay complete attention to what you are doing, saying, or hearing. Do nothing else during the interview, including smoking, drinking, eating, chewing gum, sorting papers, or communicating nonverbally with other people in your office. Say nothing you do not want the respondent to hear because the person may hear you even if you place your hand over the mouthpiece. Talk directly into the mouthpiece of the telephone and do not talk too softly or too loudly. Speak clearly, distinctly, and slowly because the respondent must rely solely on your voice. The person cannot see you, your nonverbal signals, your answer cards, or your visual materials that assist you in face-to-face interviews. State each answer option distinctly and pause between them to aid the respondent in hearing, comprehending, and recalling them. Use vocal emphasis for highlighting important words and punctuating sentences so the respondent can answer accurately: "First, (brief pause) what is the *most important* (vocal emphasis) reason for balancing the *state* (vocal emphasis) budget?" Listen to answers, and signal you are doing so with cues such as "Uh huh," "Yes," "I see." Explain any pauses or long silences of more than a few seconds: "Just a minute while I write down your answer," "I'm recording your responses," or "I'm writing down this information."

7. Coding, Tabulation, and Analysis

Once all interviews are completed, the final phase of the survey begins. This phase involves coding, tabulation, and analysis of the information you have received.

Coding and Tabulation

Begin the final phase of the survey by coding all answers that were not precoded, usually the open-ended questions. For instance, if question 10b is "Why did you not attend any of the summer concerts at The Ravine?" a variety of answers are possible. If 10b is coded 20, each answer might be coded 20 plus 1, 2, 3, and so on.

20-1   I didn't like the musical groups selected for this year.
20-2   The price was too steep.
20-3   The concerts tend to be too crowded.
20-4   Sometimes the crowd gets out of hand.
20-5   Traffic jams in and out of The Ravine are horrendous.
20-6   There was too much teenage drinking.

Answers to open-ended questions may require analysis and structuring before a coding system is developed. For example, in a study of voter perception of mudslinging in political campaigns, the interviewer asked, "What three or four words would you use to describe a politician who uses mudslinging as a tactic?" Answers included more than a hundred different words, but analysis revealed that most words tended to fit into five categories: untrustworthy, incompetent, unlikable, insecure, and immature.[21] A sixth category, "other," received words that did not fit into the five categories. All words were placed into one of these six categories and coded from one to six.

Interviewers may create chaos by recording answers in a confusing manner. For example, in a political survey, answers to the question "Who is Matthew Welsh?" were recorded as "Democrat," "governor," and "political candidate." Since Welsh was the Democratic candidate for governor and a former governor, how should you code this answer? Did "governor" mean present governor, past governor, or candidate for governor? Did "political candidate" mean for governor, senator, or representative? Did "Democrat" mean Democratic candidate for governor, Democratic governor, or just a Democrat? Data defied coding attempts and were discarded.

Analysis

Once you have coded answers and tabulated the results, begin the analysis phase. Analysis is making sense of the data you have obtained, but this task can be overwhelming.

One of the authors surveyed 354 clergy from 32 Protestant, Catholic, and Jewish groups to assess the interview training they had received during college and seminary and since entering the ministry.[22] The 48 questions in the survey times 354 respondents provided 16,992 bits of information. Attempts to compare respondents according to religious affiliation, years in the ministry, and demographic data such as age and geographical area produced hundreds of pages of computer printouts.

How can the survey interviewer/researcher handle massive amounts of information generated in most surveys? Redding suggests, first, that you be *selective.* Ask yourself "What findings are likely to be most useful?" and "What will I do with this information once I get it?" If you have no idea, do not ask for it. Second, *capitalize* upon the potential of your data by subjecting data to comparative breakdowns to discover differences between demographic subgroups. And third, *dig* for the gold that is probably hidden within your raw data and simple tabulations.[23] For instance, in polls of registered voter attitudes, interviewers often discover that female respondents favor a candidate far less than male respondents, that African-Americans have very different attitudes toward social programs than white Americans, and that the more highly educated a person is, the more likely the person is to support a tax increase. Americans who recently became citizens are likely to have very different views toward immigration than third- or fourth-generation Americans. Remember that what you do *not* find may be as important as or more important than what you *do* find. What information did you *not* obtain? What information is very different from what you had predicted?

As you analyze your data, ask a number of questions. What conclusions can you draw, and with what certainty? For what segment of your target population can you generalize? What are the constraints imposed by the sample, schedule of questions, the interviewing process, and the interviewers? Can you determine why people responded in specific ways to specific questions? Are you in danger of making mountains out of molehills of data? What unexpected events or changes have occurred since the completion of your survey? In the weeks preceding the horrendous bombing of the federal building in Oklahoma City in 1995, the consensus was that Congress would overturn gun control legislation passed in 1994, particularly the ban on assault weapons. The bombing, the accused bombers' links to heavily armed militia groups, and statements by many of these groups that armed rebellion might soon be necessary changed public attitudes and congressional plans. Any surveys preceding the bombing were outdated. And what will you do with the "undecided" and "don't know" answers and blanks on your survey forms? Your results for a question might be like the following:

Do you plan to take a vacation at least 500 miles from home this year?

Yes	45 percent	Sample = 1,000
No	39 percent	
Undecided	12 percent	
No response	4 percent	

If you eliminate "no" responses (interviewers failed to record answers or some people refused to answer), the sample equals 960, and the new percentages are "yes," 47 percent; "no," 40 percent; and "undecided," 13 percent.

What if you discard the undecideds? The sample equals 840, and the new percentages are "yes," 54 percent, and "no," 46 percent.

"Yes" looks better, but the large "undecided" figure (not to mention the earlier "no" response figure) may be the most important finding of the survey. Can you say with confidence that the majority of Americans will take vacations at least 500 miles from home, even if you ignore the undecideds? What is your margin of error? The most sophisticated survey rarely has a margin of error less than 3 percent, so "no" responses could be ahead by 2–3 percent or "yes" could be ahead by 4–5 percent.

Journalists must be cautious when writing headlines and making predictions, organizations must be cautious when basing policy decisions on survey results, voters must be cautious when casting votes according to candidate-preference poll results, and investors must be cautious when investing according to surveys of brokers or major players on the stock market. You might subject your data to a statistical analysis designed to test reliability and significance of data. Babbie and other research methodologists (see resources list) provide detailed guidelines for conducting sophisticated statistical analyses. When you have completed the analysis of your data, you must determine if you have achieved the purpose and objectives of your survey and how best to report the results.

The Respondent in Survey Interviews

The proliferation of surveys ensures that you will take part in them often. You may walk away from the market researcher at the mall, close your door to a political pollster, or hang up the telephone on a person doing an attitude survey. If you do, however, you forfeit the opportunity to play an important role in improving commercials, selecting political candidates, influencing legislation, or bettering your community.

Listen carefully to the interviewer's opening to learn who the interviewer is, who the interviewer represents, why the survey is being conducted, how answers will be used, how long the interview will take, and how you were chosen. Decide whether to take part after thorough orientation, not before the interviewer can explain the survey. If the interviewer does not provide information you think important, ask for it. For instance, one of the authors was recently visiting his daughter and her family in Portland, Oregon, more than 2,500 miles from home. During a visit to a mall, he was approached by a market researcher who explained what she was doing and why, but she did not specify that respondents had to be local residents. When the author asked if it made any difference that he was visiting from the Midwest, the interviewer said she wanted only those who visited the mall on a regular basis. The interview ended pleasantly but quickly. The opening is also the critical time when you need to determine if this is truly a survey or a slick sales effort under the guise of a survey. Is it a political preference survey or part of the persuasive campaign for a particular candidate or party? Never agree to take part to sabotage the interview.

Listen carefully to each question, particularly to answer options in interval, nominal, and ordinal questions. If you have trouble remembering a question or options, ask the interviewer to repeat the question slowly. If you do not understand the question, explain why and ask for clarification. Avoid replays of earlier answers, especially if you think you "goofed." Do not try to guess what a question is going to be from the interviewer's first words because you might be wrong and become confused, give a stupid answer, or needlessly force the interviewer to restate a perfectly clear question. If a question or a series of answer options is unclear, ask for clarification before answering. Listen to each question; think through your answer; and respond clearly and precisely. Give the answer that best represents *your* beliefs, attitudes, or actions, not the one you think the interviewer wants to hear or how other people might respond.

You have rights as a respondent. For example, you can refuse to answer a poorly constructed or leading question or to give information that seems irrelevant or an invasion of privacy. Expect and demand tactful, sensitive, and polite treatment from interviewers. Insist on adequate time to answer questions. Remember, you can always walk away, close the door, or hang up the telephone. Survey interviews can be fun, interesting, and informative if both parties treat one another fairly.

Summary

The survey interview is the most meticulously planned and executed of all interviews. Planning begins with determining a clearly defined purpose and conducting necessary background research. The general purpose of all survey interviews is to establish a solid base of fact from which to draw conclusions, make interpretations, and determine future courses of action. Only then does the survey creator structure the interview and develop questions with appropriate strategies, answer scales, coding, and recording methods. Selecting interviewees not only involves delineating a target population to survey; it almost always involves choosing a sample of this population (because of its size) that represents the whole. The creator of the survey must carefully choose appropriate sampling methods, determine the size of the sample, and plan for an acceptable margin of error. Each choice has advantages and disadvantages because there is no one correct way to handle all survey situations.

Survey respondents must determine the nature of the survey and its purposes to decide whether to take part. If the decision is to take part, then respondents have a responsibility to listen carefully to each question and answer it accurately. As a respondent, be sure you understand each question and its answer options. Demand enough time to think through your answers. And feel free to refuse to answer obviously loaded or poorly phrased questions that require you to give a biased answer or choose among options that do not include how you feel, who you are, or what you do.

A Survey Interview for Review and Analysis

As you read through this survey schedule, notice the parts of the standard opening. Identify the question strategies (filter, repeat, leaning, shuffle, and chain), the question scales (evaluative interval, frequency interval, numerical interval, nominal, ordinal, and Bogardus Social Distance), and the question sequences (funnel, inverted funnel, tunnel, and quintamensional design). Notice the built-in probing questions, instructions for interviewers, and inclusion of open questions. And note the simple, planned closing.

How might the opening be improved? How might the closing be improved? How might questions be phrased more effectively? What problems might the open-ended questions pose for both interviewers and interviewees? Could the interviewer make better use of question strategies and scales? Were the subtopics of the selected topic the most important? Are recording techniques and instructions adequate?

Issues Confronting the United States Today

(Speak to any person 18 years or older who lives in the household.)

Hello, my name is _____, from Public Opinion Research, a nationwide survey research organization located in Philadelphia. We're conducting a study of people's opinions about a number of current issues confronting the United States today. The results of our study will be supplied to members of Congress and to the public through the news media. We've been interviewing people in your neighborhood and would like to ask you a few questions.

1a.   When you think of a serious problem facing the United States today, which problem comes to mind first?

_____

1b.   What do you think is the major cause of this problem?

_____

1c.   What are other possible causes of this problem?

_____

_____

_____

2.   Many people we talk to feel that morality is a serious problem facing America today. This card *(hand card to interviewee)* gives some causes people cite for America's morality problem. Which one of these reasons do you feel is the greatest cause of immorality? *(Record answer.)* Which is the next most important cause? *(Record answer.)* And which would be the next? *(Record answer.)*

	First	**Second**	**Third**
Abortion	1	2	3
Divorce	1	2	3
Sexual promiscuity	1	2	3
Poverty	1	2	3
Immorality among leaders	1	2	3
Television	1	2	3
Outlawing prayer in schools	1	2	3
Failure of organized religion	1	2	3
Breakdown of the family	1	2	3
Drugs and alcohol	1	2	3

3.   I'm going to read several statements, and I would like you to tell me whether you strongly agree, agree, don't know, disagree, or strongly disagree with each.

(Record answers on the space below, and rotate the order in which the statements are given from interview to interview.)

a.   We should outlaw abortion in this country.

b.   We should impose a mandatory life sentence on any person committing a crime through use of a firearm.

c.   Divorce laws should be toughened.

d.   Voluntary prayer should be permitted in public schools.

e.   Sex and violence must be reduced in television programming, through federal law if necessary.

f.   Adultery should be a felony in all fifty states.

	a	b	c	d	e	f
Strongly agree	1	1	1	1	1	1
Agree	2	2	2	2	2	2
Don't know	3	3	3	3	3	3
Disagree	4	4	4	4	4	4
Strongly disagree	5	5	5	5	5	5

4.   Many people tell us they are interested in the abortion issue. This card *(hand interviewee a card)* lists several positions on abortion. Please tell me which one is closest to your feelings about abortion.

Abortions should be illegal regardless of reason.	1
Abortions should be legal only when the life of the mother is endangered.	2
Abortions should be legal when pregnancy is caused by rape or incest.	3
Abortion should be legal when the mental or physical health of the mother is endangered.	4
There should be no restrictions on abortion because it is a matter of free choice.	5

5a.   Are you familiar with the flag amendment?

Yes _____ *(If yes, ask q. 5b.)*

No _____

5b.   What do you know about the flag amendment?

_____

_____

6.   Hundreds of sex offenders are released from prison each year after serving their prison terms.

a.   Are you in favor of allowing these people to return to society?

Yes _____   No _____

b.   Are you in favor of their coming to live in this part of the country?

Yes _____   No _____

c.   Are you in favor of their coming to live in this state?

Yes _____   No _____

    d.   Are you in favor of their coming to live in this city?
        Yes ____   No ____
    e.   Are you in favor of their coming to live in this neighborhood?
        Yes ____   No ____

7a.   What do you know about what is called the religious right?

_____

_____

_____

7b.   What, if any, positive contributions do you believe the religious right has made for the United States during the past 10 years?

_____

_____

_____

7c.   Do you approve or disapprove of religious organizations being involved in selecting political candidates and aiding their campaigns?
    Approve ____   Disapprove ____

7d.   Why do you feel this way?

_____

_____

7e.   How strongly do you feel about this?
    Strongly   ____
    Very strongly   ____
    Something about which you will never change your mind   ____

8.   How would you rate the job the president is doing: excellent, good, average, not so good, poor? *(Encircle answers in the scales provided at the end of q.10.)*

9.   How would you rate the job your governor is doing: excellent, good, average, not so good, poor? *(Encircle answers in the scales provided at the end of q.10.)*

10.   How would you rate the job your mayor is doing: excellent, good, average, not so good, poor? *(Encircle answers in the scales provided below.)*

	President	**Governor**	**Mayor**
Excellent	1	1	1
Good	2	2	2
Average	3	3	3
Not so good	4	4	4
Poor	5	5	5

11.   Here is a card *(hand card to interviewee)* that lists some of the problems people say state governments must do something about. As I read each one, please tell me which political party is likely to address this problem most effectively. The first problem is _____. *(Rotate the order from one*

interview to the next.) Do you think the Republican or the Democratic Party is likely to address this problem most effectively?

	Rep.	Dem.	Either	Neither	Don't know
School funding	1	2	3	4	5
Tax relief	1	2	3	4	5
Violent crime	1	2	3	4	5
Highways	1	2	3	4	5
Welfare reform	1	2	3	4	5
Morality	1	2	3	4	5
Environment	1	2	3	4	5

Now I would like to ask you some personal questions so we can see how people with different backgrounds feel about the issues facing the United States today.

12. I'm going to read you several age ranges. Stop me when I read the one that includes your age.

    18–24 ____   50–64 ____
    25–34 ____   65 and over ____
    35–49 ____

13. How often do you attend a religious service of any type?

    More than once a week ____   Six times a year ____
    Once a week ____   Once a year ____
    Every other week ____   Less than once a year ____
    Once a month ____   Never ____

14a. Do you generally consider yourself a Democrat or Republican? *(If independent, ask q.14b.)*

    Democrat ____   Don't know ____
    Republican ____   Refuse ____

14b. Well, do you generally vote for Democratic or Republican candidates for public office?

    Independent/Democrat ____
    Independent/Republican ____
    Independent ____

15. Is your religious affiliation Protestant, Catholic, Jewish, Muslim, other, none?

    Protestant ____   Muslim ____
    Catholic ____   Other ____ _____ *(Write name.)*
    Jewish ____   None ____

16. What was the last grade level of your formal education?

    0–8 years ____   13–15 years ____
    9 to 11 years ____   College graduate ____
    12 years ____   Postgraduate ____

17.   I'm going to read several income ranges. Stop me when I read the range that
      includes your current annual family income.

0 to $14,999	____	$75,000 to $99,999	____
$15,000 to $24,999	____	$100,000 to $124,999	____
$25,000 to $49,999	____	Over $125,000	____
$50,000 to $74,999	____		

Thank you very much for your time and cooperation. The survey results should be
made public within five to six weeks.

Student Activities

1. Volunteer to be an interviewer for a survey being conducted by a company, political
    party, government agency, or religious group. What instructions and training did you
    receive? How were interviewees determined? What problems did you encounter in
    locating suitable and cooperative interviewees? What problems did you have with the
    survey schedule? What is the most important thing you have learned from this
    experience? What advice would you give the organization you volunteered to serve?

2. Try a simple interviewer bias experiment. Conduct 10 short opinion interviews on a
    current issue, using an identical question schedule for all interviews. During five of
    them, wear a conspicuous T-shirt, button, or badge that identifies membership in or
    support of an organization that advocates one side of the issue: a Republican
    elephant, a religious symbol, a T-shirt with an organization's logo or slogan on it.
    Compare results to see if your apparent identification with an organization on one
    side of the issue affected answers to identical questions.

3. Obtain a market survey schedule and a political survey schedule from the library, your
    professor, or organizations that conduct these surveys. Compare and contrast these
    surveys. How are openings and closings similar and different? Which types of
    schedules are employed? How are question types, strategies, and sequences similar
    and different? How might each have been improved?

4. Conduct an in-depth interview with a person experienced in survey interviewing. How
    does this person (or the person's organization) conduct background research? Create
    and pretest survey schedules? Determine the size of sample and sampling methods?
    Determine acceptable margins or error? Select and train interviewers? Use face-to-
    face and telephone methods? Analyze data?

Survey Role-Playing Cases

Changes in a Campus Ministry

The interviewer is a member of University Church on an eastern university campus that has
always been fairly liberal in its teaching and views. It has traditionally attracted a large following of students who have felt uncomfortable with organized religion. Two months ago,

the church's parent religious organization assigned a very conservative, traditional member of the clergy to minister to the University Church congregation. There appears to be a growing number of dissatisfied members. The interviewer has decided to conduct a survey of members to assess their attitudes toward the new minister and the changes that are taking place at University Church. A major concern is sampling.

Curriculum and Core Requirements

The interviewer is a student at a community college and has been asked by the student government to create and conduct a survey of student attitudes toward the current curriculum core requirements and proposals for revising them. The student must do background research, create a question schedule, and determine both the size and the nature of the survey sample. The college has a variety of two-year technical programs and a program preparing students to go on to four-year colleges.

Political Image Survey

Mayor Samantha Pokovic is thinking seriously about running for the U.S. congressional seat from her district in North Carolina. A major concern is a recent messy divorce from her husband of 21 years during which he accused her of having an affair with a member of her staff. The interviewer works for PolitiCom and must design an image survey that will determine how people in the congressional district feel about Mayor Pokovic and how her recent divorce and her husband's charge might affect her candidacy. A major concern is to design a survey that would assess perceptions of image without calling undue attention to the divorce and adultery charge, particularly in distant areas of the district where the news was not widespread.

Market Survey

The interviewer works for Market Studies, Inc., and must design a telephone survey instrument to assess the effectiveness of a recent advertising campaign for a new breakfast cereal. The advertising campaign consisted of three phases: videos sent to 25,000 randomly selected homes, full-page ads in major news magazines, and 30-second spots on three television networks. The interviewer must create an interview schedule and a set of instructions that others will use to train dozens of interviewers located throughout the country.

Notes

1. Paul Rosenfeld, Jack E. Edwards, and Marie D. Thomas, "Improving Organizational Surveys," *American Behavioral Scientist* 36 (1993), p. 414.

2. Earl Babbie, *The Practice of Social Research* (Belmont, CA: Wadsworth, 1995), pp. 84–86.

3. Diane K. Willimack, Howard Schuman, Beth-Ellen Pennell, and James M. Lepkowski, "Effects of a Prepaid Nonmonetary Incentive on Response Rates and Response Quality in Face-to-Face Survey," *Public Opinion Quarterly* 59 (1995), pp. 78–92.

4. Stanley L. Payne, *The Art of Asking Questions* (Princeton, NJ: Princeton University Press, 1980), p. 57.

5. Jack E. Edwards and Marie D. Thomas, "The Organizational Survey Process," *American Behavioral Scientist* 36 (1993), pp. 425–26.

6. Babbie, p. 145.

7. Norman M. Bradburn, Seymour Sudman, Ed Blair, and Carol Stocking, "Question Threat and Response Bias," *Public Opinion Quarterly* 42 (1978), pp. 221–34.

8. Sam G. McFarland, "Effects of Question Order on Survey Responses," *Public Opinion Quarterly* 45 (1981), pp. 208–15.

9. Morris James Slonim, *Sampling in a Nutshell* (New York: Simon and Schuster, 1960), p. 23.

10. Philip Meyer, *Precision Journalism* (Bloomington, IN: Indiana University Press, 1979), p. 123. See also W. Charles Redding, *How to Conduct a Readership Survey: A Guide for Organizational Editors and Communications Managers* (Chicago: Lawrence Ragan Communications, 1982), pp. 25–49.

11. Eleanor Singer, Martin R. Frankel, and Marc B. Glassman, "The Effect of Interviewer Characteristics and Expectations on Response," *Public Opinion Quarterly* 47 (1983), pp. 68–83.

12. Robin T. Peterson, "How Efficient Are Salespeople in Surveys of Buyer Intentions," *Journal of Business Forecasting* 7 (1988), pp. 11–12.

13. Singer et al., pp. 68–83.

14. Stephan Schleifer, "Trends in Attitudes Toward and Participation in Survey Research," *Public Opinion Quarterly* 50 (1986), pp. 17–26.

15. Burns W. Roper, "Evaluating Polls and Poll Data," *Public Opinion Quarterly* 50 (1986), pp. 10–16.

16. Jacques Billiet and Geert Loosveldt, "Improvement of the Quality of Responses to Factual Survey Questions by Interviewer Training," *Public Opinion Quarterly* 52 (1988), pp. 190–211.

17. Theresa F. Rogers, "Interviews by Telephone and in Person: Quality of Responses and Field Performance," *Public Opinion Quarterly* 39 (1976), pp. 51–65; and Stephen Kegeles, Clifton F. Frank, and John P. Kirscht, "Interviewing a National Sample by Long-Distance Telephone," *Public Opinion Quarterly* 33 (1969–1970), pp. 412–19.

18. Lawrence A. Jordan, Alfred C. Marcus, and Leo G. Reeder, "Response Style in Telephone and Household Interviewing," *Public Opinion Quarterly* 44 (1980), pp. 210–22; and Peter V. Miller and Charles F. Cannell, "A Study of Experimental Techniques in Telephone Interviewing," *Public Opinion Quarterly* 46 (1982), pp. 250–69.

19. William S. Aquilino, "Interview Mode Effects in Surveys on Drug and Alcohol Use," *Public Opinion Quarterly* 58 (1994), pp. 210–40.

20. Lois Okenberg, Lerita Coleman, and Charles F. Cannell, "Interviewers' Voices and Refusal Rates in Telephone Surveys," *Public Opinion Quarterly* 50 (1986), pp. 97–111.

21. Charles J. Stewart, "Voter Perception of Mudslinging in Political Communication," *Central States Speech Journal* 26 (1975), pp. 279–86.

22. Charles J. Stewart, "The Interview and the Clergy: A Survey of Training, Experiences, and Needs," *Religious Communication Today* 3 (1980), pp. 19–22.

23. Redding, pp. 119–23.

Resources

Converse, Jean M., and Stanley Presser. *Survey Questions: Handcrafting the Standardized Questionnaire.* Newbury Park, CA: Sage, 1986.

Fowler, Floyd J., Jr. *Survey Research Methods.* Newbury Park, CA: Sage, 1993.

Frey, James H. *Survey Research by Telephone.* Newbury Park, CA: Sage, 1989.

Holstein, James A., and Jaber F. Gubrium. *The Active Interview.* Newbury Park, CA: Sage, 1995.

Salant, Priscilla. *How to Conduct Your Own Survey.* New York: Wiley, 1994.

The Persuasive Interview

In previous chapters on probing and survey interviews, we have urged you to remain neutral, to use leading or loaded questions only in special situations, and to avoid interviewer bias that might cause respondents to answer as they think you want them to reply instead of as they really feel. The purpose of these interviews is to obtain information as accurately and completely as possible.

In this chapter, we focus attention not on *information getting* but on *persuasion.* The intent is to be an advocate for your product, service, organization, client, or belief, not to remain neutral or noncommittal. You take part in a persuasive interview every time you and another party attempt to affect one another's perceptions and thus to bring about changes in thinking, feeling, or acting.

You will exchange information in persuasive interviews, but this is a means to an end, not the end itself. For instance, college recruiters are interested not merely in giving and getting information but in persuading students to enroll in their colleges. Sales representatives provide information so you will buy their products and services. A campus minister might inform you about his or her religious beliefs to convert you. A neighbor may tell you about the plight of children with cancer so you will give money.

Too often we equate persuasion with sales, but as we can see from the above examples, sales is only one type of persuasive interview. And while this chapter focuses on interviews in which persuasion is the primary purpose, most interviews have persuasive elements. For example, journalists and survey takers must persuade persons to take part, cooperate, and give accurate answers. Recruiters and applicants attempt to convince one another to either offer or accept positions. Both parties in performance review interviews attempt to persuade one another and themselves about past performance and future goals. Health care providers must persuade patients to follow prescribed treatments and recommendations for healthier lifestyles, and patients may have to convince providers that they are following prescribed regimens.

It is a rare day in which you do not take part in one or more persuasive interviews or an interview with a significant persuasive element. They may be as brief and informal as an interaction with a friend about where to go for dinner or as lengthy and formal as a major business or professional venture. They may be face-to-face or over the telephone, particularly when you are trying to eat dinner or take a nap. The pervasiveness of persuasive encounters in our daily lives has led Roderick Hart to write that "one must only breathe to need to know something about persuasion."[1]

The Ethics of Persuasion

All interviewers must meet basic ethical standards such as honesty, fairness, and sincerity. But persuasive interviewers face both unique and considerable ethical responsibilities because they attempt to affect directly and indirectly our ways of thinking, feeling, and acting. It is not enough that you learn *how* to persuade; it is essential that you learn and practice *ethical* guidelines.

The formal concern for ethics and persuasion can be traced back to ancient Greece some 2,500 years ago, but our concern today is as strong as ever because of our sophisticated and technologically driven means of persuasion. A recent survey by *U.S. News & World Report* and CNN found that half of those surveyed believed people were less honest than 10 years earlier.[2] Newsmagazines have included extensive features entitled "What Ever Happened to Ethics?" "A Nation of Liars?" and "Lying. Everybody's Doin' It (Honest)."[3] *The Wall Street Journal* revealed that 25 percent of 671 managers surveyed said high ethics could hinder a successful career.[4] Powerful leaders, including some from the tobacco industry and the White House, have made emphatic denials of wrongdoing only to change their stories when evidence forced them to do so. Is it any wonder there is a concern for ethical standards in American society? In 1996, a panel of business, education, and government leaders ranked ethics ahead of technical training and communication as necessary for successful careers in the twenty-first century.[5]

Virtually every profession, from college professors to political consultants and advertisers to attorneys, has created codes of ethics to guide members' actions, but wholesale violations seem to occur before the ink dries on the announcements. It is not merely that humans seem to have difficulty being ethical, but that we as humans have great difficulty determining what is unethical. As Richard Johannesen, a recognized authority on the ethics of persuasion, writes, "Ethical issues focus on value judgments concerning degrees of right and wrong, goodness and badness, in human conduct."[6] Notice the word "degrees" in this definition. There appear to be no absolutely and universally unethical acts, and judgments tend to focus, as Johannesen claims, on degrees of rightness and wrongness. Many ethical codes are aimed at the world as we would like it to be, not as it is. Situations often appear to be so unique that ethical principles seem inappropriate or useless. Some writers argue that persuaders themselves ought to determine the ethics of their efforts according to the *end* being sought, and others claim we must judge the *means* used to reach the end. Some argue that ethics are determined by prevailing conduct in a society or personal conscience, and others argue that ethics are clearly stated in legal statutes and religious doctrines stipulated in the Bible, Torah, or Koran. Some argue that life is gamelike and thus people should adopt a buyer-beware attitude; others argue that anything that dehumanizes or cheapens persons or groups is unethical.

A confounding problem is *who* will make the value judgments concerning degrees of right and wrong, of goodness and badness, of means and ends? Every rule seems to have justified exceptions and to pose more questions than answers. For example, withholding evidence may be bad if a person is selecting an organization to join or an investment to buy but good if health or security is at stake. On the one hand, we may resent a persuader trying to scare us into a decision through use of fear appeals; on the other hand, we may use the same appeals when persuading a child not to play in the street or get in a car with a stranger. Virtually every strategy and tactic discussed in this chapter, even careful analysis and adaptation to the interviewee, may be identified by some readers as manipulative and therefore unethical.

Although there may be no single code of ethics applicable to all persuasive interviews and acceptable to all interview parties, there are guidelines to help you as interviewer and interviewee to distinguish good from bad persuasive efforts. Woodward and Denton, for example, write that "ethical communication should be fair, honest, and designed not to hurt people."[7] Take into consideration the vulnerability of the interviewee, the effect on the interviewee, and the seriousness of the results. Understand that the position of the interviewer—president, professor, physician, judge, police officer, member of the clergy—may determine the ethical standards to which he or she will be held accountable. The traits of fairness, honesty, and safety are apparent in the following commonly recommended ethical guidelines for persuaders.

1. Search for and provide accurate, complete, up-to-date, and relevant evidence to support all points made during an interview. Include both fact and opinion, but distinguish one from the other. Document or be prepared to document all evidence you use or claim to have. And avoid any "evidence" that might contain errors, be fictitious, or be distorted in some way. Do not take information out of context to enhance its effect when context is critical to its accuracy.

2. Be accurate and fair in selecting ideas, arguments, language, and tactics. Do not intentionally oversimplify complex issues, positions, or situations. Avoid attacks on the personal character of the competition, smears, or name-calling, what is commonly called *negative selling* or *mudslinging*. Do not use appeals or language that denigrates persons because of age, gender, race, culture, or sexual orientation. Develop careful arguments that avoid specious or illogical reasoning. Work toward achieving an ethical balance between your original ideas and proposals and how you alter them for persuasive effect.

3. Take into account all claims and probable consequences of the thinking, feeling, or acting proposed. Do not advocate actions that are dangerous, illegal, or unethical. Inform interviewees of the financial, psychological, social, or physical risks involved. Do not misrepresent or distort them. Do not claim certainty when probability is either low or moderate. And, although it is fashionable today to blame others for everything we do and do not do, accept responsibility for the effects of your persuasive efforts.

4. Be willing to submit your private motivations to public scrutiny. Believe in what you advocate. Balance your self-interests with those of the interviewee. And be clear, direct, and honest about your intentions and the rationales for them.

5. Be tolerant of disagreements and diverse viewpoints. Not only permit objections, challenges, and questions during interactions with interviewees but encourage them. Hear people out. You might learn something important from the other party that influences *your* thinking, feeling, or acting.

Kenneth Andersen has written: "Although we do not wish to force a given system of values or ethical code upon the reader, we do argue that he [she] has a responsibility to form one. We believe that it is desirable both for the immediate practical reasons of self-interest and for more altruistic reasons that a person accept responsibility for what he [she] does in persuasion both as receiver and as source."[8] There is no better overall guideline or code than the golden rule: Do unto others as you would have them do unto you. Which of us wants a persuader to use fictitious evidence, illogical reasoning, and racist or sexist language; to pretend dangerous consequences do not exist; to conceal private motivations; or to discourage or ignore our questions and objections? If each of us were to treat others as we wish to be treated, few unethical practices would occur in persuasive interviews.

Five Interrelated Conditions for Persuasion

Although success is never assured in persuasive interviews, the possibility of success is enhanced if your persuasive effort meets five interrelated conditions:

1. Your proposal satisfies an urgent need or one or more desires or motives, *and*
2. Your proposal and you as persuader (including your organization or profession) are consistent with the interviewee's beliefs, attitudes, and values, *and*
3. Your proposal is feasible, workable, practical, and affordable, *and*
4. Objections to your proposal are outweighed by its benefits, *and*
5. No better alternative course of action is available.

These interrelated conditions are not easy to meet, particularly when the interviewee is skeptical or hostile or aspects of the situation such as economic conditions, time of year, uncertainty about the future, or mitigating events make the interviewee reluctant to change or make commitments. Recall from Chapter 2 that you are dealing with an interviewee's *perceptions* of you, self, situation, and proposal.

Your chances are always best when you approach even simple and brief persuasive interviews systematically. Following the seven stages outlined in Figure 7.1 will help you meet the five interrelated conditions for successful persuasion.

1. Doing Your Homework

Thorough preparation is essential for persuasive interviews. Know what you are talking about, who you are talking to, the context in which the interview is taking place, and the potential influence of outside forces. Set a realistic goal, being aware that you may need two or more interviews to reach your ultimate goal.

Investigating the Topic

Be the best informed, most authoritative person in the interview. Search for solid, up-to-date information that will help persuade the interviewee that your proposal is the best to satisfy a need or desire and will enhance your credibility by showing you are well prepared, knowledgeable, and authoritative. The greater the risk or commitment involved in your proposal, the greater the likelihood an interviewee will not only expect but demand

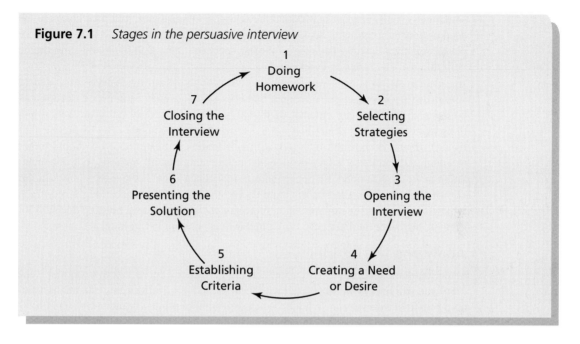

Figure 7.1   *Stages in the persuasive interview*

1
Doing
Homework

7
Closing the
Interview

2
Selecting
Strategies

6
Presenting the
Solution

3
Opening the
Interview

5
Establishing
Criteria

4
Creating a Need
or Desire

proof that what you say is worth believing and acting upon. Investigate all aspects of the topic, including events that may have contributed to the problem, reasons for and against change, evidence on all sides of an issue, and possible solutions.

The interviewee can demand support, challenge assumptions, generalizations, and claims, or ask for documentation of a source at any moment during an interview. *You are taking part in a persuasive interview, not giving a persuasive speech.* We are impressed with persuaders who reply to our inquiries with facts and documentation.

Do not overlook any potentially valuable source of information and evidence: the Internet, e-mail, interviews, letters, pamphlets, questionnaires, surveys, unpublished studies, reports, newspapers, periodicals, professional journals, and government documents. Do not overlook your own experiences and study. Check carefully all sources available to the interviewee.

Search for a variety of evidence to support the need and proposal. Collect examples, both factual and hypothetical, that may illustrate points you will make. We all like good stories, including short anecdotes and longer narratives, that make problems seem real or "in the flesh." Some writers claim that humans are storytelling animals. Gather statistics on relevant areas such as inflation, growth rates, expenses, benefits, insurance coverages, profits and losses, or causes and effects. It may be important to know the sizes and percentages of populations, demographic groups, cultural groups, organizations, memberships, families, facilities, or cities. Gather statements by acknowledged authorities on the topic as well as testimonials from those who have joined, attended, purchased, signed, or believed. Be sure none of those people have changed their minds since making the statements you have in hand. Seek comparisons and contrasts between situations, events, proposals, products, or services. For instance, you may compare the need or your proposal with actual situations, showing what has happened to other people or organizations that have faced similar decisions. And find clear and supportable definitions of key terms and concepts.

Here are a few suggestions for seeking and employing information you discover. Be sure to distinguish *opinion* (something that is assumed, usually cannot be observed, can be made at any time, and either is or should be believed tentatively) from *fact* (something that can be or has been observed, is verifiable, and is thought of as securely established). If you do not, the interviewee may! Studies indicate that you should either thoroughly document a source or give no documentation at all because poor documentation is worse than none. Evidence tends to have little effect if the audience is familiar with it or if it is presented poorly. And thorough evidence enhances long-term effect, which is important, for example, if an interviewee will not make a housing decision for months, buy a car until after the tax refund arrives, or vote in five weeks.

Analyzing the Interviewee

Once you have researched your topic thoroughly, learn everything you can about the party you will interview. As you did with the topic, do not overlook any potentially valuable source of information. What do you know from previous contacts with this party? What information is included in personal and organizational files? What can other people tell you about this party? What information is included in church, school, professional, or community directories? How and when, if at all, has the interviewee expressed an interest in this issue, problem, or proposal?

Insufficient information may be available on an interviewee, or you may have little or no opportunity to study the party ahead of time. This is common in sales and recruiting situations. In such cases, use the first few minutes of the interview to discover important information by *observing* the interviewee's dress, manner, and attitudes; by carefully *asking questions* that probe into background, interests, and purposes of this visit; and by listening insightfully to what the person says and does not say. If the party consists of more than one person, try to determine who is in charge, who will make important decisions, and who is the client, customer, recruit, or person in need.

Physical and Mental Characteristics

Consider potentially relevant physical characteristics such as age, gender, race, culture, size, health, disabilities, and physical appearance. Although any one of these characteristics may be central in a persuasive effort (choice of college, medical insurance, retirement plan, clothing, religious affiliation), be careful of stereotyping people. It is foolhardy and insulting to assume that all elderly are naive, women are more susceptible to persuasion than men, Mexican-Americans are recent immigrants, Chinese-Americans are high academic achievers, or all shabbily dressed people are economically poor. Mental health and level of intelligence may make interviewees more or less receptive to your message. Research indicates, for instance, that highly intelligent interviewees are more influenced by evidence and logical arguments but tend to be highly critical and therefore more difficult to persuade.[9]

Socioeconomic Background

Review important socioeconomic data, including the interviewee's group memberships because attitudes are strongly influenced by the groups people belong to or aspire to, and the more attached people are to groups the less they are persuaded by efforts that conflict with group norms. Investigate the interviewee's occupation, avocations and hobbies, superior/subordinate relationships, marital status, dependents, work experiences, war or military experiences, and geographical background because these affect our frames of reference—ways of viewing people, places, things, events, and issues. What is the person's income and monetary worth?

Culture

As you become increasingly a part of the global village, you will need to understand cultural differences that may affect your persuasive efforts. For instance, some cultures consider bribery a normal part of business, and others feel it is necessary to give gifts as part of the process. Bargaining is an essential part of persuasion in many cultures, often preceded by a relationship-building period over dinner or tea. "Time" in the United States, as the common saying goes, "is money," so we expect people to be on time or within a very few minutes of the time set. In Great Britain, however, it is considered "correct" to be 5–15 minutes late, and in Italy a person may arrive two hours late and not understand why you are upset.[10]

Values

Each culture has a set of generally accepted values—fundamental beliefs about ideal states of existence and modes of behavior that motivate us to think, feel, or act in particular ways.[11] These are the so-called hot buttons persuaders push because they are the foundations for our specific beliefs and attitudes. The following scheme of values includes those central to the American value system.

Survival Values

Preservation of health	Safety and security
Peace and tranquillity	Personal attractiveness

Social Values

Generosity and considerateness	Patriotism and loyalty
Affection and popularity	Sociality and belonging
Conformity and imitation	Cleanliness

Success Values

Ambition	Competition
Happiness	Pride, prestige, and social recognition
Accumulation and ownership	Sense of accomplishment
Material comfort and convenience	

Independence Values

Power and authority   Freedom from authority

Freedom from restraint   Equity and value of the individual

Progress Values

Education and knowledge   Change and advancement

Efficiency and practicality   Quantification

Science and secular rationality

As you read through this list of American values, recent experiences probably came to mind such as telephone calls urging you to change long-distance carriers, accept a Discover Card (or MasterCard, Visa, or American Express), contribute to the local symphony orchestra, help the starving children in Africa, purchase life insurance, or replace the windows in your home. Recall the visit to your door of two conservatively dressed young men who wanted to convert you to their religion. Appeals of these persuaders may have centered on values such as material comfort, accumulation of things, prestige, generosity, considerateness, security, belonging, peace, or value of the individual. As a persuader, then, you need to determine which values are relevant to the interviewee and both when and how to appeal to these values.

Beliefs

Political, economic, social, and religious beliefs emanate from our values. You need to determine which of these beliefs relate to a topic and proposal. If equity and value of the individual are important values, an interviewee is likely to support equal rights and opportunities for women, African-Americans, and Hispanics. If education and knowledge are important values, a person is likely to support increased funding for schools, give to college fund-raising campaigns, advocate continuing education for self and others, and be interested in books, trade magazines, and computer databases.

Although we tend to see ourselves as paragons of consistency in beliefs, we are in reality consistently inconsistent. For example, interviewees may decry excessive taxes and government spending but demand superhighways to every point on the map and emergency help if a natural disaster strikes; worry about permissiveness in American society but deny schools the right to punish their children in any manner; preach about fiscal responsibility while running up their credit cards; or advocate family values while on their third marriage. Discover the interviewee's beliefs and look for apparent exceptions, conflicts, or contradictions that might affect the interview.

Attitudes

Our attitudes are relatively enduring combinations of beliefs that predispose us to respond in particular ways to persons, organizations, places, ideas, and issues. If you are a conservative, you are likely to react in predictable ways to things you consider to be liberal. The reverse is true if you are a liberal. Your attitudes come from your beliefs that come from your cherished values.

It is necessary, then, to determine the interviewee's probable attitude toward the need or desire you will develop and the proposal you will make. Think of the interviewee's probable attitude or attitudes along an imaginary linear scale.

Strongly for			**Undecided/neutral**			**Strongly against**		
1	2	3	4	5	6	7	8	9

From what you have learned about the interviewee, where along this scale is this person's attitude likely to rest? If on positions 1 or 2, little persuasive effort may be required. If on positions 8 or 9, persuasion may be impossible beyond a small shift in feeling or thinking. If the attitude is on positions 4, 5, or 6, theoretically you should be able to alter ways of thinking, feeling, or acting with a good persuasive effort. This may not be the case, however, with an interviewee who is strongly committed to remaining neutral or undecided. I may be on the fence in a controversy and determined to stay there. Or I might have high ego involvement that might clash not with the need or desire you develop but with your proposal for meeting the need or desire. Researchers are also discovering that many people have very large latitudes of rejection. For these persons, an attitude scale might look like the following for a wide range of topics:

For			**R**	**e**	**j**	**e**	**c**	**t**	**i**	**o**	**n**
1	2	3	4		5	6		7	8		9

There is little room for change when dealing with such an interviewee. If you share this person's belief/attitude system, all you need to do is simple reinforcement. If you disagree, there is no room for compromise or change even in thinking or feeling.

Assess the interviewee's attitudes toward you, your profession, and perhaps the organization you represent. If an interviewee dislikes or distrusts you, your profession, or your organization, there is little chance of success unless you can alter your image or credibility during the interview. To create and maintain high credibility with most interviewees in American society, your appearance, manner, reputation, attainments, personality, and character should reveal a confident, poised person who is restrained and even-tempered, who exhibits physical energy, mental alertness, and knowledge, who is sincere in convictions, and who is fair, honest, sympathetic, and decisive in actions. Studies reveal that we pay more attention to highly credible interviewers and trust ones who are similar to us and appear to share important values, beliefs, and attitudes. At the same time, we expect highly credible interviewers to be wiser, braver, more knowledgeable, more experienced, and more insightful than we are.[12]

Studying the Situation

The persuasive situation is a context of persons, relationships, motives, events, time, place, and objects. Study carefully the situational atmosphere in which the interview will take place. Is this a regularly scheduled event such as a contact during an annual fund-raising campaign, the recruiting season, periodic sales meeting, or political campaign? Is this an urgent meeting because of an accident, illness, threat of bankruptcy, or

photo by Tim Ferguson/Photo Edit

The persuasive situation is a total context of persons, relationships, events, time, place, objects, and seating arrangement.

mechanical breakdown? Is it a moment of opportunity for you or the other party? Is there a danger that must be addressed? Is it a major event for one or both parties or merely routine? Will the atmosphere be hostile, friendly, ambivalent, or apathetic? Will you be in a superior or subordinate relationship?

Timing is often critical in persuasive interviews. For instance, a husband or wife may wait until after an annual bonus to discuss building a new home. What events have preceded this interview such as earlier interviews with this party, interviewee experiences with other members of your organization, and visits from your competitors? Few of us want to be the fourth employee of the day to ask for a raise or to request a raise from an employer who has just discovered a serious financial decline for the previous quarter. Certain times of the year (vacation time, tax time, Christmas season, back-to-school time in August) are great for some interviewers and terrible for others.

Consider carefully the physical setting in which the interview will take place. What will be the size of the room, furniture arrangement, seating, noise level, heat, and lighting? Try to provide for privacy and to control interruptions, especially telephone calls. Make an appointment if possible because not only is it often difficult to guess how much time an interview will take, but this may allow you to arrange or reserve a suitable physical setting. Will you be the host (the interview is in your office or residence); a guest (the interview is in the interviewee's place of business or residence); or on neutral ground (a conference room, restaurant, hotel, club)? If selling life insurance, for example, you might prefer to meet in the interviewee's home, surrounded by family. If selling business insurance, you might prefer to meet in the interviewee's place of business. If I am trying to recruit you for my university, I would prefer to get you on campus during a beautiful day when everything is green and in bloom and perhaps following a great sports victory.

Outside Forces

As you prepare for the interview, consider the outside forces that may affect the way you conduct the interview. These could be organizational or professional guidelines that prescribe how you must conduct persuasive interviews, appeals and arguments you can and cannot make, or authority you have in developing or proposing solutions. Also, consider the outside influences that may affect the interviewee. For example, if you are trying to convince a friend to enroll in the college you are attending, realize that others might be trying to convince that same person, the interviewee, to go to another college or different type of college. Family members may want the interviewee to attend a college that is closer to home. A significant other might want the interviewee to get a job instead of going to college. In another situation, an interviewee may want to purchase a Honda Prelude but associates are pressuring the person to "buy American." Awareness of outside influences on you and the other party may determine how you open an interview, the strategy you choose, the language you use, the arguments and evidence you select, and the courses of action you propose.

Determining Your Purpose

Only after investigating the topic, analyzing the interviewee, studying the situation, and weighing potential outside forces are you ready to determine your purpose for *this* interview. If you know the interviewee will be a hard sell because of a value/belief/attitude system, then your purpose may be only to affect thinking or feeling in minor ways. Just to get the interviewee to think about an issue or to admit there might be a problem may be a major success for a first interview. Later interviews might move the interviewee toward some significant change or action. On the other hand, if the interviewee walks into your office and tells you he or she wants a new VCR and large-screen television and is very interested in the brands you carry, you can move quickly through need/desire to solutions with a good chance of making a sale.

Be realistic in the goals you set for each interview. Be aware that major changes often come in increments and a series of interviews, not a one-shot effort. And do not give up too quickly or assume after an interview that an interviewee is not interested or will not change. We have been amazed how often salespersons have not followed up on initial efforts even when we expressed interest in their ideas, products, or services. At the same time, the old "Don't take no for an answer" adage can result in long-term ill effects for you, your organization, and others in your profession. Know when to stop.

2. Selecting Strategies

Once you have completed your homework and analyzed the interviewee and situation carefully, you are now ready to select one or more strategies for your interview. Theorists during the past half-century have developed a number of theories both to explain how persuasion comes about and to prescribe how persuaders might bring about changes in thinking, feeling, and acting. We know that most Americans consider theories to be obscure, esoteric concepts with little practical value. In fact, theories are simply efforts to explain complex human activities such as persuasion, often through careful observation of what happens in the real world. Let's think of theories as strategies and look briefly at several of them developed during the past few decades that are particularly useful in persuasive interviews.

Identification Theory

Kenneth Burke, arguably the leading rhetorical theorist of the twentieth century, claims that people persuade by *identifying* with their audience. We must strive to establish that we are consubstantially or substantially the same as the interviewee. The overlapping circles representing the interview parties in the model developed in Chapter 2 is based on Burke's notion that to communicate or persuade, we must talk the other party's language "with speech, gesture, tonality, order, image, attitude, *identifying*" our ways with theirs.[13] This is a common ground approach to persuasion.

There are several ways you can identify with a persuadee.[14] First, you may establish common ground by *associating* yourself with groups to which you both belong (National Rifle Association, Methodist Church, Libertarian Party, Elks Club), common cultural heritage (Greek, Hispanic, Polynesian Islands), programs you support (Habitat for Humanity, United Negro College Fund, Women's Shelter, Toys for Tots), or regional identification (southerner, easterner, midwesterner). You can employ the reverse of this tactic by *disassociating* yourself from groups, cultures, programs, and regions the interviewee opposes or is separated from. Second, you may identify through physical appearance, dress, hairstyle, and makeup. Third, share language with the interviewee, particularly professional jargon, slang, colloquialisms, and in-group words and phrases. Fourth, select content and appeal to values with which the interviewee identifies. And fifth, wear visual symbols you share with the interviewee such as items of clothing, political buttons, a cross, or Star of David. For these identification tactics to be effective, the interviewee must perceive commonality with you, not one you are trying to create for persuasive effect. Imagine a New Englander trying to appear and act like a Texan, a Texan trying to act like a Japanese, or a Japanese trying to act like a midwesterner.

Balance/Consistency Theory

Balance and consistency theories are based on the belief that human beings strive for a harmonious existence with self (values, beliefs, and attitudes) and that we experience psychological discomfort (dissonance) when aspects of our existence seem inconsistent or unbalanced.[15] We may experience source-proposition conflict when we like a person but detest his or her position on an issue or dislike a person but favor his or her product or service. We may experience attitude-attitude conflict when we oppose government involvement in our lives but want the government to outlaw abortion, require prayer in the public schools, and control violence and sex on television. We may experience perception-perception conflict when see Miami or New York as great places to vacation but dangerous for tourists. And we may experience a behavior-attitude conflict when we believe strongly in law and order but break the speed limits, sneak a few beers into the residence hall against college rules, or park illegally when we go shopping.

As a persuader, you may create psychological discomfort (dissonance) by attacking a source or pointing out attitude, perception, and behavioral conflicts. Then you show how the interviewee can bring these inconsistencies into balance by providing changes in sources, attitudes, perceptions, and behaviors. If you detect that an interviewee is experiencing psychological discomfort, you may bring about balance or consistency by helping the interviewee to see no inconsistency, perceive the inconsistency as insignificant, or tolerate the inconsistency. You may attack the source of the unbalance, provide social support, or offer supportive evidence.

Inoculation Theory

Inoculation theory is based on the belief that it is often more effective to prevent undesired persuasive effects from occurring than to try damage control afterward.[16] For instance, a few years ago one of the authors received a telephone call in late winter from his lawn care service. The caller warned the author of the unethical persuasive efforts of a new competitor in the area. The competitor was calling the original service's old customers with such comments as "Can we take care of your lawn again this year?" or offering ridiculously low prices for care they could not provide. The persuader hoped his call, which identified specific tactics, would keep the author from being taken in.

Police officers, building contractors, health care providers, and councils on the aging call upon people to inoculate or immunize them against persuasive efforts. Their tactic is to *forewarn* interviewees. Sometimes the interviewer will expose the interviewee to small doses of a potential persuader's language, arguments, and evidence so the interviewee can resist the effort. Or the interviewer might provide arguments and evidence the interviewee may use to mount an effective countereffort if confronted by an interviewer against which he or she is being immunized.

Forced or Induced Compliance Theory

According to forced or induced compliance theory, you can change interviewees thinking, feelings, or acting by forcing or inducing them to engage in activities counter to their values, beliefs, and attitudes.[17] Participation in counteractivities may trigger self-persuasion. It is important that you apply enough pressure so interviewees will comply with your request without feeling they have no choice. If they feel coerced, they are unlikely to change thinking, feeling, or acting.

There are a variety of ways to force or induce compliance. You might induce an interviewee to espouse a belief or attitude counter to what he or she holds so the person comes to see your point of view. You might induce an interviewee to take part in an activity to which he or she is unaccustomed or unattracted, such as hunting, taking part in a survey, or making fund-raising calls. You might induce an interviewee to play a role opposite of what he or she usually plays. The person becomes the employer instead of the applicant, the sales person instead of the customer, or interviewee instead of performance interviewer. Or you might induce the person to take part in an activity in order to receive a reward or avoid a punishment. We encounter such situations when a company offers bargains on products or services, an organization offers to give us a percentage of funds we raise for our local organization, or a government agency or college tells us how we can avoid a penalty by paying our taxes or tuition by an early date.

Psychological Reactance Theory

According to psychological reactance theory, we react negatively when someone threatens to restrict or does restrict a behavior we want to engage in.[18] We may come to value the restricted behavior more and want to engage in it more than we normally do, such as not being allowed to have a car on campus as a first-year student. We may devalue alternatives because we feel we are stuck with them instead of our preferred choice. And we often resent the restricting agent.

Books, movies, videos, and so-called assault weapons become more desirable when they are censored or outlawed. Many organizations produce limited editions of books, stamps, coins, and cars to enhance demand for them. Tickets to the NCAA basketball Final Four become of great value because they are scarce. We may be in favor of giving to the United Way campaign or joining our athletic booster club until we feel we are being forced to do so. We resent laws banning smoking or requiring us to buckle up in our cars, even though they may save our lives, because we are being forced to stop doing one and start doing the other. A person who owns several apartment buildings near one of the author's campus uses psychological reactance theory when he tries to persuade students to leave the residence halls and rent one of his apartments. He reminds them of onerous residence hall rules and dictatorial counselors that do not exist in his apartment complexes: counselors snooping into rooms or affairs; bans on alcoholic beverages, parties, and members of the opposite sex in rooms overnight; enforced quiet hours; and locked doors after midnight. "Come to one of my apartments," he in essence tells students, "and be free of oppressive rules and enforcers."

3. Opening the Interview

With homework completed and strategies selected, structure the interview to fit the interviewee and the situation. A carefully researched, planned, and structured interview is important, but you must remain flexible, ready for the unexpected, and cautious about assumptions concerning the interviewee and possible or likely reactions.

Design your opening to gain attention and interest, establish rapport, and motivate the interviewee to take part. The major advantage of the interview over public or mass persuasion is the opportunity to tailor your message to a single person or party. Therefore, it is important that you adapt the opening to each interviewee and setting, resisting the temptation to rely on a standard or traditional formula that is inappropriate or minimally appropriate for a particular interviewee. Some writers estimate that "roughly 75 percent" of all sales representatives "fail in the attention step."[19] Think of the openings in the numerous sales calls made to your home and how you reacted. Persuaders trying to interest you in yet another credit card are trained to recite a prescribed opening regardless of your age, sex, income, background, or level of interest. You may detest credit cards or have 20 of them; it makes no difference to the persuader. Little wonder that only about one in a hundred of these cold calls to our homes is successful; most do not get past the opening sentence or two.

Review the opening techniques and principles discussed in Chapter 3. Select techniques most suitable for this interviewee and situation. Begin with a warm greeting and use the interviewee's name. If the person is a stranger, do not make your greeting sound like a question: "Good evening, Ms. Ahern?" This suggests that you are unsure of the person's name or identity, unsure of yourself, and not well prepared. If you know the interviewee well enough and both the situation and your relationship warrant it, use the person's first name. As a general rule, do not greet a stranger, a superior, or a person in a formal setting by first name or nickname unless this person tells you to do so. On the other hand, being both somewhat formal and somewhat informal at the same time has its hazards. If, for example, callers greet the authors of this text as Charles or William, this is a dead giveaway that they know neither of us well enough to use our first names.

It may be necessary to introduce yourself (name, position, title, background), your organization (name, location, nature, history, products, services), and the purpose of the interview. Orientation is essential when there is no relational history between parties and no appointment or arrangements are made ahead of time. You may make *sincere* personal inquiries about family or mutual friends or small talk about the weather, sports, highway construction, or campus facilities. Do not prolong this rapport stage. Be conscious of the interviewee's situation and preferences. If a person replies immediately after the greeting, "What can I do for you?" this probably signals that the person wants to get down to business or has limited time for the interview.

Cultures differ in amount of small talk and socializing before getting to the business at hand. Most Americans want to get to the point and get the job done, preferring that people say what they mean. Japanese and other cultures desire to get acquainted, to follow interaction rituals, and to go slower on making commitments and decisions.[20] Do not prolong the rapport stage, but be sure it is appropriate. Involve the interviewee from the start so the person will play an active role throughout the interaction. Remember, persuasion is not something you do *to* a person but *with* a person. If you seem to prefer to do the talking, interviewees may remain silent and let you do so, but you will miss out on important feedback and input. And, once again, be cognizant of cultural differences. American persuaders and persuadees, particularly males, tend to take turns unevenly during interactions and to speak at length during each turn, whereas Japanese and others tend to take turns evenly and make shorter statements.

When the opening ends, both parties should be aware of the degrees of interest and warmth that will pervade the interview. They should understand the agenda, how they will share control, and the interest levels of both parties. An inappropriate opening may mislead one or both parties or create a hostile climate when unnecessary.

4. Creating a Need or Desire

The first step in creating a need or desire is to select three or four points that develop a solid case for a need or desire to change thinking, feeling, or acting. The strategy or strategies you have selected will control *how* you create this need or desire.

Selecting and Developing Main Points

The three or four points you select should maintain interest and attention, enhance comprehension, and ensure retention. Do not rely on a single reason or point. The interviewee may see little urgency in a problem that seems so simple or unidimensional or find it relatively easy to attack or reject only one point. Some research indicates that more points also enhance the persistence of persuasive effects over time.[21] On the other hand, six or eight points are likely either to make an interview too long or very superficial as you try to rush through multiple points and on to your proposed solution. An interviewee may also become overloaded with information and complex arguments and become confused or bored.

Decades of research have focused on where to place your strongest, second strongest, and weakest arguments in persuasive efforts. For instance, surveys of high school students in the process of selecting a college or university reveal seven major factors in rank order of importance: major or fields of study, tuition costs, financial aid availability, quality and academic reputation, distance from home and location, size of student body, and social atmosphere. Since major or fields of study is most important, should you place it first, in the middle, or at the end of the need stage? Unfortunately, research has resulted in a theoretical standoff—the beginning and the end seem to be about equal in effect. As a general rule, however, begin with your strongest point first because (1) you have determined that it is most central to *this interviewee's* needs or desires, (2) it is tied to important values, (3) you have solid evidence to support it, (4) you do not want it to get lost in the middle of the interview, (5) you may be able to move to the criteria/solution phases sooner than expected and want the interviewee exposed to your strongest argument, and (6) the interviewee may terminate the interview before you can present all of your points.

Develop one point at a time. Explain the point thoroughly. Provide sufficient evidence that is factually based, authoritative, recent, and well documented. Use a variety of evidence (examples, stories, authority, statistics, comparisons, definitions) so the interviewee is neither buried under an avalanche of figures nor bored with one story after another. Use a blend of logic and emotion that includes the values, beliefs, and attitudes most important to this interviewee. Encourage interaction and interviewee involvement. This is, after all, an interview, not a speech. *The more actively involved the interviewee is, the more likely you are to persuade.* Stress how each point affects this interviewee's needs and desires. Do not go to your next point until you have obtained at least tentative agreement from the interviewee. With one point developed and agreed upon, move to point two, then three, and so on. Do not rush through a point or jump to the next one if the interviewee raises objections or poses questions. Move on when the interviewee seems ready to do so. Be patient and persistent.

Developing Reasons into Acceptable Patterns

It is not enough to know which reasons or points to develop in an interview and in what order to present them. Know how to develop them into valid, acceptable patterns that coincide with the strategy selected. The most effective interview is a carefully crafted blend of the logical and the psychological. You have choices to make.

Reasoning from Accepted Belief, Assumption, or Proposition

Reasoning from accepted belief, assumption, or proposition involves three stated or implied assertions. For instance, a health care interviewer might argue this way:

> (1) Persons with high cholesterol levels have a significantly greater chance of having heart attacks and strokes; (2) your cholesterol level is very high, in the 300 range; (3) so you are a prime prospect for a heart attack or stroke.

The strength of this pattern rests on the strength and acceptance of the belief, assumption, or proposition on which it is based, assertion 1. If the interviewee does not believe that high cholesterol poses a great risk of heart attack or stroke, the person will not accept your reasoning. In most interviews, the interviewer seldom states all three parts of this pattern explicitly but allows the interviewee to supply one or more parts. A physician might say, "Your cholesterol level is very high, so you have a significant chance of having a heart attack or stroke" or "High cholesterol level means a significant risk of heart attack or stroke; your cholesterol level is very high." The patient will supply the missing reasons. The belief, assumption, or proposition is critical in this pattern because if interviewees reject the premises, they reject the conclusions.

Reasoning from Condition

Reasoning from condition is based on the assertion that if something does or does not happen, something else will or will not happen. You might reason:

> If we don't begin to control our spending on food and entertainment, we're not going to have enough money for the rent payment. I don't see us doing this, so I think we're going to be in real trouble with the rental agency.

The stated or implied condition is important to the strength of conditional reasoning. If, for instance, there is a real possibility of reducing spending, the interviewee is likely to reject your conclusion. Weigh conditions carefully and support them effectively.

Reasoning from Two Choices

Reasoning from two choices is based on the assertion that there are only two possible proposals. You remove one proposal or course of action by establishing that it does not meet major criteria or will not work and conclude the obvious. For example,

> I think you have only two choices of computer systems, the Data 5000 and the clone by Magenta, the 3.5. The Data 5000 is significantly above your budget, so you've got to go with the Magenta 3.5.

Your task is, first, to convince the interviewee that only two possibilities exist and, second, to remove one of the possibilities so your point remains.

Reasoning from Example

Reasoning from example is a generalization about a whole class of people, places, or things based on a sampling from the class. Recall the principles and methods of sampling discussed in Chapter 6. For instance, a travel agent might try to convince you to select Glacier Tours for your Alaska vacation by arguing

> Of the more than one hundred people I have booked for this vacation package with Glacier Tours during the past year, 98 percent have rated it excellent and said they would do it again.

The agent is reasoning that you are likely to be among this large percentage of satisfied vacationers.

Reasoning from Cause-Effect

Reasoning from cause-effect is related to reasoning from example because interviewers often use a sample as proof of a causal relationship. For instance,

> A study of 25 date rapes on campus revealed that 22 of the women and their
> assailants had been drinking prior to the assaults. It's obvious that alcohol causes
> most date rapes.

This reasoning relies on your ability to show the designated cause to be the only or the
major cause of the effect you are discussing. There tend to be numerous causes.

Reasoning from Facts

Reasoning from facts is offering the conclusion that seems to explain best the evidence
that is available—the best accounting for a body of facts. For instance, a campaign
worker might reason,

> Campaign workers are sending in good reports; our candidate is getting good
> turnouts for speeches; fund-raising is better than expected; the economy is
> excellent; there is general support for incumbents this year; and the polls show us
> five points ahead. I'm sure we will win.

The amount and type of evidence you can gather makes a conclusion more or less convincing to interviewees, much like the whodunits we see on television.

Reasoning from Analogy

Reasoning from analogy occurs when you point out that two things have a number of
characteristics in common and then draw a conclusion about one of them. For example,
a minister might argue,

> Five years ago I worked with a couple that reminds me very much of you two. Like
> you, they both had demanding careers; they were apart for lengthy periods each
> year; they disagreed on child care for their two children; and they felt they had
> grown apart. Today they have worked out these differences and put their careers
> and family life in proper perspective. They have the kind of strong marriage you
> can have.

Analogical reasoning is based on the assumption that if two things have a great deal in
common, they share other important traits.

Adapting to the Interviewee

Tailor each part of the persuasive interview to the values, beliefs, and attitudes of the interviewee. The first step is to determine the probable disposition of the interviewee, and
the second is to select tactics appropriate for that disposition. Here are a few interviewees you will encounter and how you might adapt to each.

Indecisive, Uninterested Interviewees

If an interviewee is likely to be indecisive, uninterested, or uncertain, you may have to
educate the person to see the reality and urgency of the problem, issue, or need. Use
opening techniques that get the interviewee's attention and generate interest in the seriousness of the situation. Then lead off with your strongest point and provide a variety of

evidence that informs as well as persuades and shows why the issue is of critical importance to *this* interviewee. Use probing questions to draw out feelings and perceptions, and involve the interviewee in the interaction. Avoid real or perceived pressure, but reveal the urgency of the problem and the necessity of acting now. You may use moderate fear appeals to awaken the interviewee to dangers to self, family, or friends, including appeals to values such as preservation of health, safety and security, freedom from restraint, ownership, and value of the individual. Exhibit some of the emotion (fear, pity, pride, sadness, anger) you want the interviewee to feel. And show how this person can make a difference in solving or reducing the problem or danger.

Hostile Interviewees

If you think an interviewee will be or appears to be hostile, first of all be sure your anticipation or impression is accurate. Do not mistake legitimate concerns or objections or a gruff demeanor for hostility. If a person is truly hostile, try to determine why. A *common-ground approach* in which you emphasize values, beliefs, and attitudes you share with the interviewee may avoid or reduce hostility. A *yes-but approach* begins with areas of agreement and similarity and gradually leads into points of disagreement. The strategy is to lessen hostility and disagreement later by establishing common ground early on. In a *yes-yes approach,* you hope that if you can get a party in the habit of agreeing, the party will keep on agreeing when you reach apparent disagreements. In an *implicative approach,* you do not state your purpose or intent explicitly because you fear a knee-jerk negative reaction. You hope interviewees will see the implications of what you are saying and proving, perhaps feeling they came up with the concerns and solutions. This beating-around-the-bush approach requires considerable skill; otherwise the interviewee may become confused or state angrily, "Please get to the point." Without realizing it, you have used this approach often with your parents when needing money, the car, permission to go to a distant music concert, or approval for attending a university in another state.

Regardless of common-ground approach, listen, be polite, and avoid defensiveness or anger when working with hostile interviewees. Be willing to accept minor points of disagreement and to admit your proposal is not perfect; no proposal is. Employ "shock-absorber" phrases that reduce the sting of critical questions: "That's a very good question, but . . . "; "I'm glad you brought that up"; "A lot of people feel that way, but . . . ." Hostility often results from lack of information, misinformation, or rumors, so respond with facts, expert testimony, examples, stories, and comparisons that clarify, prove, and resolve issues between parties.

Closed-Minded and Authoritarian Interviewees

A closed-minded or authoritarian interviewee tends to rely on trusted authorities and be more concerned about who supports your need and proposal than the proposal itself. Facts alone, particularly statistics, will not do the job; you must be able to show that the interviewee's accepted authorities support your persuasive efforts. The closed-minded and authoritarian person has strong, unchangeable central values and beliefs, and you must be able to identify yourself and your proposal with these values and beliefs.

Approach the persuasive interview in the normal, established way without bypassing hierarchical channels or altering prescribed methods. Authoritarians react negatively to interviewers who they feel don't belong in the situation or appear to be out of line, and they may demand censure or punishment of interviewers for appearing to violate accepted and valued norms.[22] Do not assume that a person is closed-minded or authoritarian because someone else says so or because of a few traits associated with these personalities. Be sure you know the party you are dealing with and adapt accordingly.

Skeptical Interviewees

The interviewee may be skeptical because of a low opinion of you, your profession (sales, public relations, recruiter, fund-raiser), or your organization. You might begin the interview by expressing some views the interviewee holds—a yes-but or yes-yes approach. Maintain positive nonverbal cues such as a firm handshake, good eye contact, a warm and friendly voice, and appropriate appearance and dress. If the interviewee feels you are young and inexperienced, allude tactfully to your qualifications, experiences, and training and provide substantial and authoritative evidence. Appear well prepared and experienced without bragging and avoid undue informality and a cocky, egotistical attitude. If the interviewee sees you as argumentative, avoid confrontations, attacks on the person's position, and demands. If the interviewee thinks you are a know-it-all, be careful when referring to your qualifications, experiences, and achievements.

When presenting the need and solution, use a two-sided approach that addresses counterarguments and competing proposals to appear objective and fair. Avoid appearances, actions, and approaches that stereotype you as a "typical" professor, attorney, sales representative, "bleeding-heart" social worker. If the interviewee dislikes or distrusts your organization, you might (1) distance yourself from it (without denying that you are part of it), (2) withhold the name of the organization until you have created good rapport with the interviewee, (3) explain how the organization has changed, or (4) try to improve the image of the organization. Realize that you may not be the best interviewer. Admissions directors tell us that they have high credibility with high school students through the freshman and sophomore years. After that, students become skeptical because recruiting is "their job." Juniors and seniors see professors and students at the university as more credible sources. It is time for the admissions staff to fade into the background and serve as support for more credible sources.

Shopping-Around Interviewees

Many interviewees will shop around before making a major purchase, a commitment to a church or temple, or a decision on an investment or contribution to a charity or who to vote for. This means they will face counterpersuasion from competing persuaders. When meeting with a "shopper" or an undecided interviewee, forewarn and prepare the person for these competitors. Provide the interviewee with supportive arguments and evidence and answers to questions or points certain to be raised in future encounters with others. Give small doses of the opposition's case (inoculation theory of persuasion) to show the strengths and weaknesses of both sides. When you discuss the competition, however, have your facts straight, avoid emotional comments or heavy-handed criticism, and neither overexaggerate nor oversimplify similarities/differences and advantages/disadvantages.

Develop a positive, factual, nonemotional approach that addresses the competition when necessary but dwells primarily on the strengths of your position and proposal.

Intelligent, Educated Interviewees

The highly intelligent or highly educated interviewee tends to be less persuasible because of knowledge level, critical ability, and faculty for seeing the implications behind arguments and proposals. Research indicates that such interviewees "are more likely to attend to and comprehend the message position but are less likely to yield to it."[23] For example, they are likely to see through the good guy–bad guy approach used in many sales situations, such as when the sales representative must get approval from the owner or manager for the deal he or she is trying to get *for you.* When working with highly intelligent and educated interviewees, support all of your ideas thoroughly, develop arguments logically, and present a two-sided approach that weighs both sides of issues. Minimize emotional appeals, particularly if the interviewee is neutral or initially disagrees with your position and proposal. Encourage the interviewee to ask questions, raise objections, and be an active participant.

If an interviewee is of low intelligence or education, develop a simple, one-sided approach to minimize confusion and maximize comprehension. A complex, two-sided approach and intricate arguments supported by a variety of evidence may confuse the interviewee. Use examples, stories, and comparisons rather than expert testimony and statistics, and appeal to basic emotions: anger, fear, pity, and pride. Do not determine intelligence or education on the basis of diplomas, degrees, grades, or appearance. A person may not be unintelligent but merely inexperienced or uninformed.

Asking Questions

Although you will rarely come to a persuasive interview with a schedule of questions, questions serve a variety of functions in persuasive interviews. Some sales professionals believe you should never *tell* when you can *ask* because this involves the interviewee as an *active participant* rather than a *passive recipient.* But you cannot rely solely on questions, particularly when an interviewee sees no need and has no idea of options available once a need or desire is established. Select appropriate questions for the moment and have a fairly accurate idea of how the interviewee will respond. Review the types and uses of questions discussed in Chapter 4.

Information Gathering Questions

If you have had little opportunity or success in analyzing an interviewee ahead of time, employ questions to ascertain an interviewee's background, needs, desires, values, beliefs, and attitudes. Ask questions to determine knowledge level and to draw out unstated concerns and objections. It is difficult to deal with that which is not on the table. Listen carefully to responses and probe for accuracy and details. Here are typical information gathering questions:

> How do you feel about . . . ?
> What do you know about . . . ?
> What experiences have you had with . . . ?

Verification Questions

Reflective, mirror, and clearinghouse probing questions may serve two important functions in persuasive interviews. First, they check the accuracy of your assumptions, impressions, and information obtained before and during an interview. For instance, you may assume you have answered an objection satisfactorily or gotten an agreement when you have not. And second, they verify that an interviewee understands what you are saying and grasps the significance of your evidence or points. Silence on the interviewee's part can indicate confusion or disagreement as well as understanding and agreement. Here are typical verification questions:

> As I understand it, you have . . . ?
> Does that answer your concern about . . . ?
> Are we in agreement, then, that . . . ?

Encouraging Interaction Questions

Use questions early in each interview to serve as a warm-up and tone-setting phase so that questioning, talking, and answering become natural for the interviewee. This interactive climate encourages the interviewee to play an active role in the interview. Interviewees will feel freer to ask questions and provide meaningful feedback once they have become an active part of the process and understand that you want them to. Employ questions to discover how a quiet or noncommittal interviewee is reacting. A poker-faced person may give no feedback except in response to direct questions. Here are samples of interaction questions:

> Well, what do you think?
> What are your reactions to . . . ?
> What questions do you have at this point about . . . ?

Attention and Interest Questions

Attention and interest questions are designed to keep the interviewee tuned in and alert to what you are saying. Many interviewees are busy or preoccupied with other concerns and their minds will wander from your presentation. Use interesting, challenging, and thought-provoking questions to maintain interest and attention.

> What would happen if . . . ?
> Suppose you or your wife lost your jobs tomorrow . . .
> Remember that incident when . . . ?

Agreement Questions

Employ questions to obtain small agreements that will lead to bigger agreements. For instance, getting agreement after each point should lead to agreement at the end of your need so you can move effectively to establishing criteria for solutions. Be careful, however, of asking for agreement or commitment before you have developed or supported a point thoroughly. Too many persuaders think a barrage of generalizations and claims "proves" a point or need when it does not. You may use a yes-response question (often in the form of a statement) to control the interview and lead to agreement if asked at the right time—after thorough development of one or more points and small agreements. For example,

> This certainly makes sense, doesn't it?
> This problem won't just go away, will it?
> I think you'll agree that this is the best way to . . . ?

Objection Questions

Use objection questions to respond tactfully to objections and to draw out unstated questions and objections. The goal is to get them on the table at a proper time. These questions can also discover what an interviewee knows about an issue and reveal the importance or reasons behind objections.

> I understand that cost is your major concern?
> Is that a major concern of yours?
> What bothers you most about . . . ?

Questions can be valuable tools in persuasive interviews if asked tactfully and strategically. Select the correct question for the specific moment and need. Beware of asking questions prematurely that call for agreements when you have established nothing upon which to agree. Use leading and loaded questions sparingly because interviewees might be turned off by high-pressure tactics. Do not substitute questions for substance. You are unlikely to recruit a person for your organization through questions only; you must present good reasons supported by information and evidence. You must know your topic and present a tailored need and solution.

5. Establishing Criteria

When you have presented the need, summarized your points, and gotten agreements from the interviewee, you are ready to establish criteria (requirements, standards, rules) that any solution should meet. If the interviewee is obviously ready to move into this phase of the interview before you have presented all of your points, move on. Do not talk interminably until the interviewee becomes impatient, unconvinced, or ends the interview because of frustration or lack of time. We too often experience interviewers who are determined to present their case whether we are convinced or not. Remember, the interview is not a speech, so you need not present everything you have prepared if it is unnecessary.

Establish a set of criteria with the interviewee for evaluating all possible solutions to the need or desire that you have established. This step "presupposes that, consciously or unconsciously, any persuadee evaluates a persuasive proposal in terms of the degree to which the proposal appears to meet various kinds of criteria."[24] This process comes natural to us, but we often do not write down a list of specific criteria even though we inevitably have them. For example, when selecting a university, you probably considered size, areas of study, reputation, nearness to your hometown and family, cost, housing, attractiveness and safety of the campus, friendliness of students and faculty you have met, athletic programs, and personal touches during the application process. In selecting an employment position, you may consider type of work, salary, hours, benefits, job security, advancement potential, geographical location, and fellow workers. Even when selecting a movie, you have criteria in mind such as type (comedy, horror, adventure), plot, reviews, ratings, cost, and recommendations.

As you think of criteria prior to the interview and develop them with the interviewee during the interview, realize that not all criteria are of equal importance to every interviewee. And most of us can readily rank order a long list of criteria. Admissions directors at large state universities, for instance, have found that quality of school is the most important criterion for out-of-state applicants while cost is number one and quality is number two for in-state students. If you want to enter law school or study engineering, however, you obviously will not consider universities without law schools or engineering programs. Persons undecided about majors will place other criteria higher. And the situation can influence criteria. For instance, cost may override all other criteria during economic recessions.

Establishing a set of criteria *with* the interviewee involves the interviewee in the process and shows that you are attempting to tailor your proposal to his or her needs, desires, and capabilities. The criteria phase provides a smooth transition from the need to the solution and reduces the impression that you are overly anxious to sell your point. Agreed-upon criteria enable you to build the interview on a foundation of agreements. When you move to the solution phase, criteria provide a clear and structured means of presenting and evaluating all proposals, including competing ones. They will also help you eliminate or handle objections. Eventually, criteria provide a means of closing the interview by summarizing how your proposal has met the requirements agreed upon.

6. Presenting the Solution

With a need established and criteria agreed upon, present your solution in detail.

Details and Evaluation

If you will consider more than one solution, deal with one at a time. Explain your solution in detail and use whatever visual aids might be available and appropriate: booklets and brochures, drawings and diagrams, graphs, letters, pictures, slides, computer printouts, sketch pads, swatches of materials, objects, or models. Some sources claim that interviewees remember only about 10 percent of what they hear but 50 percent of what they do and 90 percent of what they both see and do.[25] Visual aids are not reserved for speeches but are quite usable during interviews. They need not be large in size to be seen and analyzed. Try to anticipate objections either to address them in your presentation or respond as soon as the interviewee raises them. As you proceed through the solution phase, show how your proposal meets the criteria better than any other, and get agreements on its appropriateness, quality, and feasibility.

Approach the solution in a positive, constructive, and enthusiastic manner. *Believe* in what you are doing and *show* it. If you are not enthusiastic about your ideas,

photo by The Image Works

Explain your solution in detail and involve the interviewee in the process.

products, services, or organization, why should I be? Emphasize the strengths and benefits of your proposal rather than the weaknesses of the competition. Avoid negative selling unless the competition forces you to do so, a matter of self-defense. If I am thinking about purchasing a new CD player, I am likely to be more interested in the advantages of your product than the disadvantages of brand X.

Make no claims you cannot prove. Help interviewees make decisions that are best for them at this time. Encourage the interviewee to ask questions and be actively involved. Use repetition, what one writer calls the "heart of selling," to enhance understanding, aid memory, gain and maintain attention, and make the interviewee aware of what is most important.[26] Educate interviewees by informing them about options, requirements, time constraints, and new features. And be prepared to deal with misinformation and misconceptions.

Handling Objections

Nothing is more threatening to an interviewer than the thought of the interviewee raising unexpected or difficult objections. But you should encourage the interviewee to do so because most objections voice the need for more information or clarification and reveal the interviewee's concerns, fears, misunderstandings, and misinformation. You cannot address an objection if you do not hear it. Some people enjoy objecting because they see persuasive interviews as games in which interviewers and interviewees joust until a proposal is rejected, modified, or accepted. They may feel it is an essential part of their role, literally a duty to raise questions and objections. Or they may know that others (outside forces) will ask them if they challenged you strenuously—drove a hard bargain—or if they merely caved in; thus, many interviewees object to save face later. However, do not assume agreement because an interviewee does not raise overt questions or objections. Watch for nonverbal clues such as restlessness, fidgeting, poor eye contact, raised eyebrows, confused expressions, signs of boredom, or silences.

Possible objections are infinite, but the five big ones are procrastination, money, tradition, uncertain future, and need.

Procrastination

Why don't we get together again sometime?

Well, we have a lot of time left before we have to make that decision.

Let's sleep on it.

Money

We can't afford it right now.

That's a bit more than I had expected.

We still have a lot of expenses to meet this year.

Tradition

We've always done our banking with National Federal.

This is the way it's always been here.

All of my family have attended Baylor, starting with my grandfather.

Uncertain Future

I don't know what the future's going to bring.

With the economy the way it is, I'm not sure this is the time to act.

My job situation is a bit shaky with all of the mergers and downsizing.

Need

I already belong to one professional organization.

My computer is working just fine.

I know that the center city has a crime problem, but that doesn't affect us.

The first step in handling objections is to *anticipate* them and plan how you might respond. Planning eliminates the surprise and reduces the danger of being put on the spot, resulting in no answer or a poor answer. The second step is to *listen* carefully, completely, and objectively. Do not assume you understand the other person's point or concern until you have heard it. The third step is to *clarify* the objection, making sure you understand exactly what it is and its importance before you respond. Did the interviewee raise the objection merely out of curiosity or because it is critical to agreement? The fourth step is to *respond* appropriately, diplomatically, tactfully, and professionally. Do not become defensive or hostile. And do not treat an objection as if it is too frivolous for serious reply. *If it's serious to the interviewee, it's serious.*

There are four common strategies for handling objections: minimize, capitalize, deny, and confirm. You may combine one or more for effectiveness.

Minimize the Objection

You can minimize an objection by restating it to make it sound less important or by comparing it to other weightier matters. Providing evidence may also help reduce the importance of the objection, as in the following example:

1. **Interviewee:** We've always thought it would be great to live in the downtown of a large city in a loft like this. Quite frankly, we're afraid of the crime rate in downtown areas. The newspapers are full of stories about robberies, assaults, shootings, and break-ins in these areas.

2. **Interviewer:** That was generally true a few years ago, but crime is declining in the centers of cities and spreading to outlying areas where there are fewer police officers

and residents have a false sense of security. For example, in this area during the past three years, robberies and theft have declined by 23 percent, assaults by 43 percent, and shootings have all but disappeared. At the same time, in the outlying areas of this city, robberies and theft have increased by 27 percent, assaults by 12 percent, and shootings by 15 percent.

Capitalize on the Objection

You can capitalize on an objection by using it to clarify your own points, review the proposal's advantages, offer more evidence, or isolate the motive behind the objection. In essence, you try to convert a perceived disadvantage into an advantage.

1. **Interviewee:** I'm reluctant to buy more stocks now when the market seems too shaky and the long boom period about to end.

2. **Interviewer:** I'm getting that comment a lot from investors like you, but now is a good time to invest. The market has adjusted from its all-time high of a few months ago, and many sound stocks are lower than they should be. Investment now will pay big dividends in a few years.

Deny an Objection

You can deny an objection directly or indirectly by offering new or more accurate information, by introducing new features of your proposal, or by showing how circumstances have changed. You cannot deny an objection, however, by merely denying it. Too often we hear people say "That's just not so" or "Things have changed" without offering any proof to support these denials. If you say it isn't so, prove it. Here is an example of denying an objection:

1. **Interviewee:** Well, I've heard that HMO health plans tell you which physician you must go to and don't cover specialists you might need.

2. **Interviewer:** The first rumor is only partially true. You do need to select a physician from our lengthy list of cooperating physicians, but we never tell you which one to pick. Here's the current list of GPs. And second, your HMO physician, like all physicians, must refer you to a specialist because most specialists accept only referrals. Our HMO plan covers specialists.

Confirm an Objection

You may confirm an objection by agreeing with the interviewee or by responding and then asking if you have relieved the concern. It is better to be honest and admit problems than to offer weak defenses. Do not pretend there are no real objections, because interviewees consider their objections to be quite real. Here is a confirmation tactic:

1. **Interviewee:** But $10,000 is a lot of money for a cruise.

2. **Interviewer:** Yes it is. It's a first-class cruise on the top-rated line with the largest rooms, greatest variety of entertainment, and most ports of call. As the old saying goes, you get what you pay for. You get what you pay for on this cruise.

7. Closing the Interview

Approach the closing of the interview positively and confidently, not with a "You don't really want to do this, do you" or "You're not going join us, are you" attitude. Do not pressure the interviewee or appear too anxious for a final agreement. Interviewees hesitate to close, fearing they will make a wrong decision. And many interviewers hesitate to close, fearing they will fail to persuade. Be persistent, and remember that the average "sale" takes place after the fifth request or contact. Hesitation to ask for the sale is a major cause of failure cited by many sales professionals.

The closing of the persuasive interview usually consists of three stages: (1) trial closing, (2) filling out the contract or agreement, and (3) leave-taking.

Trial Closing

Begin the closing as soon as it seems appropriate. Do not continue talking if the interviewee is sold on your proposal. You may talk yourself out of an agreement by giving the interviewee more opportunities to ask questions, raise objections, and generate reasons not to be persuaded after all.

Be perceptive as you approach the end of the solution phase of the interview. Watch and listen for verbal and nonverbal cues that the interviewee is moving toward a decision. Verbal cues include questions and statements such as,

> How soon will these apartments be ready?
>
> This is an impressive system.
>
> What you say makes a lot of sense.

Nonverbal cues may include enthusiastic vocal expressions, nods, and smiles. Two interviewees may exchange glances at one another as if to verify interest or agreement or begin handling brochures, models, or pictures.

Ask yes-response and leading questions such as the following to verify that the interviewee is ready to close:

> This is an ideal time to upgrade, isn't it?
>
> You can see why so many golfers are joining our club?
>
> The cost seems very reasonable, don't you think?

After you ask a trial closing question, be quiet! Avoid any semblance of pressure and give the interviewee time to think and self-persuade. Your silence communicates confidence in the interviewee and gives the person an opportunity to ask questions or raise objections not yet brought out or answered fully. Often interviewees just want final verification that they are doing the right thing.

If you get a no to your trial-closing question, try to discover why. Perhaps you need to review the criteria, compare advantages and disadvantages of acting now, or provide more information. Above all, get the cause for resistance out in the open where you can deal with it. Often an interviewee is simply not ready to act. Perhaps fear of possible consequences and how others (outside forces) will react overcomes the need or desire. If you get a yes to your trial-closing question, ask a question that will lead into the contract or agreement stage:

photo by Bob Daemmrich/Stock Boston

▨ *The contract or agreement stage is critical because the interviewee knows a commitment is imminent.*

Would you like to make your donation now? I'm sure it would be a load off your shoulders to get this settled before . . . .

We can get you signed up right now and . . . .

Contract or Agreement

Once you have completed a successful trial closing, you are ready for the contract or agreement stage. This is a critical time in the persuasive interview because the interviewee knows the closing, and with it a commitment, is coming and may be frightened or anxious. Be natural and pleasant, and maintain good communication. Review the closing techniques and principles discussed in Chapter 3. You can use a variety of closing techniques during the contract or agreement stage.

In an *assumptive close,* you address part of the agreement with the phrase "I assume that . . . ." For instance, you might say, "I assume from our previous discussion that you prefer . . . ." In a *summary close,* you may summarize the need, criteria, or agreements made earlier as a basis for decisions. In an *elimination of a single objection close,* you respond to the single objection that stands in the way of an agreement, such as, "Well, I can understand your reluctance to leave a position you're comfortable with, but think of the advancement opportunities you will have with a young company that is growing and changing." In an *either-or close,* you try to limit the interviewee's choices to a manageable number, usually two, and then show that the solution you advocate has the most advantages and the fewest disadvantages, that it meets the agreed-upon criteria best. In an *I'll think it over close,* you acknowledge the interviewee's desire to think about a decision, to sleep on it, but try to discover the level of interest and why the interviewee is hesitating. You might say,

That's a good idea. This is a major step for you in your career, and I think you would be wise to make sure it's what you want. We want you on our team.

Just to clarify things, which aspect of this proposal do you want to think over?

With the urgent need of action and a proposal that you agree meets all of the criteria, how would more time help your decision?

In a *sense of urgency close,* you stress why an interviewee should act now:

This 2.6 percent finance rate will end soon.

With a possible strike looming, we may not have many of this model to choose from in a few weeks.

I understand that you want to consider other offers, but we must have your decision
by February 15.

And in a *price close*, you stress the savings possible or the bottom line of the offer:

This is the lowest price we've ever had on a 12-inch compound miter, slider saw
that normally sells for $800.
The very best offer I can make is a $35,000 annual salary and 10 percent in
commissions.

Leave-Taking

When the contract or agreement is completed, no agreement or contract can be reached,
or another interview will be necessary, conclude pleasantly and positively. Do not make
the leave-taking phase abrupt or curt. You may undo the rapport and trust you worked
so hard to establish by communicating to interviewees that they were of value only as
long as they were potential customers. The verbal and nonverbal leave-taking techniques discussed in Chapter 3 may be adapted or combined to suit each interview.
Above all, be sincere and honest in the final closing phase. And make no promises you
cannot or will not keep because of personal or authority limitations, organizational policies, laws, or time constraints.

Summary Outline

The following outline summarizes the various elements in the structure of a persuasive interview that
covers both need/desire and solution.

I. Opening the interview
   A. Select the most appropriate techniques from Chapter 3.
   B. Establish rapport according to relationship and situation.
   C. Provide appropriate orientation.

II. Creating a need or desire
   A. Provide an appropriate statement of purpose, need, or problem.
   B. Present a point-by-point development of reasons, causes, or aspects of
      the need or problem.
      1. Provide a variety of evidence and appeals to values, beliefs, and
         attitudes.
      2. Involve the interviewee in the discussion of each point.
      3. Point out how the interviewee is involved and must be concerned.
      4. Summarize the point and get at least a tentative agreement before
         moving to the next point.
   C. Summarize the need or problem and get overt agreements from the
      interviewee.

III. Establishing criteria
   A. Present the criteria you have in mind, explaining briefly the rationale
      and importance of each criterion.

   B. Encourage the interviewee to add criteria.

   C. Involve the interviewee in the discussion of criteria.

   D. Summarize and get agreement on all criteria.

 IV. Presenting the solution

   A. Present one solution at a time.

    1. Explain the solution in detail using visual aids when possible.

    2. Evaluate the solution using agreed-upon criteria.

   B. Respond to anticipated and vocalized objections.

   C. Get agreement on the appropriateness, quality, and feasibility of the preferred solution.

 V. Closing the interview

   A. Begin a trial closing as soon as it seems appropriate to do so.

   B. When the trial closing is successful, move to a contract or agreement with the interviewee.

   C. Use appropriate leave-taking techniques discussed in this chapter and Chapter 3.

Not all parts of an outline need be developed for every interview. For instance, if an interviewee agrees with the need or problem prior to the interview, you may summarize the need in the opening and move directly to criteria. An interviewee, for instance, may see the need for new divorce laws, a more powerful computer, health insurance, or more cost-efficient schools but not agree with any proposed solution or your proposed solution. Or an interviewee may feel any move now is impossible because of financial or other constraints; feasibility would be the central concern of this interview, not need or a specific proposal.

In other persuasive situations, the interviewee may like your proposal but see no need to take action at this time: The computer is still working, business is still good, no serious health problem has occurred, or retirement is still decades away. You would devote nearly all the time in your interviews with such persons to establishing urgent needs or desires. The point to remember is that you must know the interviewee and the situation well enough to design the interview accordingly. Be flexible and realistic. There is no set pattern that you must always follow.

The Interviewee in the Persuasive Interview

We have focused on your role as persuasive interviewer, but you are often in the role of interviewee. You cannot afford to be passive because the result will usually be important to you, your family, your associates, or your organization. A good offense is the best defense in persuasive interviews, so be an active and critical *participant.*

Ethical Responsibilities

You have ethical responsibilities in persuasive interviews. Too often we are more interested in quick fixes, good deals, good news, and something-for-nothing results than detailed interviews that thoroughly analyze needs, establish criteria, and weigh a number of solutions. The outcomes range from poor decisions to outright fraud. As the wise old saying goes, If an offer sounds too good to be true, it probably is. Con artists would disappear if all of us learned their tactics and played the role of critical consumer. Here are some ethical guidelines for interviewees.

First, don't be gullible. You are responsible for a reasoned skepticism about assertions, claims, and promises. If a product is far cheaper than competing products, normal and established channels are being bypassed, or outrageous claims are being made, it is not just the persuader's fault if you are taken in. You share in this responsibility. Scams work well because we are usually willing accomplices, often because of greed or the human desire to get something for nothing. Do not assume that appearance equals credibility because anyone can be neat and clean, wear a nice suit, appear sincere, and seem to be a lot like us.

Second, be an active participant in the interview. Provide thorough feedback to persuaders so they clearly understand your needs, limitations, and perception of what is taking place and being agreed to. Ask insightful and challenging questions. Raise critical objections and demand responses backed up by solid proof.

Third, do not make instant or unreasoned judgments for or against people, ideas, and proposals. Listen, question, analyze and then decide whether to accept or reject a person, idea, or proposal. Research indicates that if we like the interviewer, we tend to assume the proposal is logical and acceptable; that if a claim seems to agree with our values, beliefs, and attitudes, we will accept it regardless of how it was reached; that the *appearance* of logic or reasoning is often more important than the *substance* of it; and that we often place biased sources ahead of unbiased sources and see no difference between supermarket tabloids and the *Wall Street Journal* or *New York Times*. Obviously, we are not very good at analyzing and judging many persuasive efforts.

Tricks of the Trade

Many persuasive interviewers are aware of our inability or unwillingness to listen, think, and analyze. They know that appearances are often more important than substance, so they rely upon tactics that have always been with us. You need to be aware of these so you can recognize them and make informed decisions.

Illogical Reasoning

Earlier we identified patterns of reasoning interviewers might use to develop main points. Nearly all of these have corresponding patterns designed to short-circuit the reasoning process. The *bifurcation* tactic attempts to polarize situations, issues, or persons into only two possibilities or sides. "You're either with us or against us" is a common bifurcation tactic. We hear persuaders lump us into one of two camps nearly everyday as we are allegedly either liberal or conservative, Democrat or Republican, progun or antigun, prodevelopment or antidevelopment, proenvironment or antienvironment. Other options and degrees are ignored. Do you agree that there are only two options? If you do, do you agree with the discarding of the targeted option?

The *post hoc or scrambling cause-effect* tactic argues simplistically that since B followed A, A must have caused B. One alleged cause brought about the effect in question. For instance, "I got the flu right after I got a flu shot last year, so the shot caused the flu" or "I had trouble with my computer after I let my roommate use it, so she did something to it." Do you believe this is the only cause, the major cause, or merely a possible cause? Is coincidence being confused with cause-effect? What evidence does the interviewer provide to link the alleged cause with the effect?

The *hasty generalization* tactic generalizes to a whole group of people, places, or things from only one or a few examples. We use this tactic, for instance, when we generalize that all people at Fitzwater Consulting are jerks just because the person from Fitzwater we spoke to was a jerk. Have enough examples been considered? How, when, and where were they selected? Are these typical examples or very unusual ones? Recall the sampling guidelines discussed in Chapter 6.

The *simple comparison* tactic points out a few similarities between two people, places, or things and draws conclusions about one or the other from this superficial comparison. An interviewer might compare two persons of Italian descent, both female, same age, and same profession, and then claim they must be of the same temperament, have similar attitudes toward men, prefer certain products, or share the same economic or religious beliefs. In this case, how similar are these two people? How different are they? Which points of similarity are shared with you and which are not? For instance, one might be a second- or third-generation Italian-American and the other a recent immigrant; one might be Catholic and the other Presbyterian

When using the *thin entering wedge* tactic (the domino effect or the slippery slope), an interviewer argues that one decision, action, or law after another is leading toward some sort of disaster. Talk to a person who is against abortion, gun control, or censorship and you are likely to hear how abortion is a first step toward eliminating the right to life for other groups, how registration of handguns or outlawing of assault weapons is yet another step toward outlawing and confiscating all guns, or how censorship of books in school libraries is a dangerous step toward censoring all reading materials. Look for evidence of a string of actions that is tipping dominos, wedging into something, or sliding down a dangerous slope. Is an event or action significant enough or related to others in ways that warrant alarm? Is there evidence of intent by perpetrators to make this one victory toward winning a war against or for something?

Identification Tactics

There are a variety of tactics that attempt to link the interviewer with the interviewee. In *overt identification,* an interviewer literally says "I'm one of you" by expressing a belief, exhibiting a similar appearance, using shared language and nonverbal actions, and referring to similar backgrounds and cultures. For instance, a person recruiting members for a new country club might comment, "Hey, I was at Penn State about the same time and grew up near Reading." Ask yourself if these alleged similarities are real or merely claimed for a persuasive effect.

Interviewers use *association* to establish a connection between their proposals and an object, person, organization, cause, or idea that interviewees revere. A proposal may be supported by a church or professional organization to which you belong or is endorsed by a high-credibility source such as an astronaut, a distinguished physician, a well-known researcher, or a highly respected legal authority. Be certain that the connection is real and not merely claimed and that it signifies a major endorsement and not simply lack of opposition. Is the interviewer sincere or merely opportunistic like the politician who wears a flag in his lapel when campaigning among veterans but a Star of David when campaigning in a Jewish neighborhood? Many interviewers join all sorts of organizations merely so they can cite these associations, sort of like college students who join organizations and honoraries for "resume hits."

Interviewers employ *disassociation* to distance themselves from and sever any real or imagined connection with proposals, objects, persons, organizations, or ideas interviewees dislike. Their organization is under "new management" or is not connected in any way with a political, social, or religious group the interviewee dislikes. Ask for evidence of this disassociation. Is there a possibility the interviewer represents a group under another name? Is denial sincere or merely a ploy to obtain your approval? Why is this person no longer associated with certain ideas, groups, or proposals?

The *bandwagon* tactic urges an interviewee to follow the crowd, to do what "everyone else" is doing. It appeals to a human desire to belong and to conform and not be a loner or different. For instance, a neighbor might claim that "everyone in the neighborhood is going to decorate for the July 4 celebration." Often there is a note of urgency: "People are snapping up the choice lots, so you'd better decide soon." But how do you know everybody's doing it? Listen for qualifiers such as "nearly," "probably," "almost," and "majority." Ask for specific numbers and names of those who have signed, agreed, or joined—not merely those who have "shown an interest" or "reacted favorably." Be particularly skeptical of phrases such as "every knowledgeable person," "everyone who is someone," "all intelligent people," or "experienced investors." Do not be pressured or flattered into jumping on the bandwagon too quickly.

Attack Tactics

Some persuaders prefer to attack competing proposals, ideas, or persons rather than defend or develop their own positions on issues. In an *ad hominem* tactic, the interviewer attempts to dodge the issue, question, or objection by attacking the source, perhaps you. Thus, you may be perceived as evil or wrong for raising a question or objection, which remains unaddressed as the interviewer attempts to discredit you, an organization, a publication, or a research report. Insist that the interviewer address the issue or point, not the source. And do not be bullied by name-calling, countercharges, or efforts to make you become defensive.

Sometimes interviewers will associate a proposal, idea, or person with what tends to repel the interviewee. This is *guilt by association.* Nothing is proven or disproven by this tactic, but the interviewer hopes you will dismiss a proposal, idea, or person because of its real or alleged association with, for example, liberals or conservatives, radicals or reactionaries, or "them." For example, an affirmative action policy developed by a variety of sources may be dismissed through association with radical feminists or a school board proposal for a moment of silence may be dismissed as part of the agenda of the religious right.

An interviewer might attempt to *transfer guilt* from self or organization by making a victim, accuser, or questioner the guilty party. It is not the student's fault for failing the course; it's the instructor's fault. It is not an accident victim's fault for falling down the steps while drunk; it's the property owner's fault for not making the steps safer. It is not the date rapist's fault; it's the fault of the woman who "led him on." Do not accept guilt when it is not your fault, particularly for asking tough questions and bringing up important objections. Make interviewers share the guilt for that which they have been a party to.

Weighing Evidence

Look very closely at the evidence provided and missing when discussing the need, developing criteria, and evaluating solutions. Listen to the substance of responses to your questions and objections. Insist on satisfactory proof for assertions and claims before accepting either. Keep seven questions in mind.

First, is the reporting source *trustworthy?* Is the interviewer unbiased and reliable? Are the sources the interviewer cites unbiased and reliable?

Second, is the evidence *authoritative?* Are persons cited authorities in their fields? Were authorities in a position to have observed the facts, events, or data?

Third, is the evidence the most *recent* available? Are newer statistics or results available? Has an authority changed his or her mind on the issue? For example, in 1970 a researcher named Hawkins reported results of a study that apparently showed "subliminal perception" tactics to be effective. These are tactics such as flashing pictures or messages on a movie or television screen that you cannot see with your naked eyes or hiding messages within music that you cannot detect with your conscious hearing. In 1989, however, Hawkins reported that after years of trying to duplicate his earlier study, he had been unsuccessful in showing any effects of alleged subliminal perception. This does not stop subliminal perception enthusiasts from continuing to cite his 1970 study as evidence of its effectiveness.

Fourth, is the evidence *documented* sufficiently? Do you know where the statistics or results came from or where they were reported? Do you know when the statistics, results, or statements were made?

Fifth, is the evidence *communicated accurately?* Can you detect alterations or deletions in quotations, statistics, or documentation? Is the information quoted out of context? Many of us have remarked, "I'd give anything to know what Professor Dill is going to ask on the test." This does not mean that we would offer money for the final or that we would cheat, if possible.

Sixth, is the evidence sufficient in *quality?* Are opinions stated as facts? Is a sample used for generalizations or causal arguments satisfactory. Does proof evidence (factual illustrations, statistics, authority, detailed comparisons) outweigh clarifying evidence (hypothetical illustrations, testimonials, figurative analogies)?

Seventh, is the evidence sufficient in *quantity?* Are enough authorities cited? Are enough examples given? Are there enough points of comparison. Are adequate facts cited to draw a conclusion?

Use a variety of probing question techniques, including reflective and mirror probes, to be certain you understand what is being said, what you are agreeing with, and what commitments you are making. The following excerpt is from an interaction that took place in the office of one of the authors.

1. **Interviewer:** This test was totally unfair. No one could get an A.
2. **Interviewee:** Forty students did.

ON THE WEB

Assume you are going to purchase a new car upon graduation. You want to be thoroughly informed and prepared when you contact sales representatives so you can make an intelligent decision and get a good deal. Use the World Wide Web to access information on brands, models, features, comparative prices, and assessments by automotive experts. Sample manufacturer sites are Toyota (http://www.toyota.com), Acura (http://www.acura.com), Mazda (http://mazdausa.com), Buick (http://www.parkavenue.com), and Chrysler (http://www.chryslercars.com). What information is readily available on the Internet, and why is this so? What information is not included on the Internet, and why is this so? What are common persuasive tactics used on the Internet? What questions does your research suggest you pursue during interviews?

3. **Interviewer:** That's because you curved it. A lot of students feel the way I do.

4. **Interviewee:** You're the first to come in, and the test was two weeks ago.

5. **Interviewer:** Anyway, your test was unfair because answer options were confusing.

6. **Interviewee:** I see. Which questions do you think were unfair and confusing.

7. **Interviewer:** Look at number 47. It could be either renaming or euphemism.

8. **Interviewee:** We defined euphemism in class as using a better-sounding name, and we gave powder room for toilet as an example. That's the example given in 47. Renaming is trying to create a new vision of reality, such as replacing girl with woman for a female who is 25 years old.

9. **Interviewer:** Well, maybe that's not a good example. Let's look at 33.

Be an active participant during each persuasive interview. Use carefully phrased questions to discover an interviewer's real purpose, qualifications, and preparation and to unravel complicated or vague points and proposals. It is not impolite but intelligent to raise tough questions and objections. Do not be rushed into making a decision; you have little or nothing to gain and much to lose through haste. Insist on clear points and adequate evidence that establish a need or desire, mutually acceptable criteria by which to evaluate all proposals, and thoroughly explained and defended solutions. Do not tolerate smears, innuendos, or half-truths aimed at an interviewer's competitors. Watch for common tactics that dodge careful arguments. And remember your ultimate defenses: termination of the interview or an emphatic "No!"

Summary

Good persuasive interviews are not debates or confrontations involving categorical demands and statements; they are efforts to establish common ground during which both parties recognize the necessity of compromise and the virtues of realistic goals. Good persuasive interviews are not canned efforts designed to fit all situations; they are carefully planned and adapted to each interviewee, yet they remain flexible enough to meet unforeseen disruptions and reactions. Good persuasive interviews are not speeches to an audience of one; they are conversations involving the interviewee as an active participant and requiring the interviewer to listen as well as speak effectively. Good persuasive interviews are not aimed exclusively at either emotion or reason; they appeal to both the head and the heart. Good persuasive interviews are not efforts in which anything goes as long as the interviewee does not catch on; they are honest endeavors conducted along fundamental ethical guidelines.

The interviewee is a central part of persuasive interviews and must play an active, critical role. Good interviews are not ones in which interviewees act as passive recipients of persuasive messages; they are interactions in which interviewees listen critically, ask insightful questions, raise important objections, challenge evidence, recognize common tactics for what they are, and weigh proposals according to agreed-upon criteria.

A Persuasive Interview for Review and Analysis

This interview is between Joe Petry, district manager of a large construction firm, and Vana Black, a project engineer who has been with the firm for five years. The firm supplies each project engineer with a laptop computer that can be taken to construction sites and a docking station in the district office that allows engineers to tap into the central system and work with larger keyboards and monitors. Vana wants a new laptop and a docking station for her apartment. She is meeting with Joe in his office at 11:30 A.M. Joe has given Vana strong performance reviews and thinks she has a good future with the firm, but she can be pushy and demanding. Joe's capital budget is very tight.

How thoroughly has the interviewer done her homework? Assess the relationship between interviewer and interviewee and how this affects the interview. How satisfactory are the major parts of the interview: opening, need, criteria, solution, and closing? How well does the interviewer adapt to the interviewee's values, beliefs, and attitudes and to the situation? How does nonverbal communication affect this interview? When do exchange of persuader and persuadee roles occur, and how do these exchanges affect the interview? How effectively does the interviewee play his role as a critical and involved participant? What tactics does the interviewer use? How satisfactory is the evidence to support claims?

1. **Interviewer:** Good morning Joe. *(cheerful and smiling)* Got a few minutes to discuss a problem with me?

2. **Interviewee:** Sure Vana; *(pleasant tone of voice, looks at his watch)* have a seat. I don't have to leave for a luncheon appointment for about 15 minutes.

3. **Interviewer:** *(serious tone of voice, takes a seat in front of the interviewer's desk)* As you know Joe, I've been taking on more jobs than would normally be expected of someone in my position.

4. **Interviewee:** *(looking the interviewer directly in the eyes, serious but pleasant tone of voice)* Yes, we've been very fortunate to have you, particularly since we have been unable to replace Dan Kosko who left three months ago.

5. **Interviewer:** Well, thanks. *(smiling, glances around the office)* It's difficult to balance all the jobs I'm managing and being a single mother to growing boys.

6. **Interviewee:** Yes, I'm sure it is. *(pleasant but forceful tone of voice)* You said you wanted to talk to me about a problem? *(glances at his watch, and pulls a file from his desk)*

7. **Interviewer:** *(hurriedly, smiling)* Yes sir. I've got to have a better computer and a docking station for use at home.

8. **Interviewee:** *(pause)* Okay. You know from staff meetings that my capital budget is very tight. I'm having trouble funding repairs of current computers and meeting other equipment needs, and it's no easy task trying to balance needs.

9. **Interviewer:** *(quickly)* Hey, I'm not criticizing your leadership of this division, and I can only guess how difficult it is to meet all of our needs.

10. **Interviewee:** That's okay. *(sits back, frowns, looks at his watch)* I just want you to understand my situation and the demands of other staff and corporate headquarters. Why do you need a new computer and an extra docking station?

11. **Interviewer:** *(grave tone of voice and manner)* Well, first of all, my current laptop is not powerful enough for the new software we're introducing that will be necessary to manage our jobs, particularly the complex ones at hospitals that I'm in charge of. And my computer is beginning to have problems. I'm afraid this is just the start of a major breakdown.

12. **Interviewee:** *(appears shocked)* I thought the laptop I got you two years ago, that set us back five grand, would handle any new programs for at least four years.

13. **Interviewer:** At the time, that was true, but none of us anticipated the rapid advance in construction software or the memory the changes would need.

14. **Interviewee:** *(deliberate manner)* We're hoping to inherit some of the laptops from the Pittsburgh office when it is combined with the Columbus office this fall. That might solve some of your problems.

15. **Interviewer:** I'm afraid that's not going to help us much. It's very unlikely that any computers we would inherit would be as good as or better than the ones we have now. And it would not solve my home office needs.

16. **Interviewee:** I don't disagree with you or want to downplay your needs, but I don't see how we can afford new computers for anyone, including me, this year. Even if some money becomes available, I doubt that I could convince the people in Albany that I need to equip home offices.

17. **Interviewer:** Well, *(smiling)* if I can sell you, I think I can sell Albany. Assuming we can come up with the money, do you have time to hear my proposal?

18. **Interviewee:** Assuming you know you're dreaming, I've got a couple of minutes. *(sounds irritated)* I do have a meeting in less than five minutes.

19. **Interviewer:** Okay, here it is in a nutshell. There are two possibilities: the Comp-Data 3000 or a Magnum model. I propose we purchase a model 357 Magnum laptop and a 44 Magnum Mini-Docking Station. Believe me, I've checked them all out. *(hurried manner and fast speaking rate)*

20. **Interviewee:** I don't doubt you've done your homework, but we haven't decided on specific requirements for a new computer, or a legitimate need for a second docking station. And how do I know they're the latest, best, and cheapest?

21. **Interviewer:** Well, I know we don't have time now to go into all the details; that's why I didn't bring a lot of stuff with me. If I'm to do my job, I must have state-of-the-art equipment.

22. **Interviewee:** I'm not disinterested in your problems and proposal, but this is not something that can be proposed or brought about without a lot of research and some careful thought about criteria.

23. **Interviewer:** Oh, I agree. I've done my homework and Magnums are the best. A person at Bankcorp has had nothing but problems with the Comp-Data system.

24. **Interviewee:** Vana . . . *(sounds exasperated)* aren't you aware that the firm has a deal with Comp-Data to supply hardware and software throughout the company?

25. **Interviewer:** I know that we have purchased Comp-Data systems for some time, but I wasn't aware of any agreement that would prevent us from ordering from another electronics firm.

26. **Interviewee:** There is an agreement, and Comp-Data gives us excellent prices.

27. **Interviewer:** The Magnum systems are the best and very competitive.

28. **Interviewee:** Why do you need a second docking station?

29. **Interviewer:** It's very difficult for me to keep up with all of the projects I've been assigned without spending many evenings at the office. This is a very difficult situation for me as a single parent. If I had a docking station at home, I could work there and be near my family.

30. **Interviewee:** I can sympathize with your situation. If you can locate a 44 Magnum Mini-Doc for under $400, we might be able to handle part of your problem.

31. **Interviewer:** Well . . . this now gives *me* something to work on. It still doesn't address the computer problem.

32. **Interviewee:** Yes, that's the drawback. *(standing)* I'm late for my meeting.

33. **Interviewer:** Oh, I'm sorry. Uh, could we get together sometime in the next few days after I've looked into the 357 Magnum laptop?

34. **Interviewee:** Sure, make an appointment with Diana. Take care.

Persuasion Role-Playing Cases

Rezoning Petition for an Apartment Complex

The interviewer has been active in Citizens for the Environment, a group trying to preserve wetlands and wooded areas in and near Rockland, a city of 85,000. There are 75 acres in northern Rockland that Citizens for Development and Progress and others want to see developed into an apartment complex. The interviewer is trying to get property owners to sign a petition in favor of preserving the land and turning it into an educational park. The interviewee, a very influential member of the community, has long been involved in commercial development and would like to see more upscale apartments in Rockland. The interview is taking place in the interviewee's home at 8:00 P.M.

The interviewee, a heart surgeon, has high intelligence and belongs to local and national business groups. The interviewee enjoys all sports, is married, has two children, tends to be optimistic and open-minded, and is beginning to question the efforts and motives of many conservation groups. The interviewee believes that high-quality commercial development is essential for the growth of Rockland. Lack of upscale apartments has made it difficult to attract young physicians to the interviewee's heart clinic.

Sale to a National Chain

The interviewer is a partner in Westlake Farm and Garden, a store started 10 years ago by the interviewer and interviewee. Westlake Farm and Garden has always prided itself in being an independent, home-grown operation with very personal service, unlike the growing number of superstores that have major farm and garden departments. But competition with the superstores is taking a toll on the partners and their income. Net profits had grown slowly to nearly $225,000, divided equally between the partners, but have declined steadily during the past three years to about $175,000. The interviewer has decided to convince the interviewee that they should sell out to Green Thumb, a national chain with its own name brand products. The interview is taking place in the office area at 7:30 A.M.

The interviewee has above-average intelligence, completed two years of college in horticulture, belongs to the Westlake Optimist Club and the Small Business Club, and is a Boy Scout leader. The interviewee is optimistic, fairly open-minded, and likes to help and get along with people. The interviewee sees the interviewer as more business-minded than people-minded and thinks the interviewer's MS in agricultural economics sometimes gets in the way in a small-town, personal business like Westlake.

Adoption of a New Line of Clothing

The interviewer is 24 years old and is the assistant manager of the College Shop, a clothing store for men and women near a university campus. The interviewer's goal is to convince the manager to continue a brand of women's (or men's) clothing rather than discontinue it after the Christmas season. The interview is taking place in the manager's office after the shop closes at 8:00 P.M.

The interviewee has been with the College Shop for several years, and never forgets who is manager. Ego involvement is high because the interviewee personally selected the Shop's brands 20 years ago and had made the decision to drop the ProSportsware line after Christmas. The interviewee is generally open-minded but likes things to stay the same and tends to be very slow to change. The interviewer is perceived to be intelligent but young and inexperienced.

A New Home in the Country

The interviewer is a real estate sales representative at Oaks Realty who knows that the interviewees (husband and wife) have been looking at a variety of homes—new and used, in town and in the country—as well as plans for constructing a new home. Oaks Realty has contracted to sell a 75-year-old two-story home located on five acres of rolling land eight miles from town. The interview is taking place in the interviewees' apartment at 7:00 P.M.

The interviewees are both teachers at the local high school, with a combined income of $80,000. They have no children but plan to have one or two within the next five years. They are currently living in Riverbend Apartments and like the location's closeness to the high school. After hunting in a very systematic fashion, they are leaning toward a new modular home at the edge of town. They see the interviewer as a pleasant but "typical" real estate salesperson eager to make a sale. They know that sales commissions are the interviewer's only income and that sales have been slow.

Student Activities

1. Locate a professional (sales representative, recruiter, fund-raiser) who conducts persuasive interviews on a regular basis, and spend a day on the job with this person. Observe how this person prepares for each interview, selects strategies, opens interviews, develops needs and solutions, closes interviews, and adapts to interviewees.

2. Visit three different establishments (such as a department store, car dealer, travel agent, or bank) with persons who wish to make persuasive transactions. Observe the persuasive approaches employed in each establishment. How much information about the person did the salesperson get before making a presentation or suggestion? How did the person's personal characteristics such as age, sex, race, culture, dress, physical appearance, and apparent degree of wealth seem to affect these interactions? Which values did the interviewers appeal to?

3. Interview a college coach who actively recruits high school students for his or her program. Probe specifically into how the coach adapts to each recruit's needs and desires. What kinds of information does the coach provide? How does the coach handle objections? When and how does the coach try to close persuasive efforts?

4. Select a person you either admire or dislike—a casual acquaintance, fellow student or worker, relative, or national figure. Make a list of descriptive adjectives (such as honest/dishonest, competent/incompetent, trustworthy/untrustworthy) that you think describe this person. Which of these traits are important facets of credibility? How was this image formed in your mind? What could this person do to alter this image in your mind?

Notes

1. Roderick P. Hart, "Teaching Persuasion," in John A. Daly, Gustav W. Friedrich, and Anita L. Vangelisti, eds., *Teaching Communication: Theory, Research, and Methods* (Hillsdale, NJ: Lawrence Erlbaum, 1990), pp. 104–5.

2. "A Nation of Liars?" *U.S. News & World Report,* February 23, 1987, pp. 54–61.

3. "What Ever Happened to Ethics?" *Time,* May 25, 1987, pp. 14–29; and "Lies, Lies, Lies," *Time,* October 5, 1992, pp. 32–44.

4. *The Wall Street Journal,* September 18, 1987, pp. 1 and 5.

5. "Ethics Endorsed as Skill for 21st Century," Lafayette, Indiana, *Journal and Courier,* January 31, 1996, p. A5.

6. Richard L. Johannesen, "Perspectives on Ethics in Persuasion," in Charles U. Larson, *Persuasion: Reception and Responsibility* (Belmont, CA: Wadsworth, 1998), p. 28.

7. Gary C. Woodward and Robert E. Denton, Jr., *Persuasion and Influence in American Life* (Prospect Heights, IL: Waveland Press, 1992), p. 389.

8. Kenneth E. Andersen, *Persuasion: Theory and Practice* (Boston: Allyn and Bacon, 1971), p. 327.

9. Deirdre Johnston, *The Art and Science of Persuasion* (Madison, WI: Brown & Benchmark, 1994), p. 185; and Sharon Shavitt and Timothy Brock, *Persuasion: Psychological Insights and Perspectives* (Boston: Allyn and Bacon, 1994), pp. 152–53.

10. Michael Argyle, "Intercultural Communication," in Larry A. and Richard E. Porter, eds., *Intercultural Communication: A Reader* (Belmont, CA: Wadsworth, 1988), pp. 35–36.

11. Milton Rokeach, *Beliefs, Attitudes, and Values* (San Francisco: Jossey-Bass, 1968), p. 124.

12. Woodward and Denton, pp. 99–108 and 174–90.

13. Kenneth Burke, *A Rhetoric of Motives* (Berkeley: University of California Press, 1969), p. 55.

14. Burke, pp. 21–45; and Charles J. Stewart, Craig Allen Smith, and Robert E. Denton, Jr., *Persuasion and Social Movements* (Prospect Heights, IL: Waveland Press, 1994), pp. 165–68.

15. Woodward and Denton, pp. 161–66; and Larson, pp. 80–82.

16. Kathleen Kelley Reardon, *Persuasion in Practice* (Newbury Park, CA: Sage, 1991), pp. 54–55; and Daniel J. O'Keefe, *Persuasion: Theory and Practice* (Newbury Park, CA: Sage, 1990), pp. 179–81.

17. Woodward and Denton, pp. 163–64; and O'Keefe, pp. 71–77.

18. Erwin P. Bettinghaus and Michael J. Cody, *Persuasive Communication* (Fort Worth, TX: Harcourt Brace, 1994), pp. 57–59.

19. James F. Roberson, H. Lee Mathews, and Carl G. Stevens, *Selling* (Homewood, IL: Richard D. Irwin, 1978), p. 109.

20. William B. Gudykunst and Tsukasa Nishida, *Bridging Japanese/North American Differences* (Thousand Oaks, CA: Sage, 1994), pp. 68–73.

21. O'Keefe, p. 186.

22. Stewart et al., pp. 111–14; and Robert N. Bostrom, *Persuasion* (Englewood Cliffs, NJ: Prentice-Hall, 1983), pp. 181–82.

23. Shavitt and Brock, pp. 152–53.

24. Robert S. Goyer, W. Charles Redding, and John T. Rickey, *Interviewing Principles and Techniques: A Project Text* (Dubuque, IA: Brown, 1968), pp. 50–51.

25. Larson, pp. 200–2; and Woodward and Denton, pp. 374–75.

26. Tom Hopkins, *How to Master the Art of Selling* (Scottsdale, AZ: Champion Press, 1982).

Resources

Brennan, Charles D. *Sales Questions That Close the Sale: How to Uncover Your Customer's Real Needs.* New York: AMACOM, 1994.

Larson, Charles U. *Persuasion: Reception and Responsibility.* Belmont, CA: Wadsworth, 1995.

Shavitt, Sharon, and Timothy C. Brock. *Persuasion: Psychological Insights and Perspectives.* Boston: Allyn and Bacon, 1994.

Wilson, Larry. *Changing the Game: The New Way to Sell.* New York: Simon and Schuster, 1987.

Woodward, Gary C., and Robert E. Denton, Jr. *Persuasion and Influence in American Life.* Prospect Heights, IL: Waveland Press, 1996.

The Selection Interview: The Employer

N ot long ago, the old adage "The more things change the more they stay the same" applied to the hiring of people in organizations. The job market would expand or contract while education would lag behind market trends and catch up just in time to be behind again. Interviewing methods remained relatively unchanged from generation to generation. The chip, world economy, and demographics have changed the hiring organization so fundamentally that major changes have taken place in *who* we hire and *how* we hire them that make the process distinctly different not only from the 1960s, 1970s, and 1980s but from the early 1990s.

Steel, automobiles, and heavy equipment no longer dominate the hiring market. Technology has changed everything. And the demographics are different from a few years ago. Every seven seconds someone in the United States turns 50 as the baby boomers are passing through middle age. The workforce has changed from being dominantly populated by white males to one in which women, African-Americans, Hispanics, and Asians have made significant strides. More women have started businesses in the last 24 months than ever in history. Recent research claims that the outcomes of employment interviews are no longer directly affected by demographic factors such as age, race, gender, or ethnicity.[1]

More organizations are selling and buying goods outside of the United States than ever before. Information moves across political and geographical boundaries in milliseconds. Work done on computers in India is downloaded and available at a workstation in Minnesota the next morning. Corporate cultures that traditionally took decades to create are now in place within a few years. Recruiting and retaining highly skilled workers takes effort. Starbucks, the premier coffee house company, offers profit sharing and stock purchase plans for its *temporary* workforce.

Researchers and practitioners for decades have identified the selection interview as a poor and costly means of screening, hiring, and placing applicants.[2] Recently one of the authors gave a speech to a large audience at a midwestern university in which he presented 10 things an applicant must do to get a good position. Following his speech, the author was taken to dinner by a half-dozen faculty who have taught employment interviewing. He was stunned when they began to attack the selection interview with such comments as "Too many jobs go to the well-dressed, articulate, impression-makers" and "In a face-to-face interview, there are too many places for prejudice and personal preferences to control the selection." One faculty member asked, "Why, with computers, are we still using this old process? We should select candidates by computer to be completely objective and to eliminate all bias and prejudice." When the author suggested that the next faculty opening be filled in this fashion, he thought he would end up buying his own dinner. When faced with selecting a colleague through a computer, his dinner companions began to defend the interview. The most insightful comment was, "Face it, interviewing is a two-way choice and at the heart of it is communication, relationship, and the goodness of fit."

In spite of the selection interview's well-documented deficiencies in predicting success and its susceptibility to bias and distortion, it remains "a central component of most organizational selection procedures."[3] Selecting employees and positions is an elaborate courtship process, and few people want to select an organizational partner sight unseen. We, the authors of this text, have more than 60 years of combined experiences in hiring employees for a wide range of positions from clerical staff and pastors to deans and vice presidents. We remain amazed at how awful paper-perfect applicants are when you meet them in person and ask a few thought-provoking questions. No matter how elaborate resumes, applications forms, paper-and-pencil tests, handwriting analyses, and background searches may be, there is still no substitute for face-to-face interactions. Applicants have had much the same experience with employers after reviewing organizational propaganda and being on the receiving end of elaborate public relations campaigns.

Successful selection interviews combine all of the skills discussed thus far in this book: information getting, information giving, and persuasion. Organizations use interviews not only to select new employees and determine where they best fit into organizations but to *persuade* top applicants to join them and to create favorable images with potential consumers of products and services. Applicant decisions are significantly affected by their satisfaction with the communication that takes place during interviews.[4] And applicants use interviews not only to give and get information but to market themselves effectively, gain valuable experiences, and determine which offers to accept and reject.

Chapters 8 and 9 will *not* give you simple formulas for success, provide shortcuts in the process, or provide surefire answers to questions. There are none. These chapters, however, will prepare you for the hard work of selecting employees and obtaining positions, introduce you to the latest trends and research in selection interviewing, and provide guidelines for structuring interviews, asking and answering questions, giving information, and evaluating results. Our *short-range goal* is to help you seek and secure a good position. Our *intermediate-range goal* is to help you select employees because, unless you are a bit strange, you will play the role of employer far more often in your lifetime than the applicant role, regardless of your career fields or positions you hold. And our *long-range goal* is to help improve the selection process that is experiencing revolutionary changes, nearly all for the good.

Since the selection interview is certain to remain the central component of selecting employees and attaining positions, both employers and applicants must approach the process systematically and learn how to prepare for, participate in, and evaluate interviews. Although this chapter focuses on the employer in the selection process and you

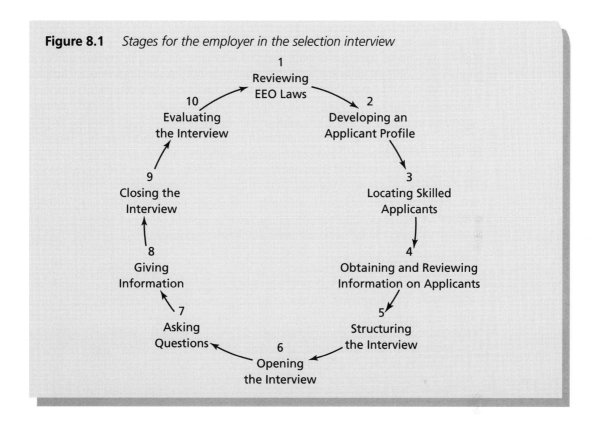

Figure 8.1   *Stages for the employer in the selection interview*

may be more interested in what the applicant should do, read this chapter carefully first because you can be a more effective applicant if you understand what employers do and why.

Organizations must make interviewing a systematic and structured part of the selection process and train all employees who will take part in any way in this process. Professionally conducted interviews not only lead to the selection of better employees but they present good impressions of organizations.[5] Figure 8.1 summarizes the stages essential for successful selection interviewing. The first stage is a thorough review of relevant equal employment opportunity (EEO) laws.

1. Reviewing EEO Laws

If you are involved in any way with hiring employees for your organization, you must be acquainted with the equal employment opportunity laws passed by states and Congress to eliminate discrimination in the hiring of employees. One writer refers to the selection interview as a "veritable minefield of potential legal liability," and another warns that "one misstatement, or poorly phrased question, can blow up into an expensive lawsuit alleging discriminatory hiring practices."[6]

Although most relevant EEO laws have been on the books for decades, interviewers continue to violate them knowingly and unknowingly. In a study of 157 organizations in Wisconsin, Springston and Keyton found that an amazing 96 percent would or might ask at least one unlawful question in each interview.[7] A study reported in *The Wall Street Journal* found that 70 percent of 200 interviewers and recruiters for Fortune 500 companies, presumably among the best trained, thought at least five of twelve unlawful questions were "safe to ask."[8] And a survey of employers and applicants discovered that 12 percent thought it was acceptable to ask questions about political beliefs, 27 percent about family background, 30 percent about the candidate's spouse, and 45 percent about the candidate's personal life.[9] Ignorance or disregard of the law can lead to noncompliance and expensive, time-consuming, and embarrassing lawsuits against your organization. And since 1991, cases may be tried by jury, and successful plaintiffs may receive back pay, benefits, compensation for lost future wages in lieu of reinstatement, and punitive damages. You do not want to be the cause of such lawsuits.

EEO Laws to Know

Become familiar with important EEO laws and Executive Orders that pertain to the employment selection interview. Federal EEO laws pertain to all organizations that (1) deal with the federal government, (2) have more than 15 employees, (3) have more than $50,000 in government contracts, and (4) engage in interstate commerce. State laws may be more stringent than federal laws. The following are laws and Executive Orders you need to know.

1. The Civil Rights Acts of 1866, 1870, and 1871 prohibit discrimination against minorities.
2. The Equal Pay Act of 1963 requires equal pay for men and women performing work that involves similar skill, effort, responsibility, and working conditions.
3. The Civil Rights Act of 1964, particularly Title VII, prohibits the selection of employees based on race, color, sex, religion, or national origin, and requires employers to discover discriminatory practices and eliminate them. Congress created the Equal Employment Opportunity Commission (EEOC) to ensure compliance and is concerned with the *results,* not the *intents,* of hiring practices.
4. Executive Order 11246, issued in 1965 and amended in 1967, prohibits discrimination and requires government contractors to take "affirmative action" to ensure that applicants are treated equally.
5. The Age Discrimination in Employment Act of 1967 prohibits employers of 25 or more persons from discriminating against persons because of age.
6. The Equal Employment Opportunity Act of 1972 extended the Civil Rights Act of 1964 to public and private educational institutions, labor organizations, and employment agencies.
7. The Rehabilitation Act of 1973 orders federal contractors to hire disabled persons, and the disabilities include alcoholism, asthma, rheumatoid arthritis, and epilepsy.
8. The Vietnam Era Veterans Readjustment Act of 1974 encourages employers to hire qualified Vietnam veterans, including those with disabilities.

9. The Immigration Reform and Control Act of 1987 prohibits discrimination on the basis of citizenship.
10. The Americans with Disabilities Act of 1990 (effective in 1992) prohibits discrimination against persons with physical or mental impairments that substantially limit or restrict the condition, manner, or duration under which they can perform one or more major life activities and requires reasonable accommodation by employers.
11. The Civil Rights Act of 1991 (often referred to as the 1992 Civil Rights Act) caps compensation and punitive damages for employers, provides for jury trial, and created a commission to investigate the "glass ceiling" for minorities and women and reward organizations that advance opportunities for minorities and women.
12. The Family and Medical Leave Act (effective in 1993) provides for an unpaid leave (12 weeks within any 12-month period or 1,250 work hours) for the birth of a child, care for an ill child, placement of a child for adoption or foster care, or care for a seriously ill spouse, child, or parent that prevents the employee from performing the functions of the job.

Compliance with EEO Laws

Compliance with state and federal EEO laws and guidelines is relatively easy. Be sure that everything you do, say, or ask during the selection process pertains to *bona fide occupational qualifications* (BFOQs), requirements essential for performing a particular job. BFOQs usually *include* work experiences, training, education, skills, lawsuits, arrest records, physical attributes, and personality traits that have a direct bearing on one's ability to perform a job effectively. BFOQs usually *exclude* marital status, family, gender, age, race, religion, physical appearance, disabilities, citizenship, and ethnic group, factors that have no bearing on one's ability to perform effectively. Exceptions are made if an employer can demonstrate that one or more normally unlawful traits are essential for a position. For example, appearance may be a BFOQ for a modeling position, religion for a pastoral position, age for performing certain tasks legally (serving alcohol, operating dangerous equipment), and physical abilities such as eyesight and manual dexterity for pilots.

A few simple guidelines will help you avoid most EEO violations and lawsuits.[10] First, meet the *test of job relatedness* by establishing legally defensible selection criteria. Second, be sure all of your questions are related to these selection criteria. Third, ask the same questions for all applicants for a specific position. If you ask certain questions only of female, disabled, older, or minority applicants, you are undoubtedly asking unlawful questions. Fourth, be cautious when probing into answers because a significant number of EEO violations occur in these created-on-the-spot questions. Fifth, be cautious of innocent chit-chat during the informal parts of interviews, usually the opening and closing or the minutes following the formal interview. This is when you are most likely to ask or comment about family, marital status, ethnic background, and nonprofessional memberships. Sixth, focus questions on the positive, what an applicant can do rather than on what an applicant cannot do. Seventh, if an applicant begins to volunteer unlawful information, tactfully steer the person back to job-related areas.

The Americans with Disabilities Act (ADA) of 1990 has created a whole new area of potential violations for the uninformed and unwary interviewer. You can avoid violating this act, first, by not requiring a medical examination prior to a job offer and, second, by *not asking about or commenting on* how the person became disabled, the nature of the disability, the severity of the disability, how the person can get to work, how the person will go to the bathroom, conditions or diseases the person has or has had, past hospitalization, past or current treatment for a mental condition, or past reception of workers' compensation. Some sources recommend that you shake hands with a disabled applicant, do not push a wheelchair unless asked, identify yourself and others involved in the interview if the interviewee is blind, and use physical signals, gestures, facial expressions, and note passing if an applicant is deaf.[11] As a general rule, however, treat a disabled person the same as you treat everyone else.

Testing Your Knowledge of EEO Laws

Test your knowledge about what you can and cannot ask during selection interviews by rating each question below as *lawful* (can be asked), *probably lawful* (may be asked under certain circumstances), or *unlawful* (cannot be asked).[12] Decide why it is lawful, probably lawful, or unlawful before looking at the answers.

1. How did you lose the fingers on your right hand?

   How a person lost fingers is not a BFOQ and none of your business. Unlawful.

2. Any marriage plans?

   Marital status or plans are rarely BFOQs. Unlawful.

3. Man, you don't look 50; how do you do it?

   This is not a BFOQ, would probably be asked only of females, and may get into health and other unlawful areas. Unlawful.

4. Who will take care of your children when they become ill?

   This question would probably be asked only of female applicants and is not a BFOQ. Unlawful.

5. Have you ever been treated for mental illness?

   This question would reveal past mental health problems, and the applicant is protected by the ADA. Unlawful.

6. Do you have friends or family who work for Microsoft?

   This question might reveal a bias toward white, middle-class males, a group that is likely to dominate the employee mix of most organizations, and thus would be unlawful. This is highly unlikely to be a BFOQ. Probably unlawful.

7. Give me an example of how you handled a stressful situation.

   If this position entails a great deal of stress and this question is asked of all applicants, it is lawful.

8. Have you pretty much settled on the size of your family?

   Female applicants are most likely to encounter this question. This is not a BFOQ and is unlawful.

9. The only wheelchair access office is in the basement. Would you mind that?

   Organizations are required to make "reasonable accommodations" if they have more than 25 employees each workday and have had such a number for 20 or more weeks this year or the preceding year. Offices must be equally available and accessible to all employees. Unlawful.

10. Would you mind if I called you Jill?

    It is often a good idea to use an applicant's first name to avoid the cumbersome and formal Ms., Miss, Mrs., or Mr. However, you should ask this of all applicants, not merely female, younger, or particularly attractive persons. Lawful.

11. Are you a citizen of the United States?

    You may ask this question if citizenship is a BFOQ. If the answer is no, you may ask, "When do you plan to become a citizen?" or "Do you have legal sanction to remain in the United States?" You may not ask how or when citizenship was obtained unless the position involves national security. Lawful.

12. Can you speak French or German?

    If speaking French or German is a BFOQ and you are not asking how or where the person learned the language, this is a lawful question.

13. What professional organizations do you belong to?

    You may ask about relevant professional organizations but not about social, religious, or political memberships. Lawful.

14. Have you ever been arrested?

    You can ask if a person has been convicted of a felony related to the position for which the person is applying. Unlawful.

15. Because of your limited vision, I assume you need a Braille keyboard for your computer.

You must be willing to make "reasonable accommodations," and specific needs such as a Braille keyboard can be determined after a person is hired. Unlawful.

16. Would your wife be available to entertain clients?

This question probes into marital status and the availability of a person who will not be on the payroll. Unlawful.

17. Could you work or travel on the weekends?

If this is a BFOQ, it is lawful. However, if it is not a justifiable BFOQ, it might probe into marital status with children and a person's religious beliefs and practices and be unlawful. Probably lawful.

18. How long would you expect to work for us?

This question is most likely to be asked of female and older applicants. Unlawful.

19. Tell me about your computer skills.

If computer skills are important to the position, this is lawful.

20. What will you do if your husband gets transferred?

Reveals gender bias and is rarely if ever asked of males about their wives being transferred. Unlawful.

21. What does your wife do?

This is the type of question that emerges during off-the-cuff comments and during informal chit-chat. Unlawful.

22. How rapidly do you expect to advance, Miss Struthers? We have recently promoted two women.

The number of people promoted, regardless of race, gender, or ethnicity, is not a BFOQ. The question is both insensitive and unlawful.

23. If you are offered this position, would you submit to a blood test?

If blood tests are required for this position, this is a BFOQ and is lawful.

24. What kinds of people do you enjoy working for the most?

This may be asked if both you and the applicant avoid such characteristics as age, sex, race, religion, and ethnic groups. However, you are opening yourself up for receiving prejudicial information and legal charges. Probably unlawful.

Keep abreast of EEO laws and interpretations, and be aware of the common areas that can get you into trouble. Studies reveal that arrest records, age, disabilities, marital and family status, and religion are the unlawful areas probed into most often.[13]

Keep a number of rules in mind when asking questions. First, federal laws supersede state laws unless the state laws are more restrictive. Second, the Equal Employment Opportunity Commission and the courts are not concerned with *intent* but with *effect.* Your organization may have to show that the "final decision maker deliberately disregarded any evaluations tainted" by stereotypical questions.[14] Third, advertise each position where *all qualified* applicants have a *reasonable opportunity* to learn about the opening: newspapers, placement centers, organizational bulletin boards and publications, the Internet, and professional journals. Fourth, your organization is liable if unlawful information is maintained or used even if you did not ask for it. Have a person not involved in the selection process review all applicant materials for potentially unlawful information such as personal data, pictures, and references. Fifth, do not write or take notes on the application form. In the past, some organizations used notes or codes to indicate race, ethnic group, age, and physical appearance of applicants. Even doodling on an application form may appear to be a code. And sixth, pose highly similar or identical questions to all applicants.

2. Developing an Applicant Profile

With EEO laws clearly in mind, conduct a thorough analysis to determine the knowledge, experiences, skills, and personal traits necessary to perform a position satisfactorily. From this analysis you should develop a *profile* of the ideal employee for a position. All applicants are then measured against this profile of BFOQs.

There are a number of ways to develop an applicant profile. You may develop, with the help of managers and human resources personnel, a competency model of traits, skills, and motives from research on individuals who do the job well. You may develop a profile by searching literature, interviewing incumbents, supervisors, and associates, observing and analyzing actual performance of the job, and standardizing requirements. You might do a systematic study of outstanding people in the field. Or you may analyze existing employee responses to performance questions to distinguish good from bad performance characteristics. Regardless of the means you use, a precise applicant profile will help you avoid EEO violations, enhance your interviewing effectiveness, and improve the hiring decisions you make.

Competency-based applicant profiles typically include specific skills, abilities, education, training, experiences, knowledge levels, personal characteristics, and interpersonal relationships. Each applicant is measured against this profile, literally a set of evaluative criteria, in an effort to choose the person who comes closest to the ideal employee. The profile approach makes the selection process more objective, encourages all interviewers to cover the same topics and traits, and reduces the effect of the birds-of-a-feather syndrome in which interviewers favor applicants who are most similar to themselves.

Some organizations, such as Bristol-Myers, have begun to employ a *behavior-based selection technique* to ensure that each interviewer matches each applicant with the ideal employee profile.[15] Four principles underlie this technique: (1) Behavior that is observed can be read; (2) behavior that is not seen must be probed for; (3) the best predictor of future behavior is past behavior; and (4) job-related behavior in the interview is a good indicator of future job performance. The behavior-based selection technique begins with a needs and position analysis to determine which *behaviors* are essential for performing a particular job. The following are observable behaviors that might be important for specific positions:

Achievement	Empathy	Persistence
Affiliation	Endurance/Stamina	Responsibility
Aggressiveness	Honesty	Responsiveness
Ambition	Impulsiveness	Self-confidence
Assertiveness	Initiative	Self-starter
Competitiveness	Leadership	Sensitivity
Consistency	Listening	Sincerity
Courage	Motivation	Sympathy
Decisiveness	Oral communication	Tenacity
Dependability	Organization-oriented	Tough-minded
Discipline	People-oriented	

Remember, behaviors being sought must be position related—BFOQs—and clearly defined so that all interviewers are looking for the same ones. Once the relevant behaviors are determined, the organization creates an appropriate schedule of questions to elicit these behaviors.

3. Locating Skilled Applicants

The development of an applicant profile allows your organization to answer the question, What kinds of skilled people do we need? The next step is to locate these ideally skilled people. Newspapers, trade journals, campus recruiting trips, and employment agencies are traditional sources. Some organizations are offering current employees between $100 and $1,000 if they hire an applicant they recommend.

Although we have had electronic search capability for resumes and positions for the last 20 years, the explosion of the services and sources in the 1990s is unprecedented. Because the security is high on some of these databases and the Internet, we recommend that you begin by establishing strong relationships with universities, departments, and professors. Networks, professional societies, and professionals can help you. Almost every college and university has its own resume services system; listed on the next page are nonacademic sources.

Career Net Graduate
643 W. Crosstown Parkway
Kalamazoo, MI 49008
Phone (616) 344-3017

Cors
One Pierce Place
Suite 300
Itasca, IL 60143
Phone (800) 323-1352 or (708) 250-8677

Electronic Job Matching
1915 N. Dale Mabry Highway
Suite 307
Tampa, FL 33607
Phone (813) 879-4100
Fax (813) 870-1883

Hispanic
360 S. Hope Avenue
Suite 300-C
Santa Barbara, CA 93105
Phone (805) 682-5843
Fax (805) 687-4546

Job Bank, USA
1420 Spring Hill Road
Suite 480
McLean, VA 22102
Phone (800) 296-1USA
Fax (703) 847-1494

MedSearch America
15254 NE 95th Street
Redmond, WA 98502
Phone (206) 883-7252
Fax (206) 883-7465

University ProNet
2445 Faber Place
Box 51820
Palo Alto, CA 94303
Fax (415) 845-4019

These are only a few of the sources available to organizations. ProNet is a private company representing 16 universities. It has a large array of graduates and alumni who can be accessed for a fee. There are specialty services for accounting, engineering, sales, human resources, and others. All of these sources charge a fee for phone calls and to use the service. A few provide CD-ROMs for a fee. Check the numbers and fees before using these services. The Internet is a potential source, but the inaccuracy of resumes and the doubtful existence of some individuals advertised on it have kept many organizations from using it.

4. Obtaining and Reviewing Information on Applicants

Obtain as much information as possible on each applicant prior to an interview through application forms, resumes, letters of recommendation, and objective tests. You want to begin to develop a "sense of the professional and personal qualities of each job applicant."[16] Design the application form with the ideal applicant profile in mind, and avoid traditional categories that violate EEO guidelines: age, marital status, physical characteristics, arrest records, type of military discharge, and request for a picture. Include a few open-ended questions similar to

photo by Spencer Grant/Photo Edit

■ *Review the applicant's credentials prior to the interview so you can devote full attention to the applicant during the interview.*

ones you will ask during the interview. And provide adequate space for applicants to answer all questions thoroughly.

Resumes

Review each resume, first, to see how well the applicant's career objective meets the applicant profile, and then how well the applicant's education, training, and experiences complement the stated career objective and the applicant profile. Look for what is and what is not included on the resume, a grade-point average, for instance. Remember that many applicants tend to exaggerate their qualifications and experiences on resumes. Be sure to delete any unlawful information from the resume (picture, age, marital status, religious organizations, and so on). You and your organization cannot be accused of using what you do not have, but if you keep this information (even though you did not request it), you can be held liable for possible discrimination based upon it.

A growing number of companies are using electronic systems to screen resumes. Resume scanning systems sort out applicants based on key words or skills listed in the system by a hiring manager or human resources department. Two widely used systems are Restrac, Inc., of Lexington, Massachusetts, and Resumix, Inc., of Sunnyvale, California. Inexpensive scanning software packages are being sold over the Internet, but their flexibility and accuracy are questionable. In Chapter 9 we will discuss the pros and cons of resume scanning systems and how candidates can prepare scannable resumes.

Who should consider a resume scanning system? If your organization receives large volumes of resumes for positions or is hiring a large number of workers, scanning systems are worth the cost. They are also of value if your organization has a central human resources structure that selects candidates for regional or multiple divisions at international locations. They save time, reduce travel expenses, and sort through a large volume of resumes. Systems can store resumes and enable you to scan this pool if another position opens. There are some disadvantages. For example, if an excellent candidate uses "personnel" instead of "human resources" or "purchasing" instead of "procurement/materials management," the candidate will be eliminated from the system and sent a rejection letter. The result is the same if an applicant's degree abbreviations do not match those in the system.

Cover Letters and Recommendations

Review each cover letter carefully. What does it reveal about career goals, adaptation to your position and organization, interest in the position, and qualifications? Is it written professionally? Is it free of spelling, grammatical, and punctuation errors?

Review letters of recommendation with skepticism because nearly all are written by friends or admirers. They rarely contain negative information. Letters do reveal who an applicant knows, who will write letters for the applicant, and bits of information about how well the applicant fits the profile. Look for hints a recommender may be dropping to signal that this is not a strong recommendation. It may be as simple as "Alicia is one of the better students I have had" rather than "Alicia is one of the best students I have had." Or a person may condemn with faint praise, such as "John was a very reliable employee" or "Marcia did her best at whatever task was assigned to her."

Tests

A growing number of organizations are using testing as a supplement in the selection process. Tests fall into three categories.

Basic skills tests attempt to assess mathematics, measurement, and reading or spelling skills. As a result of the widespread use of calculators and computers, some people have problems with answering simple math questions, such as "What is 10 percent of 166?" or "If you produced 1,886 parts in four hours and had a 2 percent rejection rate, what is your net production per hour?" Poor reading and spelling skills are posing major problems when individuals or teams are asked to write up problems on their machines or with their groups. Some tests describe a very basic problem and then ask the applicant to write five to seven sentences describing the problem. Examiners or test monitors look for spelling, sentence structure, verb tense, and readability using a common formula. Many positions require employees to convert measurement from inches, feet, ounces, and gallons to metric measurements. Organizations avoid legal problems with basic skills tests by asking applicants to sign waivers. The waivers declare that scores on tests are not the sole means used to select applicants. Tests are merely aids in placement and training.

Personality tests attempt to assess the people skills of applicants. An insurance institute claims its personality test is very successful in assessing the personality traits of applicants and predicting sales success. Many organizations use the Myers-Briggs and the Wilson Analogy tests to identify personality type and the thinking skills of applicants.[17]

Honesty tests that attempt to assess ethics, honesty, and integrity are new in the 1990s. As we noted in Chapter 7, there is a growing concern for lack of ethics and honesty in the United States. It is estimated that 6,000 organizations administer 5,000,000 integrity or honesty tests each year.[18] In addition, the rapid growth in technology has made available a wide range of information that can be stolen, sold to the competition, or destroyed. Product liability, risks, and lawsuits for negligent hiring make it important to hire honest employees. An added concern is the rise in temporary or contract workers who neither receive loyalty from nor establish loyalty with a company.

Many sources have criticized the use and validity of honesty tests. Honesty tests do identify individuals who have a high propensity for stealing in the workplace, but critics wonder about applicants who fall into the moderate to low ranges.[19] Robert Fitzpatrick, a Washington attorney who specializes in employment law, warns, "While they [honesty tests] might screen out some undesirable job candidates, they also screen out [like the old polygraph tests] a tremendous percentage of perfectly honest, upstanding citizens."[20] And Wayne Camara warns that "An honest applicant may not be the most qualified. Poor performance may mean greater losses than theft."[21] One study recommends that truth can best be determined through an analysis and comparison of factual information about the applicant, an honesty test, and a thorough probing interview.[22] That study concludes that an accurate reading of the applicant's verbal and nonverbal reactions to questions can help you separate truth from deception. Truthful applicants tend to identify in some detail the issue under investigation, acknowledge the probability of employee theft, respond without hesitation, suggest harsher punishment than deceptive counterparts, reject the idea of leniency, and expect favorable test results.

Regardless of such criticisms of honesty tests, a growing body of research is supporting such tests because they appear to predict job-related criteria.[23] Two formats are used most frequently. The first consists of highly structured interviews that focus on ethics and integrity by delving into previous work experience directly related to the position available. If previous work experience is unavailable, the interviewer poses situational questions using specific dimensions of ethical and honest behavior.[24] These interviews usually employ a five-point scale with an agreed-upon definition of the dimension. For example, in the dimension of theft, the "five" answer indicating high in theft might identify someone who would take a large portable gas-powered electric generator worth $700. The choices on the five-point scale might range from a generator to a role of transparent tape to wrap holiday packages. Other dimensions are relationship manipulation, interpersonal deception (lying), security violation (giving out trade secrets), and sexual harassment (telling dirty jokes or displaying pictures from *Playboy*). Developing ethical dimensions, making them job specific, and validating them takes a great deal of time and effort. But the time and energy might be warranted. For example, if loss prevention is critical, it would pay to check for honesty with potential employees.

Whether or not you use an honesty test, protect your organization in case you discover, after making an offer or bringing a person on board, that the individual was

ON THE WEB

Honesty tests are becoming more common during interviews as employers attempt to assess the integrity of potential employees in an age when honesty often seems the exception rather than the norm. Many employers and researchers are raising serious questions about the accuracy and value of honesty tests in the employment selection setting. Search the Internet for discussions of the uses and concerns raised by honesty tests. These sources should get you started on your search: Infoseek (http://www.infoseek.com), PsycInfo (http://www.psycinfo.com), The Monster Board (http://www.monster.com), Careermosiac (http://www.careermosiac.com), and PsychLit (http://www.psychlit.com).

dishonest during the hiring process. Place a statement such as the following on all application forms: "Falsification of information in the application or the interview will be viewed as grounds for refusal or termination of employment."

If you decide to use basic skills, personality, or honesty tests, use them as only one measure of suitability. Be sure all "objective" tests are designed to reveal relevant occupational qualifications, have been validated on a cross section of the population, and meet EEO guidelines. Ensure confidentiality of results, and obtain the applicant's written consent to be tested and a waiver of liability claims for use or reliance on test results.

Videotaping and Video-Conferencing

The use of videotaped interviews and video-conferencing is growing as part of the screening process. Half of the Fortune 500 companies are using technology to link locations.[25] Technology saves companies money and allows them to visit campuses that recruiting budgets did not permit a few years ago. If a candidate seems promising through videotape or video-conferencing, a company can bring the person on location for a follow-up interview. Kraft, Pfizer, NASA, and Cargill are using such systems.

Once a company has linked software, computer, and video together it has an interview service that can cover several cities. Dell Computer, for example, uses National Career Search "Searchlinc" to screen candidates at its headquarters and other cities.[26] A face-to-face interview costs three times as much as technological screening.

Previewing information on the applicant serves not only an initial screening step but also an important part of the total screening process. For example, the preview should give you a fairly clear notion of your relationship with the applicant by revealing how much each of you wants to take part in the interview, the degree of interest, and how control is likely to be shared. The preview also reveals areas to probe into during the interview, perhaps comparing oral and written answers to similar questions. Jablin and Miller discovered that employers who review applicant credentials thoroughly tended to ask more and a wider variety of questions and to probe more into answers.[27] Do not allow the preview to prejudice you so that favorable impressions from paper credentials or videotapes lead to favorable impressions during the interview regardless of what the applicant does or says. On the other hand, one study revealed that interviewers asked questions biased in a negative way of applicants with what they perceived to be poor credentials.[28] Base your final decision on all information gathered during the selection process.

5. Structuring the Interview

Perhaps the greatest change in selection interviews over the past 10 years has to do with structure. Interviewers traditionally approached the interview in an unstructured manner, often having no more than a few topics or favorite questions in mind, a nonscheduled interview. But research began to reveal the hazards of the unstructured and generally unplanned interview.

1. Interviewers tend to talk more than applicants in unstructured interviews rather than the preferred rate of 80 percent for applicants and 20 percent for employers.

2. Interviewers tend to make their decisions within the first four minutes in unstructured interviews, long before they have obtained all data from the interviews.

3. Only factual and biographical information (easily obtainable through written application forms and resumes) is covered consistently in unstructured interviews.

4. Since each interviewer for an organization performed a "different" interview with each applicant, ratings of applicants differ significantly among interviewers.

5. Interviewers are more susceptible to stereotyping and biases and more likely to ask EEO violation questions in unstructured interviews.

On the other hand, research has shown that the validity of interviews as a means of selecting well-qualified applicants who will prove successful with organizations depends upon a high degree of structure.[29] Structured interviews enhance the three essential ingredients of selection interviews: content, conduct of the interview, and use of appropriate, position-related criteria.

Most sources are now recommending at least a moderately scheduled interview, and a great many are recommending a highly scheduled interview in which all questions are prepared and tested ahead of time and are then posed to each applicant.[30] Structured interviews are more reliable than unstructured interviews because all applicants are asked the same or very similar questions and because they force employers to pay close attention throughout the interview instead of for just the first few minutes when a decision is often made in unstructured interviews. The chit-chat and off-the-cuff comments that have little or nothing to do with the position and may lead to EEO violations are thus eliminated from the process.

Many organizations are employing highly structured interviews tailored around specific traits in the applicant profile or around an interview guide such as (1) can the person can do the job, (2) will the person do the job, and (3) will the person fit into the organization. Fit or match with the position and organization is a growing emphasis because organizations are discovering that a well-qualified applicant who does not match the organization's ethos or culture is likely to result in poor performance and high turnover rate. Some recommend covering specific topics such as company environment, management influence, and coworkers to weed out persons not suited for their organizations.

Some organizations are developing behavior-based selection techniques. They develop highly structured interviews that provide for skillful patterning and selecting of questions, recording of responses, and rating of applicants on behaviorally defined dimensions. In the following example, the interviewer would employ a five-point scale to rate each answer according to the degree to which it exhibits or gives information about one or more behaviors: 5 = strongly present and 1 = minimally present.

Rating	Behavior	Question
_____	Initiative	Give me an example of when you have resolved conflicts between employees.
_____	Energy	How many times have you done this?

____	General intelligence	What was the outcome?
____	Decisiveness	How did you feel about the results you got?
____	Adaptability	When faced with intransigence, what did you do?

While listening to the answer to the first question, for example, you would be looking for the kinds of conflicts the applicant has addressed, their complexity, and success the applicant has had in resolving them. The answer would likely reveal a number of other characteristics, such as communication ability, sensitivity, fairness, and ability to follow prescribed procedures. Three to five interviewers may interview each applicant and rate each on a five-point scale with the goal of reaching a .5 interrater reliability or agreement.

While a behavior-based interview focuses on how an applicant handled actual work-related situations in the past, a critical incidents, hypothetical, or case approach focuses on how an applicant would handle future work-related situations. Each approach is based on a carefully prepared applicant profile and relies on a carefully structured interview. In a *critical incidents approach,* an organization selects actual critical incidents that are occurring or have occurred on the job and asks applicants how they would handle or have handled such incidents. In a *hypothetical approach,* an organization creates highly realistic but hypothetical situations and asks applicants how they would handle each. In a *case approach,* an applicant may be involved in a carefully crafted situation that will take hours to study and resolve. It could be a personnel, management, design, or production problem. All four approaches (behavior-based, critical incidents, hypothetical, and case) are based on the growing belief among organizations that responses to "How did you?" and "How would you?" questions produce more valid results than traditional interviews that rely on theoretical and philosophical questions for which applicants have already prepared answers, questions such as "What do you believe is the best way to handle conflict?" or "What qualities are essential for leadership?"[31]

6. Opening the Interview

Approach each interview in a positive manner, realizing that it is likely to be a major event in the applicant's life (even if routine for you), a great public relations opportunity for your organization, and a critical part of selecting productive employees for your organization. Give the impression that this interview is your day's top priority. There is a clear correlation between how applicants are treated and the way they talk about organizations later.

You are your organization as far as the applicant is concerned, and the applicant is more likely to accept an offer if you are perceived to be a good representative of your organization. Applicants describe ideal interviewers as warm, thoughtful, sensitive, and nondirective people who listen well, exhibit empathy, and show interest in them. Remember that you are a recruiter (persuader) as well as an information getter and evaluator. Be open and honest with each interviewee. Give a realistic picture of the position and organization, both advantages and disadvantages.

Nontraditional Interviewing Approaches

Many organizations are experimenting with nontraditional approaches. For instance, a team, panel, or board of two to five persons may interview an applicant at the same time. In some situations, panel members divide up the applicant's resume and application form, with one member asking about previous work experiences, a second asking about education and training, a third asking about technical knowledge, and a fourth asking about specific job-related skills. Although some research indicates that the panel is more effective in predicting job performance than the traditional one-on-one interview and preemployment tests, applicants and interviewers tend to prefer the traditional approach.[32] A mixed-race panel does eliminate the problem of interviewers and interviewees preferring to interview persons of the same race.[33]

Other organizations are experimenting with chain and seminar formats. In a chain format, a human resources person may take 20 minutes getting a general impression of the applicant's skills and then pass the applicant on to another person who probes into technical knowledge. This person may then pass on the applicant to a third person who probes into specific job skills. After one to three interviews, the human resources person may pick up the applicant along with written evaluations and either terminate consideration of the applicant or close the interviewing process in an upbeat manner to keep the applicant interested in the position. In the seminar format, one or more recruiters interview several applicants at the same time. This approach is subject to the pitfalls of individual interviews (if only one interviewer is present), but it takes less time, allows the organization to see several applicants at the same time, and may provide valuable insights as applicants build upon one another's comments. The openings of these experimental format interviews are critical because several people may need to be introduced, the format explained in detail, and multiple relationships addressed. Rapport and orientation will take longer.

Rapport Building

To build rapport, begin the selection interview by greeting the applicant by name in a warm, friendly voice and with a firm but not crushing handshake. Introduce yourself and your position with the organization. If appropriate, you might engage in a bit of small talk about a noncontroversial issue, but do not prolong casual conversation or fall into overworn questions such as "What do you think of this weather?" and "How was your trip?" Prolonged idle chatting may heighten tension rather than reduce it by creating anxiety and suspense. Applicants know why they are there and want to get on with it; then they can relax.

Orientation

Proceed to the orientation phase of the opening in which you tell the applicant how the interview will progress. Typically, this means, first, questions from you; second, information about the position and the organization; and third, questions from the applicant. Some interviewers, however, begin with applicant questions and then proceed to their questions. Others will give information first. You might also tell the applicant how long the interview will take and approximately how long you will devote to each part. If the interview is taking place during a plant trip, you might provide the applicant with an agenda for the visit and the names and positions of people who will be involved in the selection process.

The Opening Question

The transition from the opening to the body of the interview is usually the opening question. This open-ended, easy-to-answer first question gets the applicant talking about a familiar subject (education, experiences, background, recent internship, and so on) and sets the proper tone for the interview—the applicant talking and the employer listening. The most common opening question, "Tell me about yourself," is not a good one, however. It is so open that applicants do not know where to begin or how much information to give. Do they start with birth, grade school, high school, college, or current/recent positions? And do they talk about family, hobbies, education, work experiences, or major events? Narrow this question to a specific topic or time in the person's life.

Do not put the applicant on the spot too early because studies reveal that interviewers tend to put more weight on negative information, and the earlier it comes in the interview, the more devastating it tends to be. Thus, do not begin by asking, "What do you know about our Model 76?" or "Why are you interested in us?" Pose an easy-to-answer, reasonably open question.

7. Asking Questions

The opening question gets the body of the interview and your questioning underway. Questions are your primary tools for obtaining information and determining how well a person matches your ideal applicant profile and if he or she is a suitable fit for your organization. Questions should be open-ended, neutral, and job-specific. Open-ended questions are critical to successful selection interviews. They encourage applicants to do the talking while you listen, observe, and formulate effective probing questions. Not only do applicants give longer answers to open-ended questions, but they feel greater satisfaction with interviews that are dominated by open-ended primary and secondary questions.[34]

Question Sequences

Select one or more question sequences appropriate for the interview and the applicant; normally this means funnel or tunnel sequences. A study by Tengler and Jablin discovered that interviewers tend to use the inverted funnel sequence by asking closed primary questions during the early minutes of the interview and open-ended secondary questions in the later minutes.[35] Some interviewers apparently use the inverted sequence to test applicants and then switch to a funnel sequence with applicants they perceive to be most qualified. Since applicants tend to give short answers to closed questions while they feel out the interviewer and longer answers and more information to open questions, these interviewers are making snap judgments within the first few minutes of interviews when they have obtained very little information.[36] Also, the best way to relax an applicant is to get the person talking, but the inverted funnel sequence begins with closed questions and permits the interviewer to dominate the conversation. Begin with a funnel sequence to get the interviewee talking, relaxed, and giving maximum information from the start.

Common Question Pitfalls

Like all probing interviewers, employers create or rephrase many questions on the spot to detect relevant behaviors and probe for specifics, clarity, and implied meanings. This spontaneity makes the interview a lively conversation but leaves employers susceptible to a number of common question pitfalls. We identified some in Chapters 4 and 5, but some are unique to the selection interview.

1. *The bipolar trap:* The interviewer asks questions with only two options such as yes or no, agree or disagree, like or dislike.

   Bad: Have you traveled much in your previous positions?
   Good: To what extent have you traveled in your previous positions?

2. *The open-to-closed switch:* The interviewer asks an open-ended question but rephrases it to a closed question before the applicant can respond.

   Bad: Tell me about your projects in computer graphics. Did you design mechanical systems?
   Good: Tell me about your projects in computer graphics.

3. *The double-barreled question:* The interviewer asks two or more questions at a time.

   Bad: Tell me about your course work and projects in journalistic writing.
   Good: Tell me about your course work in journalistic writing.

4. *The leading push:* The interviewer suggests how the applicant ought to respond.

   Bad: I assume you would be willing to move to another location if necessary?

   Good: How would you feel about moving to another location?

5. *The guessing game:* The interviewer tries to guess information instead of asking for it.

   Bad: Did you leave IBM because of downsizing?
   Good: Why did you leave IBM?

6. *The evaluative response:* The interviewer expresses judgmental feelings about an answer.

   Bad: That wasn't very wise was it?
   Good: How do you feel now about your whistle-blowing?

7. *EEO violation:* The interviewer asks an unlawful question.

   Bad: Do you attend church or synagogue regularly?
   Good: (no good revision)

8. *Yes (or no) response:* The interviewer in reality gives the applicant only one option.

    Bad: Do you think you're a good fit for this position?
    Good: Why do you think you're a good fit for this position?

9. *The resume–application form question:* The interviewer asks a question that is already answered on the resume or application form.

    Bad: What offices have you held in student organizations?
    Good: Tell me about the offices you have held in student organizations.

Standard Employer Questions

The following are typical selection questions that avoid pitfalls and gather important job-related information.

Interest in the Organization

1. Why would you like to work for us?
2. How did you hear about this opening?
3. What materials have you read about our organization?
4. What do you know about our products and services?
5. What do you know about the history of our organization?

Work Related (General)

1. Tell me about the position that has given you the most satisfaction.
2. How have your previous work experiences prepared you for this position?
3. Why did you choose this career?
4. What did you do that was innovative in your last position?
5. What do you think your previous supervisors would cite as your strengths?

Work Related (Specific)

1. What tactics do you use to get your point across?
2. Describe a typical strategy you would use in a sales call.
3. What criteria do you use when assigning work to others?
4. Tell me about a situation in which you made a wrong decision and how you corrected it.
5. How do you follow up on work assigned to subordinates?

Teams and Teamwork

1. What kinds of work experiences have you had in teams?
2. How do you feel about your compensation being based in part on team results?

3. In order to reduce errors and improve productivity, we often switch people around on teams. How do you feel about trying different positions or jobs within a team's areas of responsibility?

4. What does the word "teamwork" mean to you?

5. Here at Bluefield Electronics we use integrated, cross-functional teams, so we may have marketing, sales, engineering, and purchasing representatives on the same team. How would you feel about working on such a team?

Education and Training

1. What computer skills do you have?

2. What aspects of your education have prepared you for this position?

3. What courses did you like most (least) in college?

4. If you had your education to do over, what would you do differently?

5. Why did you choose . . . as your major?

Career Plans and Goals

1. What are your long-range career goals?

2. If you join our organization, what would you like to be doing five years from now?

3. How do you feel about the way your career has gone so far?

4. What are you doing to prepare yourself for advancement?

5. Who influenced you most in your career choice?

Performance

1. What do you believe are the most important performance criteria in your area of expertise?

2. How do you ensure that you are receiving feedback pertaining to your performance?

3. All of us have pluses and minuses in our performance, what are some of your pluses (minuses)?

4. What criteria do you use when making difficult decisions?

5. How were you evaluated during your last two evaluations?

Salary and Benefits

1. What kind of salary would you need to join us?

2. What would you consider to be a good annual salary increase?

3. Which fringe benefits are most important to you?

4. How does our salary range compare to your last position?

5. If you had to do without a fringe benefit, which would it be?

Career Field

1. What do you think is the greatest challenge facing your field today?

2. What do you think will be the next major breakthrough in your field?

3. Which area of your field do you think will grow the most during the next five years?

4. How do you feel about environmental regulations in your field?

5. What do you see as major trends in your field?

On-the-Job Questions

As we noted earlier in this chapter, many interviewers are employing information getting tactics beyond the typical interview question. Some are employing *critical incident, hypothetical,* and *case* questions. In addition to these question tactics, some organizations create *idealistic employee policy statements* and observe the reactions of applicants as the statements are read. Only about 20 percent of reactions are considered positive. Others employ *job simulations* that involve the applicant in actual job tasks related to the position. A variation of the simulation is an actual *role-playing* exercise with the interviewer acting as a reluctant prospect, a hostile employee, or an angry client. And some organizations ask applicants to make *presentations* to members of the organization who evaluate the presentations according to criteria such as oral presentation, organization, knowledge, and adaptation to the position and organization.

All on-the-job questions are based on the belief that the best way to assess ability to perform a job is to observe the applicant *doing* the job. Employers have discovered that many applicants can tell you about the theories and principles they would use, but they are unable to put these theories and principles into practice. It is one thing to say how you might confront a hostile employee but quite another to do it. Studying how to interview effectively, for instance, is not the same as conducting effective interviews. That is why all interviewing courses combine both study and practice.

Regardless of the questioning methods you use, design the questioning phase of the interview to explore how well the applicant meets the ideal employee profile and would fit into your organization. Get specifics, explore suggestions or implications in responses, clarify meanings, and force the applicant to get beyond safe, superficial Level 1 responses to reveal feelings, preferences, knowledge, and expertise. Review the questioning techniques discussed in Chapters 4 and 5, particularly silent, nudging, clearinghouse, informational, restatement, reflective, and mirror probes.

Use all available tools to get the information necessary to select the best applicants. Remember there are always two applicants in each interview, *the real* and *the make-believe.* Your task is to determine how much of what you see and hear is a facade and how much is genuine. Get beneath the surface of rehearsed and planned answers to find the real person. Research indicates that interviewers have difficulty doing this. Listen carefully to all that is said and not said. Be responsive. Silent and nudging probes are effective because applicants feel less threatened and more respected when interviewers respond with simple verbal and nonverbal signals and do not interrupt them. Do not become a cheerleader by saying "Good!" after every answer.

8. Giving Information

Interviewers tend to focus on questioning as their role in interviews, but giving information is also an essential ingredient in successful interviews. Before you begin to give information, however, ask applicants two important transition questions: (1) What do you know about this position? (2) What do you know about our organization? Answers to these questions show, first, how much homework the applicant has done, thus revealing the applicant's level of interest and work ethic. And second, they tell you how much and what the applicant already knows about the position and organization so you can begin where the person's knowledge leaves off. This prevents you from wasting valuable interview time giving the applicant information the person already knows. Do not be surprised, however, if an applicant is unfamiliar with a very recent story, event, or introduction of a new product or service.

Give adequate information to facilitate the matching process between your organization and the applicant. Information about your organization's reputation, the position, organizational environment, and advancement opportunities tend to be the most important factors in acceptance of job offers. Compare your organization to your competitors, but do not be negative. Sell the *advantages* of your position and organization. Do not lie to applicants, intentionally hide negative aspects of the position or organization, or inflate applicant expectations. These practices result in high rates of employee dissatisfaction and turnover. Tell applicants what a typical workday would be like. Avoid gossip. Do not talk too much about yourself, a common problem in selection interviews.

While you want to inform applicants thoroughly, do not allow your information giving to dominate an interview. Some studies have found that applicants speak for only 10 minutes in a typical 30-minute screening interview.[37] Reverse this figure, because you will learn more about the applicant by listening than by talking. Review the guidelines for giving information in Chapter 12. Here are a few important suggestions for giving information. Practice good communication skills because applicants may judge the authenticity of information you give by how it is communicated verbally and nonverbally. Encourage applicants to ask questions about information you are giving so you know it is being communicated accurately and effectively. Do not overload applicants with information, much of which may be available in organizational pamphlets and reports. Organize your information systematically and logically.

9. Closing the Interview

If you have the authority to hire on the spot (rare in most interviews), either offer the position or terminate further consideration. If you do not have hiring authority or do not want to make an immediate decision, explain specifically what the applicant can expect after the completion of the interview. For example,

> Well, Phil, as you know, we are interviewing a number of people for this position and will invite four or five to go through an additional interview at our facility in Dallas. You will be notified from my office by mail within the next 10 days as to whether or not you will be asked to come for the next round of interviews. If you

need to talk to me for some reason before then, you can reach me or one of my associates by calling 800-439-6909, extension 33. Any final questions?

Thank applicants for their time and interest in your organization, give them your address, telephone number, and e-mail address on a business card, and encourage them to write or call you personally if they have any questions.

Do not encourage or discourage applicants needlessly. If you have many excellent applicants for a position, do not give each the impression that he or she is at the top of the list. If you know an applicant will not be considered further, do not string the person along with false hope. Let the individual down gently. An applicant you cannot use at this time may prove to be ideal for a future opening.

And watch what you do, say, and ask following the formal closing as you walk with the person to the door or to the parking lot, take the person to the airport, or escort the person to meet another member of your organization. As noted earlier, these informal times can lead easily to EEO violations. Do not do or say anything that adversely affects the relationship you have developed carefully during the interview.

Be sure you or your office follows up on all prospects. If possible, have all letters typed and signed by you or your representative. A personal touch, even when rejecting an applicant, can maintain a feeling of goodwill toward you and your organization.

10. Evaluating the Interview

Record your reactions to each applicant as soon as possible after each interview. It is wise to build in time between interviews for this purpose. Many organizations provide interviewers with standardized evaluation forms to match applicants with the ideal applicant profile for each position. If the interview is a screening interview, you must decide whether to invite the applicant for a second round of interviews. If the interview is a determinate interview, you must decide whether to make an offer or send a rejection letter (the infamous "ding letter").

The interview evaluation often consists of two parts: a set of standardized questions and a set of open questions. See the sample interview evaluation form in Figure 8.2. The standardized part should consist of bona fide occupational qualifications for each position and be extensive enough to allow you to determine how well the applicant matches these qualifications.

The following are typical open-ended questions:

1. What are the applicant's strengths for this position?
2. What are the applicant's weaknesses for this position?
3. How does this applicant compare to other applicants for this position?
4. What makes this applicant a good or poor fit with our organization?
5. How accurate is the applicant's conception of what this position entails?

You should also use the evaluation stage to assess your own interviewing skills and performance. The following are typical self-evaluation questions:

Figure 8.2   *Interviewer's evaluation report*

Interviewer's Evaluation Report

Applicant _____ Position _____

Interviewer _____ Date _____ Location _____

	Poor	Fair	Good	Very Good	Excellent
Interest in This Position	___	___	___	___	___
Knowledge of the Company	___	___	___	___	___
Education/Training	___	___	___	___	___
Experiences	___	___	___	___	___
Maturity	___	___	___	___	___
Adaptability	___	___	___	___	___
Assertiveness	___	___	___	___	___
Ability to Communicate	___	___	___	___	___
Appearance	___	___	___	___	___

1. What are the applicant's major strengths?

2. What are the applicant's major weaknesses?

3. How does this applicant compare to other applicants for this position?

Overall rating: Unfavorable   1   2   3   4   5   Favorable

1. How successfully did I create an informal, relaxed atmosphere?
2. How effectively did I open the interview?
3. How effectively did I encourage the applicant to speak openly and freely?
4. How thoroughly did I explore the applicant's qualifications for this position with primary and secondary questions?
5. How effectively did I listen to the applicant?
6. How adequate was the information I provided on the position and organization?
7. Did I reserve adequate time for the applicant to ask questions?
8. How well did I respond to the applicant's questions?
9. How effectively did I close the interview?
10. Did I reserve judgment until the interview was completed?

Summary

The selection interview can be an effective means of selecting employees, but it takes preparation that includes becoming familiar with state and federal EEO laws, developing an applicant profile, obtaining and reviewing information on applicants, and developing a carefully structured interview. And preparation must be followed by a thoroughly professional interview that includes an effective opening, skillful questioning, probing into answers, thorough information giving, honest and detailed answers to questions, and an effective closing. And you must practice effective communication skills that include language selection, nonverbal communication (silence, voice, eye contact, facial expressions, posture, and gestures), listening, and empathy. And when the interview is concluded, you should conduct evaluations of the applicant and yourself, the first for suitability and fit and the second for effectiveness as applicant evaluator and recruiter.

A Selection Interview for Review and Analysis

In this interview, Rachel McSween is applying for a position as a management trainee with Everything for the Office, Inc., a national outlet for office supplies, equipment, computers, and furniture. Dieter Vosterbeck is a college recruiter for Everything for the Office. The interview is taking place at the campus placement center.

How satisfactory are the rapport and orientation stages of the opening? How well do the employer's questions meet EEO guidelines and avoid common question pitfalls? How effectively does the employer probe into answers? Does the employer appear to have an ideal applicant profile in mind? How adequate is the employer's information giving? Does the employer control the interview too much, too little, or about right? How satisfactory is the closing?

1. **Employer:** Good afternoon. It's a beautiful day, isn't it? You're Rachel McSween, my 2:45 appointment?

2. **Applicant:** Yes, I am.

3. **Employer:** Won't you have a seat. I'm Dieter Vosterbeck. Please call me Dieter.

4. **Applicant:** Okay.

5. **Employer:** How's everything at school?

6. **Applicant:** Okay, thanks.

7. **Employer:** What I would like to do today is, first of all, ask you some questions concerning yourself and your interests, then I would like to tell you a bit about what Everything for the Office, Inc., has to offer you, and finally, I will be more than happy to answer any questions you have for me.

8. **Applicant:** Okay. I have been looking forward to this interview.

9. **Employer:** First of all, tell me how you became interested in management.

10. **Applicant:** Okay. Well, it started in high school when I needed a part-time job to buy a car and clothes. I started working for Burger King as a junior and gradually worked my way up to night manager during college. I like management because it is a people-oriented major and career. I guess I like to work with people.

11. **Employer:** Why do you like to work with people?

12. **Applicant:** Well, it seems like my whole life has been centered on people. Through the activities and the things I have done, I see that I am a very people-oriented person. I can't explain why; I just enjoy working with people.

13. **Employer:** Tell me what enables you to work well with people?

14. **Applicant:** Okay. Well I come from a big family; I have three brothers and four sisters. And my neighborhood in Memphis had all kinds of people from all over the world and some very interesting characters. I learned to understand different people. When I came to college, I decided to live in the dorm, and our dorm had people from all over the United States and the world. My roommate was from Thailand. You learn to live with and to work with many different types of people.

15. **Employer:** Um-hmm. What work experiences have you had with different types of people, besides Burger King?

16. **Applicant:** During the school years, I worked in the cafeteria at the dorm with people of both sexes, different ages, and from lots of different cultures.

17. **Employer:** You have been a night manager at Burger King during the summers for about three years, right?

18. **Applicant:** Right.

19. **Employer:** Tell me the most difficult situation you have had to deal with.

20. **Applicant:** Okay. That was a night about a year ago when we were held up just after closing by two men who were acting like customers.

21. **Employer:** That sounds difficult and dangerous.

22. **Applicant:** Yes, it was scary.

23. **Employer:** And what did you do?

24. **Applicant:** Well, they ordered all of us into the walk-in freezer and made me open the cash drawers. I followed many of the company's procedures for such situations. I gave the robbers money and tried to keep everyone calm. It's scary to have someone aiming a loaded gun at you.

25. **Employer:** Then what happened?

26. **Applicant:** They closed the door of the freezer and warned us not to come out for five minutes. After waiting a couple of minutes, I came out and called 911. The police came within a minute or two. One of the hold-up men was caught a few days later trying to hold up another fast-food restaurant.

27. **Employer:** How do you feel your personal qualities and characteristics, as well as experiences, will help you in a management training position with Everything?

28. **Applicant:** I feel these equip me to work in many jobs. Specifically relating to Everything for the Office, I feel they are going to help me in working with people.

29. **Employer:** Very good. Rachel, why are you interested in a position with Everything?

30. **Applicant:** My major in management has prepared me well for a manager position in a large retail setting like Everything for the Office. It is a growing company in a very competitive field that is changing rapidly from mom and pop–run office stores to giant outlets. I think this will be exciting.

31. **Employer:** So why should we choose you over the other applicants?

32. **Applicant:** That's a tough question. I feel that my work experience places me at the top of most applicant lists.

33. **Employer:** Let me tell you a little bit about Everything for the Office. We were founded in 1987 with the consolidation of three small office supply chains in Alabama and Mississippi. We currently have 47 mega stores in seven states and are opening a new store once every two months. Our sales place us among the top five office supply chains. We are probably the fastest growing. Do you have any questions for me?

34. **Applicant:** Yes. The stock market has fluctuated tremendously during the last several months. How is this going to affect Everything in the long run?

35. **Employer:** We will not be affected like many companies because we are in a business that is essential. Companies are going to have to have supplies, furniture, and electronic equipment that becomes dated very quickly.

36. **Applicant:** I know Everything for the Office is expanding throughout the South. What about other areas of the country?

37. **Employer:** We are recruiting heavily right now because we are moving people around with the company as new stores come on line. We plan to expand out of the South soon.

38. **Applicant:** I would like to know more about your training program.

39. **Employer:** Well, it's basically an orientation program. You'd be meeting people, getting familiar with our policies and procedures, working with different individuals within different departments, and getting familiar with the surroundings. We also do a seminar to orient new employees.

40. **Applicant:** What about specific training in management?

41. **Employer:** Not in the sense of classes. We try to hire people who have extensive training in management and, hopefully, some actual management experience. You will work, however, with different managers during your training to learn their styles.

42. **Applicant:** That's all the questions I have. I would like to add, Mr. Vosterbeck, that I'm very interested in a position with Everything for the Office.

43. **Employer:** I'm glad to hear that. I should be getting in touch with you by mail no later than the fifteenth of this month. I notice that you have no specific geographic location preference on your application.

44. **Applicant:** That's correct. I will be looking forward to hearing from you.

45. **Employer:** You should hear from me within two weeks.

46. **Applicant:** Okay.

47. **Employer:** Have a good day.

Selection Role-Playing Cases

An Accountant for a Metal Company

You have an opening in the Human Resources Department at Midwest Metalworking. This position requires a full knowledge of human resources, initiative, and loyalty to the company. With not much immediate opportunity for promotion from this position, the person hired will be in a dead-end spot for some years. The Human Resources Department has good morale, and the workers get along well with each other and with the department head. You know little about the applicant except information on a resume that the person will graduate in the spring with extensive course work in the human resources area. This applicant would be a good person for this position, except that he or she is inexperienced and might be eager for advancement.

A Travel Agency Position

You have an opening in your travel agency, King and Associates, for a top-notch salesperson. The position requires a person with experience in sales, knowledge of the travel industry, willingness to travel to gain first hand information on destinations, and ability to talk easily and persuasively with people. King and Associates is run on a commission basis and offers opportunity for advancement. The applicant has a degree in advertising and public relations and has worked for four different firms in the past eight years. During a brief telephone conversation, the applicant seemed pleasant, easy to talk to, and skilled in verbal and nonverbal communication. You are unsure why this person is interested in a position out of public relations and advertising. The person appears to have traveled extensively while growing up with a father in the Air Force.

A Broadcast News Reporter

You are the new owner-manager of radio station WWWZ in a city of 90,000. This station has changed owners a number of times, and with each new owner there has been a new format: classic rock, pop, jazz, country and western, a mixture of everything, and talk. The news department has been the one consistently bright spot in WWWZ because it has retained veteran reporters and anchors. Retirements are now threatening the quality of the news department. You want to hire a first-rate news reporter who can develop good relationships with the local university, government, police departments, political leaders, and groups and do some in-depth stories. The applicant's background and sample tape are impressive, but the applicant is a recent college graduate whose only experience is at the college radio station. You are not sure the applicant is ready to jump into a commercial station and meet your high expectations.

Student Activities

1. Contact your state employment office. Ask the office to recommend a list of tests that do not violate state or federal laws. How can these tests help to focus interviews? What questions might test results suggest?

2. Contact a local temporary employment agency in your community. Ask a person about employment trends in this area. What tools do they use to select appropriate applicants? How do interviews with temporary workers differ from those with permanent workers? On average, how many applicants do they send to an employer before the position is filled?

3. Interview a person in your profession who conducts selection interviews. Ask about the advantages and disadvantages of videotaping employment interviews, both standard interviews and video-conference interviews. How does the person prepare for each? How might evaluative procedures change when an interview is videotaped?

4. Interview an experienced recruiter about his or her questioning techniques and strategies. What opening questions does the person use and how are these determined? What probing or secondary question techniques does the person use? What question sequences, if any, does this recruiter employ? What application questions such as critical incident, hypothetical, and role-playing has this person used? How have his or her questioning types and strategies changed during the past five or ten years?

Notes

1. K. Michele Kacmar and Wayne A. Hochwarter, "The Interview as a Communication Event: A Field Examination of Demographic Effects on Interview Outcomes," *Journal of Business Communication* 32 (1995), pp. 207–32.

2. Paula C. Morrow, "Physical Attractiveness and Selection Decision Making," *Journal of Management* 16 (1990), pp. 45–60; and George E. Gercken, "Preconception-Misconception, or Why We Interview So Ineffectively," *Manage,* October 1993, pp. 34–35.

3. Michael A. Campion, David K. Palmer, and James E. Campion, "A Review of Structure in the Selection Interview," *Personnel Psychology* 50 (1997), pp. 655–702; and Peter Herriot, "Commentary: A Paradigm Bursting at the Seams," *Journal of Organizational Behavior* 14 (1993), pp. 371–75.

4. Steven M. Ralston and Robert Brady, "The Relative Influence of Interview Communication Satisfaction on Applicants' Recruitment Decisions," *Journal of Business Communication* 31 (1994), pp. 61–77.

5. Michael A. McDaniel, Deborah H. Whetzel, Frank L. Schmidt, and Steven D. Mauer, "The Validity of Employment Interviews: A Comprehensive Review and Meta-Analysis," *Journal of Applied Psychology* 79 (1994), pp. 599–616.

6. Janine S. Pouliot, "Topics to Avoid with Applicants," *Nation's Business,* July 1992, pp. 57–58; and David K. Lindo, "Are You Asking for a Lawsuit?" *Supervision,* December 1993, pp. 17–19.

7. Jeffery Springston and Joann Keyton, "Defining and Quantifying Potentially Discriminating Questions in Employment Interviewing," unpublished paper, Annual Convention of the National Communication Association, San Francisco, 1989.

8. Junda Woo, "Job Interviews Pose Risk to Employers," *The Wall Street Journal,* March 11, 1992, pp. B1 and B5.

9. Clive Fletcher, "Ethics and the Job Interview," *Personnel Management,* March 1992, pp. 36–39.

10. Phillip M. Perry, "Your Most Dangerous Legal Traps When Interviewing Job Applicants," *Law Practice Management,* March 1994, pp. 50–56.

11. "Etiquette for Interviewing Candidates with Disabilities," *Personnel Journal,* supplement, September 1992, p. 6.

12. According to Rochelle Kaplan, legal counsel for the College Placement Council, no question is technically unlawful. The use of a question may be unlawful because courts assume that if you ask such a question, you will use it for unlawful purposes.

13. Perry, 1994, pp. 50–56; and Phillip M. Perry, "Foolproofing the Job Interview," *Folio,* January 1, 1993, pp. 83–84.

14. Heather K. Gerken, "Understanding Mixed Motives Claims under the Civil Rights Act of 1991: An Analysis of Intentional Discrimination Claims Based on Sex-Stereotyped Interview Questions," *Michigan Law Review* 91 (1993), pp. 1824–53.

15. George F. Dreher, Ronald A. Ash, and Priscilla Hancock, "The Role of the Traditional Research Design in Underestimating the Validity of the Employment Interview," *Personnel Psychology* 41 (1988), pp. 315–27.

16. "Hiring: An Expert Explains How to Choose the Best Applicant," *Effective Manager* 6 (1982), pp. 4–5.

17. Patrick H. Raymark, Mark J. Schmit, and Robert M. Guion, "Identifying Potentially Useful Personality Constructs for Employee Selection," *Personnel Psychology* 50 (1997), pp. 723–36.

18. Wayne J. Camara and Dianne L. Schneider, "Integrity Tests: Facts and Unresolved Issues," *American Psychologist* 49 (1994), p. 112.

19. Paul R. Sackett and James E. Wanek, "New Developments in the Use of Measures of Honesty, Integrity, Conscientiousness, Dependability, Trustworthiness, and Reliability for Personnel Selection," *Personnel Psychology* 49 (1996), pp. 787–829.

20. Carol Kleiman, "From Genetics to Honesty, Firms Expand Employee Tests, Screening," *Chicago Tribune,* February 9, 1992, p. 8, 1:1.

21. Wayne J. Camara, "Employee Honesty Testing: Traps and Opportunities," *Boardroom Reports,* December 15, 1991, pp. 7–8.

22. Anita Gates, "The Secrets of Making a Good Hire," *Working Woman* 17 (1992), pp. 70–72.

23. K. R. Murphy, *Honesty in the Workplace* (Pacific Grove, CA: Brooks/Cole, 1993); and D. Z. Ones, C. Viswesvaran, and F. L. Schmidt, "Comprehensive Meta-Analysis of Integrity Test Validities: Findings and Implications for Personnel Selection and Theories of Job Performance," *Journal of Applied Psychology* 70 (1993), pp. 774–76.

24. I. M. Shepard and R. Duston, *Thieves at Work: An Employer's Guide to Combating Dishonesty* (Washington, DC: Bureau of National Affairs, 1988). John C. Hollwitz and Donna P. Pawlowski in the Department of Communication Studies at Creighton University have developed a behavior and situational interview that focuses on honesty dimensions.

25. Karl Magnusen, O. Kroeck, K. Galen, and Elizabeth Shelley, "Video-Conferencing: Maximizing Recruiting," *HR Magazine,* August 1995, p. 70.

26. Julia King, "Dell Facilities Recruiting via Video Services," *Computerworld,* September 15, 1997, p. 14.

27. Fredric M. Jablin and Vernon D. Miller, "Interviewer and Applicant Questioning Behavior in Employment Interviews," *Management Communication Quarterly* 4 (1990), pp. 51–86.

28. Therese H. Macan and Robert L. Dipboye, "The Effects of Interviewer's Initial Impressions on Information Gathering," *Organizational Behavior and Human Decision Processes* 42 (1988), pp. 364–87.

29. Allen I. Huffcutt and Winfred Arthus, "Hunter and Hunter (1984) Revisited: Interview Validity for Entry-Level Jobs," *Journal of Applied Psychology* 79 (1994), pp. 184–90.

30. Philip Roth and Jeffrey J. McMillan, "The Behavior Description Interview," *CPA Journal,* December 1993, pp. 76–79.

31. Michael M. Harris, "Reconsidering the Employment Interview: A Review of Recent Literature and Suggestions for Future Research," *Personnel Psychology* 42 (1989), pp. 691–726; and Phillip E. Lowry, "The Structured Interview: An Alternative to the Assessment Center," *Public Personnel Management* 23 (1994), pp. 201–15.

32. Philip L. Roth and James E. Campion, "An Analysis of the Predictive Power of the Panel Interview and Pre-Employment Tests," *Journal of Occupational & Organizational Psychology* 65 (1992), pp. 51–60; and Dennis Warmke and David J. Weston, "Success Dispels Myths about Panel Interviewing," *Personnel Journal* 71 (1992), pp. 120–26.

33. Thung-Rung Lin, Gregory H. Dobbins, and Jiing-Lih Farh, "A Field Study of Race and Age Similarity Effects on Interview Ratings in Conventional and Situational Interviews," *Journal of Applied Psychology* 77 (1992), pp. 363–71.

34. Jablin and Miller, pp. 51–86; and Gerald Vinton, "Open versus Closed Questions—An Open Issue?" *Management Decision* 33 (1995), pp. 27–32.

35. Craig D. Tengler and Fredric M. Jablin, "Effects of Question Type, Orientation, and Sequencing in the Employment Screening Interview," *Communication Monographs* 50 (1983), pp. 245–63.

36. M. Ronald Buckley and Robert W. Eder, "B. M. Springbelt and the Notion of 'Snap Decision' in the Interview," *Journal of Management* 14 (1988), pp. 59–67.

37. Thomas Gergmann and M. Susan Taylor, "College Recruitment: What Attracts Students to Organizations?" *Personnel* 61 (1984), pp. 34–36; and Fredric M. Jablin, "Organizational Entry, Assimilation, and Exit," *Handbook of Organizational Communication* (Beverly Hills, CA: Sage, 1987).

Resources

Adams Media Corporation. *Job Almanac.* Holbrook, MA: Adams Media Corporation, 1998.

Dixon, Pam. *Job Searching Online for Dummies.* Foster City, CA: IDG Books Worldwide, 1998.

Kanter, Arnold B. *The Complete Book of Interviewing: Everything You Need to Know from Both Sides of the Table.* New York: Times Books, 1995.

Weitzul, James B. *Evaluating Interpersonal Skills in the Job Interview: A Guide for Human Resources Professionals.* New York: Quorum Books, 1992.

Yates, James B. *Hiring the Best.* Holbrook, MA: Adams Media Corporation, 1994.

The Selection Interview: The Applicant

T he changes in the world economy are remarkable. The merger and acquisition frenzy that took place in the 1980s has continued through the late 1990s. The U.S. stock market, in spite of declines at times, has grown an average of 16 percent each year since 1982.[1] This expansion and change in the United States has been magnified by the loss of Smith Corona, our last typewriter company, the purchase of Zenith by a Korean company and its ultimate bankruptcy, the merger of Chrysler with a German company, and the purchase of Amoco by British Petroleum (BP).

The Changing World of Work

The employment future has never been brighter for those with college degrees in technical fields. The employment market is so in need of information-technology-trained engineers and both software and hardware programmers that Congress may extend the stay of technically educated immigrants and increase the number of immigrants allowed to enter the United States. There are not enough engineers to fill available positions.

In the past we have offered encouraging words for majors in liberal arts, education, and nontechnical fields, but the market was not as good for them. Today, a college degree or degrees can open many exciting employment opportunities regardless of major. Those who do not seek four-year degrees can find employment in tool-making, mold-making, and a wide variety of services. Employment is no longer limited to the technically educated.

Peter Drucker's world of the knowledgeable worker has arrived. The changes in employment are apparent in the lists of good positions and places to seek employment. By reviewing Drucker's knowledge-service worker paradigm and the "best job" lists from such sources as *Money Magazine, Time, U.S. News & World Report,* and *The Wall Street Journal* and realizing that a large portion of positions after the turn of the century will deal with high-tech products and services, we believe there are 12 areas of significant potential for today's and tomorrow's college graduates.[2] Six will be in high-technical/manufacturing areas and six in service areas.

High-Technical/Manufacturing

1. Computer programming: software and hardware design, application, and repair.

2. Computer application technology: phones, automobiles, smart homes and offices, space, air transportation.

3. Engineering: chemical, civil, electrical, mechanical, manufacturing, robotics, aeronautical, environmental.

4. Telecommunication: networks, integration, broadcasting, cable, interactive entertainment and education.

5. Scientific research: biology, chemistry, environmental studies, conservation, meteorology, gerontology.

6. Medicine: primary care, specializations of all types, home care.

Services

1. Sales/marketing/merchandising: retail, wholesale, home delivery.

2. Accounting and financial service: international finance, investment and retirement consulting, financial analysis, financial planning.

3. Consulting: computer systems, training, organizational development, finance, employee assistance programs, family and personal counseling.

4. Corrections and law enforcement: police, private security, for-profit prison operations, criminology, law.

5. Human resources/education: employment benefits and compensation, training and development, elementary, secondary, college, and university teaching, guidance counseling.

6. Advertising and public relations: creative consulting, corporate imaging, public relations, creative writing.

These lists do not include all employment opportunities. With unemployment at or below 5 percent, persons remaining unemployed are often unemployable.

Organizations are targeting skills, degrees, and applicant groups. Cultural diversity is reality for most organizations engaged in national and world markets. Every seven seconds someone turns 50 in the United States. If that person is a white male, there are more women and minorities capable of replacing him than ever before. Today, the workforce in many organizations consists of women and men of diverse cultures, languages, and countries. Here is *Fortune*'s top "diversity elite":[3]

1. Pacific Enterprises, Los Angeles—a public utility that has the highest percentage of minority officials and managers of any company on the list.

2. Advantica, Spartanburg, South Carolina—the parent company of Denny's now has a culturally diverse group of suppliers and franchisers.

3. BankAmerica, San Francisco—recognized for its approach to provide a comfortable place for everyone to work.

4. Fannie May, Washington D.C.—in breaking down barriers to home ownership for blacks and Hispanics it has found a new growth business.

5. Marriott International, Bethesda, Maryland—minority ownership of Marriott franchises increased from 1 to 29 in one year.

6. Applied Materials, Santa Clara, California—actively recruits at historically black Howard University and the National Hispanic University in San Jose.

7. Edison International, Rosemead, California—settled a large discrimination suit and increased corporate minority officers from one to five.

8. Computer Associates, Islandia, New York—founder and CEO is from China, president is from Sri Lanka, donated $25 million to State University of New York for an Asian-American center.

9. Ryder System, Miami, Florida—tied with Applied Materials for most minorities among the 25 highest-paid employees.

10. Pitney Bowes, Stamford, Connecticut—goal of spending $52 million with minority and women suppliers, minorities accounted for half of all hires in 1997.

The variety of employers and types of positions in *Fortune*'s diversity elite is astonishing, and they are a fraction of excellent American companies. It is a seller's market. Attracting and retaining good employees is essential today. Organizations are offering signing bonuses, stock options, tuition reimbursement, health insurance, and profit sharing to top applicants. The competition for good employees has created excellent financial opportunities, and you should be encouraged if an interviewer tells you in a screening interview about benefits the organization has to offer.[4]

Organizational flattening during the 1970s, 1980s, and 1990s, illustrated in Figure 9.1, has eliminated millions of middle-management positions and made upward movement slower. The smallest rectangle represents a Japanese division of a multi-billion

Figure 9.1 *Organizational flattening*

1960s to Mid-1980s	**1990s**	**2000s**
1. Chair of the board	1. Chair	1. President
2. President	2. CEO	2. Managers
3/4. Senior or executive vice president	3. Vice president	3. Associates
5. Vice president	4. Director	
6. Director	5. Manager	
7. Manager	6. Supervisor	
8. Supervisor	7. Associate	
9. Assistant supervisor		
10. Group leader		
11. Lead person		
12. Misc. increase		
13/14. College entry level		
15. Employee entry level		

dollar corporation doing $800 million of business in the United States with fewer than 120 employees at three levels: a president, eight managers, and everyone else. You are likely to remain in the same position longer, and your development is likely to be a widening of job responsibilities and skills rather than promotion to a new level as in the past.

Right-sizing, downsizing, and reengineering continue among some of the world's largest corporations. These shakeouts are coming about because of massive, worldwide economic changes. Japan, for the first time since World War II, has experienced a severe economic downturn that has impacted Asian countries such as Malaysia, China, and Thailand. Russia, after moving to a market economy, has encountered major political and economic problems. If an organization exports to or manufactures in these countries, economic events will affect hirings. Every company or organization is for sale, depending on price and circumstances. Efforts to fend off mergers and buyouts are being challenged.

One of the authors was recently asked during a campus visit, "How do I stay away from organizations that are targets for mergers and acquisitions in order to make my job more secure?" The response was simply, "You cannot." Job security is not only a function of the organization but of the employee's skills and flexibility. While employees of your grandparents' and parents' generations often remained with the same organizations for 30 or more years and received the legendary gold watch, you are likely to work for six to eight different organizations and change careers three times.

This does not mean that Fortune 500 companies are not seeking long-term employees, but changes in ownership, direction, product lines, and services that affect employment are the rule rather than the exception.[5] Reconstruction, mergers, outsourcing, and use of contingency workers (formerly called temporary) will continue to be part of the changing organizational landscape. In a recent study by Clarke, Poynton, and Associates, 57 percent of companies surveyed reported being more careful in their selection of employees to maintain and retain their workforce.[6]

Applicants, like organizations, must make interviewing a systematic and structured part of the search for and selection of a suitable position. This involves a series of stages, illustrated in Figure 9.2. Be ready for honesty tests, skills tests, and personality inventories. Prepare thoroughly for each selection interview because no two interviews, positions, or organizations will be exactly the same. Do not be surprised if your interview is videotaped or the screening interview is done through a conference call. If you decide to wing it, to learn as you go, you will face many disappointments both in searching for a position and in the position you are able to select. Preparation includes the first four stages of the search process.

1. Analyzing Yourself

The essential first step in locating and obtaining the position you want is a thorough and insightful self-analysis. First, you must know yourself—including education, training, experiences, needs, desires, strengths and weaknesses, likes and dislikes—so you can determine ideal positions and ideal organizations for *you*. And second, nearly all interview questions

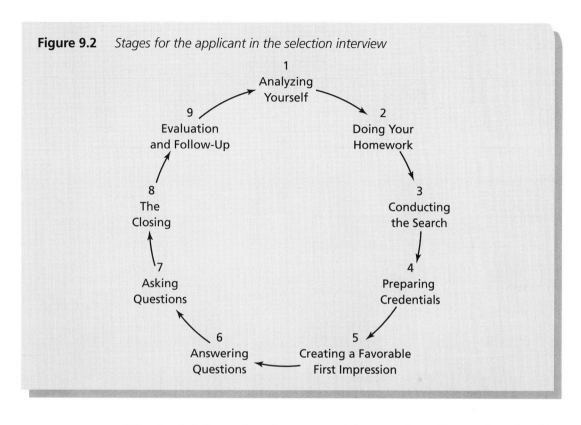

Figure 9.2   *Stages for the applicant in the selection interview*

will be aimed at discovering who *you* are, what *you* can do, and how well *you* fit with a specific position with a specific organization. You cannot answer most questions insightfully and persuasively if *you don't know who you are.* Simply put, you cannot sell you if you don't know you.

Self-analysis may be painful because most of us do not want to probe deeply and honestly into our strengths and weaknesses, successes and failures. No one needs to see your self-analysis but you, so be painfully honest with yourself. The following questions can serve as guides for your personal inventory.[7]

1. What are your *personality* strengths and weaknesses?

Reliability	Values
Motivation	Maturity
Open-mindedness	Flexibility
Adaptability to change	Ability to accept criticism
Integrity	Moral standards
Assertiveness	Ambition
Self-control	Work under pressure

2. What are your *intellectual* strengths and weaknesses?

Intelligence   Ease of learning

Organizing   Analyzing

Creating   Evaluating

Planning   Reasoning

3. What are your *communicative* strengths and weaknesses?

Oral communication skills   Written communication skills

Listening skills   Interpersonal skills

With superiors   With subordinates?

With coworkers   With persons of different sex, age, race, ethnic group, nationality

4. What have been your *accomplishments and failures*?

Academic   Extracurricular activities, hobbies, avocations

Work   Professional

Goals set and met

5. What are your *professional* strengths and weaknesses?

Education   Training

Experiences   Specific skills

Talents

6. What do you want in a *position* and *organization?*

Responsibility   Contact with people

Independence   Authority

Type of work   Security

Prestige of organization   Variety

Decision making   Benefits

Coworkers   Income

7. What are your *most valued needs* as a person?

Family   Home

Possessions   Free time

Relationships   Recreation opportunities

Geographical location   Prestige

Recognition   Success

8. What are your *professional* interests?

Short-range goals   Long-range goals

Advancement   Recognition

Growth

9. Why did you attend _____ college/university and how happy are you with this decision?

10. Why did you major in _____, and how happy are you with this decision?

11. Why did you accept positions at (1) _____, (2) _____, (3) _____?

12. Why did you leave (1) _____, (2) _____, (3) _____?

By the time you thoroughly and honestly answer questions such as these, you should have a detailed self-inventory and a good idea of who you are, what you are qualified to do, and what you would like to do. Determine how well you are prepared for the 10 universal skills and attitudes essential to work in the twenty-first century.

You will need to deal comfortably *with numbers.* Voluntary compliance with ISO-9000 and other measurement standards and increased importing and exporting into other currencies make this an important skill. You may be required to track units made per hour per machine, customer response time, and cost per unit of hire or sales per hour per store. With the help of computers and calculators, you may not need to write down these numbers, but you may be required to interpret them, formulate ratios, and change costs from lira to francs. You may need to interpret the methods and results of quantitative research.

You will need to be *computer literate.* Much of what you do—from paying bills, ordering books from the library, and chatting on the Internet, to sending e-mail, doing word processing, and creating graphics—will require continually updated computer literacy. You may need to be comfortable with spreadsheets such as Excel.

You will need to be *customer- and quality-oriented.* Every organization will be driven by these goals. For instance, every division of the Motorola Corporation has one overriding objective: total customer satisfaction.

You will need to have a *global and diverse perspective.* You will increasingly be a part of the global village. Merely look around your classroom or lunchroom to see how diverse our workforce has become in a few short years.

You will need to speak a *second language.* As the world grows smaller and the United States becomes more diverse, the need to speak a second or third language will increase. Notice in newspaper want ads or electronic bulletin boards how often they require the ability to speak Spanish. According to some demographers, states such as California, Florida, and Texas will have Hispanic majorities by the year 2005. American Honda and other Japanese-owned companies are offering language training for their employees.

You will need strong *interpersonal skills.* Verbal and nonverbal communication, listening, and ability to understand and work with others will be essential in whatever position you choose. Such skills will also enable you to make effective presentations.

You will need to deal with *change and job ambiguity.* Every career area will face continual changes in technology, structure, management, and marketing and your job will require continual adaptation, adjustment, and flexibility. The organization may give you a minimal job description or ask you to shape or write your own description.

You will need to nourish a *willingness to learn.* Organizations are committed to ongoing training, development, and education. Your college commencement is merely the beginning of your lifelong learning process. While organizations will invest in your knowledge base, you should plan to invest a portion of your income in books, tapes, discs, computer hardware and software, CD-ROMs, and seminars.

You will need to take on a *team perspective.* The growing diversity of the workforce and complexity of the problems organizations encounter require teamwork in study groups, self-managed workforces, cross-functional teams, and problem-solving task forces.

You will need to be a *problem solver,* not a problem creator or distractor. Organizations need doers who resolve problems and issues. They will no longer tolerate employees who create morale problems or complain, some would say whine, "I don't want to do that," "That's not my job," or "That's not what I was hired to do."

Your personal inventory will help you write down a list of short-term and long-term goals and then a career goal or life mission statement. If you know who you are, what you want, where you are, and where you want to go, your chances of determining how to get there are pretty good. Do not settle too quickly on a position title or a narrow description. Focus rather on kinds of activities and achievements that give you satisfaction because you are unlikely to be aware of all the opportunities open to you now and in the future.

2. Doing Your Homework

Once you know who you are, what you are qualified to do, and what you want to do, it is time to do your homework. Study the changing workplace, your field or fields, the organizations you will apply to, the positions you will apply for, current events, and the interviewing process.

Your Field, Organizations, and Positions

Learn everything you can about your *field* before you start searching for positions and developing resumes because this knowledge should influence both. What are your field's history, developments, trends, areas of specialization, leaders, challenges, current and future problems, and employment opportunities? What education (including degrees and specializations) and experiences are essential for entering this field? Develop a mature, realistic perception of what your field is like and what people do during typical workdays.

Employers expect you to be acquainted with organizational life and have positive attitudes toward a career in business, management, teaching, medicine, law, engineering, or another profession. They expect you to know why you want to enter a field.

Interview friends and professionals about their fields. Internships, cooperative arrangements, part-time positions, observational visits, and volunteer activities with researchers, veterinarians, law firms, advertising agencies, and newspapers are excellent ways to discover what a field is all about.

Learn everything you can about *each organization* to which you apply. Investigate its leaders and staff, products and services (old, new, future), geographical locations (plants, divisions, offices), expansion or downsizing plans, potential mergers and growth. Discover the organization's major competitors, financial status, nature of ownership, and its reputation in the field, particularly with its own employees, customers, clients, patients, or students. Only through this research can you answer a critical question, "Why do you want to work for us?" And only through research can you determine if your personality and interests are a good fit with the organization's culture.[8]

You can discover information about the organization by writing to the organization or by talking to current and former employees and clients, professors, and friends. An organization's publications, recruiting literature, and annual reports are valuable sources of information. See if there is a mission statement or long-range plan available. And check the library for sources such as the following:

The Career Guide: Dun's Employment Opportunities Directory

College Placement Annual

Dictionary of Occupational Titles

Dictionary of Professional Trade Organizations

Dun and Bradstreet's Middle Market Directory

Dun and Bradstreet's Million Dollar Directory

Encyclopedia of Business Information Sources

Encyclopedia of Careers and Vocational Guidance

Guide for Occupational Exploration

Moody's Industrial Manual

Occupational Outlook Handbook

Open the Book: How to Research a Corporation

Standard and Poor's Corporation Records

Standard and Poor's Industry Surveys

Standard and Poor's Register of Corporations, Directors and Executives

The One Hundred Best Companies to Work for in America

The Wall Street Journal

Thomas' Register of American Manufacturers

Ward's Directory of Public and Private Corporations

In addition to these resources, there are specialized publications on nearly every major career field from acting and advertising to visual arts and writing. Check them out. Some sources are:

Career Opportunities Directory Volume II: Business Administration

Job Opportunities in the Environment

Marketing and Sales Career Directory

National Directory of Corporate Training Programs

Peterson's Job Opportunities for Business and Liberal Arts Graduates

Do not overlook Web pages and the growing number of databases, many on CD-ROM, such as American Business Disc, Company ProFile, Disclosure Database, Dun's Electronic Business Directory, Dun's Million Dollar CD-ROM Collection, and ABI/Inform Ondisc.

It may be difficult to research the person or persons who will conduct your interview because you may not know the identity of the interviewer or interviewers until an interview begins. If you do know the identity of the person ahead of time, talk to friends, associates, professors, placement center personnel, and members of the interviewer's organization to discover the interviewer's position, professional background, personality, and interviewing characteristics, and the organizations to which the interviewer belongs. What types of persons has this interviewer hired in the past? An interviewer may have a dry sense of humor, come from a different culture, or be all business. It is helpful to know such characteristics ahead of time.

Learn everything you can about the *position* for which you are applying. Your research should include responsibilities, duties, necessary skills, required education, training, experiences, type of supervision, advancement potential, amount of travel involved, locations, organizational culture and climate, job security, fringe benefits, training programs, salary and commissions, relocation possibilities and policies, rate of turnover, coworkers, and starting date. After you complete your research on a position, see how well this position matches your self-analysis. For example, if a position entails frequent travel, locating a thousand miles from your home, relocation, and high turnover rate, but you value home life, your family and friends, and stability in location and employment, this position is not a good fit or match for you. A thorough knowledge of the position for which you are applying will prepare you to answer the employer's questions effectively, ask meaningful questions of your own, and determine if you, the position, and the organization are a good fit. The position search model in Figure 9.3 will help you analyze each position and determine if it suits your needs and desires.

Current Events

Learn everything you can about current events. Read a good daily newspaper and such news periodicals as *Newsweek, Time, U.S. New & World Report, Business Week,* and *Fortune.* Employers expect mature applicants to be aware of what is going on around them and in the world—local, state, nation, abroad—and to have formed intelligent, rational positions on important issues. Be well informed on all current events that may affect your field or profession. For instance, if you are going into the pharmaceutical field, be aware of any controversies concerning new drugs. If you are going into research that involves animals, be aware of the animal rights movement and initiatives at the state and national levels. If you are interested in working for an organization with facilities in India, for instance, be aware of American and organizational relations with India and how

Figure 9.3   *The Cash position search model*

All positions are comprised of these elements:

Your
talents/skills
and abilities

The position—
What must be done
daily/weekly/monthly

The organization's
needs/wants/desires

What you like about:

the organization
the position
the people
the work itself

What you dislike about:

the organization
the position
the supervisor
the pay

You get paid for <u>effort</u>, <u>attitude</u>, and <u>results</u>.

Effort—Showing up ahead of time and prepared to work

Attitude—Being a positive influence on others

Results—Doing what needs to be done

Indian culture differs from the American culture. *The Wall Street Journal* and its Web page provide insights into job trends, mergers, and acquisitions. Its *National Employment Weekly* combines its four regional editions into one employment source for experienced professionals.

The Interview Process

Learn everything you can about what happens during interviews. Read Chapter 8 on the employer in the selection interview if you have not done so. This chapter will give you insights into what to expect in interviews. Review pamphlets and handouts available at your college placement service. Check up-to-date library sources because the selection process is undergoing major changes. Talk to friends and acquaintances who have recently been through the interviewing process, professors who are involved in interviewing and keep track of what is taking place in their fields, and recruiters. Notice that all of these are stated in the plural. There is no *single* or *standard* means of conducting interviews, so talking to one person, even a highly skilled corporate recruiter, will give you only one view of the process. That is why many of us teaching interviewing skills do not bring a recruiter to class to "show how it is done." There is no single source that can speak for the hundreds of variations in selection interviews.

Costs, a more rapid response to openings, and the need to fill many positions have forced organizations to implement a number of screening processes and new approaches. Some companies employ video or telephone conferencing so several representatives of the organization, perhaps at different sites, can talk with you at the same time. Recordings allow representatives to review your interview at their convenience. Not long ago the custom was to screen applicants during campus interviews, invite three to five finalists to the plant or regional office, and then bring one or two back for determinate (decision-making) interviews. This custom is changing. Because of cost and a shortage of applicants in critical fields such as information technology and engineering, you may go through only two interviews, a screening interview with reference checks, transcripts, drug test, and a Myers-Briggs assessment and then a determinate interview. Do not be shocked if you are asked to take a drug test. This is becoming commonplace.

Integrity or honesty tests, as we discussed in Chapter 8, are common in areas that require security and safety. An employer may ask you to answer a series of written questions (as many as 40 to 80) or go through a preemployment interview dealing with degrees of honesty. Be honest and forthcoming because all of us have done things that, by a strict definition, are morally or ethically wrong. For example, have you kept too much change from a purchase and you knew it? An examiner may give you amounts to choose from, such as under a dollar, two dollars, five dollars, or twenty dollars. Many of us don't count our change when leaving a restaurant or busy store and discover the excess change when we get to our cars or homes. Assume you got home and discovered that the cashier had given you five dollars too much in change. A follow-up question in the honesty test might be, "Would you return to where you made the purchase, wait until you went back again, call to see if the cashier came up short, or see their loss as your gain?" This process looks at degrees of honesty. Usually an employer looks at casual mistakes, such as keeping a small amount of change, placing a company pen or pencil in your pocket, or taking a small pad of Post-it notes, as acceptable and natural. Major examples of dishonesty are taking company tools, calculators, or products; planning a theft; or plotting to injure someone or damage property. Be honest and do not try to hide past behaviors.

As you do your research into the interview, ask such questions as: What do employers look for? What turns employers off? What kinds of questions do they ask? Why do they ask these questions? What kinds of information do they give? What do they want to see and hear in applicant questions? What kinds of interviewers will you face: age, gender, race, ethnic group, American and non-American, skilled and unskilled? Will interviewers be familiar with your areas of expertise and interests? How likely is it that you will face a panel or seminar situation? How long do interviews last? How are interviews during plant trips (or any second or third interview) similar to and different from screening or first interviews?

Your research may uncover some surprising answers. For example, recent studies have revealed the following: 50 percent of "speech acts" in a sample of interviews were declarative statements rather than questions and answers. Most interviewers have no training in interviewing. In a study of 49 interviews, 10 interviewers did not give applicants opportunities to ask questions (an unforgivable oversight). Interviewers are increasingly viewing the interview as a work sample and look for relevant job behaviors from applicants. They usually have three questions in mind: Can you do the job, will you do the job, and how well will you fit into the organization?[9] Employers also want to see evidence that you have researched their organization and position prior to the interview—that you have done your homework.

When supervisors at Hughes Aircraft were asked to list behaviors and information they looked for when interviewing applicants, they produced a pyramid (see Figure 9.4) with the most important behaviors and information at the bottom, as foundations, and the least important at the top.[10] Many observers were shocked by the apparent unimportance placed on specific abilities, the ones that relate most directly to your education and training in management, sales, engineering, finances, computer technology, and so on. The supervisors explained that integrity was most important because, for example, a highly trained and skilled salesperson or manager without honesty, morals, and sincerity would quickly become a detriment to most organizations, other employees, and clients. The same holds true, they argued, for employees narrow in knowledge, unable to communicate orally and in writing, immature, and unambitious. They want well-trained engineers and computer specialists, for instance, but thorough training, education, and skills alone do not make a strong employee. The Hughes Aircraft pyramid visualizes what most employers have espoused for a long time: that the best employees are honest, intelligent, mature, creative, well-educated persons who can think, communicate, and work well with others.[11] These are the traits employers look for during interviews and reviewing credentials.

3. Conducting the Search

With your homework completed, you should be ready to begin the job search in earnest. Be selective in the positions for which you apply, but choose a range of positions you would be happy with. For instance, instead of being set on a position as a cost accountant, public relations director, or editorial writer, try for a position with a good firm or newspaper, with the hope of moving into cost accounting or a director's or an op-ed position. The changing labor market is leading to recommendations that you consider a part-time or "temp" position in which to gain experience and work your way into a full-time position. A survey of 476 human resources executives revealed that 63 percent use temporary-help services to compete for qualified employees.[12] For example, some teachers serve as substitute teachers or time-share in which they teach a class for a half-day while another teacher teaches the other half. Many hope this arrangement will evolve into a full-time position.

Networking

Despite all of the new electronic sources for conducting searches, *networking* remains a major source for locating positions. Fifty-seven percent of human resources executives

Figure 9.4   *Criteria for evaluating applicants*

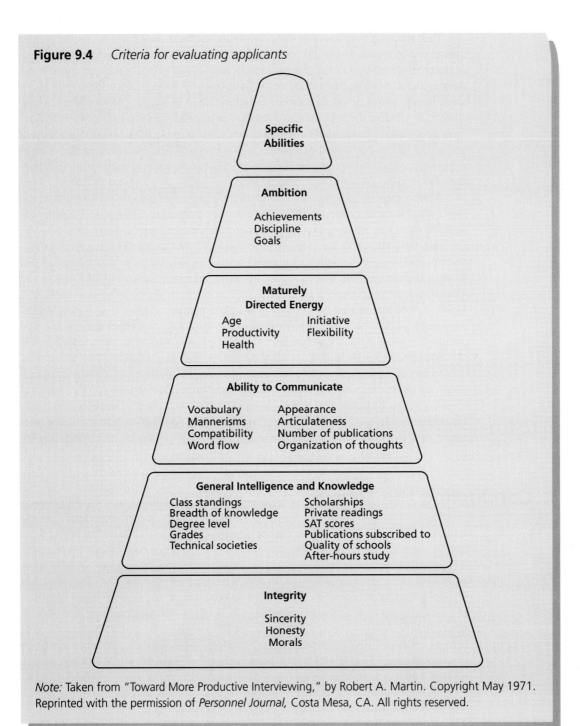

report they rely on networking to locate qualified applicants.[13] Many students are using internships as the basis for starting their networks. If you have made a career decision early in college, the summer internship may serve as entry into a full-time position. Be flexible as you begin your search.

Here are suggestions for beginning a network. Take a sheet of paper and begin a "network tree" with names on one side and addresses and telephone numbers on the other. Start your tree with the most readily available sources: friends, acquaintances, relatives, former employers, alumni, internship directors, teachers, professors, insurance agents, real estate brokers, family connections, and others you might think of. Your primary contacts may be as many as 50, but you can never have too many.

Call the person in slot number one and say you are looking for a *career opportunity,* never a *job.* The word "job" often signals the negative impression that you are looking for anything that pays money, not something you turn into a career. If this contact gives you a lead, write it down under this individual's name so you can recall who made the suggestion; the *who* may be the major factor in a lead's willingness and enthusiasm to help you. Be sure to get the lead's full name, position, and telephone number. If this contact has no opportunities, ask for three or four names of persons who might know of career possibilities. Everyone knows at least three possible leads if they think a bit or check their computer or Rolodex.

Your original list of 50 may soon become 100 or more. Be sure to thank each primary contact and ask, "You don't mind if I use your name with Dirk Tanaka do you?" This leading question is likely to obtain a positive response. When a networking contact leads to an interview or a very good prospect, be sure to send a thank you note to show your gratitude.

The Obvious Places

Do not overlook the obvious places for positions. Newspaper classified sections have become good places to locate positions because organizations know that if they advertise there, their opening will meet the EEO test of making it known to those who are interested and qualified. *The Wall Street Journal* is an excellent source for openings around the country. Check organizational bulletin boards and printed materials that announce personnel openings. Subscribe to professional publications, such as *The Chronicle of Higher Education,* that include ads for a variety of positions. And contact organizations directly to see if they have current or future openings.

The Placement Service or Agency

Another source is the placement service or agency. Almost every college and university has a free agency for students and alumni. These agencies not only provide contacts for on-campus interviews but offer free counseling services that will help you analyze yourself (including the careers you seem most interested in and qualified for), discover career fields, obtain information on organizations and positions, develop resumes, and write cover letters. Other placement services are associated with professional organizations for teachers, management majors, communication majors, civil engineering majors, and so on. The cost is minimal.

Many "percentage" agencies will help to place you for a fee, often a percentage of your first year's salary, payable upon assuming a position they helped you obtain. Most of these agencies have fee-paid positions, which means that an organization has retained them on a fee basis to locate quality applicants. You pay nothing. If you use a percentage agency, be aware that they may charge a registration fee to process your credentials. Check the contract carefully, and do not allow them to send you to interview for positions in which you are not interested or qualified.

Most agencies are ethical and want to find excellent positions for their clients, but use reasoned skepticism. If they want a great deal of money in advance just to process your resume or make claims of placing nearly all of their applicants in very high paying positions, you would be wise to go elsewhere. Be careful of agencies that want to produce videotapes and other expensive "credentials" for you. A favorite scam in today's global village is the promise to find you a position overseas in Germany, Australia, Saudi Arabia, or other allegedly lucrative job markets. Most often the applicant's money disappears into a post office box. Check an agency thoroughly before making any monetary commitment or signing any contract. Use agencies, career counselors, and resume firms that charge for their services at your own risk.

Publications

There are a variety of publications in your college placement center or library that will guide you to career opportunities and services. *Jobs,* published annually and written by Kathryn and Ross Petras, contains some 600 pages of addresses, toll-free numbers, and industry groupings. At the beginning of each industry grouping, they provide a brief employment history, list the best bets for growth and job opportunities, and provide names of associations, directories, and professional journals for that grouping. This source is ideal for entry-level positions.

The Kennedy publications are helpful for those with 10 or more years of experience, particularly their *Executive Directory of Search Firms* and *Directory of Executive Recruiters 1999* (published annually). Entry-level applicants will not find these sources very helpful. Other Kennedy publications include *Consultants News, Executive Recruiter News, Directory of Management Consultants,* and *Directory of Outplacement Firms.*

Career Communication Incorporated publishes a number of useful sources, particularly the *Job Market Directory National Edition.* This large-format paperback provides general career information helpful to those getting their first positions and those recently terminated. After describing the basics of job searches, this directory includes sections focusing on job market data, federal, state, and city job centers, nontraditional training, and employment programs serving women. A spin-off publication entitled *Job Hotlines USA* lists 1,000 organizations that post openings by telephone, including some banks, hospitals, insurance companies, school districts, and colleges. Perhaps their most helpful publication is the *Job Hunters Yellow Pages,* which includes more than 15,000 employment agencies and services.

The Internet

The Internet is growing rapidly into a major source for positions and tips on how to obtain them. Colleges and other organizations are using the pages of the World Wide Web to advertise positions and seek high-quality applicants. You should check an up-to-date copy of *The Guide to Internet Job Searching,* compiled by Margaret Riley Dikel, Frances Rodney, and Steve Oserman, and published by VGM Career Horizons. The following are some Internet resources:[14]

America's Job Bank (http://www.ajb.dni.us)

Catapult (http://www.wm.edu/catapult/catapult.html)

E-Span (http://espan.com)

Job Hunt (http://www.job-hunt.org)

Jobtrak (http://www.jobtrak.com)

National Association of Colleges and Employers' Jobweb (http://www.jobweb.org)

North American Classifacts (http://www.classifacts.com)

OnLine Career Center (http://www.careermosiac/com)

The Riley Guide (http://www.dbm.com/jobguide)

Career Fairs

Career fairs held on your campus or around the country are excellent for networking and making contacts with organizations for internships and postgraduate employment. Many are limited to specific majors or areas such as liberal arts, engineering, or agriculture; others are open to all fields of interest. Some large companies conduct their own career fairs. Listed below are two major contacts for information on fairs:

photo by Michael Newman/Photo Edit

■ *Use the Internet to search for positions and then research organizations and positions prior to taking part in interviews.*

American Job Fairs
Phone (516) 681-9200

Career Fairs International
311 S. Wacker Drive, Suite 4550
Chicago, IL 60606
Phone (312) 697-4717
Fax (312) 697-4769

4. Preparing Credentials

Once you have analyzed yourself thoroughly, completed your homework, and searched for positions, it is time to prepare your credentials. Your credentials consist of resumes, portfolios, and cover letters.

Resumes

Once you have analyzed yourself thoroughly, prepare different resumes for each type of position for which you apply. Your resume is your silent sales representative, and it is most persuasive when tailored to the skills and expectations of each position and prepared in a highly professional manner. It is the first opportunity for an organization to "see" you. Since most employers will spend only two to four minutes scanning each resume, yours must gain and maintain *positive* attention if you hope to get beyond the application stage in the selection process. Campion recommends that you "think like the boss" if you want the job.[15]

Content of Resumes

Do not include a title such as "Resume"—the employer knows what it is. Place your full name at the top center of the page in bold print; no nicknames.

Provide one or two complete addresses (with zip codes), telephone numbers (with area codes), and if available, an e-mail address and fax number so the employer can reach you easily and quickly. Multiple addresses and telephone numbers are important for applicants who are in college or in transition between addresses and are difficult to contact, particularly during the workday. If you list a campus telephone, provide a date when it will no longer be operable.

Your career objective usually comes next, and may be critical, particularly if the employer does not have a cover letter from you or chooses to review resumes alone. The majority of employers will read no further if your career objective does not fit the opening or is unimpressive. *Impressive career objectives* are brief (one- or two-line phrases), precise, singular, adapted to a specific position, and targeted to a specific organization; they communicate the type of position you are most interested in and are not self-centered. *Unimpressive career objectives* are multiple (a shotgun or Jack/Jill-of-all-trades approach), vague, imply the position is a mere stepping-stone to another position, mention going to graduate school, and include words such as "job" instead of "career" (implies you merely want to earn money) or "exciting" or "progressive" when describing type of targeted organization (which organization is unexciting or regressive?). If your career objective seems to be a good fit, the employer is likely to read further to see if you are qualified for the opening. A career objective is less important if it is highlighted in your cover letter and all interviewers have access to the letter.

If you are just completing your education or training and your work experiences are minimal or unrelated to the position, your educational record usually comes next. In a survey of 188 college recruiters, 57 percent preferred education to be listed first, even when the college applicant had significant work experiences.[16] List your degrees or training in reverse chronological order so the employer can detect quickly what you are doing now or what you recently completed. List degree, diploma, or certificate, date of graduation or completion, school, location of the school if name is insufficient for accurate identification (many universities have multiple campuses and there are several universities called Loyola), and majors and minors. You might provide a selective list of courses relevant to the opening, particularly if you are short on experience. However, courses often take up too much space and reveal the obvious. List your grade point average (GPA) if it is a B or better, and be sure you indicate the numerical system used at your college, for example: 3.4 (4.0 scale) or 3.4/4.0. Do not use abbreviations for courses, majors, or degrees. For example, an interviewer may not know if Eng. refers to English or engineering. And be sure to list any relevant certificates or licenses. These are essential for applicants in professions such as health care, law, teaching, accounting, and engineering.

After education and training, if you have selected this order, present your *experiences* relevant to the specific position for which you are applying. If you entitle this section "Experiences," you can include more than work or salary-earning situations, an advantage if you are young and just completing your education or training. Volunteer activities may be highly relevant and impressive. If you are developing a *chronological format,* list your experiences (including internships, co-op arrangements, assistant unpaid positions, organizational activities) in reverse chronological order so the employer can see quickly what you have been up to most recently. See Figure 9.5 for a sample chronological format resume.[17] List organization, title of your position or positions, dates, and, above all, what you did in each position, emphasizing the skills and experiences most relevant for the opening. Studies indicate that the primary concern of interviewers is applicant achievement and accomplishment, the belief being that the best predictor of future performance is past performance. Caution: Do not exaggerate your experiences and accomplishments, only to be shot down during the interview. Be honest! Use action verbs, such as the following, to show you are a *doer:*

Administered	Coached	Designed
Advised	Consulted	Devised
Arbitrated	Coordinated	Directed
Arranged	Counseled	Edited
Budgeted	Created	Eliminated
Built	Delegated	Evaluated

Figure 9.5   *Chronological resume*

Joshua H. Mullins

Campus Address   Permanent Address
2712 Dodge Street   706 Hard Rock Creek
West Lafayette, IN 47906   Chatham, IL 62629
(765) 743-1213   (217) 973-2044
E-mail: jhmul@dodge.com

Objective: A management position requiring strong interpersonal and
                     communication skills.

Education: **Purdue University**
                     Bachelor of Science Degree, August 2001
                     Major: Management
                     Minor: Public Relations
                     GPA: 3.25/4.0 (Overall) 3.45/4.0 (Major)

Experience: **Guest Relations Intern**—Summer 1999
                     Six Flags Great America, Gurnee, IL
                     • Evaluated and replied to guest concerns
                     • Provided assistance to guests

                     Public Relations Assistant—Summer 1998
                     Illinois Department of Tourism, Springfield, IL
                     • Created and implemented PageMaker charts
                     • Edited brochures of fall festivals
                     • Updated records on attendance at festivals
                     • Composed letters for Director of Public Relations

Computer Skills: WordPerfect 6.0, Windows 1998, PageMaker, Lotus 1-2-3,
                     World Wide Web, Home Page, PowerPoint

Activities: **President**—Travel Club, 1998–1999
                     • Conducted monthly meetings
                     • Chaired Travel Planning Committee
                     • Developed Web page for the Travel Club

                     Activities Director—Management Student Council
                     • Planned monthly meetings
                     • Arranged for guest speakers
                     • Organized field trips

Examined	Maintained	Reconfigured
Facilitated	Managed	Researched
Fashioned	Modified	Scheduled
Formulated	Negotiated	Sold
Founded	Operated	Solved
Gathered	Organized	Supervised
Generated	Oversaw	Tested
Improved	Performed	Trained
Increased	Persuaded	Updated
Instituted	Planned	Won
Instructed	Produced	Wrote
Lectured	Received	
Led	Recommended	

If you are developing a *functional format,* place your experiences under headings that highlight your qualifications for the position (see Figure 9.6). Typical major headings are management, sales, advertising, training, counseling, team building, organizational development, recruiting, finance, teaching, administration, supervision, project manager, and marketing. You can include a variety of experiences from different positions, internships, and organizations under each heading. Be sure to use action verbs when identifying your experiences, such as "Wrote press releases for . . . " and "Developed training modules for . . . . " Do not include too many headings and subheadings. Focus attention on important qualifications such as communication and people skills.

If you are using a *chronological format,* the next section may list relevant organizational memberships and activities, including college, professional, and community. Be selective. High school activities are excluded for college graduates, and college activities will be excluded after a few years in your career. It is a continual updating process. Emphasize with action verbs your responsibilities, leadership positions, achievements, and awards. A long list of organizations without leadership roles is likely to give a *negative* impression. *Show you are a doer.* Include honorary organizations such as Phi Beta Kappa and Golden Key, and provide a brief description of organizations with which the interviewer might be unfamiliar. If you are using a functional format, you may list organizations or include them within various major headings under experience. A functional format may include this section or blend it within your skills and experiences. Realize that your outside activities can indicate motivation, communication skills, ability to work with people, work ethic, and ability to lead. Employers are concerned about narrow specialists, such as the finance major whose only involvement in four college years was the Finance Club.

A *chronological format,* such as the one in Figure 9.5 and not the bare-bones outline common 10 years ago, has a number of advantages. It is easy to write and organize, emphasizes experiences, is most common, and is easy for an employer to scan for relevant experiences. A *functional format,* such as the one in Figure 9.6, also has a number

Figure 9.6 *Functional resume*

Anna S. Selfridge

7125 W. Lamar Parkway
Philadelphia, PA 19122
(215) 678-2456
E-mail: anself@temple.com

Objective: Production manager and director for a video production company.

Education: **Temple University**
Bachelor of Arts, December 2000
Major: Radio, Television, Film
Minor: Theatre
GPA: 3.1/4.0 (Overall) 3.75/4.0 (Major)

Experience: **Management**
- Developed operating budgets for student productions.
- Supervised the staff of a student production.
- Provided liaison between students and faculty.

Production
- Scheduled television programming for a BS station.
- Directed radio and television commercials.
- Produced and directed basketball half-time television shows.

Writing
- Developed equipment manuals for the television studios.
- Assisted professor in writing a textbook for the production sequence.
- Wrote advertising copy for student productions.
- Wrote press releases and brochures for productions.

**Work
Experience:** **Merchandising Associate** October 1998–January 1999
Home Depot, Pittsburgh, PA

Showroom Sales Associate May 1999–August 1999
Macy's, Philadelphia, PA

Honors:
- Outstanding Television Documentary
- Superior Achievement Award for Public Relations Announcement
- Dean's List, Temple University
- Who's Who Among American College Students

of advantages. It focuses attention on relevant skills to match the ideal applicant profile, dates are less important, and seemingly unrelated positions and education are not highlighted. And functional resumes do not repeat the same skills and experiences under different positions, so it can be tighter and shorter. Most resumes today are blends of the two formats, as is apparent in Figures 9.5 and 9.6.

Do not include a list of references or note "References upon request." The second is a given today. Do not list political, religious, ethnic, or social memberships and activities that can identify your race, religion, political affiliation, or ethnic group, are irrelevant to the position for which you are applying, and may lead to discrimination. Do not include a picture or give personal data such as age, marital status, number of children, parental status, height, or weight. You do not break any law if you do so, but you are providing information apart from bona fide occupational qualifications and assuming that an employer may hire you from unlawful criteria. Realize that you may *not* get a position because of this information. Employers are keenly aware of their liability for unlawful information sent to them even when they do not ask for it. They employ gatekeepers such as secretaries and staff members to review all credentials, with instructions to discard pictures and place heavy black lines through such information as age, marital status, religion, and so on. As a result, your interviewer may not see the highly professional resume you have prepared so meticulously but a mutilated version with a picture cut off and several black lines through it.

Mechanics of Resumes

Although content is most important in resumes, do not overlook the effects of appearance and layout. Have your resumes professionally printed on white, off-white, light gray, or light beige bond paper. Although attention-getting colors such as yellow or orange may be suitable for a few creative positions in advertising and graphics, most employers are likely to consider them inappropriate and unprofessional.

Pay attention to how the resume is blocked so it looks neat, attractive, organized, carefully planned, and uncrowded. Employers like white space on resumes, so indent sections carefully, double-space parts, and leave at least one-inch margins all around. Center your name at the top in bold letters so it stands out. Use different printer fonts so headings guide the reader through important information about you. Employers prefer resumes with bullets that separate and call attention to important information because this helps them scan the resume more efficiently. If you provide two addresses, place one on each side under your name. If you provide one address, place it in the center or on the right side away from staples and paper clips.

A large majority of employers prefer a *single-page resume*. A two-page resume may be acceptable, however, if it is less crowded and provides valuable information about experiences, skills, awards, and organizational activity and leadership that will not fit on a single page. Do not repeat the same information anywhere on the resume. If you develop a two-page resume, consider having it printed front to back on one sheet of paper because a second page may get misplaced or ripped off when your resume is taken from a file or briefcase. Be sure you signal with a page number or notation such as "page one of two" that there is more on the back. If you prepare two pages, be sure your name is repeated at the top on the left and a page number is on the top right.

Use perfect grammar. Select language carefully, avoiding turnoffs such as the word "job" and including action verbs. Check all spellings and punctuation. Check for typographical errors. Be precise but persuasive in how you phrase education, experiences, skills, accomplishments, and awards.

The Electronically Scanned Resume

A small but growing number of organizations are using electronic systems to scan resumes. Those that do so tend to have large numbers of openings that attract a great many applicants. This saves time and money.

If one of your resumes is likely to be electronically scanned, follow some basic rules. Figure 9.7 is a scannable resume. Do not use colored paper. Use only one or two print fonts. Do not underline anything except a blocked format. Be sure your resume contains up-to-date terms, labels, and names the scanner is designed to detect. The following are examples of correct and incorrect terms:

Yes	No
Human resources	Personnel
Administrative assistant	Secretary
Sales associate	Sales clerk
Information systems	Data processing
Environmental services	Housekeeping
Accountant	Bookkeeper
Facilities engineering	Maintenance
Inside sales	Customer relations

To prevent resumes from being rejected by scanning software, some applicants have placed key skills along the bottom of the resume using the same typeface as the resume. This trick works *sometimes.*

Most organizations reject candidates that have less than 50 percent of the required skills. Save yourself frustration by not applying for positions unless your qualifications and the position are an obvious match.

In every Barnes and Noble and Borders bookstore and on Amazon.com, you can find hundreds of books on creating surefire resumes and cover letters. It seems that everyone has a secret formula for success, but there is no simple formula. If you follow the guidelines we have suggested and adapt your resume to your field, the employer, and the position, you will get interviews and job offers. Realize, however, that your *record,* the *substance* of your resume, is what really counts, not beautiful paper, striking fonts, well-placed bullets, and careful blocking.

The Portfolio

Portfolios are essential if you are in fields such as photography, advertising, public relations, art and design, journalism, architecture, and professional writing. Your portfolio should be a small and yet varied collection of your best work. Organize your portfolio

Figure 9.7   *Scannable resume*

Nathan Mason

1408 E. Main Street
Norwalk, Ohio 23320
Home Phone (215) 796-4420
Fax (215) 796-4441

Objective: To obtain a position in retail store management and merchandising.

Experience:

1993–1999   Regional Store Manager and Buyer
- Manager of 5 regional stores in Northwestern Ohio
- Buyer of all retail shoes sold in the store
- Design specific store displays in line with corporate guidelines and plans
- Directly supervise 9 employees—5 full-time, 4 part-time
- Indirectly supervise 4 managers, 4 assistant managers, and 37 part-time employees
- Responsible for all financial and sales reporting and verifications

1991–1993   Manager, Payless Shoe Source
349 Erie Street
Sandusky, Ohio
- Promoted from Assistant Manager to Manager, Fall 1993

1990–1991   Sales Associate
- Worked full-time from 1991 to promotion in 1993
- Responsible for weekly inventory for 3 departments (men's, children's, athletic)

1989–1990   Sales Associate
- Hired full-time in Fall 1989

1986–1989   Pizza Hut Host and Server
- Part-time during the year and 2 summers full-time

Education: B.S. in Marketing and Merchandising, 1990
- Member, American Marketing Association
- Theta Chi Social Fraternity

thematically. Make it visually attractive. Have excellent copies of your work, not faded, soiled, marked-up, or wrinkled samples. Employers want to see how well you write, design, photograph, edit, and create, and the well-designed and presented portfolio is the best means of doing this.

If you are going into broadcasting, your portfolio is likely to be an audio- or videotape of selections that show your best oral and video work. Again, select your best work. Quality, not quantity, is what sells. The portfolio is an ideal way to exhibit your skills and experiences.

The Cover Letter

Your cover letter is a third-party introduction to future employers. Design it to open the employment door by showing interest in the organization's products or services. Make them want to read your resume by making a pleasant and professional impression. Send an original, creative cover letter along with each resume to any lead that might prove fruitful. Form cover letters or ones aimed at a number of positions impress no one. You must tailor each letter to each position and organization.

Whenever possible, address your letter to a specific person who will be actively involved in the selection process. "To whom it may concern" letters rarely get responses, and imagine how a female recruiter would react to a letter addressed to "Gentlemen." Yes, this is still a common occurrence at the turn of the century. Sending a letter to a person uninvolved in recruiting will, at best, delay reaching the correct person. Be sure your letter has the correct and complete address.

The letter should be brief, usually three or four paragraphs—8–12 declarative sentences—and never more than one page. Figures 9.8 and 9.9 illustrate typical cover letters. As with the resume, the cover letter must be neat, typed on good bond paper, and contain no typos, misspellings, grammatical errors, or punctuation errors. Provide at least one-inch margins all around. Be sure the font is professional and easy to read.

Explain why you are writing. Specify the position in which you are interested and why. Reveal how you discovered the opening and what you know about the organization.

Explain how your education and training, experiences, and organizational memberships and activities make you an ideal fit with the applicant profile. You can refer to your resume, but do not merely repeat it. You must persuade the reader that you are well suited for *this position* with *this organization* at *this time*. Relatively few applicants are able to do this. One of the authors recently chaired a national search for a new director of admissions for his university, and the search generated more than 100 applications from military officers (retired and soon to be retired), executives, administrators, and directors of admissions. Although the published description of the position emphasized such skills as marketing, communication, networking, and management and experiences with new technologies, mass media, strategic planning, and recruiting, most applicants emphasized the millions of dollars they had managed, their rise through management, or leadership of military units. None of these were relevant for redesigning and leading the university's recruitment efforts into the twenty-first century. Your career objective and the position must be a good fit.

Emphasize your interest in and enthusiasm for this position with this particular organization. Show that you have researched both thoroughly and are not merely sending

Figure 9.8   *Sample cover letter*

3379 North Cumberland Avenue
Athens, GA 30601
January 14, 1999

Ms. Elizabeth George
The Westin Peachtree Plaza
Atlanta, GA 30343

Dear Ms. George:

Professor John Williams at the University of Georgia has informed me that the Westin Peachtree Plaza will soon be hiring managers for its expanded convention and resort programs. I have attended several conferences held at the Peachtree and have always been impressed with its facilities, services, and staff. Since my career goal is to manage convention and resort facilities at a major hotel, I am very interested in the possibility of interviewing for a position with you.

My academic program in Hotel, Institutional Management at the University of Georgia has given me a firm foundation in labor-management relations, marketing, property management, computer systems, and communication. This background will enable me to work effectively with employees, guests, the public, and organizations interested in holding conventions at the Westin Peachtree Plaza. In addition, my summer internships at the Hyatt-Regency in Louisville and the Opryland Hotel in Nashville have provided me with experiences in managing conventions, customer relations, and the operations of large hotels.

I would thoroughly enjoy an opportunity to talk with you about how my training and experiences have prepared me for a position with the Westin Peachtree Plaza. Since Athens is only a short drive from Atlanta, I could come for an interview at your convenience.

I look forward to hearing from you.

Sincerely,

Diana Johnson

Enclosure: Resume

out dozens of letters and resumes in a blind fashion. It is deadly to show that you not only know little about the position or organization but that you have wrong information about both. Sometimes applicants confuse one organization with another through lack of research. Every time the authors' departments have a number of very different faculty openings at the same time, numerous letters will be placed in a "question mark" file because it is impossible to tell after reading the cover letters which position or positions these persons are applying for.

Figure 9.9   *Sample cover letter*

321 Ferguson Road
Santa Clara, CA 95052
September 21, 1999

Mr. Lou Gaffney
Motorola Energy Products Division
4412 Industrial Avenue
Mundelein, IL 60019

Dear Mr. Gaffney:

I am writing in response to your advertisement in the *Wall Street Journal* for an industrial engineer with 3–5 years of experience and a background in sonic welding.

It is my understanding that the Energy Division is a spin-off division of the Cellular Phone Division and supplies batteries for that division.

My B.S. degree is in industrial engineering from the University of California at Los Angeles (UCLA). I have spent the last three years working at Mattel Toys providing engineering support for their mini-toy division (matchbox cars), which uses Unitek Sonic Welders.

I look forward to discussing the opportunity that this position affords someone with my qualifications and experiences. Please feel free to contact me at my home telephone number because my answering machine is on 24 hours a day.

Sincerely,

Robert J. Jeffries

Enclosure: Resume

Close the cover letter by restating your interest in the position and organization. Ask for an interview and state when you might be available for an interview. If, for instance, you will be in the Dallas area where the organization is located during the third week of April, state your willingness to meet with them at that time.

If the position is listed on a Web site or in a newspaper or journal, use the ad's language. Do not merely repeat the words but show you fit the requirements. Good and bad responses to advertised positions are illustrated below.

Advertisement 1

We want a self-starting Regional Manager who can take charge of the store, merchandising, displays, and staff scheduling.

Good Reply: I have been a district manager for the last three years. I establish my own store visitation schedule, interview all new hires at the management level, and take the lead in store layout and staff scheduling based on store traffic.

Bad Reply: I have three years of district manager experience. I visit the store every month and help when needed.

Advertisement 2

Entry level human resources recruiter in a large high tech company. Must be able to work with higher management. Computer literacy is a necessity.

Good Reply: Being a part of the selection process and working with decision makers would be a real opportunity for me. With a course in interviewing and a working knowledge of Microsoft 98, Excel, and Power-Point, I believe I am prepared for this position.

Bad Reply: I have taken a course in interviewing, can work with all types of people, and can operate a computer.

Use the cover letter to sell the skills, abilities, and experiences you possess that make you a good match for the position. Be positive and to the point. And show enthusiasm for the position and organization.

5. Creating a Favorable First Impression

As you approach the interview, realize that your attitudes are a critical ingredient in your success or failure. Be thoroughly prepared. Anxiety is heightened when you feel you do not know enough about the position or the organization, are unready to answer tough questions, or do not know what questions to ask. If you feel you are not going to do well in an interview, you won't. If you cannot sell you to you, how can you sell you to someone else? Be positive about yourself, current and past employers, associates, professors, and clients. Never bad-mouth others, especially employers because this signals that you are likely to bad-mouth future employers. Never reveal confidences. Your candidacy for a position will end quickly if you do either. One recent study revealed that good first impressions lead interviewers to show positive regard toward applicants, give important job information, sell the organization to them, and spend less time gathering information.[18]

Relationship of the Interview Parties

Assess the relationship that is likely to exist between you and the interviewer. How will control be shared? Degree of control is often determined by the job market, how eager the organization is to fill the position, the strengths and weaknesses of your background, and how much you desire and need this position. Successful applicants dominate interviews but also know when to let the interviewer control the conversation, whereas unsuccessful applicants are submissive or try to dominate when the employer clearly wants to do so.

To what extent do you and the interviewer want to take part in this interview? You may find it difficult to get fired up for an interview if you have been turned down a number of times during previous months or you are not really interested in this position or organization. For instance, you may be interviewing for a sales position only because you cannot get into management, teaching, human resources, or broadcasting. An interviewer may find it equally difficult to get excited about the tenth interview of the day or when an applicant is not a good fit for the position. Perhaps the interviewer believes he or she has more important things to do at the office or plant.

What degree of liking (mutual trust, respect, friendship) is there between you and the interviewer as revealed in previous encounters, telephone contacts, and letters? How similar are you to the interviewer in age, sex, race, ethnic group, background, education, and profession, and how might these similarities affect the interview positively and negatively? A recent study revealed that the same-race effect remains in selection interviews. Candidates racially similar to interviewers (black and white) received higher interviewer ratings.[19] Results were the same for panel interviews in which the majority of interviewers were the same race as the candidate.

Both parties must cooperate, disclose strengths and weaknesses (of self and organization), be honest, and provide meaningful feedback. Understand the relationship between you and the employer, and adapt accordingly.

Dress and Appearance

Dress and appearance are important elements in a favorable first impression. Although we all believe we know how to dress appropriately and prepare ourselves for selection interviews, the following are five common mistakes men and women make.[20]

Men

1. Dirty and wrinkled clothes that do not fit properly.
2. Shirts that are too tight at the collar or around the waist.
3. Dirty hands, nails, or hair.

Women

1. Too much or inappropriate jewelry.
2. Too much or too little makeup, particularly overpowering perfume.
3. Scuffed or inappropriate shoes.

4. Shoes wrong color for clothes or dirty and scuffed.

4. Clothing inappropriate for the workplace.

5. Wrong style for body shape.

5. Ill-fitting clothing.

Your budget may limit the clothing you have to wear, but there is no excuse for dirty hands, nails, and hair or rumpled, dirty, and inappropriate attire. Be sure your hair is neatly combed or brushed and is trimmed neatly. Facial hair for men, beards and mustaches, is generally acceptable but should be neat and trimmed.

Advice for Men

Standard interviewing apparel for men is a dark suit (blue, gray, black, charcoal) with a white or pastel solid shirt and a contrasting but not wild tie. The rule of thumb is to wear conservative, professional, and formal apparel to the interview, even if the interviewer (who has a job by the way) may be dressed informally. Levi Strauss, a maker of casual clothing, began a newsletter in 1994 for human resource departments suggesting how to have a casual Friday or a comfortable Monday. Although many organizations now have a casual day sometime during the week, perhaps the day you arrive for an interview, you should dress for a formal business meeting.

Try the sit-down test to check for fit. Almost anyone can wear clothes that are a bit too tight when standing, but sitting down quickly reveals if the jacket, waistband, seat, or collar is too tight or the shirt gaps at the waist. Insert one finger into the collar of your shirt. If the collar is too tight, you need a larger shirt; if it is too loose, you need a smaller shirt to avoid the sloppy look of a drooping collar.

Wear brown shoes only with a brown suit; wear black or cordovan (deep wine color) with blue, gray, charcoal, or black suits. Be sure shoes are clean and polished. Wear dark socks that complement your suit and cover at least half a leg so when you sit down and cross your legs, no skin is visible. Tie size and age depend upon what is in style, but it is always safe to wear a wide stripe, polka dot, or conservative pattern tie that is blue, red, gray, or burgundy. Avoid trendy colors and sizes or ties with patterns, pictures, and drawings that signify immaturity or inappropriateness. When in doubt, ask a friendly person at a clothing store or department.

Men also need to choose clothing that is appropriate for their body shapes: regular, thin or slender, heavy or muscular, and tall or

photo by John Coletti/Stock Boston

■ *Be neat, well groomed, and dressed professionally to make a good first impression.*

short. For example, a heavy, muscular male should not wear large plaids, thick stripes, or bright colors. Better choices are dark shades with pinstripes. For less formal settings, such as dinner during the interviewing process, you might wear a blue blazer with light gray or tan slacks. A thin or slender male may wear a greater variety of clothing, and some plaids might add size and depth to the physical appearance.

Colors have both psychological and physiological effects on interview parties. It is claimed that black projects power and sophistication; gray projects security; blue projects harmony; red projects energy and arouses emotions; brown projects friendliness and approachability; and yellow projects intelligence and optimism.

Jewelry for men should be minimal and professional. A gold or silver watch and a gold or silver ballpoint or fountain pen are more impressive than plastic ones. Do not wear bracelets (unless for health reasons) or gold chains. One or more earrings may negatively affect some interviewers but, if earrings are important to you, you may want to take the risk.

Advice for Women

Makeup, hairstyle, and clothing are personal decisions that reveal a great deal about your personality—who you are, your self-concept, and what you think of others. Take them seriously. No makeup is probably too little, but if makeup calls attention to itself, it is too much. Recruiters suggest small (not dangling) earrings with one per ear, one ring per hand, and no bracelets. Coloring is essential, and a cosmetic counselor can help you determine what is professionally appropriate for you and your clothing.

Select a business suit or jacket with a skirt rather than slacks. Pantsuits were once very controversial, then seemed to gain acceptance in many organizations, particularly government agencies and not-for-profit groups, and have now declined. It would be a good idea to ask the prospective employer if a pantsuit is appropriate before wearing one to an interview. A conservative jacket that is not too informal and an appropriate-length skirt give a professional rather than a casual appearance. Wear a conservative blouse that matches the suit. Low, comfortable pumps are more appropriate than high heels or flats.

Tight clothes do not look attractive. Try the sit-down and one-finger-in-the-collar tests recommended for men. Avoid see-through blouses or ones with plunging necklines. Avoid short skirts and ones with long slits. Avoid baggy panty hose or ones with runs or snags. Wear clear or plain-color stockings appropriate for your outfit. In all matters of clothing, be neat, clean, comfortable, and professional.

Nonverbal Communication

Nonverbal communication, such as voice, eye contact, gestures, and posture, are important ingredients throughout selection interviews, but they are critical in making good first impressions.[21] Interviewers react more favorably toward applicants and rate them higher if they smile, have expressive facial expressions, are enthusiastic, maintain steady eye contact without staring, and match the interviewer's pace. Dynamism and energy level are communicated through the way you shake hands, sit, walk, stand, gesture, and move your body. Use a firm but not crushing handshake. Try to appear (and be) calm and relaxed, but sharp and in control, by avoiding nervous gestures, fidgets, movements, and playing with pens or objects on the interviewer's desk. Respond crisply and confidently.

Speak in a normal conversational tone with vocal variety that exhibits confidence and interpersonal skills. Interviewers prefer *standard* or *prestigious* accents. Studies reveal that applicants with regional, ethnic, or racial accents receive lower evaluations, get shorter interviews, and receive fewer offers.[22] If English is your second language or you have an accent developed since birth, you are unlikely to desire or be able to eliminate it when taking part in interviews. However, you must work on your accent and pronunciation so interviewers can understand you clearly and effectively. Realize that the interviewer may be wondering how the organization's staff, clients, customers, or others will be able to understand you if hired. Communication skills are important in all positions.

Do not hesitate to pause before answering difficult critical incident and hypothetical questions, but be aware that frequent pauses may make you appear hesitant, unprepared, or slow. Interviewers interpret pauses of one second or less as signs of ambition, self-confidence, organization, and intelligence. Remember that nonverbal communication or body language can validate or negate *what* you are saying.

Arrival and Opening

Arrive for the interview a few minutes ahead of time. If you are late, there may be no interview or you may receive a very cool reception. After all, if you cannot be on time for the interview, will you be on time for work? Do not arrive too early. The employer may have other tasks to perform or interviews to conduct and does not want to assign staff to entertain you until the scheduled interview time. Be courteous to everyone you meet, first, because it is polite to do so and, second, because you never know who will be involved in the selection process.

Greet the employer pleasantly and dynamically. Do not use the interviewer's first name unless invited to do so. Sit when asked to do so and never sit down before the interviewer does. Be an active participant during the opening, avoiding a string of yes and no answers. You will become more relaxed once you get into the flow of the interview, so respond to opening, icebreaker questions as you would in any normal conversation. How you handle yourself during the first few minutes with a stranger tells the interviewer a great deal about your communication and people skills.

6. Answering Questions

Although dress, appearance, and nonverbal communication are important ingredients in the selection process, do not *overestimate* their importance. A number of studies suggest that the final decision is most often based on a combination of verbal and nonverbal impressions, with the verbal (language, answers, questions) having a clear edge over the nonverbal.[23]

Preparing to Respond

Be ready and eager to answer questions effectively. Nervousness is natural, and will disappear if you concentrate on answering questions confidently and thoroughly. All successful applicants are ready to handle frequently asked questions such as,

1. Tell me about yourself.

2. Why do you want to work for us?

3. What are your greatest strengths? Your weaknesses?

4. What are your short-range career goals? Your long-range goals?

5. Why did you leave your position with _____?

6. What do you do in your spare time?

7. What did you like best in your position at _____? Like least?

8. What is the most difficult decision you have made in the past six months?

9. Who else have you interviewed with?

10. Why should we select you over the other applicants we have for this position?

11. How do you motivate yourself?

12. What do you know about our organization?

13. What is the greatest challenge facing our field today?

14. Tell me about your experiences in working on teams.

15. What do you do when you're not studying?

These traditional questions continue to play major roles in selection interviews, particularly during the opening minutes to get applicants talking and to learn about them as human beings and budding professionals.

As we mentioned in Chapter 8, however, the nature of questioning in selection interviews is changing rapidly. Interviewers are asking more challenging questions and placing applicants in joblike situations to see how they might fit in and function as employees. The philosophy is simple: Employers can determine best how applicants might operate in specific positions by placing them in these positions during the interview process. A *critical incidents* question might go like this: "We are facing a situation in which we . . . . If you were on our team, what would you recommend we do to resolve this situation?" Some critical incidents questions are historical, such as: "Two years ago we had a conflict between . . . . If you had been the supervisor in this situation, what would you have done?" Other questions are *hypothetical:* "Suppose you had a customer who claimed his computer hardware was damaged in shipment. How would you handle this?" Or the interviewer might ask, "If we hired you and you saw one of our employees, perhaps a supervisor, doing something you considered unethical, what would you do?" Other questions are *task oriented:* "Here's a sheet of paper. Write a policy statement for the assignment of overtime." Interviewers have been known to take out a ballpoint pen and say to an applicant not interviewing for a sales position, "Sell this to me." Such questions assess thinking and communication abilities and how well an applicant can operate in stressful or surprise situations. Many questions probe into the *applicant's experiences:* "Tell me about a time when you have operated as part of a team to solve a vexing technical problem" or "Tell me about the most difficult decision you have ever had to make and how you went about making the decision."

Many employers are requiring would-be teachers to teach, salespersons to sell, engineers to engineer, managers to manage, and designers to design. Job simulations, role-playing, presentations, and day-long case studies challenge applicants to demonstrate their knowledge, skills, experiences, maturity, and integrity.

Responding: Successful Applicants

Successful applicants *listen* carefully to the whole question without interrupting or trying to second-guess the interviewer.[24] They *think* before replying, and then give answers that are succinct, specific, and to the point of the question. Many applicants miss the mark of questions, such as in the following example:

1. **Interviewer:** Why do you want to work for Feeble Construction?
2. **Interviewee:** I've always been interested in construction, particularly large commercial projects. This interest was heightened in my internship last summer with Rocky Mountain Construction in Denver.

This applicant emphasizes interest in commercial construction, but does not address the question: Why Feeble Construction? Present carefully organized responses with clear arguments, relevant content, good grammar, and action verbs that show you are a doer. Use professional jargon when appropriate. If you are short of actual work experiences, provide relevant illustrations from other experiences. Be honest because any hint of dishonesty, insincerity, unethical behavior, or evasion will be fatal. Do not reply with canned answers, prepared in advance to sound good, that an interviewer can destroy with a single, well-placed probing question, such as,

1. **Interviewer:** Why are you interested in sales?
2. **Interviewee:** I believe sales would be exciting, stimulating, and rewarding.
3. **Interviewer:** What would be exciting about a sales position?
4. **Interviewee:** Well, uh, you would be meeting interesting people and be on your own, and uh . . . .

Remember, there is no single, correct answer for each question. Five different interviewers asking the same question may be looking for somewhat different answers. Show enthusiasm and dynamism. Speak positively about your experiences. Have clear goals and career plans. Exhibit direct interest in both the position and the organization. Successful applicants do nothing merely for the sake of making a good impression. They do not play act but act themselves. After all, good interviewers can easily detect phoniness. Accept responsibilities for past actions; give reasons, not excuses. Blame yourself for mistakes, not others. Show in everything you do and say that you are a mature man or woman, not an immature boy or girl. Neither undersell nor oversell what you have done, who you are, and what you are capable of doing. And successful applicants demonstrate the characteristics of the interviewer's ideal applicant profile through communication skills, answers, and actions.

Answer questions thoroughly, but know when to shut up. Knowing when enough is enough is particularly difficult to determine during conference telephone calls, which are becoming widely used in narrowing applicants to a reasonably short list. You do not have the usual interviewer nonverbal cues (leaning forward, looking at notes, facial expressions, gestures) present in face-to-face interviews to tell you when to stop.

Successful applicants know when to follow up questions with questions. If you are asked a vague question or one you do not understand, paraphrase it in your own words or ask tactfully for clarification. Interviewers assume applicants understand questions unless they state otherwise. If you are asked a difficult critical incidents, hypothetical, or problem-solving question, not only think your answer through carefully but consider the ramifications of your response for you and the organization. For example, you might be wise to ask about organizational policies or legal constraints that have a bearing on the problem. Ask for additional details you need to know before framing a response. Ask what authority you would have in this situation. Asking for such information is likely to impress the interviewer with your professionalism and understanding of organizational situations and caution about acting with haste that might have negative ramifications for the organization.

Responding: Unsuccessful Applicants

Unsuccessful applicants tend to give brief answers that indicate they are nonassertive, passive, and cautious. Their answers contain qualifiers such as "perhaps" and "maybe" and nonfluencies such as "you know" and "and uh," which display tentativeness and powerlessness. They seem evasive and use less active, concrete, and positive language and less technical jargon.

Unsuccessful applicants appear uncertain about the kinds of positions they want and where they hope to be in the next five or ten years. They are unable to identify with the interests and needs of the interviewer and the organization. They fail to show interest in and enthusiasm for the position and organization. They do not ask for the position. They appear to know little about the position or organization.

Unsuccessful applicants play passive roles in both openings and closings. The reverse of passive, and perhaps even less likely to be hired, are applicants who attempt to manipulate interviewers by name-dropping or insincere flattery. In short, unsuccessful applicants exhibit few of the qualities interviewers are seeking.

Identifying Unlawful Questions

As we noted in Chapter 8, many applicants, particularly women, are still asked unlawful questions even though federal and state laws have existed for decades and most organizations train employees to follow EEO guidelines when interviewing applicants. You must be able to identify an unlawful question when it occurs and respond to it tactfully and effectively.

Violations range from mild infractions such as "What does your husband do?" to sexual harassment. Some are accidental during informal chatting with applicants, and others occur as a result of curiosity, tradition, and ignorance of the laws. Others occur, however, because interviewers have exaggerated feelings of power over applicants or they desire to violate laws that they perceive as infringements on their rights to do as they please, regardless of effects on others. Some continue to ask unlawful questions because they know that the EEOC cannot sue them. Only applicants can sue for violations of EEO laws, and only if the court decision is in the applicant's favor can the EEOC apply a fine. Thus, some interviewers believe erroneously that few applicants will go to the trouble and expense of suing. At a briefing in Chicago, the EEOC reported a backlog, its pending file, of 97,000 cases that include age, race, or sexual discrimination. Bias against overweight applicants, particularly females, seems to be a growing EEO violation.[25]

Regardless of why interviewers violate EEO laws and guidelines, such questions pose serious dilemmas for applicants. If you answer unlawful questions honestly, you may lose positions for irrelevant and unlawful reasons. If you refuse to answer such questions, you may lose positions because you appear to be uncooperative, evasive, hostile, or "one of those." There is no gracious way to refuse to answer a question even though this is the usual recommendation.

You must be able to recognize an unlawful question when it occurs. Most applicants are unaware of what constitutes an unlawful question and, regardless of knowledge level, feel they must answer whatever question an interviewer asks. Review the EEO laws and unlawful questions identified in Chapter 8. You must also be aware of tricks employers use to get unlawful information without appearing to ask for it. For example, a low-level clerk may ask you which health insurance plan you would choose if hired, and your answer may reveal that you are married and have children, perhaps even that you are a single parent. During lunch or dinner or a tour of the organization's facilities when you are least expecting and prepared for serious questions, an employer may address an unlawful area indirectly. For instance, an employer, perhaps a female, may probe into child care under the guise of talking about her own problems: "What a day! My daughter Emily woke up this morning with a fever, my husband is out of town, and I had an eight o'clock conference downtown. Do you ever have days like this?" You may begin to tell problems you have had with your children or family members and, in the process, reveal a great deal of irrelevant, unlawful, and perhaps damaging information without knowing it.

Employers have learned how to get unlawful information through lawful questions. Instead of asking, "Do you have children?" an employer asks, "Is there any limit on your ability to work overtime (evenings, weekends, holidays)?" Others use coded questions and comments. For example, "Our employees put a lot into their work" means "Older workers like you don't have much energy." "We have a very young staff" means "You won't fit in." And "I'm sure your former company had its own corporate culture, just as we do here" means "You can't teach an old dog new tricks."

Responding to Unlawful Questions

What, then, should you do when asked an unlawful question? First, determine how important the position is for you. How much do you want and need it? Your primary goal is to get a good position, and if you are hired, you may be able to change organizational attitudes and recruiters' practices. You cannot do anything from the outside. And second, determine the severity of the EEO violation. If it is a gross violation, consider not only refusing to answer the question but reporting the interviewer to his or her superior or to placement center or employment agency authorities.

If a question is a minor or moderate violation and you are interested in the position, consider a number of answer tactics. You may try a *tactful refusal,* such as the following:

1. **Interviewer:** How old are you?

   Interviewee: I don't think age is important if you are well qualified for a position.

2. **Interviewer:** Do you plan to have children?

   Interviewee: My plans to have a family will not interfere with my ability to perform the requirements of this position.

3. **Interviewer:** What do you do on Sunday mornings?

   Interviewee: If working on Sundays or weekends is a requirement of this position, I would prefer to discuss that after we determine whether or not I am the person you want for this position.

Note than none of the above is a simple refusal, such as "I will not answer that question because it is unlawful." You may choose to *answer directly but briefly,* in the hope the interviewer will move on to relevant, lawful questions, such as the following:

1. **Interviewer:** What does your wife do?

   Interviewee: She's a pharmacist.

2. **Interviewer:** Do you attend church regularly?

   Interviewee: Yes, I do.

You may pose a *tactful inquiry* such as the following:

1. **Interviewer:** What does your husband do?

   Interviewee: Why do you ask?

2. **Interviewer:** Apparently you are confined to a wheelchair; how might this affect your work performance?

   Interviewee: How is my disability relevant for a position as a computer programmer?

You might answer by trying to *neutralize* the interviewer's apparent concern, such as,

1. **Interviewer:** Do you plan on having a family?

   Interviewee: Yes, I do. I'm looking forward to the challenges of both family and career. I've observed many of my women professors and fellow workers handling both quite satisfactorily.

2. **Interviewer:** Who will take care of your children while you are at work?

   Interviewee: *Our* children will attend good day care centers and preschools until they are in the primary grades.

3. **Interviewer:** What happens if your husband gets transferred or needs to relocate?

   Interviewee: The same that would happen if I would get transferred or need to relocate. We would discuss location moves that *either* of us might have to consider and make the best decision.

You might try to *take advantage* of the question to support your candidacy:

1. **Interviewer:** Where were you born?

   Interviewee: I am quite proud that my background is _____ because it has helped me work effectively with people of diverse backgrounds.

2. **Interviewer:** How would you feel about working for a person younger than you?

   Interviewee: I have worked for and with people younger and older than I am. This has never posed a problem for me because I admire competence regardless of age.

3. **Interviewer:** Are you married?

   Interviewee: Yes I am, and I believe that is a plus. As you know, many studies show that married employees are more stable and dependable than unmarried employees.

You might try what Bernice Sandler, an authority on discrimination in hiring, calls a *tongue-in-cheek test response* that sends an unmistakable signal to the interviewer that he or she has asked an unlawful question. This tactic must be accompanied by appropriate nonverbal signals to avoid offending the interviewer.

1. **Interviewer:** Who will take care of your children?

   Interviewee: *(smiling, pleasant tone of voice)* Is this a test to see if I can recognize an unlawful question in the selection process?

2. **Interviewer:** How long do you expect to work for us?

   Interviewee: *(smiling, pleasant tone of voice)* Is this a test to see how I might reply to an unlawful question?

These are a few examples of tactics you might use when confronting unlawful questions during selection interviews. Unlawful questions are never easy to answer, but you can handle them more effectively if you are prepared to do so. Remember, you need not answer every question an interviewer asks.

7. Asking Questions

While nearly every applicant checks lists of employer questions and mulls over appropriate and effective answers, too few spend more than a few minutes planning questions *they* will ask. Most interviewers will give you an opportunity to ask questions, and some, like the authors, often begin selection interviews with applicant questions. Your questioning portion of the interview is a critical time not only to get information to help you make an important life decision but to reveal preparation, maturity, intelligence, professionalism, interests, motivation, and values.

You control this part of the interview, so make the most of it. Not having any or having too few questions is a major common mistake of applicants. Your questions can help persuade the interviewer that you are an ideal person for this position and organization or destroy the favorable impression you made during the opening and while answering questions. If you had a number of questions prepared when you arrived but the interviewer has answered all of them during the information giving portion of the interview, resist the urge to ask a question just to ask a question. There is a good likelihood it will be a poor question. Remember the old adage: You can remain silent and be thought stupid; or you can open your mouth and remove all doubt.

Successful applicants tend to ask more questions than unsuccessful applicants. And the questions of successful applicants are open-ended and probe into the position, the organization, and the interviewer's opinions. They also ask more follow-up or secondary questions to get complete and insightful answers. Unsuccessful applicants ask closed questions and miscellaneous information questions.

Follow the guidelines presented in Chapter 4 for effective questions and some specific ones for the selection interview. First, avoid the "me . . . me . . . me . . . " syndrome in which all of your questions inquire as to what you will get, how much you will get, and when you will get it. Second, avoid questions about salary, promotion, vacation, and retirement during screening interviews and never as your first questions. Interviewers assume that you will ask your most important questions first, so if your first question is about salary, for instance, they will assume your major, perhaps only, concern is money. If you are a 22-year-old recent college graduate, why are you greatly concerned about retirement? Third, do not waste time asking for information that is readily available in the organization's publications on the Web or in the library. If you have done your homework, you should know this information without asking for it.

When asking questions, you are acting as a probing interviewer, and you may be prone to tumble into the common question pitfalls discussed in previous chapters: double-barreled, leading, yes/no response, bipolar, guessing game, and open-to-closed switch. For instance, how do you expect an employer to respond to these yes (no) questions: "Do you encourage your employees to find new and better means of performing their jobs?" or "Are you a progressive bank?" Applicants have a few question pitfalls of their own.

1. The *have-to question* in which you make it sound as if you will be an uncooperative employee if hired or unwilling to perform a major requirement of the position.

   Bad: Would I have to travel much?
   Good: How much travel would this position entail?

2. The *typology question* in which you ask for type when you really want an open-ended answer.

   Bad: What type of training program do you have?
   Good: Tell me about your training program for this position.

3. The *pleading question* (often a series of them) in which you seem to beg for an answer.

   Bad: Could you please tell me about the expansion plans for the Jacksonville plant?
   Good: Tell me about the expansion plans for the Jacksonville plant.

4. The *little bitty question* in which you seem to indicate lack of interest in detailed information, perhaps asking a question merely to ask a question.

Bad: Tell me a little bit about your operation in Flint.
Good: Tell me about your operation in Flint.

5. The *uninformed question* that shows lack of professional maturity.

    Bad: Do you have any benefits?
    Good: Tell me about the stock-sharing plan you have for employees.

Phrase your questions carefully to avoid common mistakes and pitfalls. And listen to yourself because nonverbal communication can aid in making a question neutral and professional or threatening and unprofessional.

Take the time to prepare a moderate schedule of questions in advance so you have them phrased effectively and ordered according to importance. Do not place a critical question fifth or sixth on your list because you may not get the opportunity to ask five or six questions in a 20- to 25-minute interview, particularly if your questions are open-ended and obtain in-depth answers. The following sample applicant questions show interest in the position and the organization, are not overly self-centered, and meet question guidelines:

1. Describe your ideal employee for me.
2. Tell me about the culture of your organization.
3. How does your organization encourage employees to come up with new ideas?
4. What is the history of this position?
5. How much choice would I have in selecting geographical location?
6. How computerized is this operation?
7. Tell me about a typical workday for this position.
8. What is the possibility of flexible working hours?
9. How does your organization evaluate employees?
10. What characteristics are you looking for in applicants for this position?
11. How might your organization support me if I wanted to pursue an MBA?
12. How much supervision would I get as a new employee?
13. How often would I be working as part of a team?
14. What, in your estimation, is the most unique characteristic of your organization?
15. How might an advanced degree affect my position in your organization?
16. How does the cost of living in Milwaukee compare to Green Bay?
17. Tell me about where other persons who have held this position have advanced within the organization.
18. What have you liked most about working for this organization?
19. What can you tell me about the possible merger with CentralTel?
20. I noticed in *The Wall Street Journal* last week that your organization was listed among the 200 fastest-growing midsize corporations in the United States. How can you account for such growth?

21. How much involvement would I have with research and development?

22. Tell me about the people I would be working with in this division.

23. What training would I receive for this position?

24. What major changes do you anticipate for this organization within five years?

25. What will be the most important criterion for selecting a person for this position?

8. The Closing

The closing stage of the selection interview is usually brief, rarely more than a few minutes. Be careful of everything you say and do. This is not the time to say or do something that will detract from an impressive performance. Take an active part in the closing, not merely a nod and a handshake. Be sure you ask for the position implicitly and explicitly. Discover what will happen next and when. If you need to get in touch with the organization about your candidacy, whom should you contact and how?

There is a major rule for all interview closings: It's not over till it's over. If any member of the organization walks you to the outer office, the elevator, or the parking lot, it isn't over. If a person takes you on a tour of the organization or the area, it isn't over. If a person takes you to lunch or dinner, it isn't over. If a person drives you to the airport or train station, it isn't over. The employer is likely to note everything you do and say. Positions are lost because of the way applicants react during a tour, converse informally, meet other people, eat dinner, or handle alcoholic beverages.

9. Evaluation and Follow-Up

Following each interview, do a thorough review with the goals of repeating strengths and eliminating weaknesses in future interviews. Be careful not to overreact to your impressions and the interviewer's feedback. Your perceptions of what happened during an interview, how the interviewer reacted, or what nonverbal actions meant may be greatly exaggerated or wrong. The interview is more art than science, so do not believe you can assign specific meanings to each verbal and nonverbal signal.

Ask questions such as the following during your postinterview evaluation:

1. How adequate was my preparation: background study, resume, cover letter, answers, questions?

2. How effective was I during the opening?

3. How comfortable was I during the interview?

4. How appropriate was my dress?

5. Which questions did I handle well? Which poorly?

6. What opportunities to sell myself did I miss?

7. How thorough and to the point were my answers?

8. How well did I adapt my questions to this organization and position?

9. How effectively did I show interest in this organization and position?

10. Did I obtain enough information on this position and organization to determine if I should remain interested?

Be sure to follow up the interview with a brief, professional letter thanking the interviewer for the time given you. Emphasize your interest in this position and organization. The thank-you letter provides an excuse to contact the interviewer, keep your name alive, and provide additional information that might help the organization decide in your favor. And, after all, it is the polite thing to do. As in your cover letter, be sure your word choice, grammar, spelling, and punctuation are excellent.

Summary

Technology has allowed us to communicate instantly and to send and check information immediately. The scanning of resumes and the use of the Internet as sources for positions and resume storage will change the face of searching for positions. Personality, integrity, and drug tests are adding a new dimension to the process.

We have become a part of the global economy and are undergoing a second industrial revolution, moving from a manufacturing to a service and information-oriented society. The best positions in the future will go to those who understand and are prepared for the selection process. You must know yourself, the position, and the organization in order to persuade an employer to select you from hundreds of other applicants. The job search must be extensive and rely more on networking and hard work than merely appearing at your college placement center for an interview. Your resumes and cover letters must be thorough, professional, attractive, adapted to specific positions with specific organizations, and persuasive.

Interviewing skills are increasingly important because employers are looking for employees with communication, interpersonal, and people skills. You can exhibit these best during the interview. Take an active part in the opening, answer questions thoroughly and to the point, and ask carefully phrased questions about the position and the organization. Take an active part in the closing, and be sure the interviewer knows you want this position. Close on a high note.

In a survey of 188 college recruiters, Cunningham discovered a number of ways applicants can slip up during interviews.[26] Notice how the ones listed below summarize (in a negative way) the suggestions presented in this chapter.

1. Lack of awareness about the company and position.
2. No interest or enthusiasm.
3. Lying or telling the recruiter what you think he or she wants to hear.
4. Poor communication skills.
5. Too money-oriented.
6. Unclear or unrealistic goals.

7. No relevant experience.

8. No campus involvement.

9. Poor appearance.

10. Not having any questions to ask.

11. Bad attitude.

12. Inflexible.

13. Arriving late for the interview.

14. Poor listening skills.

15. Arrogant or cocky.

Follow up the interview with a carefully crafted thank-you letter that expresses again your interest in this position and organization. And do an insightful postinterview evaluation that addresses strengths and weaknesses with future interviews in mind.

A Selection Interview for Review and Analysis

This interview is between a senior in organizational communication and a college recruiter for Transnational Consulting, a firm that helps a wide variety of organizations in business, government, and education with their management and communication needs. Transnational has been growing rapidly as increasing numbers of organizations are outsourcing rather than having full-time experts as part of their organizations.

How active and effective is the applicant during the opening? What image does the applicant present during the interview? How appropriate, thorough, to-the-point, and persuasive are the applicant's answers? Has the applicant done adequate homework? How persuasively does the applicant demonstrate an interest in and fit for the position as a consultant for Transnational Consulting? How well do the applicant's questions meet the criteria presented in this chapter? How active and effective is the applicant during the closing?

1. **Interviewer:** Good afternoon Kathryn. *(shaking hands)* Please be seated.

2. **Interviewee:** Thank you.

3. **Interviewer:** I hope you've enjoyed your visit to our campus here in Atlanta. We've really enjoyed the area and the campus-like atmosphere. And it's very convenient to the airport when you travel as much as we do.

4. **Interviewee:** Yes, I certainly found it easy flying here from Little Rock.

5. **Interviewer:** I want to talk to you for about 20–25 minutes and then introduce you to other members of our firm. Let me begin by asking why you chose the University of Texas and organizational communication rather than management.

6. **Interviewee:** I've always been a great Texas fan, growing up near Houston, and I wanted to go to a major university.

7. **Interviewer:** And why organizational communication?

8. **Interviewee:** Well, during my freshman year, I realized that I was more people-oriented than theory-oriented. The management program is very theoretical and mathematical. After taking some communication courses and speaking to students and faculty, I decided to switch majors to a program that, I felt, was more to my liking and prepared me well for a consulting position.

9. **Interviewer:** Describe an ideal position for me.

10. **Interviewee:** I guess it would be like my internship with Andersen Consulting. It would give me an opportunity to work closely with people, develop and present training seminars, and work one-on-one with clients who need our help.

11. **Interviewer:** Tell me about the most difficult problem you have ever faced.

12. **Interviewee:** Well, it was the death of my father when I was a junior. We were very close, and he was my role model. I wasn't sure I wanted to continue school. It was very difficult getting motivated again to read and do class projects and cram for tests. School didn't seem important anymore.

13. **Interviewer:** What happened?

14. **Interviewee:** My mother and older brother sat down with me and reminded me that my degree had been my father's dream, as well as mine, and that he would want me to continue and graduate on time.

15. **Interviewer:** And?

16. **Interviewee:** I went back to Austin, made the dean's list, and got the internship with Andersen.

17. **Interviewer:** How much travel are you willing to do?

18. **Interviewee:** I'm looking forward to traveling around the country, and maybe abroad, and seeing areas I have not been to in the northeast and northwest.

19. **Interviewer:** What experience have you had working with teams?

20. **Interviewee:** Quite a bit actually. Nearly all of my organizational communication classes involved team or group projects. And I worked with teams quite often in my internship and activities on campus.

21. **Interviewer:** What would you do if a client called to complain about a presentation on conflict resolution made by a person under your supervision?

22. **Interviewee:** Well, first, I would try to get specifics on the situation and discover why the client is dissatisfied.

23. **Interviewer:** And then?

24. **Interviewee:** I would call the consultant in and get his or her side of the story. In my experiences, I have seen situations in which the client got what was asked for but somehow expected more without the consultant knowing it.

25. **Interviewer:** And once you have both sides of the story, then what?

26. **Interviewee:** I would urge both parties to sit down and decide what Transnational might do to satisfy all expectations. A consulting firm cannot afford to disappoint or anger clients.

27. **Interviewer:** Why would you like to work for Transnational Consulting?

28. **Interviewee:** Well, everything I have read indicates that you are one of the fastest-growing consulting firms and are hiring a lot of young people like myself. I think I would fit in real well.

29. **Interviewer:** What else?

30. **Interviewee:** I like doing different things and meeting new challenges. This is what I've always enjoyed and why I would really like to work for Transnational. I get bored with doing the same thing all the time and just sitting at a desk.

31. **Interviewer:** Why should we hire you for this position?

32. **Interviewee:** Well, first, I have received an excellent education at the University of Texas. And second, I think my experiences have prepared me for this job.

33. **Interviewer:** What do you know about Transnational?

34. **Interviewee:** Let's see. You were originally a division of American School Supplies to work with school systems. Then in the early 1980s you began to work for major universities and corporations throughout the country, including most of the Big 12. That's when you spun off into an independent company. You now have offices here in Houston, San Francisco, St. Louis, and Baltimore.

35. **Interviewer:** We do have nearly 1,500 employees nationwide, about 350 connected with this office. Although we do have staff who work here most of the time on special projects, most of our staff work with clients on-site and may be around here only a few hours a week. We were recently listed in *The Wall Street Journal* among the fastest-growing consulting firms in the country and mentioned in *Business Week* as one of the firms to watch. What questions do you have?

36. **Interviewee:** I'm interested in the stock-sharing plan mentioned in one of your brochures.

37. **Interviewer:** After you've been with us for six months, you are eligible to purchase stock in the company. We believe this is a good way for all of us to have a stake in what we do.

38. **Interviewee:** Would I be provided with a car for travel?

39. **Interviewer:** No, we prefer to give employees a monthly travel allotment.

40. **Interviewee:** If advanced training is needed, perhaps an MBA, would Transnational help with this?

41. **Interviewer:** We would help if we required this training, but not if you decide to do graduate work on your own.

42. **Interviewee:** What do you like best about working for Transnational?

43. **Interviewer:** I like the variety of work, the freedom we have when working with clients, and the team atmosphere that pervades Transnational.

44. **Interviewee:** What's the salary range for this position?

45. **Interviewer:** It's competitive, depending upon the cost of living in the area where you might be assigned.

46. **Interviewee:** That's all the questions I have. Transnational sounds like a great place to work.

47. **Interviewer:** We hope to make a decision in about two or three weeks. It's been good talking with you and getting acquainted.

48. **Interviewee:** Thank you for the interview. It's been a pleasure meeting with someone from Transnational.

49. **Interviewer:** Good. Let me introduce you to Ralph Stein, who came to us two years ago from Purdue University.

Selection Role-Playing Cases

An Accountant with a Metal Company

You are a 30-year-old production supervisor with Rolled Aluminum. You enjoy working for Rolled Aluminum and have enjoyed your position. Unfortunately, your chance of advancement is slight because the people above you are in their 30s and show no signs of leaving. You have decided to look elsewhere for advancement possibilities.

You have made an appointment with the vice president for human resources at All-Metal Stamping about a position above the one you hold at Rolled Aluminum. You have a degree in leadership and supervision and introduced a number of innovations while at Rolled Aluminum. You are not quite sure what to say if the interviewer asks why you want to leave your current position. You want to appear ambitious but not excessively so.

A Real Estate Salesperson

You are in your late 20s and worked as a salesperson of women's clothing in a major Chicago department store for six years. You had a very good record, and many of your customers requested help with purchases. The store did not want you to leave. After becoming dissatisfied with your low salary and no opportunity for advancement, you decided to enroll in a training course in real estate. You took the test recently and passed with a very high grade.

You have an interview with the owner of a large residential and commercial real estate firm. You have a pleasant personality and can talk easily with people. However, when you become nervous or feel you are under stress, you tend to stutter. Should you mention this problem to the interviewer? What should you do if you begin to stutter during the interview?

Photo Journalist

You are a recent college graduate about to interview for a position as a photo journalist with a major newspaper with a regional circulation. This paper rarely hires reporters or photo journalists just out of college, but your journalism professors have recommended you highly to the publisher, who has agreed to interview you because the paper's veteran photo journalist was recently killed in an auto accident. The interviewer might be looking for a temporary replacement until a more experienced photo journalist can be hired.

You must decide what to include in your portfolio of photo samples and how to introduce it effectively. You have had two internships with midsize city dailies and have worked for two years on your college newspaper as reporter and photo journalist. How might you work in these experiences to show you are qualified without seeming to think a college or midsize city daily are the same as a major newspaper? How and when, if at all, should you use the names of professors who have recommended you without seeming to name-drop?

Student Activities

1. Call 10 organizations you would like to work for. Ask about their dress codes during working hours. Then ask them if they would consider it appropriate dress if you came to interview with them wearing a comfortable pantsuit (for women) or a sport coat, tie, colored shirt, and wash pants (for men).

2. There are many organizations that make products or parts for other organizations. They are often unknown to the public because their products or parts are unavailable through retail outlets or direct sales. Select a company such as Molex, Tellabs, Cherry Electric, Sonoco, or Platinum Technology and use their Web pages to discover the positions they have available.

3. Create a series of sentences or short paragraphs you could use to sell your skills and abilities. Consider interpersonal skills, writing skills, computer skills, and skills specific to your discipline. How can you phrase them effectively without exaggerating them or underselling yourself?

4. Identify the part of the United States or the world in which you want to work after graduation. Use the resources of this chapter, local bookstores, library, and campus career center to select a dozen Internet addresses that would help you locate positions most suitable to your interests, education, and experiences.

Notes

1. Harry Dent, *The Roaring 2000s* (New York: Simon and Schuster, 1998), pp. 3–38.

2. "The 50 Hottest Jobs in America," *Money,* March 1995, pp. 114–17; "Where the Action Is," *U.S. News & World Report,* October 31, 1994, pp. 86–93; "Jobs in an Age of Insecurity," *Time,* November 22, 1993, pp. 32–39; and "Looking Good: Where the Fast Growth Is and Will Be," *The Wall Street Journal,* February 27, 1995, p. R5.

3. Lixandra Urresta and Jonathan Hickman, "The Diversity Elite," *Fortune,* August 3, 1998, pp. 114–15.

4. Lisa Holton, "Courting the Candidates in a Tight Job Market," *Chicago Tribune,* August 16, 1998, p. 6, 1:6.

5. Peter L. Brill and Richard Worth, *The Four Levels of Corporate Change* (New York: AMACOM, 1997), pp. 3–45; and Bruce A. Pasternak and Albert J. Viscio, *The Centerless Corporation: A New Model for Transforming Your Organization for Growth and Prosperity* (New York: Simon and Schuster, 1998).

6. "No Job Openings? Set Up an Interview Anyway," *Chicago Tribune,* August 16, 1998, Jobs Section, p. 6, 1:2.

7. Lois Einhorn, *Interviewing . . . A Job in Itself* (Bloomington, IN: The Career Center, 1977), pp. 3–5; and Charles J. Stewart, *Interviewing Principles and Practices: Applications and Exercises* (Dubuque, IA: Kendall/Hunt, 1997), pp. 119–22

8. Timothy A. Judge and Daniel M. Cable, "Applicant Personality, Organizational Culture, and Organization Attraction," *Personnel Psychology* 50 (1997), pp. 359–94.

9. Fredric M. Jablin and Vernon D. Miller, "Interviewer and Applicant Questioning Behavior in Employment Interviews," *Management Communication Quarterly* 4 (1990), pp. 51–86.

10. Robert A. Martin, "Toward More Productive Interviewing," *Personnel Journal* 50 (1971), pp. 359–62.

11. Steve D. Ugbah and Randall E. Majors, "Influential Communication Factors in Employment Interviews," *Journal of Business Communication* 29 (1992), pp. 145–59.

12. Robert L. Rose, "A Foot in the Door," *The Wall Street Journal,* February 27, 1995, p. R7.

13. Catherine Smith MacDermott, "Networking and Interviewing: An Art in Effective Communication," *Business Communication Quarterly,* December 1995, pp. 58–59.

14. An excellent listing of Internet resources can be found in John R. Cunningham, *The Inside Scoop: Recruiters Tell College Students Their Secrets in the Job Search* (New York: McGraw-Hill, 1998), pp. 45–58.

15. "Extra Touches Help Resume Dazzle," Lafayette, Indiana, *Journal and Courier,* May 21, 1995, p. C3.

16. Cunningham, p. 68; and Kevin Hutchinson and Diane S. Brefka, "Personnel Administrators' Preferences for Resume Content: Ten Years After," *Business Communication Quarterly,* June 1997, pp. 67–75.

17. We wish to thank Rebecca Parker, assistant professor, Department of Communication, Western Illinois University, for assisting us with the sample chronological and functional resumes included in Figures 9.5 and 9.6.

18. Thomas W. Dougherty, Daniel B. Turban, and John C. Callender, "Confirming First Impressions in the Employment Interview: A Field Study of Interviewer Behavior," *Journal of Applied Psychology* 79 (1994), pp. 659–65.

19. Amelia J. Prewett-Livingston, Hubert S. Field, John G. Veres III, and Philip M. Lewis, "Effects of Race on Interview Ratings in a Situational Panel Interview," *Journal of Applied Psychology* 81 (1996), pp. 178–86.

20. Richard J. Ilkka, "Applicant Appearance and Selection Decision Making: Revitalizing Employment Interview Education," *Business Communication Quarterly,* September 1995, pp. 11–18.

21. Neil R. Anderson, "Decision Making in the Graduate Selection Interview: An Experimental Investigation," *Human Relations,* April 1991, pp. 403–17; and Ronald E.

Riggio and Barbara Throckmorton, "The Relative Effects of Verbal and Nonverbal Behavior, Appearance, and Social Skills on Evaluations Made in Hiring Interviews," *Journal of Applied Psychology* 18 (1988), pp. 331–48.

22. R. Gifford, C. F. Ng, and M. Wilkinson, "Nonverbal Cues in the Employment Interview: Links between Applicant Qualities and Interviewer Judgments," *Journal of Applied Psychology* 70 (1985), pp. 729–36.

23. Richard L. Street, "Interaction Processes and Outcomes in Interviews," in M. L. McLaughlin, ed., *Communication Yearbook 9* (Beverly Hills, CA: Sage, 1985), pp. 217–18; Keith G. Rasmussen, "Nonverbal Behavior, Verbal Behavior, Resume Credentials, and Selection Interview Outcomes," *Journal of Applied Psychology* 69 (1984), pp. 551–56; and "Verbal Skills More Important Than Experience," *CA Magazine,* May 1993, p. 10.

24. Lois J. Einhorn, "An Inner View of the Job Interview: An Investigation of Successful Communicative Behaviors," *Communication Education* 30 (1981), pp. 217–28; Street, pp. 216–18; and Patricia Stubs, "Some Hints to Those Who Are Interviewed," *Management World* 13 (1984), pp. 17–18.

25. Regina Pingitore, Bernard Dugoni, R. Scott Tindale, and Bonnie Spring, "Bias against Overweight Job Applicants in a Simulated Employment Interview," *Journal of Applied Psychology* 79 (1994), pp. 909–17.

26. Cunningham, p. 184.

Resources

Bolles, Richard N. *What Color Is Your Parachute?* Berkeley, CA: Ten Speed Press, 1995.

Cunningham, John R. *The Inside Scoop: Recruiters Tell College Students Their Secrets for Success in the Job Search.* New York: McGraw-Hill, 1998.

Dikel, Margaret Riley; Frances Roehm; and Steve Oserman. *The Guide to Internet Searching.* Lincolnwood, IL: VGM Career Horizons, 1998.

Gale, Linda. *Discover What You're Best At.* New York: Fireside Press, 1998.

Kennedy, Joyce Lain. *Electronic Job Search Revolution.* New York: John Wiley and Sons, 1995.

McDonnell, Sharon. *You're Hired!: Secrets to Successful Job Interviews.* New York: Macmillan, 1995.

Yeager, Neil, and Lee Hough. *Power Interviews.* New York: John Wiley and Sons, 1998.

The Performance Interview

The two Rs of employment—recruitment and retention—play a major role in the success of all organizations. Unless a position is highly specialized, organizations must invest time, money, and knowledge to bring employees up to speed in necessary skills or success is unlikely. The Cash-Stewart development cycle involves nine steps: recruitment, selection, orientation, skills assessment, training, review, evaluation, promotion, and retention.

The organization must *recruit* the right persons. During recruitment, interviewers must sort out those who do not fit the position description and *select* one or perhaps two in case an applicant rejects an offer. The review process begins with *orientation* that includes polices and procedures for doing things within the organization. If benefits were not employed to generate interest among good applicants in the position, they are explained during orientation. New employees often must wait six months to a year for benefits such as bonuses, profit sharing, stock options, interest-free personal loans, cars, and stock purchases.

Depending on organizational structure, *skills assessment* begins almost immediately with computer skills. If teams are in place between six weeks and three months, a new employee may be reviewed regarding problem solving, decision making, team contribution, and style. Individuals are often directed to *training* programs that will improve specific abilities. The organization can then *review, evaluate,* and *promote.* Careful review and evaluation resulting in appropriate and meaningful promotion will enable the organization to *retain* high-quality employees. A promotion today often means more lateral responsibilities rather than a move up. This employee development process is influenced by 360-degree or multisource feedback.

It seems at times that the more things change, the more they stay the same. The performance review process had its heyday in the 60s, 70s, and 80s and was conducted by the supervisor. Initially the person used a blank sheet of paper, then a checklist, and then a checklist with a five-point Likert scale. The interview was the most dreaded part of the process. Few liked to conduct the interviews, and fewer liked to take them. With EEO laws being more strictly enforced and observed in the 1970s, the trend was toward goal setting and an opportunity for the employee to write responses. The multisource feedback process came from the use of assessment center technology. The use of self-evaluation instruments and questionnaires completed by a supervisor and several staff members outside the functional area became the model. At first, this process erred in the same two directions as the old appraisal model. The review turned into "love discussions" or "you got me so I will get you" sessions. Criticisms leveled at the old system are being leveled at the 360-degree process:

1. Supervisors are biased.

2. Supervisors are too critical.

3. One process serves too many purposes: raises, promotions, evaluations, feedback, and development.

4. The process encourages passive compliance behavior.

5. Supervisors do not have enough training to perform the process correctly.

An interviewing instructor commented to one of the authors that he did not bother with performance review interviews because the 360-degree approach made them unnecessary. This is not true. Even in the group-oriented process, the leader of the feedback session is called the interviewer/facilitator. The interviewer role is more important than ever. The performance interview serves important functions for both organizations and employees if both interviewer and interviewee learn the purposes of the interview, the keys to success, how to prepare for it, and how to take part in it. Figure 10.1 illustrates the stages for planning and taking part in performance interviews.

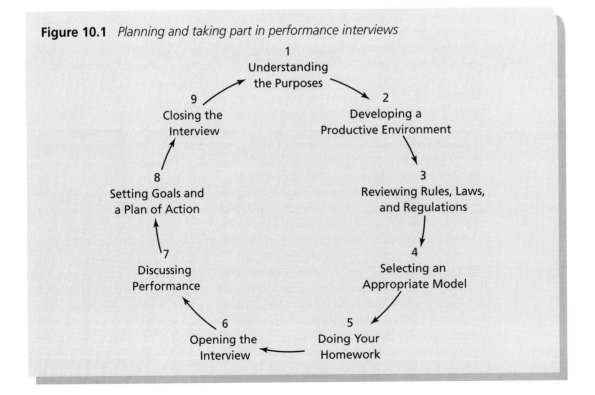

Figure 10.1 *Planning and taking part in performance interviews*

1. Understand the Purposes of the Interview

The performance review interview is essentially a feedback mechanism that may serve multiple purposes for both parties.[1] The most important purpose for the employer is not to review and judge past performance but to bring about better future performance. This is best accomplished by using a total performance and development plan to make equitable and objective decisions about pay raises, assignments, promotions, demotions, and discharges. This plan should emphasize prospects for advancement, meaningful feedback, and the employee's strengths and accomplishments. Thus, an effective performance review system enables organizations to assess training and development needs, enhance superior-subordinate communication, build stronger staff relationships, and create a positive, results-oriented atmosphere by recognizing good work and achievement of goals.

The most important purpose for employees is to assess their performances of predetermined and verifiable goals. Self-evaluations combined with employer evaluations tell employees exactly how they are doing on specific tasks, where they stand within organizations, and where they might be going. Employees should seek ongoing feedback and clarification of the extent of their authority and control of personal and organizational resources.

2. Developing a Productive Organizational Environment

Of the many keys to successful interviews, according to Douglas McGregor, the most critical is the organizational environment that reflects the organization's basic "assumptions about human nature and human behavior."[2] These assumptions, McGregor adds, "are frequently implicit, sometimes quite unconscious, often conflicting; nevertheless, they determine our predictions that if we do A, B will occur." McGregor uses these assumptions for what he calls Theory X and Theory Y. For instance, a Theory X manager assumes:

1. Human beings have an inherent dislike of work and will avoid it when they can.
2. Because human beings dislike work, they must be coerced, controlled, directed, or threatened with punishment to get them to put forth adequate effort toward the achievement of organizational objectives.
3. Human beings prefer to be directed, wish to avoid responsibility, have relatively little ambition, and want security above all.

A Theory Y manager assumes that:

1. The expenditure of physical and mental effort in work is as natural as play and rest.
2. Human beings, without external control or threat of punishment, will exercise self-direction and self-control in the service of objectives to which they are committed.
3. Commitment to objectives is a function of the rewards associated with their achievement.

4. Human beings, under proper conditions, not only accept but seek responsibility.

5. The capacity to exercise a relatively high degree of imagination, ingenuity, and creativity in the solution of organizational problems is widely, not narrowly, distributed in the population.

6. Under the conditions of modern life, the intellectual potentialities of the average human being are only partially utilized.

Performance interviewers acting on Theory X assumptions are likely to provide a *defensive climate,* whereas interviewers acting from Theory Y assumptions are likely to provide a *supportive climate.* Gibb suggests that defensive and supportive climates have these characteristics:[3]

Defensive Climates

1. Evaluation
2. Control
3. Strategy
4. Neutrality
5. Superiority
6. Certainty

Supportive Climates

1. Description
2. Problem orientation
3. Spontaneity
4. Empathy
5. Equality
6. Provisionalism

As our society moves from an industrial to an information and service environment, Theory X and its defensive climate must give way to a supportive climate that values independence, mutual trust and respect, and creativity. There must be fewer superior-subordinate relationships and more associate and team relationships. Meyer writes: "A performance review discussion based on the subordinate's self-review is more appropriate for the new climate. Research indicates that performance review discussions based on self-review are more productive and satisfying than traditional manager-initiated appraisal discussions."[4] The modern organization that Meyer addresses attempts to create a partnership with employee participation and involvement in supervisory management and to send a strong message that individual performance is highly important to the success of the organization.

Employees prefer a supportive climate that includes mutual trust, well-defined job descriptions, subordinate input, and a planning and review process. They want to be treated sensitively by a supportive, nonjudgmental interviewer. Employees want to contribute to each aspect of the review, get credit for their ideas, and know what to expect during and after the review process. The performance review is likely to be successful if an employee knows what to expect during the interview, has the ability to do what is expected, receives regular feedback, and is rewarded for a job well done.

As an interviewer, you can create a relaxed, positive, and supportive climate by continually monitoring the employee's progress, offering psychological support in the forms of praise and encouragement, helping to correct mistakes, and offering substantial feedback.[5] Above all, do not dwell on negative aspects of performance. Base your review on performance, not on the individual—attack the problem, not the person. Provide performance-related information, and measure performance against specific

standards agreed upon during the previous review. How many sales has the person made or how many claims has the person settled, and how do these compare with the standards set during the most recent review session? Studies reveal that subordinates see supervisors as helpful, constructive, and willing to help them solve performance-related problems when these supervisors encourage them to express their ideas and feelings and participate equally in performance review interviews.[6]

Supervisors at all levels have found it useful to talk periodically with each subordinate about personal and work-related issues.

photo by Steven Rubin/The Image Works

Frequency of interviews is a major key to success. Providing feedback on a regular basis, literally as a day-to-day responsibility, can avoid formal, once-a-year "tooth pulling" reviews dreaded by both parties. Once a year is too infrequent, and twice is a minimum. Evaluate poor performance immediately before damage to the organization and the employee is irreparable. Avoid surprises during the interview caused by withholding criticisms until the formal review session. And be sure to conduct as many sessions as necessary to do the job right; do not try to handle everything in one marathon session.

Training of interviewers is essential for successful reviews. Interviewers must know how to create a genuine dialogue between themselves and interviewees. They must realize that playing the role of evaluator will reduce the two-way communication process and negatively affect a relationship that is critical to the review process. Subordinates perceive interviewers who have learned how to handle performance-related information, assign goals, and give feedback to be equitable, accurate, and clear during performance interviews.

A primary employee complaint is the sloppy, casual attitude of too many employers toward documentation that affects their work lives, career progress, and financial gain. They want interviewers and others involved in the review to take them, their work, and their roles within the organization seriously. Interviewers must be trained and committed to the review process so that it enhances future performance.[7]

3. Reviewing Rules, Laws, and Regulations

There are no shortcuts to successful performance interviews. Each must be thoroughly researched and prepared. Begin by reading your organization's regulations and policies for reviewing employees, and then turn to laws, specifically Title VII of the 1964 Civil Rights Act (as amended) and Equal Employment Opportunity Commission guidelines and interpretations. Be careful of assessing traits such as honesty, integrity, appearance, initiative, leadership, attitude, and loyalty that are difficult to judge objectively and fairly.

Remember that all aspects of the employment process, including hiring, promoting, transferring, training, and discharging, are covered by civil rights legislation and EEO guidelines. Laws do not require performance reviews, but guidelines state that ones conducted must be standardized in form and administration, measure actual work performance, and be applied equally to all employees. Employees with equal experience or seniority in jobs requiring the same skills, effort, responsibility, and working conditions must receive equal compensation. Compensation based on gender, race, age, or ethnic group is unlawful.

The rapidly changing demographics of the workforce requires a keen familiarity with EEO laws, the nature of the review interaction, and questionable assumptions that have governed organizational interactions for too long. Increasing numbers of the disabled, females, and minorities are entering the workforce each year. Review carefully the EEO laws outlined in Chapter 8. Goodall, Wilson, and Waagen warn that communication between "superiors" and "inferiors" in the review process leads to ritual forms of address "that are guided by commonly understood cultural and social stereotypes, traditional etiquette, and gender-specific rules."[8] If this is so, then we should not be surprised that performance interviewers often violate EEO laws and guidelines. The American workforce is increasingly older, and some authorities predict that age discrimination will be the most prominent area of litigation in the twenty-first century. Incidentally, contrary to popular assumptions, older workers perform better than younger workers.[9]

4. Selecting an Appropriate Review Model

To meet EEO guidelines and conduct fair and objective performance-centered interviews, theorists and organizations have developed a number of models during the past 20 years. Because of the cost associated with training and developing effective employees, it is essential that organizations help them grow and improve by informing them about what they do well and how they can correct what they do wrong.

Person-Product-Service Model

According to the *person-product-service model,* managerial competencies lead to effective behaviors that then lead to effective performance. A competency may be a motive, trait, skill, aspect of self-image, social role, or body of knowledge that leads to effective performance. Supporters of this model argue that reviews of persons in terms of competencies have two major advantages: (1) a single competency is manifest in several different actions, and (2) a manager's particular behavior is typically affected by several competencies.

Behaviorally Anchored Rating Scales (BARS) Model

In the *behaviorally anchored rating scales (BARS) model,* skills essential to a specific job are identified through a job analysis, and standards are set, often with the aid of industrial engineers. Typical jobs for which behaviors have been identified and standards set include telephone survey takers (at so many telephone calls per hour), meter readers for utility companies (at so many meters per hour), and data entry staff or programmers (at so many lines of entry per hour). Usually job analysts identify specific skills and weigh their relative worth and usage. Each job can have specific measurable skills that eliminate game-playing or subjective interpretation by interviewers.

Employees whose interviewers use BARS report high levels of review satisfaction, feel they have greater impact upon the process, and perceive their interviewers as supportive.[10] They know what skills they are expected to have, their relative worth to the organization, and how their performance will be measured. However, not every job has measurable or easily identifiable skills, and arguments often arise over when, how, and by whom specific standards are set. One study suggests that using the BARS model results in more accurate performance ratings than does using the mixed standard scale model.[11]

Management by Objectives (MBO) Model

The *management by objectives (MBO) model* involves the manager and the subordinate in a mutual (50–50) setting of results-oriented goals rather than activities to be performed. Advocates of the MBO model contend that behaviorally based measures can (1) account for more job complexity; (2) be rated more directly to what the employee actually does; (3) minimize irrelevant factors not under the employee's control; (4) encompass cost-related measures; (5) be less ambiguous and subjective than person-based measures; (6) reduce employee role ambiguity by making clear what behaviors are required in a given job; and (7) facilitate explicit performance feedback and goal setting by encouraging meaningful employer-employee discussions regarding the employee's strengths and weaknesses.

The MBO model classifies all work in terms of four major elements: (1) inputs, (2) activities, (3) outputs, and (4) feedback.[12] *Inputs* include equipment, tools, materials, money, and staff needed to do the work. *Activities* refer to the actual work performed. *Outputs* are results, end products, dollars, reports prepared, or services rendered. *Feedback* refers to subsequent supervisor reaction (or lack of it) to the output. Figure 10.2 shows how the four major work elements interact.

If you serve as a performance review interviewer using an MBO model, keep several principles in mind. First, always consider quality, quantity, time, and cost. Almost any job can be measured by these four criteria. The more of these criteria you use, the greater the chances that the measurement will be accurate. If you want to measure the effectiveness of a recruiter, for instance, you might count the number of interviews conducted by that recruiter per hire. By comparing the number of interviews per hire, you obtain the quality and quantity measure needed. You can calculate the cost in terms of time taken to fill a position, and measure quantity and quality by noting the number of people hired who received outstanding performance ratings.

Second, state results in terms of ranges rather than absolutes. Whether you use minimum, maximum, or achievable, or five- or seven-point scales, allow for freedom of movement and adjustment. Do not try to fine-tune the performance measure at the start, but begin with a broad range that you can adjust as the performance period continues.

Third, keep the number of objectives small and set a mutual environment. If you are measuring a year's performance with quarterly or semiannual reviews, measure no more

Figure 10.2 *MBO performance appraisal model*

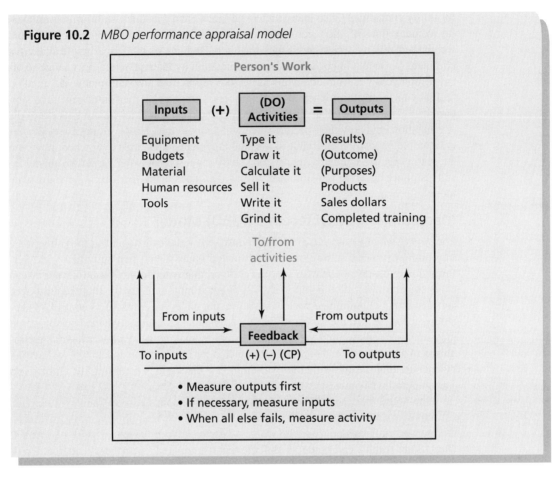

than six to eight major or critical aspects of performance. Positions such as research or development may have only one objective. The agreed-upon objectives should comprise about 70 percent of the work, with 30 percent kept in reserve to measure performance of assignments that come up unexpectedly.

Fourth, try for trade-offs between mutually exclusive aims and measures. An objective that is too complex may be self-defeating. For example, if you attempt to reduce labor and decrease cost at the same time, you may create more problems than you solve. Job performance is somewhat like performance in sports—when you concentrate on one aspect of the game, other parts may deteriorate. The best action might be to work on a goal step-by-step until you have achieved it.

Fifth, when the value of the performance is abstract, initiate practices that make it measurable. Measuring is often difficult, but anyone or anything that works can be measured. In a legal department, you might measure performance in terms of the number of cases won or lost or in terms of dollars lost to the organization. In graphic arts, you might measure response time, cost, and consumer satisfaction.

And sixth, if you cannot predict conditions on which performance success depends, use a floating or gliding goal. As one part of the target grows or moves, the other part does the same. This comparative measure works, for example, with production changes when people say, "You can't measure us because the production schedules change so often." You simply measure the amount produced versus the amount scheduled.

Universal Performance Interviewing Model

William Cash has developed and tested a *universal performance interviewing model* in more than 40 organizations during the past seven years. This model begins with four basic questions that are followed by six important words.

1. What is not being done that should be?
2. What expectations are not being met at what standard?
3. Could the person do it if he or she really wanted to?
4. Does the individual have the skills to perform as needed?

Too often personality clashes, prejudices, or politics result in unfair interviews that may lead to termination. If an interviewer says "I do not like how she is doing . . . " or "I cannot put my finger on it, but he is just not doing . . . ," the four questions set up in columns on a blank piece of paper can serve as guidelines for fairness and comparisons of one employee to another. The interviewer must be able to specify what is missing or not being done well, such as "She does not fill out the customer complaint form when she is on the telephone and often leaves off the customer's number." This is feedback that can lead to change and need not wait until an annual review.

The bulk of performance problems fall into two broad categories: training (Does the person have the skills, knowledge, or education?) and motivation (Are there positive or negative consequences for doing a job correctly and does the person want to?). It is reasonable and logical to ask if a person knows how to do a job and, if so, why the person is not doing it. There are as many answers to these questions as there are people. You can record and assess only the behavior that you can hear or observe. Good intentions cannot be recorded or measured.

Narrow each problem down to a coachable answer. Maybe no one has emphasized that getting 100 percent of customers' numbers at the beginning of calls is critical because the customer number drives the system and makes it easier to access billing or other pieces of information under that number. Perhaps the employee cannot type fast enough to enter the number or knows the customer's number by heart and intends to place it in the correct position on the screen after the customer hangs up. The observation-judgment dilemma has been a problem for performance reviewers. A problem like the above may require only a quick reminder and not a lengthy discussion. Correct such problems on the spot rather than waiting for an appointed review period.

The four questions in conjunction with six key words shown in Figure 10.3 allow interviewers to make a number of observations about performance. This model can be employed with others (the increasingly popular 360-degree review process) with separate observations by supervisors, peers, and customers (internal and external) that can

Figure 10.3 *Six key words in the universal performance interviewing model*

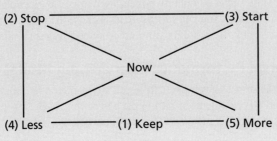

be compared to one another for consistency, trends, and rater reliability. An 11" by 14" sheet of paper with the four questions in columns can provide the bases for quarterly or annual reviews or brief coaching sessions. Many organizations are eliminating the annual performance review or making it a part of a coaching process that takes place weekly for production workers and monthly for professionals. A summary session may be done quarterly with an annual review to set goals for the coming year, review progress, and look at developmental needs.[13]

Once you have answered the four basic questions, start on the model with "keep." When an employee is doing something well, you need to make sure the person knows you appreciate a job well done. Start with "keep" and then go to "stop," followed by "start," "less," "more," finishing with the time frame for improving performance. The word "now" emphasizes the importance of making appropriate changes immediately. Performance problems do not resolve themselves. Define "now" in terms of weeks or perhaps months. Be specific. If you do not want a problem resolved "now," why discuss it?

The universal performance interviewing model enables you as coach to start with positive behavior you wish the employee to maintain, followed immediately by behaviors you wish corrected now. This begins the interview on a positive note. Your "stop" list should be the shortest and reserved for those behaviors that place an employee or product at risk, are destructive to others or the work environment, or are qualitatively and procedurally incorrect.

The interviewer can deliver each of the four questions and the six words at different verbal and nonverbal levels, including hints, suggestions, and corrections. For example, the interviewer might say:

I want you to stop doing	You must do more of . . . .
You must stop doing	You must do less of . . . .
I want you to start doing	You must do . . . . now.

Many highly sophisticated systems spend too much time on the analytical end and almost no time on the specific behavior to be altered and how. We believe strongly that if you cannot provide a specific alternative behavior and explain how to achieve it, then there is no need for a performance review.

Let us use the customer service representative mentioned earlier as an example. Assume that she knows many customer numbers because of the frequency of calls from them and has the numbers memorized. She thinks it is unnecessary to log each number in the system until she has finished discussing specific problems with customers. After all, she often has several lines ringing and wants to get to other customers as quickly as possible because of the four-ring objective—every incoming call must be answered within four rings. She is above average (four on a five-point scale). Instead of making this problem an issue that requires lengthy interviews, you might use one of the following styles to present the problem without making it a bigger problem.

Hint: *(smiling pleasantly)* I noticed you were busy this morning when I stopped by to observe you, and I just thought it might be easier for you to record each customer's number while this person is at the beginning of the conversation with you.

Suggestion: *(neutral facial expression and matter-of-fact vocal inflections)* Just one little idea came to mind from my observation this morning. I would like to see you try to record each customer's number early so it does not get lost in the shuffle of answers to other callers and you won't forget to record it.

Correction: *(stern voice and face)* Based on my observation this morning, you must be sure to record each customer's number before you do anything else on the system for that number. This number drives our entire system, and problems result when a number is not recorded immediately.

The purpose of every performance interview is to provide accurate feedback to the employee about what must be altered, changed, or eliminated and when. Most employees want to do a good job, and the performance mentor or coach must provide direction. Imagine if the following comments were made to our customer representative:

1. **Interviewer:** *(matter-of-fact face and voice)* You need to get better on that system.

2. **Interviewer:** *(uncaring)* I would like to see some improvement before I observe you again.

3. **Interviewer:** *(uncaring and angry)* After my observation this morning, what do you think I found wrong with your performance?

Feedback such as the above builds walls of resentment between coach and employee. If everything is a major problem, the wall grows.

This brings us to another part of the model that is crucial in performance interviews. The two Ss in the model are "specific" and "several," and these are important in every review session even if it is a brief exchange and not an annual performance review. Performance interviews must not be guessing games. Attempts at mind-reading cause relationship problems. The two Ss enable interviewers to provide specific examples to show the problem is not a onetime incident but a trend. Our three examples above violate both Ss because they are neither specific nor several. Example 1 does not reveal what or how much. This is why measurement—an established yardstick—of clearly established objectives is extremely important. Example 2 is similar to example 1. And example 3 does nothing to improve performance and may retard an ongoing relationship. The two Ss are

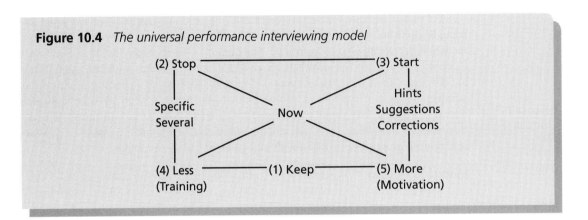

Figure 10.4 *The universal performance interviewing model*

important because they indicate the severity and frequency of an error or behavior and whether a lengthy exploration or brief on-the-job adjustment is most appropriate. Figure 10.4 includes all parts of the universal performance interviewing model. The advantage of this model is that it allows you to measure or observe on-the-job behavior and either compare it to goals or quickly correct the smallest error.

Coaching is the centerpiece of all performance review processes. The variety of approaches used today ranges from the old one-page checklist with five-point scales to group coaching sessions after each team process or event. The amount of time, the number of individuals involved, and the depth of data and feedback vary widely. Regardless, employee review processes are aimed at improving individual performance.

Several authors give advice at various levels. Shula and Blanchard offer a set of basic principles that spell coach:[14]

Conviction-driven—Never compromise your beliefs.

Overlearning—Practice until it's perfect.

Audible ready—Respond predictably to performance.

Consistency of leadership—Consistency in performance.

Honesty based—Walk the talk.

Fournies offers advice, help, and a checklist.[15] His chapter on why managers fail and his coach analysis decision tree are excellent. Hargroves's *Masterful Coaching* takes a team approach to learning, growing, and improving.[16] Rummler and Brache take a more integrated systems approach by looking at the organizational level, the process level, and the job/performer level.[17] The learning organization approach places coaching at the center of the process for organizational growth.

The 360-Degree Approach

Lipsinger and Lucia provide the most complete book on the 360-degree approach to performance review.[18] The basic differences between the old check sheet followed by the annual review and the 360-degree approach are the number of people involved, collection of data, and how the data are used during the interview session designed for improvement. The concept is logical: Get as many views of a person's performance as possible from observers who interact with a person on a regular basis from three months to a year. Questionnaires are used to collect input from 6 to 10 sources on skills, knowledge, and style. Evaluators are trained in behavioral observation, interviewing, and listening.

Each firm employs a somewhat unique 360-degree process, questionnaires, and interview schedules, but we can describe the general tests used. The employee in question works with his or her supervisor to select a number of evaluators, such as one direct supervisor, someone at the same level as the employee, two colleagues, and two individuals from departments the employee interacts with on a regular basis. The number of evaluators depends on the extent to which the employee interacts with others in the organization.

Let's assume that B.K. is in charge of human resources data entry, and the manager is in charge of employee relations. B.K. interacts with payroll and internal auditing almost daily. She tells the manager she would like to include Don from payroll; Susan from auditing; Brenda, who works for the manager; Donna, the receptionist who is cross-training in the manager's department; and Rob, the manager of employment, because she works with him on all new hires. B.K. and her manager select projects, events, and so forth, to be evaluated. Questionnaires covering skills, knowledge, and style are sent to each of the evaluators. Several questionnaires may be used if the projects are very different.

The completed questionnaires are summarized, and in some cases, scores are displayed on a spreadsheet. The manager selects two or three individuals from the original six to serve as a panel to conduct a feedback interview with B.K. The interviewer/facilitator may take the raw data from the questionnaires and interview the evaluators. B.K. receives the data in advance of the meeting. Each participant is asked to come with coaching or behavior-change input. The purpose of the session is not to attack, blame, or hurt the employee but to provide objective, behavior-based feedback with suggestions where necessary for improvement. B.K. may not need much improvement, so compliments are acceptable.

The interviewer/facilitator may ask B.K. to start the meeting with reactions to the data. The interviewer/facilitator's role is to ask open questions with neutral probes. For example:

> Tell me about your responsibilities in SAP training.
>> Tell me more.
>> Explain it to me
>> Describe your frustrations with the consultants' training manual.
> If you were going to take a similar project, what would you do more or less of?
> When you identified those people in _____ department as "rockheads," what did you mean?
>> How did they behave?
>> What did they say?
>> What did they do?

Once the feedback session is completed, the interviewer/facilitator and B.K. formulate a plan for improvement. This would probably be B.K.'s direct supervisor. If not, her team would develop improvement goals and objectives.

The use of multisource feedback for employee development works best in organizations that use a goal-setting process from the top down.[19] Goal setting, positive feedback from several perspectives, and a plan to improve make multisourcing a productive experience. This approach has advantages and disadvantages, however.

Advantages

1. The single process is useful for both improvement and development.
2. Questionnaires and interviews provide objective data and the feedback needed for employee development.
3. Raises and bonuses are not based on a single performance, so a poor supervisor will not prevent employee development.
4. The employee has control over who gives feedback.
5. The employee reads, hears, and discusses the data, so data are more than numbers on a form.
6. The process provides documentation for dealing with performance problems.

Disadvantages

1. It takes a great deal of time and training.
2. It is costly.
3. It may give more feedback that some people can handle.
4. The employee may simply see his or her work style as "my personality," "my persona," or "just the way I am."
5. The employee may see it as his or her turn to be shot down.
6. Follow-up coaching is necessary to ensure that necessary change occurs.

In Chapter 9, we talked about the 10 universal skills and attitudes employees must have for work in the new century. Two are interpersonal skills and team perspective. Just

ON THE WEB

As you begin to think seriously about specific careers and organizations, you should investigate how organizations assess the performance of employees. Use the Internet to discover the types of performance review models used by employers in which you have a career interest. Access two types of resources. First, research employers through general resources such as Career Mosaic (http://www.careermosaic.com), Jobtrak (http://www.jobtrak.com), and Monster Board (http://www.beast.monster.com). Second, check the Web sites of specific organizations such as Price Waterhouse (http://www.pw.com/mcs), Ford (http://www.ford.com), and Electronic Data Systems (http://www.eds.com).

as employee selection is becoming a group process, so is the performance review. You must have the ability to ask and answer questions, develop serious purposes, listen, and speak effectively in the review process.

5. Doing Your Homework

Regardless of the review model you select, you must do thorough homework. Study the employee's past record and most recent performance evaluation. Review the employee's self-evaluation. Understand the nature of the employee's position and work. Pay particular attention to the fit between the employee, the position, and the organization. Identify well in advance the primary purpose of the interview, especially if it is one of several with an employee. Prepare possible questions and forms you will use pertaining to measurable goals.

Know yourself and the employee as persons. For example, will you approach the interview from an appraisal or a developmental perspective? From an appraisal point of view, the interview is seen as required and scheduled by the organization, superior-conducted and -directed, top-down controlled, results-based, past-oriented, concerned with *what* rather than *how,* adversarial, and organizationally satisfying. By contrast, from a developmental perspective, the interview is initiated by individuals whenever needed, subordinate-conducted and -directed, bottom-up controlled, skill-based, now- and future-oriented, concerned with *how,* cooperative, and self-satisfying.[20]

Understand the relationship that is likely to exist between you and the employee. How will control be shared during the interview? How willing are both parties to take part in the interview? Are you the best person to play the role of interviewer? Would the interviewee prefer someone else? How much do you like one another? What is the history of your relationship? Realize that your relationship with the employee will affect the interview because research reveals that two or more employers often evaluate the same employee differently because their relationships differ. Prepare a possible action plan to be implemented following the interview. Finally, schedule the interview several days in advance so that both parties can prepare and the employee realizes it is not a spur-of-the-moment crisis or discipline interview.

6. Opening the Interview

Try to put the interviewee at ease with a pleasant, friendly greeting. Get the person seated in an arrangement that is nonthreatening and not superior-subordinate. Researchers agree that fear of what performance interviews might yield "interferes with communication between interviewer and interviewee and keeps the review process from achieving its full potential."[21] Consider offering a soft drink or a cup of coffee.

Establish rapport by showing support for the employee and engaging in a few minutes of small talk, but do not prolong this stage. You might orient the employee by giving a brief outline of how you want to conduct the interview. If there is something the employee would rather talk about first, do so. A slight alteration of your interview plan is worth the improved communication climate it may create. Encourage the employee not to wait for a turn or the correct moment to ask a question or bring up a topic but to participate actively throughout the interview.

7. Discussing Performance

Communication skills are critical to successful performance interviews. Be aware of your own nonverbal cues and observe those emanating from the interviewee. As noted in Chapter 2, it is often not so much *what* is said but *how* it is said. Listen carefully to the interviewee, and adapt your listening approach to the changing needs of the interview, listening for comprehension when you need to understand, for evaluation when you must appraise, with empathy when you must show sensitivity and understanding, and for resolution when developing courses of action to enhance performance.

"Be an active listener" is good, commonsense advice; but Goodall and colleagues warn that interviewers must know *why* they are listening actively: "Motives may include a desire to exhibit efficient appraisal behavior, to show a concern for the interviewee's well-being, or to collect evidence of talk that may be used for or against the subordinate at a later date."[22] The first two are positive, but the third may be detrimental both to the interview and future interactions with the interviewee.

Maintain an atmosphere that will ensure two-way communication beyond Level 1 by being sensitive, providing feedback and positive reinforcement, reflecting feelings, and exchanging information. Feedback may be your most important skill. Use a team of interviewers rather than a single interviewer. Research suggests that the panel approach produces higher validation in judgment, better developmental action planning, greater compliance with antidiscrimination laws, and more realistic promotions expectations, and it reduces perception of favoritism. Employees tend to give favorable ratings to good interviewers and unfavorable ratings to poor interviewers.

Allow for full and open discussion about performance between both parties; the discussion should aim at improving both individual and organizational performance. Critical keys to the success of the appraisal interview are your abilities to communicate information effectively and encourage open dialogue. Strive to be a counselor, coach, or partner in career management and development rather than an authoritarian judge.

Discuss the interviewee's total performance, not just one event or a specific portion of the review period. Begin with areas of excellence so you can focus on the person's strengths. Strive for an objective, positive integration of work and results. Cover standards that are met, and encourage the interviewee to identify strengths. Communicate factual, performance-related information, and give specific examples.

If an employee takes special pride in a certain accomplishment and then you criticize that area, you will compound the problem. When employees believe you are attacking their personality, character, or integrity, you are left with no basis upon which to help them improve performance. The tendency of supervisors to inflate negative information when giving feedback may create conflict and reduce trust, disclosure, and cooperation. When one of the authors asked managers from a large federal agency to list the characteristics of the best manager they had ever had, the list included the following:

fair, open-minded, caring, sincere, good listener, encouraging, trusting, informative, precise, knowledgeable, and a "straight shooter."

Excessive and prolonged praise can create anxiety and distrust because employees not only expect but desire to discuss their performance weaknesses. An employee who receives no negative feedback or suggestions of ways to improve will not know which behavior to change. Discuss needed improvements in terms of specific expected behaviors in a constructive, nondirective, problem-solving manner. Employees are likely to know what they are not doing satisfactorily but unlikely to know what they should do differently. Let the employee provide much of the input. Probe tactfully and sensitively for causes of problems.

Do not heap criticism upon the employee. The more you point out shortcomings, the more threatened, anxious, and defensive the employee will become. As the perceived threat grows, so will the person's negative attitude toward you and the review process. Unfortunately, perceptions of employee and supervisor are not the best yardsticks for measuring performance. Where comments, suggestions, and criticisms are concerned, it is often not what is intended that counts but what the other party believes is intended. If a fault cannot be corrected by positive suggestions, do not mention it during the interview.

Whether giving positive or negative feedback, you must be constantly aware of the potential effects of your biases. For example, if interviewers like certain individuals or perceive them to be similar to themselves, they tend to treat them more positively and to rate their performances higher. Males continue to discriminate against women where promotions, development, or supervision are concerned—the so-called glass ceiling. Women tend to rate achievements by other women less favorably than similar ones by men unless outside recognition influences them otherwise. You can control your biases more effectively by using objective criteria for all persons who do the same work and by being aware of common appraisal pitfalls.

Lowe identifies eight ways to ruin a performance review.[23] The *halo effect* comes about when an interviewer gives favorable ratings to all job duties when the interviewee excels in only one. The *pitchfork effect* leads to negative ratings for all facets of performance because of a particular trait the interviewer dislikes in others. The *central tendency* causes interviewers to refrain from assigning extreme ratings to facets of performance. The *recency error* occurs when an interviewer relies too heavily on the most recent events or performance levels. The *length of service* of an interviewee may lead the interviewer to assume that present performance is high because performance was high in the past. The *loose rater* is reluctant to point out weak areas and dwells on the average or better areas of performance. The *tight rater* believes that no one can perform at the necessary standards. And the *competitive rater* believes than no one can perform higher than his or her levels of performance.

Do not begin establishing goals without first summarizing the performance discussion and making sure that the employee has had ample opportunity to ask questions and make comments. Use reflective probes and mirror questions to verify information received and feedback given. Use clearinghouse questions to be sure the employee has no further concerns or comments.

8. Setting New Goals and a Plan of Action

Authorities agree that goal setting is the key to successful performance reviews and should constitute 75 percent of the interview.[24] Focus on future performance and career development rather than dwelling on the past, and the interviewer should be an adviser, supporter, and facilitator rather than a judge. Hill writes that "Although it is important to evaluate on the basis of past performance, it is just as important to anticipate future growth, set goals, and establish career paths."[25]

Review the last period's goals before going on to new ones. Performance is best when employees set their own goals. Never intentionally or unintentionally impose goals. Avoid either/or statements, demands, and ultimatums. The goals should be few, specific, well defined, practical, and measurable. Avoid ambiguous language such as teamwork, cooperation, unity, and group effectiveness.

Both employer and employee must be able to determine when goals have been accomplished and why. Do not make the goals too easy or too difficult, but allow the employee to stretch a bit. Do not directly relate improved performance to salary increases, even though the overall evaluation may lead to a promotion or raise. Get the employee to suggest and agree on programs for improvement, because without cooperation the review has failed. Decide on follow-up procedures and how they will be implemented. Feedback combined with clear goal setting produces the highest employee satisfaction.

9. Closing the Interview

Do not rush the closing. Be sure the employee understands all that has transpired. Conclude on a note of trust and open communication. End with the feeling that this has been an important session for interviewee, interviewer, and the organization. Do not leave the impression that you are "Glad this is over until next year" or "Well, now I can get to something important." If you have filled out a form such as the one in Figure 10.5, sign off the agreements. If organizational policy allows, permit the employee to put notes by items he or she feels strongly about. Give the employee a copy of the signed form as a record of the plan for the coming performance period.

The Employee in the Performance Review

As an employee, prepare for your performance review interview by reviewing the objectives you were to reach during the period and the standards by which your performance will be measured. Study production, attendance, and other records. Make a list of your accomplishments and problem areas. Analyze the causes of your strengths and weaknesses, and be prepared to respond to possible corrective actions with ideas for ways to improve on your own. Self-criticism often softens criticism from others, particularly superiors. Understand your relationship with the interviewer and his or her appraisal style. Check into the interviewer's mood prior to the interview. Be aware that a significant degree of sexual harassment occurs in organizations and that employees who have submitted to it tend to be judged more harshly than those who have resisted when such cases come to trial.

Figure 10.5 *Performance appraisal review form*

Name: _____	Date of Appraisal: _____
Performance Expectations	Performance Accomplishments
Employee Signature _____	Employee Signature _____
Supervisor Signature _____	Supervisor Signature _____
Manager Review _____	Manager Review _____

Realize that while the interviewer runs the interview, at least half of the responsibility for making the interview a success rests with you. Approach the performance interview as a valuable source of information on prospects for advancement, a chance to get meaningful feedback about how the organization views your performance and future, and an opportunity to display your strengths and accomplishments.

Be prepared to give concrete examples of your performance and how you have met or exceeded expectations. Prepare intelligent, well-thought-out questions. Be ready to discuss your career goals.

When taking part in the interview, try to maintain a productive, positive relationship with the interviewer. Do not be eager to defend yourself unless there is something to be defensive about. If you are put on the defensive, maintain direct eye contact and clarify the facts before answering charges. You might ask, "How did this information come to your attention?" or "Who compiled these sales statistics?" This tactic will give you time to formulate a thorough and reasonable response based on complete understanding of the situation. Answer all questions thoroughly, and ask for clarification of those you do not understand. Offer explanations, but do not make excessive excuses or try to fix blame. Assess your performance and abilities reasonably, and be honest with yourself and your supervisor. Realize that what you are, what you think you are, what others think you are, and what you would like to be may describe different people.

The performance review interview is not a time to be shy or self-effacing. Be sure to mention achievements such as special or extra projects, help you have given other employees, and community involvement on behalf of the organization. Be honest about challenges or problems you expect to encounter in the future. On the other hand, do not be afraid to ask for help. Correct any of the interviewer's false impressions or mistaken assumptions.

If you are confronted with a serious problem, discover how much time is available to solve it. Suggest or request ways to solve your differences as soon as possible. The interviewer is not out to humiliate you but to help you grow for your own sake and that of the organization. Keep your cool. Telling your supervisor off may give you a brief sense of satisfaction, but after the blast, the person will still be your supervisor and the problem may have worsened. Do not try to improve everything at once. Set priorities with both short- and long-range goals.

As the closing approaches, do not be in a hurry to get the interview over with. Summarize or restate problems, solutions, and new goals in your own words. Be sure you understand all that has taken place and the agreements you are signing off for the next review period. Do not leave if major questions remain unaddressed or unanswered. Close on a positive note with a determination to meet the new goals.

The Performance Problem Interview

The term "discipline," while still used in some union contracts and outdated employee handbooks, is no longer an appropriate label. When an employer has problems with an employee in an "at will" state or a state that requires "just cause," the situation today is handled as a "performance problem." The negative connotation and implication of "discipline" implies guilt, and organizations are reluctant to imply guilt. Usually there is an implied or stated probationary period.

In states such as Illinois that are "at will" states, an employer may terminate an employee at any time. However, after a reasonable time, usually six months to a year, a contract between employer and employee exists.[26] Whether a contract is implied or in writing, an employer must show just cause to terminate an employee who is not in a probationary period or designated a temporary or contract worker.

Determining Just Cause

What is just cause? Just cause means fair and equitable treatment of each employee in a job class. Many organizations are using behavioral selection interview processes and behavioral performance reviews to provide documentation in case a performance problem arises. A number of interviewers or reviewers provide more and better insights, spread the blame among several members of the organization, and, should termination occur, make it difficult for the dismissed employee to counter four, five, or six points of view. The following tests of just cause are tests of logic and reasoning that come from union contracts and attorneys involved in termination cases.

1. *Did the employee violate reasonable rules or orders?* For instance, if you had an employee who had been working on a specific machine, cash register, or phone-answering system, his or her supervisor could request the employee to move to a similar piece of equipment until the current one undergoes needed repairs. If the employee refuses this request, you have grounds for discharge.
2. *Was the employee given clear and unambiguous notice?* If this employee has been with your organization for six months to a year, follow an oral warning with a written warning within a short time.
3. *Was the investigation timely?* In most union contracts and employee appeals policies, a specific length of time and procedures are outlined for investigating performance problems. Timely usually means within one to three days. If there is a refusal to work or a confrontation, the supervisor or manager may want to have a witness present and obtain a written statement from this witness. Security cameras may be used to tape confrontations.
4. *Was the investigation conducted fairly?* Did the supervisor interview all parties involved? Did the supervisor obtain all necessary documentation? If there is a union contract, was a union representative included in all interviews or discussions?
5. *Were all employees given equal treatment?* You have undoubtedly heard the phrase "equal treatment under the law." It is essential that each organizational investigation of performance problems be conducted in exactly the same manner.
6. *Is there proof and documentation that a performance problem occurred?* Most failures are due to a supervisor's unwillingness to take the time to write down the problem and obtain necessary records before disciplinary action or termination occurs. There are three things you need for termination: documentation, documentation, documentation.
7. *Is the penalty fair?* The longer an employee is with an organization, the longer the termination process. Union contracts and organizational policies usually have designated steps before an employee can be disciplined or terminated. If an offense is minor, a day off without pay or a written warning may be appropriate. A number of infractions within a short time may end in termination. Punishment should be progressive rather than regressive. An organization can get into trouble if it brings up a number of offenses from the past. Most contracts or policies cover one year with the record wiped clean at the end of the year.

Preparing for the Interview

A helpful way to prepare for performance problem interviews is to take part in realistic role-playing cases. These rehearsals can alleviate some of your anxiety and help you anticipate employee reactions, questions, and rebuttals. The variety of situations and interviewees encountered, without the pressures of a real organizational and employee crisis, can help you refine your case-making, questioning, and responding while sticking to the facts and documenting all claims with solid evidence.

Role-playing cases, literature reviews on performance problem situations, and discussions with experienced interviewers will help you learn what to expect. For example, a study by Monroe, Barzi, and DiSalvo discovered four common responses from subjects in behavior conflict situations.[27]

1. *Apparent compliance:* Overpoliteness and deference, apologies, promises, or statements of good intentions followed by the same old difficult or problem behaviors.

2. *Relational leverage:* Statements that they have been with the organization longer than the interviewer and therefore know best, or that they are the best and thus can't be fired or disciplined, reference to friends or relatives within the organization or to a close relationship with the interviewer.

3. *Alibis:* Claims of tiredness, sickness, being overworked, budget cuts, family problems, it's someone else's fault, or poor instructions or information.

4. *Avoidance:* Disappearing on sick leave or vacation, failure to respond to memos or phone calls, or failure to make an appointment.

These four response types accounted for 93 percent of total incidents derived in their study.

Begin to prepare yourself by reviewing *how* you know the employee has committed an infraction that warrants an interview. Did you see the infraction directly, as in the case of absenteeism, theft, poor workmanship, intoxication, fighting, harassing another employee, or insubordination? Did you find out indirectly through a third party or by observing the results (such as lateness of a report, poor-quality products, or goals unmet)? Were you anticipating an infraction because of a previous incident, behavior, or stereotype? For example, African-Americans and other minorities are often watched more closely than others because supervisors believe they are more likely to violate rules. On the other hand, supervisors tend to be lenient with persons they perceive as likable, similar to themselves, or possessing high status or exceptional talent. And supervisors may avoid confronting persons who they suspect will "explode" if confronted; not confronting is the easy way out.

Next, decide whether the perceived problem warrants a confrontation or punitive action. Absenteeism and low performance are generally considered more serious than tardiness and horseplay. Try to determine the *cause* of the infraction because this will affect how you conduct the interview and what action to take. For example, interviewers are more likely to fire, suspend, or demote employees (1) when they feel the poor work is due to lack of motivation, interest, or drive rather than to lack of ability or technical competence and (2) when they think an employee should have been able to control the problem. Review the employee's past performance and history.

The two basic reasons for corrective action are poor performance or a troubled employee. When a person's performance gradually or suddenly declines, the cause may be motivational, personal, work-related, or supervisory. Drops in performance are indicated by swings in the employee's behavior—a friendly employee may suddenly become nasty, aggressive, or uncooperative. Keep an eye on other performance indicators such as attendance, quality and quantity of work, willingness to take instructions, and cooperation with other employees. A troubled employee may have an alcohol or drug dependency, a marital disturbance, problem with a child, or an emotional problem such as depression or anxiety. An employee may be stealing from your organization to support a gambling habit, drug or alcohol addiction, or a boyfriend or girlfriend. Such employees need counseling, not discipline, but few organizations have effective counseling programs, and many employees refuse to take part if they do.

For principles applicable to the performance problem interview, review the performance portion of this chapter and Chapter 11 on the counseling interview. Consider the relational dimensions discussed in Chapter 2 that affect performance problem interviews. Often neither party wants to take part, and, as supervisor, you may have delayed the interview until there was no other recourse and multiple problems piled up. As a specific problem comes to a head, you and the employee may come to dislike and mistrust one another, even to the point of verbal and nonverbal abuse. Both may see one another as very dissimilar. You may decide to reprimand, punish, demote, or dismiss the employee or the employee may become belligerent or resign. Your options are generally the most potent, unless the employee is very valuable to your organization at this time. Trust, cooperation, and disclosure are difficult to attain in a threatening environment.

Keeping Yourself and the Situation under Control

You are the supervisor, and while you want to head off a problem before it becomes critical, you must not lose your temper or let the situation get out of hand. Never conduct a performance problem interview when you are angry. You will be unable to control the interview if you have difficulty controlling yourself, including language, voice, facial expressions, and gestures.

Hold the interview in a private location. Performance problem interviews are often ego shattering, so do not worsen the situation by reprimanding the employee in the presence of peers. Meet in a place where you and the employee can discuss the problem freely and neither must play to an audience.

When severe problems arise, consider delaying a confrontation and obtaining assistance. For example, if two employees are caught fighting on a dock, have them report to your office or send them home and talk with each the next day. Let all tempers cool down. Depending on the situation, you may want to consult a counselor or call security before acting. Do not overreact, but be aware of the many incidents during the past few years when disgruntled current or former employees have returned with guns and killed employees and supervisors.

Include a witness or union representative. The witness should be another supervisor because using one employee as a witness who

photo by Michael Newman/Photo Edit

■ *Never conduct a performance review interview when you are angry, and conduct the interview in a private location.*

might testify against another employee is dangerous for all parties involved. If the union contract or organizational policies spell out the employee's right to representation, be sure to follow this procedure to the letter. You may ask the witness to write down names, dates, locations, and other details relevant to the incident.

Focusing on the Problem

Deal in specific *facts,* such as absences, witnesses to the event, departmental records, and previous disciplinary actions. Do not allow the situation to become a trading contest: "Well, look at all the times I have been on time" or "How come others get away with it?" Talk about this situation and this employee.

Record all available facts. Unions, the EEOC, and attorneys often require complete and accurate records. Take detailed notes, record the time and date on all material that might be used later, and obtain the interviewee's signature or initials for legal protection. A paper trail is often critical in future encounters.

Try not to be accusatory. Avoid words such as troublemaker, drunk, thief, or liar; avoid statements such as "Admit you stole those tools." You as supervisor cannot make medical diagnoses of alcoholism or drug addiction, so do not use these terms. Point to facts and leave physical and psychological judgments to professionals.

Preface remarks carefully. For example, you may begin comments with such phrases as "From what I know . . . ," "According to your attendance report . . . ," "As I understand it . . . ," or "I have observed . . . ." These phrases force you to be factual and keep you from accusing an employee of being guilty until proven innocent.

Ask questions that allow the person to express feelings and explain behavior. Begin questions with "Tell me what happened . . . ," "When he said that, what did you . . . ," or "Why do you feel that . . . ?" Open-ended questions allow you to get facts as well as feelings and explanations from the employee. Strive to establish the facts of the case and reach a common agreement with the employee regarding the alleged problem.

Avoiding Conclusions during the Interview

Avoid verbalizing conclusions during the interview. A hastily drawn conclusion may create more problems than it solves. Some organizations train supervisors to use standard statements under particular circumstances. If you are sending an employee off the job, you may say, "I do not believe you are in a condition to work, so I am sending you home. Report to me tomorrow at . . . ." Or "I want you to go to medical services and have a test made; bring me a slip from the physician when you return to my office." Or "I'm sending you off the job. Call me tomorrow morning at nine, and I will tell what action I will take." This last statement gives you time to talk to others about possible actions and provides a cooling-off period for all concerned.

Closing the Interview

Conclude the interview in neutral. If action is required to address the performance problem or termination is appropriate, do it; but realize that delaying action may enable you to think more clearly about the incident. Be consistent with organizational policies, the union contract, this employee, and all other employees. Refer to your organization's prescribed actions for specific offenses. Theft, except under unusual circumstances, is usually grounds for dismissal; employees with alcohol and drug problems may be counseled the first time and fired the second time. Apply all rules and actions equally to all employees.

Summary

Evaluate an employee's performance on the basis of standards mutually agreed upon ahead of time. Apply the same objectives equally to all employees performing a specific job. Research and good sense dictate that performance, promotion, and problem issues be discussed in separate interview sessions. Performance review interviews should occur at least semiannually; but promotion, salary, and performance problem interviews usually take place when needed. Deal with performance problems before they disrupt the employee's work or association with your organization. Select a performance review model most appropriate for your organization, employees, and positions.

For both employer and employee, flexibility and open-mindedness are important keys in successful performance review interviews. Flexibility should be tempered with understanding and tolerance of individual differences. The performance process must be ongoing, with no particular beginning or end. Supervisors and subordinates are constantly judged by the people around them. By gaining insights into their own behavior and how it affects others, both parties can become better persons and organization members.

A Performance Interview for Review and Analysis

AGF Learning Systems develops custom training programs—video, audio, programmed instruction, and computer simulations—both for domestic and international clients. Nancy Jamieson is manager of Account Services (customer relations), and Jack Doyle has worked for Nancy for more than three years. AGF uses an MBO system mutually agreed to by supervisor and employee. The following key objectives are measured 70 percent by the employee's work and 30 percent by the supervisor: day-to-day duties, response to change, working with others, and so on. Each objective is measured on a five-point scale, with 5 being high and 1 being low; the higher the score, the greater the percentage of salary increase.

How effective is the opening in establishing rapport and orienting the employee? Which type of climate prevails, supportive or defensive? How effectively do supervisor and subordinate deal with positive aspects of performance first before getting into negative aspects? Does either party get into nonperformance aspects of the employee's behavior? How effectively do the parties set goals for the next review period? Does either party dominate a specific phase of the interview? How effectively is the interview closed? How skilled are the supervisor as an interviewer and the subordinate as an interviewee? How prepared are both parties?

1. **Interviewer:** Hi Jack; have a seat.
2. **Interviewee:** Thanks. This is some office. I can see where money goes.
3. **Interviewer:** It is nice. A lot of the furnishings are mine.

4. **Interviewee:** Good taste.

5. **Interviewer:** Thanks. Let me just refresh my memory and summarize where we left off last time, Jack. At the end of the third quarter when we discussed your five key objectives, you were not only on target but ahead of schedule on number one. Objectives two and three were close to being reached. The real problems were in numbers four and five. Is that about what you recall?

6. **Interviewee:** Yeah, pretty much.

7. **Interviewer:** Number four was to notify your customer base at least 90 days prior to the time their materials needed updating in order to give programming, production, and printing a maximum of 180 days lead time, with 150 days being ideal but 120 being acceptable. This one seems to be really off target.

8. **Interviewee:** Yeah, but that's not my fault. The lead time is unrealistic. When I call clients before sending out the Suggested Revision Lists and then make follow-up calls to make sure they have received the lists, it irritates them.

9. **Interviewer:** Do you have the notes we made on this last quarter?

10. **Interviewee:** Yeah.

11. **Interviewer:** Good. We agreed to the call-write-call strategy because too many customers were calling in complaining about our lack of response time once they had asked for revisions. *(pause)* Why do you think this is irritating *your* clients?

12. **Interviewee:** Well, first, it's not just irritating *my* clients. I've talked this over with Omar, Joy, and Gary, and they're all having similar problems. I've had a few customers tell me that our account representatives had told them to ignore Account Services and call them when they were ready for revisions or updates.

13. **Interviewer:** What did you say to them?

14. **Interviewee:** I told them we wanted to make sure that their revisions and updates didn't get lost in the busy day-to-day business and that this new system was to their advantage.

15. **Interviewer:** Nice way to handle an awkward situation, Jack! I have a feeling that Sales is trying to sell up to customers, and we are trying to revise current materials. Let me take this up with Matt in Sales. Between now and year-end, let's adjust this objective to read, "When customers respond positively or give us permission to revise materials, we will . . . *(Jack interrupts)*

16. **Interviewee:** No problem!

17. **Interviewer:** If you can't control it, then it's hard to hold you responsible for it. This adjustment should help.

18. **Interviewee:** Yeah, that's okay, but I see no real help on number five. I've been off target for three quarters and don't see any way to get back within budget.

19. **Interviewer:** I'm sorry to hear that. Why not?

20. **Interviewee:** *(laughing)* Why not? Hey, I'm way over budget on customer complaint corrections and if I can't charge back some of the special request customers, there is no chance for me to make budget.

21. **Interviewer:** Jack . . . you do good work! There seem to be only two areas of slippage. The SRC budget items and your relationship with Accounting. Now . . . *(Jack interrupts)*

22. **Interviewee:** Great, but here's my predicament. When a customer calls me or one of my six operators and wants an extra tape or CD-ROM, one more manual, a few copies of Tab II materials, I can't just say no, I can't bill them, and I can't charge Sales. So I eat the cost and catch it from you.

23. **Interviewer:** Jack! Come on; you're too nice to your customers. Why not say, "Okay, but we will need to bill you X?"

24. **Interviewee:** I've tried that! They slam down the phone or contact one of our competitors. After I stop swearing, I usually pick up the phone myself and put NC on the bill. If I lose good customers because of these charges, then my next performance review will really be a hoot.

25. **Interviewer:** *(silence)*

26. **Interviewee:** Look, what do you want me to do? You're the boss.

27. **Interviewer:** I was going to save this for the end, but maybe now is a good time. Jack, overall your performance has been outstanding. Here is a survey we took of customers. You and your group came out on top, but the survey indicates some interesting findings. Read some of these comments.

28. **Interviewee:** *(after a few minutes)* The ratings are great, but I'm not sure I like the handle "Easy Jack"! Maybe I try too hard, but . . . *(Nancy interrupts)*

29. **Interviewer:** Jack, customer service is art and science. You have a reasonable budget, but you are way over. This is a tough area that requires a delicate sense of judgment. You need to ask yourself, "Am I doing too much to please the customer?" It may sound harsh, and I don't mean to be, but we're in the business of selling products and services. You simply must charge the customers for all of those extra services and products. Now let's see if we can't keep this item under $120,000 for the year.

30. **Interviewee:** That's only $2,000 for nearly three months. I can't do it!

31. **Interviewer:** Try. You're meeting all other objectives well, so just focus on this one. I've got another appointment now, but let's talk again soon.

32. **Interviewee:** Okay, but I'm going to make a lot of customers unhappy. Don't blame me if I'm right.

Performance and Problem Role-Playing Cases

A Recreation Department Assistant

The interviewer is director of a city recreation department. The assistant director is a young college graduate with a major in recreation studies. There are eight full-time members on the recreation staff and a large group of part-time or volunteer workers. The interviewer is in his mid-40s and has been involved in physical education, recreation, and industrial education most of his life. He has built a good working relationship with the local high schools and industries. His assistant has been with the department for one year and has been eased into dealing with local industry. Much to the interviewer's surprise, he has had a number of phone calls complaining that his assistant has shown favoritism to a few out-of-town companies. Since a performance review is scheduled, he has chosen this time to deal with this problem.

The interviewee would like the recreation department to have better and more up-to-date equipment. He thinks local merchants and industries have taken advantage of their local connections in the past and have charged higher prices than warranted for equipment and supplies. He has also hinted that kids ought to support only those who support them, supplying them with catalogs from out-of-town companies. He is up for a scheduled performance review and, while not unhappy with his job, feels he could use more help and support.

A Clerical Staff Member

The interviewer is the manager of an office with a clerical staff of eight in a company than makes products for office and commercial use and has a dozen salespersons on the road. Each member of the clerical staff is assigned one or two salespersons and several distributors and must be able to handle the telephone and deal with people. When an account calls directly to the factory, the salesperson assigned to that territory is given the commission. It is important that the clerical staff member be accurate in recording the order and crediting the commission to the right person. The interviewer is about to conduct a quarterly performance review with a member of the staff for nearly two years who performed above average in all previous periods. Recently, however, she has cost the company money by inaccurately recording phone numbers, causing wrong quantities and items to be shipped. There are rumors that this staff member may be in the early stages of Alzheimer's disease. The interviewer must decide whether to ask about this rumored condition and its possible effects on performance.

The interviewee is in her early 40s. She turns out twice the volume of most employees, but some of it must be done over. She is pleasant, enjoys her work, and loves to talk to salespersons on the telephone, especially concerning large accounts. Lately, however, she has experienced fatigue and dizzy spells. She has had trouble remembering to record important information on sales. She knows her work has been affected, but does not know how to handle it during the performance review.

An Hourly Worker

The interviewer is a former production supervisor recently promoted to assistant personnel manager. Because of a recent turnover in plant personnel, she has been assigned to conduct performance reviews for several hourly workers. The person she is interviewing has just completed his six-month probation period. The interviewee's record is above average, his waste is well within prescribed limits, and his attendance is normal. But he is a chronic complainer, a persistent cloud of gloom and doom. He complains about the insurance plan, the vending machines, the material handlers, the water fountains, and the supervision. He is constantly placing suggestions in the suggestion box.

The interviewee had to go to work before completing high school because of his father's health problems. While he did not mind leaving school at first, he has a growing resentment toward a younger brother and sister who are now attending a local college and heading toward promising careers; he feels he is stuck in a monotonous factory job supporting the family. He dislikes people who do not speak their minds. He feels that while this is not a bad place to work, it is not a good one either. He is surprised that some of his coworkers have been, as he puts it, "chained to their jobs" for 10, 15, or 20 years. He complains a lot but does not really mean to. Lately, some of his colleagues on the 3:00 to 12:00 shift have been giving him the cold shoulder.

A Fashion Manager

The interviewer is the manager of a large men's department in a major department store. He is ambitious, competitive, and hopes to become the head buyer for the entire department store chain. He has 43 people working for him in three areas. The big turnover is in the College Shop where the new team leader is a young college graduate who is beautiful, efficient, and bossy. She had two years of experience with a competitor before joining this store where she improved her area's business 13 percent in just one year. The interviewee is an excellent merchandiser, but complaints have reached the interviewer that she spends considerable company time with male trainees and is occasionally more than friendly with some management. How can the interviewer address these concerns without losing her?

The interviewee is 25 and looks 19, is very proud of her figure, and dresses to show it off. After all, she feels, people in the fashion business should be a picture of fashion. She wants to be a big success in fashion retailing and spends long hours at night keeping up on the latest fabrics, trends, and designs. She works closely with trainees because she feels they are the future of the company. Her feeling toward her supervisor is not warm. She feels that if the interviewer would order some of the things she suggests, she could improve business 25 percent. She plans to mention this during the upcoming performance review interview.

Student Activities

1. Select a company in your hometown or where you go to school. Call the company to arrange an interview in which you can discuss the type of performance review process they employ. Ask for copies of the forms they use, and discuss how they are used as part of the review process.

2. When we think of performance reviews, we usually think of positions for which we receive monetary awards. Consider instead your performance as a student. If this performance were to be evaluated by a team of three to six feedback interviewers, whom would you select and why?

3. Assume that a member of one of your student groups or a fellow employee constantly interrupts during team meetings, corrects others concerning their opinions, and criticizes conclusions the team reaches. Write 10 questions and appropriate neutral probing questions under each that you as team leader might use to review this person's performance.

4. Terminated employees often sue organizations for alleged discrimination based on age, sex, race, and ethnic group. What behaviors could justify termination regardless of length of employment, position, or protected status such as age, sex, and race? Check your list with two organizations in your area for accuracy and conditions.

Notes

1. Bruce R. McAfee and Mark L. Chadwin, "How Can Performance Evaluations Be Used to Motivate Employees?" *Management Quarterly* 24 (1983), pp. 30–35.

2. Douglas McGregor, *The Human Side of Enterprise* (New York: McGraw-Hill, 1960), pp. 6, 33–34, and 47–48.

3. Jack R. Gibb, "Defensive Communication," *Journal of Communication* 11 (1961), p. 141.

4. Herbert H. Meyer, "A Solution to the Performance Appraisal Feedback Enigma," *Academy of Management Executive,* February 1991, pp. 68–76.

5. O. L. Hill, "Time to Evaluate Evaluations," *Supervisory Management,* March 1992, p. 7.

6. Ronald J. Burke, William F. Weitzell, and Tamara Weir, "Characteristics of Effective Employee Performance Review and Development Interviews: One More Time," *Psychological Reports* 47 (1980), pp. 683–95; and H. Kent Baker and Philip I. Morgan, "Two Goals in Every Performance Appraisal," *Personnel Journal* 63 (1984), pp. 74–78.

7. Bob Losyk, "Face to Face: How to Conduct an Employee Appraisal Interview," *Credit Union Executive,* Winter 1990–1991, pp. 24–26.

8. H. Lloyd Goodall, Jr., Gerald L. Wilson, and Christopher F. Waagen, "The Performance Appraisal Interview: An Interpretive Reassessment," *Quarterly Journal of Speech* 72 (1986), pp. 74–75.

9. Gerald R. Ferris and Thomas R. King, "The Politics of Age Discrimination in Organizations," *Journal of Business Ethics* 11 (1992), pp. 342–50.

10. Stanley Silverman and Kenneth N. Wexley, "Reaction of Employees to Performance Appraisal Interviews as a Function of Their Participation in Rating Scale Development," *Personnel Psychology* 37 (1984), pp. 703–10.

11. Phillip G. Benson, M. Ronald Buckley, and Sid Hall, "The Impact of Rating Scale Format on Rater Accuracy: An Evaluation of the Mixed Standard Scale," *Journal of Management* 14 (1988), pp. 415–23.

12. This model and explanation come from a booklet prepared by Baxter/Travenol Laboratories entitled *Performance Measurement Guide.* The model and system were developed by William B. Cash, Jr., Chris Janiak, and Sandy Mauch. The model is reprinted with permission of Baxter/Travenol, Deerfield, IL.

13. Jack Zigon, "Making Performance Appraisals Work for Teams," *Training,* June 1994, pp. 58–63; and John M. Ivancevich, "Subordinates' Reactions to Performance Appraisal Interviews: A Test of Feedback and Goal-Setting Techniques," *Journal of Applied Psychology* 67 (1982), pp. 561–67.

14. Taken from Don Shula and Ken Blanchard, *Everyone's a Coach.* Copyright 1995 by Shula Enterprises and Blanchard Family Partnership. Used by permission of Zondervan Publishing House (www.zondervan.com).

15. Ferdinand Fournies, *Coaching for Improved Work Performance* (New York: Liberty Hall Press, 1987).

16. Robert Hargrove, *Masterful Coaching* (San Francisco: Jossey-Bass, 1998).

17. Geary Rummler and Alan P. Brache, *Improving Performance: How to Manage the White Space on the Organizational Chart* (San Francisco: Jossey-Bass, 1995).

18. Richard Lipsinger and Anntoinette D. Lucia, *The Art and Science of 360 Feedback* (San Francisco: Jossey-Bass, 1998).

19. Anthony T. Dalession, "Multi-Source Feedback for Employee Development and Personnel Decisions," in James W. Smitter, ed., *Performance Appraisal: State of the Art in Practice* (San Francisco: Jossey-Bass, 1998), Ch. 8, pp. 278–330.

20. From a speech to a client briefing on September 30, 1983, in San Francisco by Buck Blessing of Blessing and White, Inc., a leading international career development company.

21. Goodall, et al., pp. 74–87; Arthur Pell, "Benefiting from the Performance Appraisal," *Bottomline* 3 (1996), pp. 51–52; and H. Kent Baker and Philip I. Morgan, "Two Goals in Every Performance Appraisal," *Personnel Journal* 63 (1984), pp. 74–78.

22. Goodall, et al., p. 76.

23. Terry R. Lowe, "Eight Ways to Ruin a Performance Review," *Personnel Journal* 65 (1986), pp. 60–62.

24. Willard M. Oliver, "I/O Psych and You," *Security Management,* March 1991, pp. 41–44; and William Umiker, "Performance Review Interviews: Planning for the Future," *Health Care Supervisor* 10 (1992), pp. 28–35.

25. Hill, p. 7.

26. Kate Barbara Repa, *Your Rights in the Workplace* (Berkeley, CA: Nolo Press, 1996), p. 10.2.

27. Craig Monroe, Mark G. Barzi, and Vincent DiSalvo, "Conflict Behaviors of Difficult Subordinates," *Southern Communication Journal* 54 (1989), pp. 311–29.

Resources

Hale, Judith. *The Performance Consultant's Fieldbook: Tools and Techniques for Improving Organizations and People.* San Francisco: Jossey-Bass, 1998.

Hargrove, Robert. *Masterful Coaching.* San Francisco: Jossey-Bass, 1998.

Kaufman, Roger; Thia Garajan Sivasailam; and Paula MacGillis. *The Guidebook for Performance Improvement: Working with Individuals and Organizations.* San Francisco: Jossey-Bass, 1998.

Lipsinger, Richard, and Anntoinette D. Lucia. *The Art and Science of 360 Feedback.* San Francisco: Jossey-Bass, 1998.

Rossett, Allison, and Jeanette Ganiter-Downes. *A Handbook of Job Aids.* San Francisco: Jossey-Bass, 1997.

Rummler, Geary, and Alan P. Brache. *Improving Performance: How to Manage the White Space on the Organizational Chart.* San Francisco: Jossey-Bass, 1995.

Schula, Don, and Ken Blanchard. *Everyone's a Coach.* New York: Harper Business, 1995.

Smitter, James W., ed. *Performance Appraisal: State of the Art in Practice.* San Francisco: Jossey-Bass, 1998.

The Counseling Interview

Although few of us have ever had the title of "counselor," we are called on frequently to help people gain insights into and cope with physical, emotional, financial, academic, or personal problems. Most counseling interviews, including highly sensitive and critical ones, are conducted by persons in fields where training in counseling may be minimal: physicians, clergy, lawyers, teachers, funeral directors, and supervisors. We often turn to associates and friends (fellow workers, students, and club members) and family members for counsel. Interviewer training may range from extensive course work to a few hours of intensive training to none at all beyond having counseled in the past. Fortunately, the lay counselor has proven remarkably successful, particularly in urban and campus crisis centers. Persons in need of help often seem to trust people more like themselves who are nonthreatening and willing to listen.[1]

The counseling interview may be the most sensitive of interviews because it occurs when a person feels incapable of handling a problem alone or when a counselor decides that help is needed. Either situation may be a blow to a person's ego. In addition, the problem is likely to be personal, involving finances, intimacy, emotional stability, physical health, drug or alcohol abuse, marriage, morals, grief, grades, or work performance. The counseling interview requires a high degree of *trust* and *openness* if the interviewee is to understand the problem and determine how to resolve it.

This chapter introduces you to the fundamental principles of counseling interviewing so you can work more effectively with those who come to you with problems they need to talk about. It is not intended to make you an instant psychotherapist ready to treat persons with psychological disorders. Approach each counseling interview systematically with considerable attention to preparation and planning. Figure 11.1 illustrates the six-stage process counselors should follow in helping interviewees understand and resolve problems themselves. Counselors can rarely resolve problems for other people.

1. Preparing for the Counseling Interview

Begin your preparation with a detailed and insightful self-analysis. Although self-analysis is rarely easy, you will have difficulty understanding and helping others if you do not know yourself. And you will have difficulty understanding and helping others if you know little or nothing about them and their situations. Only after these preinterview analyses can you determine which interviewing approach will be most appropriate.

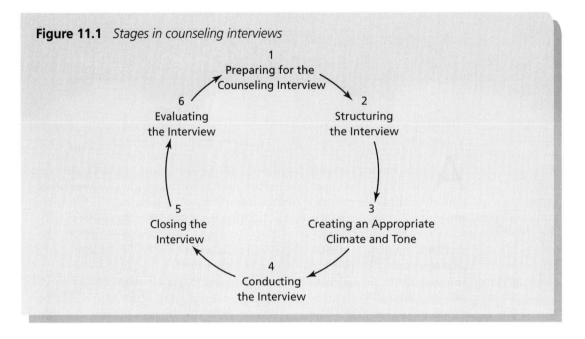

Figure 11.1 *Stages in counseling interviews*

Analyzing Self: The Interviewer

Begin your self-analysis by assessing your personality characteristics. Research indicates that qualities intrinsic to the personalities, attitudes, and nonverbal behavior of counselors—rather than sex or ethnic group membership—largely account for counseling effectiveness.[2] Be open-minded, optimistic, serious, self-assured, relaxed, and patient. Do not be argumentative or defensive when there is no need for either. A recent study indicates that counselors have higher credibility with clients if they share beliefs in the causes of the person's problem.[3] Feel comfortable with disclosing your motives, feelings, values, beliefs, and attitudes if you expect others to be open with you. Research suggests that an interviewer's self-disclosure of personal experiences and background helps the interviewee gain insights and new perspectives for making changes because of an equalized relationship and reassurance.[4]

As interviewer, you must not dominate interpersonal interactions; rather, you must have a sincere desire to help others. You must be *people-oriented* rather than *problem-oriented.* Unfortunately, most of your education and professional training are geared toward solving problems, with the emphasis on taking charge and doing it yourself. But in nearly all counseling interviews, the problems are attached to people who need assistance, not prescriptions, in solving the problems themselves. You as counselor must be *people-centered* to be sensitive to the interviewee's needs and communicate understanding, comfort, reassurance, and warmth. Above all you need to communicate empathy, that you truly understand the interviewee's situation and feelings.

Assess your intellectual, communicative, and professional strengths. You must be imaginative, analytical, and organized. You must be able to learn quickly and recall information accurately and completely. You must be able to communicate in a variety of settings by being a good listener (for understanding, empathy, evaluation, resolution) and skilled in verbal and nonverbal communication. You must be comfortable with persons who reveal highly personal and perhaps embarrassing problems and incidents; who express intense emotions such as sorrow, depression, anger, fear, and hatred; and who show their feelings through tears and shouting.

Interviewers must have realistic views of their counseling skills. Do not try to handle counseling situations for which you have neither the experience nor the training. Know when to refer the interviewee to a person with more skills and expertise. Prepare yourself by reading and taking courses and seminars in counseling. Keep up to date in your field, including research, trends, changes. Know how other people, the present interviewee in particular, view you and your position, organization, and profession.

Analyzing Other: The Interviewee

Review everything you know about the interviewee: ethnicity, education, work history, academic record, family background, group memberships, medical and psychological histories, test results, previous counseling sessions, and information about past problems and solutions. Talk to other people about the interviewee. Instructors, supervisors, family members, friends, acquaintances, other counselors, and fellow workers may give you keen insights into the person and why the person needs assistance. Be careful, however, of how this information might affect your attitudes and the pending interaction. Think of times others have warned you about a supervisor, roommate, or professor, but you found the person to be just the opposite: helpful, friendly, and understanding. Be informed but keep an open mind.

How might past situational variables be affecting this person: death in the family, recent divorce of parents, failure in courses, loss of a job, illness? How might future situational variables be affecting this person: pending graduation, marriage, surgery, job loss or search, retirement? We are often held hostage by the past and future to the point where we cannot thrive in the present.

What is your relationship with the interviewee? Consider the critical dimensions of relationships we discussed in Chapter 2: similarity, inclusion/involvement, affection/liking, control/dominance, and trust. What social, family, professional, religious, commercial, or political relations do you have in common with the interviewee? What values, beliefs, and attitudes do you share? Have you counseled this person before, and if so, have you and the interviewee done everything agreed to? Do each of you want to take part in a counseling session at this time? What are your positive and negative feelings toward one another? How much control must you impose if the session is to be productive? One study found that those not yet contemplating change (compared to those who were contemplating change, already engaged in change, or maintaining previous changes) have significantly lower expectations of help and the interviewer's acceptance, genuineness, and trustworthiness.[5]

If you know an interviewee thoroughly prior to the interview, you will be better able to anticipate and respond effectively to common questions and comments. The following are ones we have all heard (and used) at one time or another:

I don't need your help.

If I need help, I'll let you know.

I can take care of myself.

Get off my back.

Let's get this over with so I can get back to work.

Why should I discuss my personal problems with you?

You wouldn't understand.

Don't tell mom and dad.

Just tell me what you want me to do.

I can't afford to take time off.

You've never been married, so how can you help me?

No one knows how I feel.

No one cares.

You don't know what it's like being a student (parent, patient, teenager).

The more thoroughly you have analyzed the interviewee, the more likely you will know why a person is reacting in a particular way and how you might reply effectively.

An interviewee may ask for help without notice or explanation. You get a telephone call in the middle of the night from your brother or sister, a friend drops in at your office or home, a business associate reveals a problem during a round of golf or over a drink, or a significant other makes an unexpected comment or introduces a topic during an interaction totally unrelated to the personal problem. You must rely on your training and experiences to discover what is bothering the person and how you might help. *Listen* rather than *talk*. Do not assume you know why a person is calling, showing up at your door, or bringing up a topic such as a personal relationship, dissatisfaction with a major, illness of a parent, or fear of failure.

Determining the Interviewing Approach

After carefully analyzing yourself and the interviewee, you should be able to determine an appropriate interviewing approach. In Chapter 2, we introduced you to two fundamental approaches, directive and nondirective, and discussed their advantages and disadvantages. The sensitive and potentially explosive nature of the counseling interview necessitates a careful selection of interview approach, so review the principles and assumptions that underlie each before the interview.

Directive Approach

In the directive approach, the interviewer controls the structure of the interview, subject matter attended to and avoided, pace of interactions, and length of the interview. You collect and share information, define and analyze problems, suggest and evaluate solutions, and provide guidelines for actions. In brief, the directive interviewer serves as an expert or consultant who analyzes problems and provides guidelines for actions. The interviewee is involved more as a reactor and recipient than an equal or major player in the interaction. The directive approach is based on the assumption that the interviewer knows more about the problem than the interviewee and is better suited to analyze it and recommend solutions. An experienced academic counselor, for example, rarely hears a new or unique problem and knows better than most students the university's requirements, rules, procedures, student rights, and penalties for infractions. The accuracy of this assumption, of course, depends on the interviewer, the interviewee, and the situation. The interviewee, for instance, may not be hampered by illness, injury, emotions, or lack of information about problems and solutions.

Nondirective Approach

In the nondirective approach, the interviewee controls the structure of the interview, determining the topics, when and how they will be discussed, and the pace and length of the interview. The interviewer acts as a passive aide and helper, not as an expert or adviser. The interviewer *helps* the interviewee obtain information, gain insights, define and analyze problems, and discover and evaluate solutions. The interviewer listens, observes, and encourages but does not impose or dictate ideas. The nondirective approach is based on the assumption that the interviewee is more capable than the interviewer of analyzing problems, assessing solutions, and making correct decisions. After all, the interviewee must implement recommendations and solutions. In the extreme, this assumption questions the right of another person to "meddle" in another person's problems or to serve as more than an indirect helper. The accuracy of this assumption, like the directive assumption, depends on the interviewer, interviewee, and situation. The interviewee may know nothing about the problem or potential solutions, or worse, may be misinformed about both. Professors often discover that students believe a variety of academic myths, such as,

> If I stop going to class, I will get an incomplete.
> The two lowest quiz grades will be dropped.
> If we don't discuss a topic in class, it will not be on the test.
> If I can get a good set of class notes, I don't need to go to class.
> A grading curve will always help me get a better grade.
> There are exceptions to all the rules.

The interviewee's problem may not be lack of information or misinformation. The person may be incapable of expressing or visualizing a problem, making sound decisions, or considering the ramifications of decisions. An interviewee may refuse to admit there is or will be a problem with smoking, drinking alcoholic beverages, having an affair, or cutting class. An interviewee party of two or more persons—husband and wife, roommates, workers—may be hopelessly divided over what to do or how to do it. At such times, the interviewer may serve as an objective, neutral referee, presenting pros and cons of specific courses of action. Distinguish between when you are serving as expert adviser and when, quite subtly and unintentionally perhaps, you are imposing personal preferences on an interviewee.

Combination of Approaches

In many counseling interviews, you will find it necessary to employ a combination of directive and nondirective approaches. You may, for instance, begin with a nondirective approach to encourage the interviewee to talk and thereby reveal the problem and its causes. Then you may switch to a more directive approach when discussing possible solutions or courses of action. A directive approach is best for obtaining facts, giving information, and making diagnoses, whereas a nondirective approach tends to open up large areas and bring out a great deal of spontaneous information. The difficult task is to determine which approach is most appropriate at the moment and when a change in approach is necessary during an interview.

2. Structuring the Interview

Although there is no standard structural format for counseling interviews, Echterling, Hartsough, and Zarle's sequential phase model, originally created for handling calls to a campus or community crisis center, is applicable to most counseling situations.[6] It can also help you determine when to use a directive, nondirective, or combination approach. Figure 11.2 illustrates the sequential phase model. The *affective* or emotional phases, boxes 1 and 3, involve the interviewee's feelings of trust in the counselor and feelings about self and the problem encountered. A nondirective approach is usually best for the affective phases of the interview. The *cognitive* or thinking phases, boxes 2 and 4, involve thinking about the

Figure 11.2 *Phases of counseling interviews*

Affective	Cognitive

1. Establishment of a helpful climate
   a. Making contact
   b. Defining roles
   c. Developing a relationship
	2. Assessment of crisis
	   a. Accepting information
	   b. Encouraging information
	   c. Restating information
	   d. Questioning for information

3. Affect integration
   a. Accepting feelings
   b. Encouraging feelings
   c. Reflecting feelings
   d. Questioning for feelings
   e. Relating feelings to consequences or precedents
	4. Problem solving
	   a. Offering information or explanations
	   b. Generating alternatives
	   c. Decision making
	   d. Mobilizing resources

problem and taking action. A directive or combination approach is usually best for cognitive phases.

The typical interview begins with establishing rapport and a feeling of trust (phase 1), proceeds to discovering the nature of the interviewee's problem (phase 2), probes more deeply into the interviewee's feelings (phase 3), and comes to a decision about a course of action (phase 4). Except in emergencies, do not move from phase 1 to phase 4, or omit phase 3, without careful thought. If you do not discover the depth of the interviewee's feelings, you may not understand the problem or possible solutions.

Do not expect to move through all four phases in every counseling interview or to proceed uninterrupted in numerical order. You may go back and forth between phases 2 and 3, or between 3 and 4, as different aspects of the problem are revealed or disclosed, feelings increase or decrease in intensity, and a variety of solutions are introduced and weighed. Unless the interviewee wants specific information (where to get medical assistance, how to drop a course and add another, how to get an emergency monetary loan), you may not get to phase 4 until a second, third, or fourth interview. Be patient!

3. Creating an Appropriate Climate and Tone

Consider carefully the climate and tone of the counseling interview for which you are preparing. Climate and tone will affect the levels of communication that will take place, particularly the willingness of both parties to disclose feelings and attitudes as well as information.

The Setting

Provide a climate conducive to good counseling—a quiet, comfortable, private location, free of interruptions. You cannot expect an interviewee to be open and honest and communicate at Levels 2 and 3 if other employees, students, workers, or clients can overhear the conversation. Consider selecting a neutral location such as a restaurant, lounge, park, or organization's cafeteria where the interviewee might feel less threatened and more relaxed. Some interviewees feel comfortable or safe only on their own turf, so consider meeting in the person's room, home, office, or place of business.

When possible, arrange the seating so that both interviewer and interviewee are at ease and able to communicate freely. Studies suggest that the situation is the most important variable in determining level of self-disclosure and that an optimal interpersonal distance is 3.5 feet. Review the discussion of seating arrangements in Chapter 2. Many students and others comment that an interviewer behind a desk makes them ill at ease, as though the "mighty one" is sitting in judgment. They prefer to sit in a chair at the end of the desk—at a right angle to the interviewer—or in chairs facing one another with no desk in between. Arrangements of furniture can contribute to or detract from the informal, conversational atmosphere so important in counseling sessions. Many counseling interviewers are discovering that a round table, similar to a dining room or kitchen table, is preferred by interviewees because it includes no power or leader position. This setup also allows both parties to take notes and pass materials to the interviewer or more than one interviewee more easily than when seated at a desk or coffee table. Interviewees

photo by Bob Daemmrich/The Image Works

■ *Provide a climate conducive to effective counseling, which is a quiet, comfortable, private location, free of interruptions.*

also seem to like this arrangement because they have often handled family matters around the dining or kitchen table.

The Opening

The first few minutes of a counseling session set the verbal and psychological tone for the remainder. Greet the interviewee by name in a warm, friendly manner, being natural and sincere. Show that you want to be involved and to help. Do not be condescending or patronizing. As counselor, you might want to say, "Well, it's about time you decided to get some help" or "It must be pretty bad if you came to see me." Stifle such inclinations. Accept the interviewee as he or she is.

Do not try to second-guess the interviewee's reason for making an appointment or dropping by. It is natural and tempting to make such statements as,

> I'm not going to discuss test results.
> I think I know why you're here.
> I suppose you want to discuss your family
>   problems again.
> I assume you want to talk about your
>   performance.

The interviewee may not have initiated this contact for any of these reasons but may feel threatened or angry by your comment and attitude or feel pressured into agreeing to some extent with your guess. At the least, your interruption and comment, sometimes interpreted as a put-down, may ruin an opening the interviewee has prepared that would have revealed the *primary* concern and proceeded to the start preferred. Avoid tactless and leading reactions all too common in interactions with family members, friends, and associates. All of us have been on the receiving end of such statements as,

> Looks like you've put on some weight.
> Where did you get that outfit?
> Have you been taking your medicine?
> You look terrible!
> What have you done to your hair?
> You have been going to class, haven't you?

Comments and questions such as these do not create the climate and tone necessary for a successful counseling interview.

When you initiate a counseling session, state clearly, precisely, and honestly what you want to talk about. If there is a specific amount of time allotted for the interview, make this known so you and the interviewee can work within it. The interviewee will be more at ease knowing how much time is available. Be concerned about the quality rather than the length of time spent with an interviewee.[7] Your attire and role behavior will significantly affect the interviewee's perceptions of your attractiveness and level of expertise and help determine how closely the person is drawn to you.

The counseling interview often consumes considerable time getting acquainted and establishing a working relationship with the interviewee. This time may be necessary even when your relationship with the interviewee has a long and positive history. The counseling interview is somehow different and more threatening than many other interactions. An interviewee may begin by talking about the building, your office, books on the shelves, pictures on the walls, the view out the window, the weather, a recent event, or sports unrelated to the interview topic and purpose. Be patient. Do not rush this seemingly frivolous process. The interviewee is sizing up you, the situation, and the setting and is, perhaps, building up the nerve to introduce the issue of concern.

The rapport stage, in which you attempt to establish a feeling of goodwill with the interviewee, is your chance to show attention, interest, fairness, willingness to listen, and ability to maintain confidences. You can discover the interviewee's expectations and apprehensions about the interview and attitudes toward you, your position or organization, and counseling sessions in general. You must be comfortable with the situation, which may include an embarrassing topic such as sex, a taboo topic such as death, a crying interviewee, or one who talks about everything but the real problem. If you are obviously uncomfortable, the interviewee will be uncomfortable.

Disclosure of information, beliefs, attitudes, concerns, and feelings usually determines the success of the counseling interview. The climate conducive for this disclosure begins during the opening minutes of the interaction. Some factors may be beyond your control. For instance, females tend to disclose significantly more about themselves and their problems than do males, especially on intimate topics such as sex, and a person's self-disclosure history often affects disclosure in other interviews.[8] Males often have psychological defenses to protect themselves from feelings of weakness and to restrict emotional reactions.[9] But you can encourage interviewee disclosure, for example, by disclosing your own feelings and attitudes, by ensuring confidentiality, and by reducing the interviewee's perception of risk in providing information. Realize, however, that interviewees may benefit from hiding some undesirable facets of themselves from you.[10] Appropriate humor can release tensions of both parties and help to create a good working alliance.

4. Conducting the Interview

When rapport is established and orientation completed, you may let the interviewee begin with the topic that seems of most interest, particularly if the interviewee initiated the contact. This is the first step (as seen in the sequential phase model) toward discovering the precise nature of the problem and why a person has been unable to face or resolve it. Do not rush the interviewee.

Persons or parties will usually tell you what they want you to know when they are ready to do so. Above all, do not rush in with solutions as soon as you think you have discovered the problem. Observe the interviewee's nonverbal cues carefully because apparently insignificant cues may reveal inner feelings and their intensity. If you initiated the contact or the interviewee seems incapable of getting to the point, you may take charge and guide the interviewee toward discovering the nature of the problem.

Listening, Observing, and Questioning

Although you will play many roles in each counseling interview, five dominate: listening, observing, questioning, responding, and informing. In each of these roles, strive to help, empathize, and inform.

Listening

Listening (for comprehension, empathy, evaluation, and resolution) may be the most important skill for counselors to master. To get to the heart of a problem, you must give undivided attention to the interviewee's words and their implications, as well as to what is intentionally or unintentionally left unmentioned. Be genuinely interested in what the person is saying. Do not interrupt or take over the conversation. Beware of interjecting personal opinions, experiences, or problems. Too often, for example, a person may want to talk about a serious illness of a father or mother, but the counselor takes over with a story about his or her own family illness. Maintain the focus on the interviewee and the interviewee's problem, not yours.

If the interviewee pauses or stops talking for a few moments, do not chatter to fill in the silence. Use silence for a variety of purposes, an important one being to encourage the interviewee to continue talking. Review Chapters 2 and 4 for uses of silence and listening principles. Leonard suggests several nonverbal behaviors that communicate a willingness to listen: facing the other person squarely, adopting an open posture, leaning toward the other person, being relatively relaxed, maintaining good eye contact, reflecting attention through facial expressions, and attending with vocal cues such as "um-hmm" and "yes."[11] Interviewees tend to interpret smiles, attentive body postures, and gestures as evidence of warmth and enthusiasm.

Observing

Observe how the interviewee sits, gestures, fidgets, and maintains eye contact. Pay attention to the voice for loudness, timidity, evidence of tenseness, and changes. These observations may provide clues about the seriousness of the problem and the interviewee's state of mind. How disturbed or relaxed does the person appear to be? How comfortable is the person with you? Deceptive answers may be lengthier, more hesitant, and characterized by longer pauses; however, some people may maintain eye contact longer when they lie. If you are going to take notes or record the interview, explain why, and stop if you detect that either activity is affecting the interview adversely. Many people are hesitant to leave a taped record that others might hear; although they may be willing to confide in you, they fear reactions from undetermined others.

Questioning

Questions play important roles in counseling interviews, but asking too many questions is a common mistake. Too many questions interrupt interviews, change topics prematurely, and break the flow of self-disclosure. Numerous questions, often asked in a rapid-fire manner, reduce the interviewee to a mere respondent and may stifle the interviewee's own questions. Open questions, both primary and secondary, encourage talkativeness and emotional expression, very important for phases 2 and 3. Ask one question at a time because multiple or double-barreled questions tend to result in ambiguous answers with neither portion answered clearly and thoroughly. Use encouragement probes such as,

And?	I see.
Uh-huh?	Go on.
Then what happened?	And then?

Avoid curious probes into feelings and embarrassing incidents, especially if the interviewee seems hesitant to elaborate. Beware of questions that communicate disapproval, displeasure, or mistrust and make the interviewee less open and trusting. Avoid leading questions except under unusual circumstances. Be careful of "why" questions that appear to demand explanations and justifications and put the interviewee on the defensive. Imagine how an interviewee might react to the following questions:

Why bother?	*Why* did that happen?
Why didn't you follow the rules?	*Why* haven't you seen a physician?
Why didn't you come in sooner?	*Why* did you do that?

Review the question tools discussed in Chapter 4 and the probing skills discussed in Chapter 5 for questioning guidelines useful in counseling interviews.

Responding and Informing

Interviewers in counseling interviews spend more time responding to questions and information requests than in other types of interviews. Selecting an appropriate response may be difficult.

A Client-Centered Approach

Turner and Lombard summarize a client-centered approach in Figure 11.3 that shows the information potentially available to the interviewer and the general ways the interviewer might respond.[12] These types of information and responses may occur in any of Echterling, Hartsough, and Zarle's four interaction phases. Turner and Lombard say the interviewee is likely to talk about (1) objects, events, ideas, concepts, and so on, (2) other people, or (3) self. As an interviewer presented with these kinds of information, you should respond to what the interviewee is saying about self because self is the primary focus of counseling interviews.

You may respond to information on self by (1) giving opinions, advice, or suggestions, (2) interpreting what the interviewee is saying, or (3) accepting or clarifying what the interviewee has been saying from his or her perceptions. With these choices, you

Figure 11.3 *Information and responses in counseling interviews*

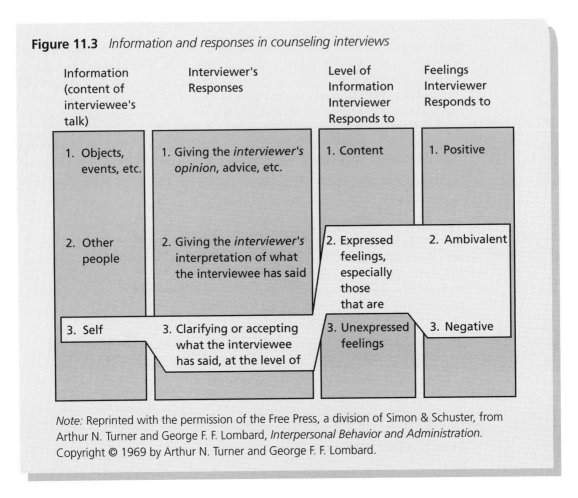

Note: Reprinted with the permission of the Free Press, a division of Simon & Schuster, from Arthur N. Turner and George F. F. Lombard, *Interpersonal Behavior and Administration.* Copyright © 1969 by Arthur N. Turner and George F. F. Lombard.

should accept or clarify what the interviewee has been saying about self, maintaining focus on the interviewee.

You may respond to the interviewee's talk about self at the level of (1) content, (2) expressed feelings, or (3) unexpressed feelings. Respond to expressed feelings the interviewee is willing and able to reveal and apparently believes are important.

Expressed feelings provide a fourth decision. Should you respond to feelings that are (1) positive, (2) ambivalent, or (3) negative. Turner and Lombard recommend that you respond to ambivalent and negative feelings rather than to positive ones to gain insights into the interviewee's problem.

Turner and Lombard's suggestions should not be interpreted as fixed rules. The interviewee, the situation, and the phase of the interview will determine what kinds of information become available and which ones have priority. Phase 4 in Echterling, Hartsough, and Zarle's sequence may require advice rather than clarification of what the interviewee has said, but use Turner and Lombard's suggestions as guidelines. Interviewers may respond to interviewee information, questions, comments, and feelings in

Interviewer responses may range from highly nondirective to nondirective, directive, and highly directive.

an infinite variety of ways. These responses may be placed along a continuum from highly nondirective to nondirective, directive, and highly directive.

Highly Nondirective Reactions and Responses

Highly nondirective reactions and responses encourage interviewees to continue commenting, to analyze ideas and solutions, and to be self-reliant. As an interviewer, you offer no information, assistance, or evaluation of the interviewee, the interviewee's ideas, or possible courses of action. Highly nondirective reactions and responses are used in phases 1, 2, and 3 of the interaction phase model. You may even remain silent, thus encouraging interviewees to continue or to answer their own questions, as in the following example:

1. **Interviewee:** I don't know what to do.
2. **Interviewer:** *(silence)*
3. **Interviewee:** Maybe I should consider a tech school.

You may encourage an interviewee to continue speaking by employing semiverbal phrases:

1. **Interviewee:** There doesn't seem to be an end to it.
2. **Interviewer:** Um-hmm.
3. **Interviewee:** First, my computer hard drive crashed. Then my air conditioner went out. And last week someone backed into the side of my car at the mall.

When reacting and responding in a highly nondirective manner, be aware of your nonverbal behaviors. Face, tone of voice, speaking rate, and gestures must express sincere interest and reveal a high level of empathy. Show you are listening. Interviewees look for minute as well as overt signs of approval or disapproval, interest or disinterest. For instance, Purtilo discusses five kinds of smiles:[13]

> I know something you don't know.
> Poor, poor you.
> Don't tell me.
> I'm smarter than you.
> I don't like you either.

If a person asks, "When will this end?" the interviewer merely smiles and sends some very clear messages. Holding one's hand or a simple touch may reassure a person and show that you care and understand. An "um-hmm!" may signal a positive or negative reaction and frighten an interviewee. Simple nonverbal reactions—rolling your eyes, raising an eyebrow, crossing your arms, sitting forward on your chair—may adversely affect an interview by making the interviewee wary of expressing true or intense feelings or desires or by encouraging the person to express feelings and desires apparently acceptable to you. Silence must not be prolonged or awkward. If an interview party seems unable to continue or to go it alone, switch to more appropriate responses.

A variety of question techniques may serve as highly nondirective responses. Silent, nudging, and clearinghouse probes are quite useful. You may *restate* or *repeat* an interviewee's question or statement instead of providing answers or volunteering information, ideas, evaluations, or solutions. The attempt is to urge the person to elaborate or come up with ideas alone.

1. **Interviewee:** I don't know what to do.
2. **Interviewer:** You're unaware of options available to you?

Restatement and repetition questions must be tactful and purposeful. An interviewee may become upset by a constant echo during a counseling interview. You may *return* a question rather than answer it. Once again the attempt is to encourage the interviewee to analyze problems and select from among possible solutions. A return question looks like this:

1. **Interviewee:** Should I try to apologize for what I said?
2. **Interviewer:** How do *you* feel about that?

Do not continue to push a decision back if you detect that the individual has insufficient information or is confused, misinformed, genuinely undecided, or unable to make a choice. To continue with a highly nondirective approach would be nonproductive and potentially harmful to the interviewer-interviewee relationship.

You might *invite* the interviewee to discuss a problem or idea. The following is a typical invitation question in counseling interviews:

1. **Interviewee:** I'm having second thoughts about our relationship.
2. **Interviewer:** Want to talk about it?

In highly nondirective interviews, the interviewee may refrain from elaborating or keep feelings concealed. The invitation question asks if the person is willing or interested in discussing, explaining, or revealing. The interviewer does not intrude with more demanding questions such as "Tell me about it" or "Such as?"

Reflective and mirror questions are valuable techniques to make sure, in a nondirective manner, that you understand what the interviewee has just said or agreed to. As discussed in Chapter 4, reflective questions are designed to clarify and verify questions and statements, not to lead a person toward your preferred point of view. Here is a reflective response:

1. **Interviewee:** We first noticed negative behavior around fourth grade.

2. **Interviewer:** He was about 10 at the time?

Reflective questions require careful listening and a concerted verbal and nonverbal effort not to lead the interviewee. Interviewees are often highly vulnerable and easily swayed, even when you do not intend to influence them.

Nondirective Reactions and Responses

Nondirective reactions and responses inform and encourage. No *imposition* of either information or encouragement is intended. These reactions occur primarily in phase 4 but may appear in phase 2. The following is an example of information giving:

1. **Interviewee:** Well, what can I do now?

2. **Interviewer:** You can plead guilty and explain your situation or you can take your chances with a trial.

Be specific in answers whenever possible. If you do not have the information, say so and promise to get it or refer the interviewee to a better qualified source. You need not have all the answers. As interviewer, you may encourage or reassure the interviewee by noting that certain feelings, reactions, or symptoms are normal and to be expected, such as,

1. **Interviewee:** I seem to get angry over nothing.

2. **Interviewer:** That's not unusual when someone is under constant stress.

There are quick ways to lose the trust and respect of an interviewee facing a difficult situation. You may give unrealistic assurances such as "There's nothing to worry about," "I'm sure everything will be just fine," or "Everything works for the best." You may "preach" to the person with "in the old days" comments such as, "You think you have it tough? When I was your age, I had to . . . " or "When we were first married, we faced . . . ." And avoid clichés:

> Every cloud has a silver lining.
> You'll look back and laugh at this someday.
> We all have to go sometime.
> It's always darkest before the dawn.
> You're a lucky person; why I know of a person who . . . .
> It could have been worse, you know.

Be careful of falling into the "we" trap. Think of when you experienced these all-too-common we'isms from counselors, teachers, health care providers, and parents:

> How are *we* feeling today?
> I think *we'll* make it.
> *We* must take it one step at a time.
> Are *we* ready for the final exam?

You may have felt like shouting, "What do you mean *we?* I'm the one taking the test (getting the shot, undergoing therapy, overcoming grief)!"

Directive Reactions and Responses

Directive reactions and responses go beyond encouragement and information to mild advice and evaluations or judgments. Directive reactions are employed in phases 2 and 4 and sometimes in phase 3. In the following interchange, the interviewer supports the interviewee's ideas and urges action:

1. **Interviewee:** I don't know if I can handle that kind of workload.
2. **Interviewer:** Why don't you try it?

A second type of directive response mildly questions the interviewee's comments or ideas. Be tactful and cautious when employing this technique:

1. **Interviewee:** I can't tell Janet I cheated on her.
2. **Interviewer:** Don't you think she has suspicions?

In a third type of directive response, the interviewer provides information and personal preference when asked, such as,

1. **Interviewee:** Would you work for a few years before deciding on an MBA?
2. **Interviewer:** Yes, I would, because I believe experience is valuable when studying for an MBA.

Directive reactions and responses may challenge an interviewee's actions, ideas, or judgments, or urge the person to pursue a specific course or to accept information or ideas. Both are mild, however. It is usually wise to employ directive responses only if nondirective responses do not appear to be working.

Highly Directive Reactions and Responses

Reserve highly directive reactions and responses for special circumstances. Exhaust all less directive means first. Suggestions and mild advice are replaced with ultimatums and strong advice that should be reserved for phase 4. The following are examples of highly directive responses and reactions:

1. **Interviewee:** I can't break my smoking habit. I've smoked all my life.
   Interviewer: Then there's not much reason for us to meet again. You've got to try.
2. **Interviewee:** What should I do?
   Interviewer: Here's what you've got to do. Cut up your credit cards. Make a careful monthly budget and stick to it. Buy no new clothes for a year. And limit entertainment expenses to $20.00 per week.

Highly directive responses are most appropriate for simple behavioral problems and least appropriate for complex ones that are based on long-time habits or firmly held beliefs and attitudes. Try to be a helper, not a dictator, because the change or solution must

ON THE WEB

Selecting counseling approaches and responses most appropriate for a particular interviewee and problem may be critical to the outcome of the interview. Philosophies and practices differ among counselors and counseling agencies. Use the Internet to explore the interviewing approaches currently advocated and illustrated by researchers, practitioners, and agencies when dealing with a variety of clients and problems. Useful sources are the Pamphlet Page (http://uhs.uchicago.edu/scrs/vpc/virtulets.html), the Counseling Center Village (http://ub-counseling.buffalo.edu/ccv.html), and Counseling and Psychological Services at Purdue University (http://www.purdue.edu/caps).

come from the interviewee. A hostile or stubborn person may turn you into a highly directive counselor and thus receive less understanding and reassurance and more evaluations and prescriptions. You can rarely force people to comply with instructions and regimens, even when you have the authority or power to punish or fire them.

Interviewer reactions and responses may enhance self-disclosure during interviews, so it is important that you select an appropriate directive or nondirective response. For example, use highly directive responses only after you have established a close relationship with the interviewee. Do not be shocked by what you hear, or do not show it. Preparation can reduce the number of surprises, making extreme or unusual reactions or comments less likely to shock you. Do not try to dodge unpleasant facts. Be honest and tactful, and let your voice, facial expressions, eye contact, and gestures communicate a relaxed, unhurried, confident, warm, and caring image. If you have a good working relationship with the interviewee, you can release tensions with tasteful and tactful humorous interventions and responses. Talk as little as possible, do not interrupt the interviewee, and listen empathically.

Actively seek agreement from the interviewee on the problem and possible remedies. But getting agreement is not enough; you must also work toward compliance with what has been agreed to. Compliance is best achieved by responding appropriately and by giving adequate information about what a person should and should not do, and why. A recent study revealed that question types do not seem to affect compliance, but interviewees who receive positive feedback comply more with the interviewer's requests and recommendations, return more often for counseling, and arrive earlier. These findings led the researcher to conclude that "how interviewers respond seems to make a crucial difference."[14] And another study discovered that interviewees are more likely to implement interviewer recommendations when there is a good match between the recommendation and the problem, the recommendation is not too difficult to implement, and the recommendation is built on the interviewee's strengths.[15]

5. Closing the Interview

The closing of the counseling interview is vital to the success of the entire interaction. If interviewees feel they have imposed on you or been pushed out the door as though on an assembly line, progress made during the interview may be erased, including the positive relationship established so carefully throughout.

The verbal and nonverbal leave-taking actions discussed in Chapter 3 explain how interviews are closed both consciously and unconsciously. Decide which means or combination of means best suits you and the other party.

There are a number of guidelines for closing counseling interviews. For instance, both parties should be able to tell when the real closing is taking place. Do not begin new topics when the interview has already come to a close, either in fact or psychologically. Do not expect to finish with a solution all worked out like a neatly wrapped package. Be content that thought has been stirred or that the interviewee was able and willing to discuss the problem or express feelings. Do not be overly concerned about not meeting all expectations; remember that you and the interviewee are human beings with failings. Leave the door open for further conversation. And be sincere and honest in the ways you close interviews.

6. Evaluating the Interview

Think carefully and critically about the counseling interviews you take part in. Only through perceptive analysis will you begin to improve your helping interactions with others. Be realistic, however, because you cannot expect complete success in all counseling interviews. They are interactions between complex human beings, at least one of whom has a serious problem and may not know or admit it. Many people, men in particular, have difficulty expressing feelings and emotions. Remember that your perceptions of how the interview went and how the interviewee reacted may be exaggerated or incorrect. You will be greatly surprised by your successes and your failures in attempting to help others. And some of each will be short-lived.

The following questions may serve as guides for your postinterview evaluations.

Preinterview Preparation

1. How thoroughly did I review available materials concerning the interviewee before the interview?
2. How well did I know myself and assess my level of counseling expertise?
3. How effectively did I assess how I communicate and come across with others, particularly this party?
4. How thoroughly did I review questions I might ask to get necessary information and make informed decisions?
5. How thoroughly did I review questions the interviewee might ask and how I might respond?
6. How successfully did I prepare a climate and setting in which openness and disclosure would be fostered?

Structuring the Interview

1. How effective was the opening?

2. How effectively did I blend directive and nondirective approaches?

3. How effectively and completely did I explain all options?

4. How effective was the closing?

Interviewing Skills

1. How skillful were my question techniques?

2. How appropriate were my responses and reactions?

3. How was the pace of the interview—too fast or too slow?

4. How effectively did I communicate with all members of a multiple-person party?

5. How effectively did I motivate the interviewee to communicate at Levels 2 and 3?

6. Did I take adequate notes without disturbing the interviewee or the process?

7. How effectively did I listen for comprehension, empathy, evaluation, and resolution?

Counseling Skills

1. How well did I adapt to this party and situation?

2. How effectively did I help the interviewee gain insights and make decisions?

3. How effectively did I discover the real problem?

4. Was I too eager to be liked by the interviewee?

5. Did I make promises I will not be able to keep?

6. Did I agree with the interviewee when I should have disagreed?

7. Did I try to handle a problem beyond my level of expertise?

8. How did my responses, feedback, and presentation of recommendations enhance the likelihood of interviewee compliance?

Your experiences and specific situations may add to or subtract from these lists of postinterview questions. The important point is to evaluate what you do in order to improve your helping skills.

Summary

You take part in a counseling interview whenever you try to help a person gain insights into a physical, mental, emotional, or social problem and discover ways to cope. The counseling interview may be the most sensitive of interview settings because it usually does not occur until a person feels incapable of handling a problem or a counselor decides that a helping session is needed. Preparation helps you determine how to listen, question, inform, explain, respond, and relate to each interviewee. No two interviews are identical because no two interviewees and situations are identical. Thus, many suggestions but few rules are available for selecting interview approaches, types of responses, questions, and structures.

A Counseling Interview for Review and Analysis

This interview is between a college student and a professor who teaches a course that is part of a qualifying system for majors. Students need an A or B in this course if they hope to declare a major. The student is retaking this course after getting a D the previous semester. His work to date indicates he will get a C this time around. He wants to see what he needs to do to improve his grade.

How effectively does the professor handle the opening? Which approach or approaches (directive, nondirective, or a combination) does she use? How appropriate is this choice? How effectively does the professor follow the four phases of counseling interviews developed by Echterling, Hartsough, and Zarle? How appropriate are the professor's reactions and responses? How appropriate is her use of questions? At which levels of disclosure (Level 1, 2, 3) are most of the student's revelations? How effective is the professor as a listener? How adequate is the closing? What are the chances of the student's compliance with suggestions and agreements?

1. **Student:** Professor Carter?

2. **Professor:** Yes, Jim, come on in. I've been waiting for you since nine o'clock.

3. **Student:** Oh, I'm sorry. I studied late last night and slept in.

4. **Professor:** Uh-huh. I haven't seen you in class this week.

5. **Student:** Well, uh, this is a hectic time of the semester. I've had trouble getting to most classes.

6. **Professor:** As I recall, you told me at the beginning of the semester that this is a do-or-die semester for you and that you were going to give it your best shot.

7. **Student:** Well, yeah, and I've been doing a lot better this semester.

8. **Professor:** What can I do for you this morning?

9. **Student:** Well, I've been checking out my grade situation in your class, and it looks like I'm heading toward a C. I really need at least a B.

10. **Professor:** I know.

11. **Student:** I study really hard for your exams, but my grades don't show the effort I put into them. I don't understand what's wrong.

12. **Professor:** Let me ask you some questions and see if the answers can give you some insights. Do you take detailed and carefully structured notes each day of class?

13. **Student:** Yeah, most of the time, but I have trouble keeping up with you sometimes.

14. **Professor:** Lecture notes are shown on the overhead and remain up for several minutes. Do you read assigned readings as each topic is being discussed in class or wait until exam time to read?

15. **Student:** I try, but I find I do best if I cram just before a test because I forget what I read weeks ago.

16. **Professor:** That strategy doesn't seem to be working, does it? Do you review class notes from the previous lecture-discussion before the next class begins?

17. **Student:** Sometimes.

18. **Professor:** Do you study with a good study group?

19. **Student:** No, I work best alone.

20. **Professor:** Do you attend help sessions before exams and remain for the question-answer period?

21. **Student:** I get to most help sessions, but I don't find the question-answer periods to be of much help.

22. **Professor:** Yes, I noticed you left early during the last help session. You would be surprised at the excellent questions other students raise that will be on the exams. One last question. Following an exam, do you meet with one of my assistants to see what you missed and why?

23. **Student:** I know you're busy and I don't want to take up your time. I don't find going over an old exam that I will not take again to be of much help.

24. **Professor:** You seem set on a series of strategies that have not been very successful.

25. **Student:** Well, yeah, I guess that's sort of true, but I really need help.

26. **Professor:** What do you think you need to do?

27. **Student:** I'm stumped. That's why I came in today. I need help.

28. **Professor:** What kind of help do you want?

29. **Student:** I need to figure out how to answer the questions on your exams. They seem vague and contradictory.

30. **Professor:** I see.

31. **Student:** I do really well on other exams in my major.

32. **Professor:** "Really well" means?

33. **Student:** I get 70s and some 80s as a rule in other classes.

34. **Professor:** Those are C and B– grades I imagine.

35. **Student:** Yeah, but that's all you need in other classes.

36. **Professor:** You know you need a B or better in my course to qualify as a major.

37. **Student:** Of course! That's why I'm here.

38. **Professor:** I have a class in just a few minutes. I'd like for you to think carefully about what you might do in the next few weeks to prepare more thoroughly for the next exam. Then come see me, and let's discuss what you have in mind.

39. **Student:** Well, okay, but I hoped you could give me some real help today.

40. **Professor:** I think I did. Think carefully about my earlier questions and your study strategies. I hope to see you in class tomorrow.

41. **Student:** Okay. I'll call you in a week or so.

Counseling Role-Playing Cases

Cheating on a Paper

The interviewee is a sophomore in college who has never cheated before. He recently has been having trouble with grades and needs an A in a sociology class to keep from going on probation. He found an excellent term paper done for this course several years ago and decided to hand it in as his own. The day after turning in the paper, the interviewee's conscience began to bother him, and he decided to talk with a professor in another department whom he knows quite well. The student must decide whether to tell the professor and apologize or let it go because the professor will never discover the truth. If he tells, the professor might fail him for the entire course and report him to the Dean of Students.

The interviewer has the reputation of being a good teacher and counselor. He knows the interviewee very well and finds it hard to believe that he handed in someone else's work. The interviewer has never had anyone come to him with a problem quite like this one.

An Employee-Employer Relationship

The interviewee is a legal secretary in her early 20s and has been working for a well-known attorney. She has discovered what she considers to be some unethical practices pertaining to a high-profile case. The interviewee has decided to quit working for the attorney because she does not want to get involved in an unethical and perhaps illegal situation. In addition, she does not want to create trouble for her employer, who is a nice person, an excellent attorney, and pays the interviewee well. When she tells him she is quitting, should she tell him the truth or make up a story? The interviewee decides to talk the matter over with a lifelong friend who is in human relations with a department store chain.

The interviewer is a 30-year-old human relations manager for the Hicks Department Store chain. The interviewee has asked to discuss a serious personal problem over lunch. The interviewer has a vague idea that the problem relates to the interviewee's work and knows that the interviewee enjoys her position.

Class Attendance

The interviewer is a counselor in a college residence hall where he has worked for nearly a year. The interviewee is one of 45 first-year students on his floor. The interviewee is girl-crazy, does not like to study, loves beer, and is thoroughly enjoying the freedom of not living at home. The residence hall where the interviewee lives is a coed unit that suits the interviewee just fine since his latest girlfriend lives in the same building. About the middle of the first semester, the interviewer received a report from the Dean of Students, office stating that the interviewee had not been attending classes for weeks.

The interviewee does not know why his floor counselor has asked to see him. He has broken no residence hall rules and gets along well with everyone on his floor. He does not know that residence hall counselors receive reports of students missing from classes.

Too Many Credit Cards

The interviewee is 23 years old and graduated from college two years ago in computer technology. While in college, she had very little money because she was paying nearly 75 percent of her college expenses. In addition to some loans, she became very dependent on credit cards to purchase books and supplies and to pay tuition. At first she could keep up with credit card payments, but then car trouble and dental expenses resulted in getting further and further behind. Now she is desperate. Several credit card companies are threatening action. She has decided to see a financial counselor to see what she can do and is seriously thinking of declaring bankruptcy.

The interviewer is 30 years old and sees young and old people who have gotten themselves caught in the easy credit trap. Many have become addicted to their credit cards. She does not like people to declare bankruptcy.

Student Activities

1. Visit a crisis center in your community or on your campus. Observe how volunteer counselors handle telephone counseling. Talk with counselors about their training techniques and self-evaluations. How does telephone counseling differ from face-to-face counseling?

2. Interview three kinds of counselors: a marriage counselor, a student counselor, and a financial counselor. How are their approaches and techniques similar and different? What kinds of training have they had and what kinds would they recommend for counselors in their occupations? In their estimation, what is a successful counselor?

3. Pick one of the counseling role-playing cases and develop a complete approach to the case, beginning with setting and furniture arrangement. How would you begin the interview? What questions would you ask? How much would you disclose about yourself—training, background, experiences, and so on? What kinds of reactions and responses would you use? What solution would you suggest? What would you do and not do to aid interviewee compliance? How would you close the interview?

4. You have undoubtedly been an interviewee in many counseling sessions during your lifetime, with interviewers ranging from parents, teachers, and employers to clergy, academic counselors, financial advisers, and health care providers. Pick out two or three of the best and two or three of the worst counselors you have encountered. Then make two lists, one of the counseling and communication characteristics of the best and one of the characteristics of the worst. Compare these to the research, principles, and techniques offered in this chapter.

Notes

1. Donald R. Atkinson, Francisco Q. Ponce, and Francine M. Martinez, "Effects of Ethnic, Sex, and Attitude Similarity on Counselor Credibility," *Journal of Counseling Psychology* 31 (1984), pp. 589–91.

2. Barbara Goldberg and Romeria Tidwell, "Ethnicity and Gender Similarity: The Effectiveness of Counseling for Adolescents," *Journal of Youth and Adolescents* 19 (1990), pp. 589–603.

3. Roger L. Worthington and Donald R. Atkinson, "Effects of Perceived Etiology Attribution Similarity on Client Ratings of Counselor Credibility," *Journal of Counseling Psychology* 43 (1996), pp. 423–29.

4. Sarah Knox, Shirley A. Hess, David A. Petersen, and Clara E. Hill, "A Qualitative Analysis of Client Perceptions of the Effects of Helpful Therapist Self-Disclosure in Long-Term Therapy," *Journal of Counseling Psychology* 44 (1997), pp. 274–83.

5. William A. Satterfield, Sidne A. Buelow, William J. Lyddon, and J. T. Johnson, "Client Stages of Change and Expectations About Counseling," *Journal of Counseling Psychology* 42 (1995), pp. 476–78.

6. Lennis G. Echterling, Don M. Hartsough, and H. Zarle, "Testing a Model for the Process of Telephone Crisis Intervention," *American Journal of Community Psychiatrists* 8 (1980), pp. 715–25.

7. Paul R. Turner, Mary Valtierra, Tammy R. Talken, Vivian I. Miller, and Jose R DeAnda, "Effect of Session Length on Treatment Outcome for College Students in Brief Therapy," *Journal of Counseling Psychology* 43 (1996), pp. 228–32.

8. Timothy P. Johnson, James G. Hougland, and Robert W. Moore, "Sex Differences in Reporting Sensitive Behavior: A Comparison of Interview Methods," *Sex Roles* 24 (1991), pp. 669–80; and Judy Cornelia Pearson, Richard L. West, and Lynn H. Turner, *Gender and Communication* (Madison, WI: Brown & Benchmark, 1995), pp. 149–52.

9. James R. Mahalik, Robert J. Cournoyer, William DeFranc, Marcus Cherry, and Jeffrey M. Napolitano, "Men's Gender Role Conflict and Use of Psychological Defenses," *Journal of Counseling Psychology* 45 (1998), pp. 247–55.

10. Anita E. Kelly, "Clients' Secret Keeping in Outpatient Therapy," *Journal of Counseling Psychology* 45 (1998), pp. 50–57.

11. Rebecca Leonard, "Attending: Letting the Patient Know You Are Listening," *Journal of Practical Nursing* 33 (1983), pp. 28–29; and Ginger Schafer Wlody, "Effective Communication Techniques," *Nursing Management,* October 1981, pp. 19–23.

12. Reprinted with permission of the Free Press, a Division of Simon and Schuster, from Arthur N. Turner and George F. F. Lombard, *Interpersonal Behavior and Administration.* Copyright 1969 by Arthur N. Turner and George F. F. Lombard.

13. Ruth Purtilo, *The Allied Health Professional and the Patient: Techniques of Effective Interaction* (Philadelphia: Saunders, 1973), pp. 96–97.

14. Peter Chang, "Effects of Interviewer Questions and Response Type on Compliance: An Analogue Study," *Journal of Counseling Psychology* 41 (1994), pp. 74–82.

15. Collie W. Conolly, Marjorie A. Padula, Darryl S. Payton, and Jeffrey A. Daniels, "Predictors of Client Implementation of Counselor Recommendations: Match with Problem, Difficulty Level, and Building on Client Strengths," *Journal of Counseling Psychology* 41 (1994), pp. 3–7.

Resources

Atkinson, D. R.; G. Morten; and D. W. Sue. *Counseling American Minorities: A Cross-Cultural Perspective.* Dubuque, IA: Brown and Benchmark, 1993.

Hansen, James C. *Counseling: Theory and Practice.* Boston: Allyn and Bacon, 1994.

Maple, Frank F. *Goal Focused Interviewing.* Thousand Oaks, CA: Sage, 1997.

Okun, Barbara F. *Effective Helping: Interviewing and Counseling Techniques.* Pacific Grove, CA: Brooks/Cole, 1997.

Palmer, Stephen, and Windy Dryden. *Counseling for Stress Problems.* Thousand Oaks, CA: Sage, 1995.

Ridley, Charles R. *Overcoming Unintentional Racism in Counseling and Therapy.* Newbury Park, CA: Sage, 1995.

The Health Care Interview

W e suspect that only a few of you are majoring in pharmacy, nursing, and health sciences or preparing to enter professional schools to become dentists, physicians, or veterinarians. However, each of you takes part in health care interviews several times a year as patients or consumers. Your participation will increase in the years ahead as you grow older and preventive medicine becomes increasingly important to catch medical problems early and to reduce health care costs.

Health care interviews can involve a wide variety of situations, ranging from treatment for poison ivy, the filling of a cavity, a routine physical checkup, an eye examination, the setting of a broken arm, and minor surgery, to major surgery and long-term care for a curable disease such as breast cancer or a currently incurable disease such as AIDS or Alzheimer's. Your interview may be scheduled days, weeks, or months in advance or occur without warning because of an accident, act of violence, heart attack, virus, or food poisoning.

Health care interviews are often tense and emotional, whether involving the embarrassment of a gynecological examination, the happiness of childbirth, the trauma of cancer detection, or fear of a diagnosis. For example, one of our students a few years ago was greatly embarrassed to admit that he had broken his arm while playing badminton. Another student was embarrassed because she was losing her hair during chemotherapy. And nearly all health care interviews are influenced by anxiety over the unknown, traditions, societal expectations, the medical bureaucracy, and health maintenance organizations (HMOs). Relationships may last for minutes (a brief consultation with a bone specialist or a blood pressure check by a nurse practitioner) or years (examinations and treatments by the family dentist, optometrist, or physician).

During the past few decades, research has revealed that communication between providers and patients plays a major role in health care delivery and patient satisfaction.[1] In a study on critical incidents in health care, Rubin notes that the findings "argue persuasively that patients in a variety of health care settings place a very high premium on personal treatment" and interpersonal communication.[2] In Great Britain, a study of communication between medical personnel and couples facing the death of a partner concluded that "poor communication causes more suffering than any other problem except unrelieved pain."[3] We as patients tend to be most satisfied when we are fully informed, treatments or problems are explained, both parties share personal information, and the provider uses humor.[4]

Many health care providers have assumed they and their colleagues would "acquire interpersonal skills through role-modeling or by trial and error without exposure to a formal teaching program."[5] Research indicates otherwise. Studies have revealed that the communication skills of medical students actually deteriorate when not exposed to training even though they have increasing experience with patients. Effective communication is too often taken for granted, with many health care professionals believing they communicate better than they do. Research by Moore and Schwartz discovered, for example, that nurses "*report* they communicate effectively verbally and nonverbally" but they are not always "*observed* to do so."[6] Experience alone has proven to be insufficient; skills need to be continually checked and refined. When training does take place, some medical professors argue, "too much emphasis has been given to the content of the interview and not enough to the process of the interview."[7]

The apparent shortcomings of health care providers have led researchers to focus on the professional as *the cause* of all communication problems between patients and medical personnel. As we have stressed throughout this book, however, interviews are two-way processes in which both parties share responsibility for the success and failure of interactions. Thompson emphasizes that "patients play an equally important role in both effective and ineffective communication."[8] She has discovered, for instance, that provider and consumer fail to ask questions at critical times during interviews. For example, a relative of one of the authors had been treated for years for recurring "indigestion" problems and had undergone all sorts of tests with little satisfaction. Her physician was shocked recently to discover in casual conversation about exercising that her family had a history of early deaths from heart attacks. She had never mentioned this history and the physician had never asked for it. Both parties shared the blame for this missed diagnosis. Sometimes we withhold information, consciously or unconsciously, unless an interviewer asks for it specifically so we can avoid bad news during a diagnosis.

Although the medical interviewer may play a dominant role in an interview, such as gathering information during an intake interview or a counseling session following surgery, the interviewer is most likely to switch hats frequently, depending upon the need of the moment. Within a 10- to 15-minute interaction with a patient, a physician, nurse, or dentist might act as an information seeker, information giver, counselor, and persuader—all of the major roles we have discussed in this book.

Because the interviewer plays so many roles in a typical health care interview, no series of stages as outlined in previous chapters is possible for health care interactions. This chapter begins with an extensive review and analysis of the health care relationship because it is critical for patient satisfaction and compliance. Then the chapter focuses on three tasks interviewers encounter most often in health care interviews: information getting, information giving, and counseling.

The Health Care Relationship

Although the relationship between interviewer and interviewee is important in all interview settings, its importance is greatly magnified in the health care interview. Some researchers argue that "the physician-patient relationship is perhaps the most critical component of the health care delivery process."[9] A person's apprehension before a selection interview or a performance review pales in comparison to a pending pelvic examination or revelation of test results for cancer or AIDS.[10] And the status of the interview parties in the health care interview cannot be matched in any counseling, persuasive, or journalistic setting. This relationship tends to be seriously lopsided. The medical professional is highly trained, speaks in scientific terms few understand, appears to be in control of both self and situation that is seen as routine, is seldom emotionally involved, and is fully clothed in a suit or uniform. The patient (literally one who bears or endures pain or suffering with composure and without complaint) is usually uninformed, has little medical knowledge or familiarity with medical language, has little or no control over self, is in an unfamiliar and threatening environment, sees the situation as a crisis, and may be partially nude, highly medicated, in severe pain, or anxious about life-and-death matters. The relationship between provider and patient is important to the medical interview because, as Kreps concludes, it "facilitates exchange of relevant health information, coordination of efforts, and provision of emotional support between interdependent health care consumers and providers."[11]

The history of health care in the United States has influenced communication between provider and consumer and thus the relationship between them. During the nineteenth century when physicians could do little scientifically to combat germs and bring people back to health, they established relationships by being always available and through caring and listening skills. During the twentieth century as science and technology enabled physicians to attack germs that cause diseases, caring and listening seemed less important and, for a time, scientific language, manner, and procedures brought new respect to providers. Unfortunately, this biomedical model also brought a power imbalance between patient and provider.[12] During the past 25 years, however, consumers have become increasingly dissatisfied with medical care and the communication that accompanies it. In a recent study that asked patients to describe their most memorable medical experiences, 39 percent expressed dissatisfaction with nurses, 36 percent with physicians, and 44 percent with receptionists and nontechnical personnel.[13] Unfortunately, health care providers see themselves as effective communicators who exude caring and empathy.

Ineffective communication and relationship building have led to dissatisfaction with health care services and alienation between providers and patients. Patients complain of lack of friendliness and warmth, lack of communication with themselves and their families, excessive technical language and jargon, and inadequate explanations. On the other hand, health care professionals complain of unrealistic expectations, control struggles, and failure of patients to comply with instructions. It is important to become aware of the perceptions, roles, and forces that mold the health care relationship to understand and improve communication in the health care setting.

The Provider's Perspective

Health care providers learn from training, role models, peer pressure, and the actions and comments of their superiors that they are to be "in control" at all times.[14] Many are understandably reluctant to share this control with patients and their families or even with other professionals, particularly physicians, nurses, emergency medical technicians, or staff members who are lower in the medical hierarchy. To maintain control under difficult and emotional circumstances, health care providers often adopt a professional distance or an impersonal attitude toward patients and their associates. They tend to be busy, task-oriented individuals who are reluctant to waste time on inconsequential chats with patients; time is a critical concern of providers. They want to diagnose and treat the disease as quickly and efficiently as possible so they can treat the next patient because they assess the quality of health care based on clinical and technical criteria, medical skills, and the manner in which patients are treated medically. Researchers have found that physicians tend to view most medical visits as *relatively routine,* and in routine situations, interviewers assume "their behavior is appropriate and their interpretations are accurate."[15]

Health care providers often stereotype patients. Patients are seen as being emotionally disturbed, having personality disorders, being childlike, and lacking in knowledge, understanding, and intelligence. The perception of the patient as a childlike dependent is often revealed in condescending attitudes and baby talk with adults. And, although the physician or nurse may call the patient by his or her first name or nickname, the patient nearly always refers to the provider as "the EMT," "the nurse," or "the doctor" and usually uses terms of address such as Dr., Miss, or Mr. Thus, the patient is partially to blame for the parent-child relationship. Health care providers often have very positive attitudes toward certain kinds of patients such as the middle-aged and very negative attitudes toward others such as adolescents. The "good patient" is cooperative, quiet, obedient, grateful, unaggressive, considerate, and dispassionate. "Good patients" tend to get better treatment than "bad patients." Patients seen as lower class tend to get more pessimistic diagnoses and prognoses. Overweight patients are deemed *less* likable, seductive, well educated, in need of help, or likely to benefit from help and *more* emotional, defensive, sincere, warm, and likely to have continuing problems. Balint writes that the doctor's individuality rather than the patient's needs or problems determines the nature and longevity of the doctor-patient relationship.[16]

The Patient's Perspective

Unlike providers who see most medical visits as routine, patients or consumers view visits "with apprehension and uncertainty, especially if they normally experience good health," and when people are uncertain and anxious, they closely monitor their own and the provider's behavior and communication.[17] When people seek medical care, often as a last resort because the pain has become unbearable, they openly admit that their health problems are beyond their control and they must turn to others for help. People in this position are disappointed with themselves and feel guilty, weak, or inadequate. If the problem affects their looks or results in the removal of an organ or limb, patients may not feel like "whole persons" and may experience changes in personality, ego, self-image, and identity.

Hospitalized patients often feel exceedingly vulnerable because they lose the security and familiarity of homes, jobs, routines, and normal relationships. They find themselves in threatening environments, deprived of their dignity, autonomy, authority, and freedom. A person who is a president of a university or a corporate executive one minute may not be able to decide when and where to go to the bathroom the next. Unlike the health care provider who focuses on diagnoses, technology, and treatment, the patient focuses on being ill and the *care* received. And good care is most often equated with

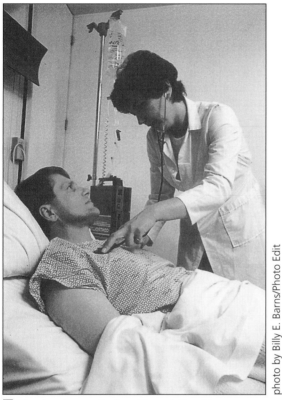

photo by Billy E. Barns/Photo Edit

■ *The development of positive relationships between health care providers and receivers is essential for effective communication and health care.*

personal treatment, interpersonal communication, and relationship building: listening, empathy, warmth, ease of communication, and ability to explain things in understandable ways rather than scientific efficiency.

Facing the unknown or an uncertain future frightens patients and their families and affects their perspectives. As Barnlund writes, "To be uninformed is to be communicatively impotent, and this dependent state is not one mature people tolerate gracefully."[18] To make matters worse, patients are surrounded by authority figures in lab coats, uniforms, and suits who appear to have unlimited power to foster or deny the simplest of requests and sharing of information. Life itself may be out of their control. It seems dangerous to displease medical authorities in any way, and since patients detect that time must not be wasted, they generally try to be patient, brave, and above all, cooperative; this often means silence.

People react to their altered and threatening circumstances in a variety of ways. Many become self-centered and develop unrealistic expectations of health care providers from receptionists to physicians. Some become overly conservative, rigid, and suspicious. They see small incidents they would have ignored when well as affronts or signs of rejection. Others react angrily and lash out at nurses, technicians, staff members, and visitors. Still others withdraw into themselves or become overly dependent; some may even want to remain ill to get attention, escape from the world, or achieve personal ends.

Poor interpersonal communication is a major factor in patient dissatisfaction, patient noncompliance, and incidence of malpractice litigation. Dissatisfied patients often change physicians on this basis alone, sometimes even turning to medical quacks in search of reassurance, kindness, consideration, and communication. On the other hand, we all know of family members who have stuck with "good old Doc" who was hopelessly behind the times and incapable of giving them the specialized care needed; but old Doc communicated with them, took the time to listen, and seemed to care.

Positive relationships between health care providers and patients are essential for effective communication and good health care. Mutual trust, cooperation, maximum self-disclosure, meaningful feedback, and a sharing of content are needed. However, too many situations are characterized by one-sided control and an impersonal setting, with neither party wanting to be involved in the interview. Such an atmosphere produces relationships in which conflict and fear prevail. Too often patients tend to agree with medical authorities during interviews and then ignore prescriptions, regimens, and advice afterward. The provider-patient relationship can be positive when both parties work at it.

Ways to Enhance Interview Relationships

The good news is that recent research indicates that health care providers are beginning to see the importance of relational communication and believe that it is their responsibility to establish effective relationships.[19] At the same time, consumers of health care are beginning to exert more control in medical interviews and, as a result, are complying more with recommendations and prescriptions.[20] Patient-centered care (PCC), in which patient "needs, preferences, and beliefs are respected at all times," is a growing movement in the United States.[21] These trends can be enhanced if both parties learn and practice good interpersonal communication principles.

Health care providers and consumers must realize that both interview parties, while unique in some ways, also share many perceptions, needs, values, beliefs, attitudes, and experiences. Both are real persons, not medical magicians or miracle workers and not disease carriers or chronic whiners. Both need to maintain a degree of control, dignity, privacy, self-respect, and comfort. Providers and consumers can enhance relationships. For instance, each party must strive to understand and identify with the other. Health care providers must realize how their messages can frighten and confuse consumers, and consumers must realize how important it is for them to explain their symptoms clearly and fully to receive appropriate treatment. The health care interview must be a collaborative effort.[22]

Training can enhance the caregiver's communication skills and significantly increase patient satisfaction. A recent study revealed that personnel who underwent training in communication (unlike those in a control group who did not) provided effective openings and closings, listened effectively, interrupted only when necessary, observed and responded to verbal and nonverbal cues, used appropriate question techniques, and exhibited warmth, concern, and interest. A growing number of medical programs are encouraging students to spend a day lying in a hospital bed or using a wheelchair or crutches to experience the feelings of helplessness and dependency patients experience. Some medical schools are using mock patients to test the competence and compassion of students. Others are replacing plastic models with real people, sometimes medical students themselves, to train students how to conduct physical examinations.

Health care consumers can benefit from visits to hospitals and nursing homes and stints as volunteers to see what it is like to be in the receptionist's, nurse's, technician's, and physician's shoes. While medical personnel can reduce relational distance by not hiding behind uniforms and policies, patients can do the same by not hiding behind hospital gowns and their inability to communicate because of their conditions. Both can reduce emotional distance by encouraging two-way dialogues about feelings rather than one-way monologues about technical matters. Neither party, however, should push the relationship too quickly—before either is ready to talk about personal matters and concerns. Zakus and others suggest five ways for health care providers to enhance relationships with patients, and this is good advice for patients as well: (1) Try to be relaxed, confident, and comfortable; (2) show interest in the patient as an individual; (3) maintain objectivity; (4) be sincere and honest; and (5) maintain appropriate control over the

O N   T H E   W E B

Because the quality of communication directly affects the relationships and outcomes of health care interviews, it is important for you to understand communication problems unique to the health care situation. Use the Internet to identify a number of these problems addressed in recent and ongoing research, and note the solutions or actions proposed or implied in this research. Pay particular attention to problems caused by sex, age, and cultural differences between interviewer and interviewee. Begin your search with Internet resources such as Health Communication around the World (http://www.sla.purdue.edu/health-comm/), Third International Conference on Communication, Aging and Health (http://uxl.eiu/~cfdgb/welcome.html), *Journal of Health Communication* (http://www.tandf.co.uk/jnls/hcm.htm), Health Communication Network (http://www.hcn.net.au).

structure of the interview without shutting off the other party.[23] It is not surprising that communication between health care givers and receivers with relational histories is both different from and better than communication between those with no relational history. The former tend to practice the suggestions listed above.

All of our suggestions for improving health care relationships and communication must be tempered, of course, with the realization that people—providers and consumers of health care—are not the same. Gender, for instance, may make a difference. Some studies have discovered that women tend to be more concerned about health (perhaps a learned difference), are more verbal in interactions (perhaps because they know more about health-related matters), have more communication time with providers (but their concerns are taken less seriously), and are more active communicators.[24] Older patients tend to be more reluctant to "challenge the physician's authority" than are younger patients,[25] and physicians (most under 65) are "significantly less egalitarian, less patient, less attentive, and less respectful with older patients," and are "less likely to raise psychosocial issues with them."[26] In one study, African-American and Puerto Rican respondents indicated that their race, ethnicity, and lower economic status impacted negatively on their information seeking (particularly HIV-related information) and health care.[27] As we noted in earlier chapters, cultural differences affect interpersonal communication. For instance, Arab cultures practice close proximity and kissing among men; both could be seen as offensive in American or European health care interactions. American Indian and Asian cultures prize nonverbal communication, whereas American and German cultures prize verbal communication. Many societies, particularly those in Asia, are less assertive, and this affects their communicative roles and control-sharing in medical interviews. Kreps and Thornton discuss the differences in medical philosophies in different countries and suggest the difficulties these might pose for nonnative caregivers and consumers working or being treated in them. French physicians tend to discount statistics and studies and emphasize logic; German physicians tend to be authoritarian romantics; English physicians tend to be paternalistic; and American physicians tend to be aggressive and want to "do something."[28] Both consumers and providers of health care can enhance communication and relationships by being aware of how different people perceive each role and its purposes.

The remainder of this chapter focuses on principles and practices that enable health care providers to get information, give information, and counsel effectively.

Getting Information in the Health Care Interview

Health care providers spend a great deal of time trying to get vital information from patients to diagnose problems and prescribe treatments. This is not an easy task. We begin first by identifying and illustrating barriers to getting information and then by offering suggestions for getting information more effectively.

Barriers to Getting Information

Physical or emotional factors often make it difficult for interviewees to remember or articulate information accurately and completely. For example, frightened and anxious patients often unintentionally leave out significant parts of their medical histories or intentionally minimize symptoms to get a good diagnosis. Mothers spontaneously recall only about half of their children's major illnesses. When patients feel ashamed or embarrassed, they may camouflage the real problem and make rationalizing statements such as, "You know how women (men, teenagers, elderly) are." Depth of self-disclosure, often with Level 1 interactions, is likely to be shallow if the patient does not trust the medical technician, nurse, or physician or is not assured of strict confidentiality, a difficult guarantee to give in a crowded emergency room or multiple-bed room. An interviewee may give short answers in hopes of ending an uncomfortable interview as soon as possible. And some patients give answers they think interviewers want to hear to please revered or feared medical authorities or to avoid receiving bad news in return.

The traditional history-taking interview, with its long inventory of closed questions, has produced more problems than it has solved. The manner is typically impersonal, and the questions often have little if anything to do with a patient's current problem. As one patient remarked after such an experience, "He spent so long on things not wrong with me—two pages of lists—that it made me feel the interview had nothing to do with my illness at all."[29] It is not surprising that patients in great pain or discomfort become angry or numbed, what one researcher calls "negative weakening,"[30] when responding to a series of seemingly irrelevant questions. We have all been in situations like the following:

1. **Doctor:** Any chest pains?

2. **Patient:** No. *(strongly)*

3. **Doctor:** Any irregular breathing?

4. **Patient:** No. *(fairly strong)*

5. **Doctor:** Any trouble swallowing?

6. **Patient:** No. *(average stress)*

7. **Doctor:** Any high blood pressure?

8. **Patient:** No. *(weak)*
9. **Doctor:** Any allergies?
10. **Patient:** (shaking head)

One of the authors, while visiting a family member in a nursing home in Florida, witnessed this same wearing-down process. A very elderly, ill, confused, and somewhat angry patient had just been admitted to a bed in the room with the family member. Two medical personnel entered soon thereafter and began to ask a very long list of questions; many would have been difficult for a medically fit person to answer adequately. It did not take long to see that the patient was exhausted and increasingly confused. The interview droned on, even though one of the medical questioners turned to the other and remarked, "I don't know why we don't do this over two or three days. It's not like she's going anywhere." The "interview" continued.

A series of rapid-fire closed questions (sometimes referred to as the Spanish Inquisition approach) clearly sets the tone for the health care relationship: The interviewer is in charge and wants short answers (usually yes or no), is in a hurry, and is not interested in explanations. But simple yes or no answers may not reveal potentially tragic misunderstandings of simple medical terms. Too many health care providers assume that everyone is familiar with medical jargon, or they feel that it is useful only for communication between medical professionals. The following real examples, although somewhat comical, illustrate not only patient misunderstanding of simple jargon but the dangers of bipolar questions.[31] What if the patients had simply answered yes or no? The interviewers would not have detected any problems.

1. **Provider:** Have you ever had a history of cardiac arrest in your family?

   Patient: We never had no trouble with the police.

2. **Provider:** Multiple births?

   Patient: *(after a long pause)* I had a retarded child once. *(Perhaps thinking multiple meant Siamese twins)*

3. **Provider:** Do you have dentures?

   Patient: No. I have schizophrenia.

A recent study discovered that 20 percent or more of respondents did not know the meaning of such common medical terms as abscess, sutures, tumor, and cervix, and the percentages jumped as soon as more uncommon terms were used, such as edema and triglyceride. Persons over 65 are less knowledgeable that ones between 45 and 64, and more educated respondents are most familiar with medical terms.[32] While jargon gets more attention from researchers, ambiguous questions pose equally serious problems. During nearly every medical interview, health care providers ask such questions as:

Do you have regular bowel movements?
Do you feel tired?
Are you ever short of breath?

What does "regular" mean? Who doesn't feel tired? Who hasn't been short of breath? We witness 18- and 19-year-old college students breathing "heavily" from "shortness of breath" after they walk two flights of steps to our offices.

Medicine has yet to reach the point scientifically or medically where simple check-lists are sufficient to determine diagnoses, prognoses, or treatments. Neither have patients, despite television dramas, public discussions, and health care campaigns, become familiar or comfortable with medical jargon and abbreviations. Too many health care providers fear that if they push the right buttons, they will end up with a 30-minute conversation when they are already four patients behind. Thus, closed questions and abrupt cutoffs of answers are more the rule than the exception. Studies indicate that patients rarely ask for clarification or repetition of questions or words in questions. They simply defer to the provider's expertise and authority.[33]

Ways to Improve Getting Information

Many techniques can improve getting information in health care interviews. First, provide an atmosphere in which the interviewee feels free to express opinions, feelings, and attitudes—even ones with which you might disagree. Because health care providers and consumers rely so heavily on interviews to get information, the process is simply taken for granted, and both parties fail to realize that cooperation is necessary for a *sharing* of information. A sense of collaboration leads to more information as well as greater patient satisfaction and compliance with instructions. Select, if at all possible, a comfortable, attractive, quiet, nonthreatening, private location free of interruptions, where questions and answers will remain confidential. Check out a typical pediatrics area and one for adults of all ages and conditions. The first will be designed thoughtfully in every detail (pictures, aquarium, toys, plants, books) for the young patient and parents to minimize fear and anxiety and maximize communication and cooperation. The second is most likely to be a stark treatment room with a few medical gadgets and a small stack of ancient magazines of little interest to anyone.

Second, open the interview with a pleasant greeting. Introduce yourself (name and position) if unacquainted with the patient or family, and explain what is needed and why. Realize that if you address the patient by first name ("Hi Mary Lou") while you address yourself by title ("I'm Doctor Tatloff"), you are setting a superior-subordinate relationship from the start. Although these may seem like commonsense actions, many health care providers without training in communication skills tend to do none of them. A simple orientation can reduce anxiety, satisfy curiosity, and allay suspicions. Do not prolong rapport building unless trust is very low because most patients prefer to get to the point after a brief, pleasant orientation. If you are late for an appointment or the patient has been waiting for some time, apologize for the inconvenience and explain the reason for it. Simple politeness—treating people the way you like to be treated—can defuse an angry or impatient interviewee and show that you value other's time and are sensitive to the person's perceptions and needs. Too many medical personnel and institutions treat individuals like numbers (even calling them by number from the waiting room) or objects on an assembly line, then cannot understand why they encounter hostility or lack of cooperation. Spiers has shown the relevance of "politeness theory" and how its use can enhance communication in the health care interaction:

> Politeness is used primarily to ease social interaction by providing a ritualistic form of verbal interaction that cushions the stark nature of many interactions such as requests, commands, or questioning. Politeness provides a means for covering embarrassment, anger, or fear in situations in which it would not be to one's advantage to show these emotions either as a reflection of one's self or because of the reaction of the other.[34]

Spiers offers excellent advice on how to help health care receivers "save face" in a threatening situation over which they have little control.

Third, employ individualized rather than routine approaches. Try to adapt to each patient. Be aware of communication apprehension common in medical interviews, particularly ones dealing with sensitive or embarrassing topics. You can reduce apprehension by carefully explaining examination procedures, being attentive and relaxed, treating patients as equals, and talking to them in their street clothes rather than backless hospital gowns.

Fourth, enhance turn-taking during health care interviews so patients feel free to ask questions, provide more extensive information, and comment on what you are saying. You can encourage turn-taking by pausing, maintaining eye contact, nodding your head, and using verbal responses that invite interactions. Be careful of verbal routines that give patients false cues for turn-taking. These include such verbal reactions as "Okay?" "Right," and "Uh-huh" that appear to invite responses but actually may stifle turn-taking, particularly when the receiver detects a pattern of false cues. Turn-taking is essential if the interview is to be a collaborative effort.

Fifth, employ a funnel sequence that begins with open-ended questions and gradually narrows to specific symptoms, diagnoses, and treatments. Open-ended questions communicate interest in what the interviewee has to say and show you trust the interviewee to give valuable information, information you might not think to ask for. Such questions may evoke a wide range of information and are relatively free of interviewer bias. Open questions invite rather than demand answers and give patients a greater sense of control over what is being volunteered and discussed.

Early questions should not be too open-ended, however. A patient experiencing fear, pain, or confusion may have difficulty responding to "How are you today?" "Tell me about yourself," or "Well, what seems to be the problem?" Use more focused questions such as "What kind of difficulties are you having with your back?" "What sort of night did you have?" or "Tell me about the stress in your life right now." Watch out for the open-to-closed switch in which you ruin a perfectly good open question with a quick bipolar follow-up before the patient can reply, such as the following:

1. **Interviewer:** What problems are you having with your back? Pain in the hip?
2. **Interviewer:** What have they given you for that? A painkiller?
3. **Interviewer:** Well, how do you feel? Any more problems with you shoulder?
4. **Interviewer:** How long have you had that? Since you fell from the ladder?

Use an inverted funnel sequence with caution because closed questions early in an interview may set a superior-to-subordinate tone and communicate desire (if not determination) of the provider to maintain control of the interaction. Closed questions communicate that you want simple, specific answers. And that is what most patients will provide—and nothing more. It is easy to hide fears, feelings, and symptoms you do not want to share in short answers. By the time you reach the open questions in the inverted funnel sequence, respondents may be unable or unwilling to adjust to new expectations and continue giving brief answers.

And sixth, as patients respond to questions, listen carefully and actively. Listen for hidden as well as obvious answers and requests and for evidence of confusion, hesitation, apprehension, or uncertainty. Very few activities in medical interactions are as important as listening for comprehension, empathy, evaluation, and resolution. Most people will respond if you appear interested, attentive, and relaxed. Research indicates that what patients want most is an opportunity to tell their stories, but they are often interrupted within 18 seconds by interviewers who ignore what they are saying and try to transform stories into medical terms and logic. Kreps and Thornton emphasize the importance of stories in health care:

> Stories are used by consumers of health care to explain to their doctors or nurses what their ailments are and how they feel about these health problems. . . . By listening to the stories a person tells about his or her health condition, the provider can learn a great deal about the person's cultural orientation, health belief system, and psychological orientation toward the condition.[35]

Patients often try in vain to get health care providers to pay attention to their personal sense of illness rather than technical cause and treatment. Avoid unnecessary interruptions, especially if the interviewee becomes overwhelmed with emotion. Some writers suggest that the success of medical interviews may be due to the number of words the provider does *not* say. Health care interviewers tend to control interviews, and the consumer's main, and sometimes only, opportunity to give the facts he or she wishes is at the beginning when answering the opening question. A recent study discovered that physicians tend to control interactions through questioning and topic change, that is, by introducing, developing, and dissolving topics.[36] Some providers use "empathic opportunity terminators" to redirect interviews and cut off further revelations of patients' emotional concerns.[37] Here are two examples. In the first, the physician changes the subject.

1. **Patient:** I'm in the process of retiring . . . .
2. **Physician:** You are?
3. **Patient:** Yeah. I'll be 66 in February.
4. **Physician:** Do you have Medicare?

In this second example, the physician retreats to the earlier, less emotional concern.

1. **Patient:** And right now I'm just real nauseous and sick. I lost 10 pounds in 6 days.
2. **Physician:** Okay. And you lost 10 pounds.

3. **Patient:** And I'm getting, and I'm getting worse. I'm not getting any better.
4. **Physician:** Okay . . . and right now you are not able to eat anything, you said?

Be patient, and use nudging probes to encourage interviewees to continue answering. Avoid irritating interjections such as "right," "fine," "okay," and "good." Avoid guessing games. Ask, "When does your knee hurt?" not "Does it hurt early in the morning? When you walk? When you sit for a while? How about climbing the stairs?" The patient may go along with whatever your questions suggest. Be careful of multiple or double-barreled questions such as the following.

1. **Interviewer:** And in your family, had there been high blood pressure or strokes? And what about cancer?
    Interviewee: No.
2. **Interviewer:** Did you ever have mumps, chicken pox, or measles? Have a rash?
    Interviewee: Yes.

What do the no and yes responses mean in these exchanges? Are the patients saying yes or no to all parts of the questions or only to the last one in a series?

If you have any doubt about what a person has said, employ reflective and mirror probes to be sure you understand thoroughly and accurately. Use these probing questions carefully, however. Some people will go along with your reflectives or mirrors even if their answers are error-filled, feeling that you as a medical authority know what they should have said. Thus, a neutral reflective has become a leading question, perhaps without you knowing it. Listen for important cues in answers, what patients are suggesting or inferring verbally and nonverbally. A study of medical students at Oxford University revealed how important it is to learn the art of cue detection:

> All the patients provided many useful cues about the nature of their problems. Hence, it was disconcerting that 74 percent of the students failed to pick up more than a fraction of these. Only 4 percent of the students were able consistently to detect and use the cues given them. Patients were often forced to repeat key phrases such as "I was feeling very low" as many as 10 times to get the students to acknowledge their mood disturbance.[38]

Learn to listen and observe. Do not be in a hurry to ask your next question. Ask one question at a time and avoid the open-to-closed switch pitfall discussed earlier. Ask an open question and don't talk until the patient has responded. At times you may have to make it clear to parents, spouses, relatives, or friends present that you want the *patient* to answer. This is particularly prevalent when interviewing children in the presence of a mother or father. Stifle helpful others tactfully and sensitively.

Sometimes, like a good journalist, you must ask a closed question (who, what, when, where, how, or why) to make thorough diagnoses and recommend courses of action. It takes skill to ask the appropriate type of question at the proper time as well as to know when to remain silent and let the patient talk. Remember that active interviewees not only volunteer more information and opinions but understand more clearly what is taking place and experience a better medical outcome than inactive, passive interviewees.[39] Patients are also more satisfied with their health care.

As a general rule, avoid leading questions such as "You are staying on your diet, aren't you?" Few patients will say no when the interviewer clearly wants a yes or will give a different answer when a question reveals the *correct* or *expected* answer. Leading questions may be necessary to persuade some patients to follow regimens and take prescriptions properly. Harres discusses the importance of "tag questions" in health care interviews.[40] She offers as examples, "You can bend your knee, can't you?" and "You've been here before, haven't you?" Although these look like common leading questions, Harres discovered that they elicit information, summarize and confirm information, express empathy, and provide positive feedback. The key is to *encourage* rather than *lead* the interviewee.

Giving Information in the Health Care Interview

Giving information seems so simple, but it is a deceptively complex and difficult process. Health care settings nearly always involve the giving of vital information and instructions, and it is essential that consumers of health care understand, remember, and act upon this information satisfactorily. One study reveals that within 10 to 80 minutes, less than 25 percent of patients remembered everything they had been told, and patients who remembered most had received only two items of information. Another study of 25 patients discovered that within a short time, 10 showed significant distortions of information and 4 showed minimum distortions.[41] Several studies have focused on prescribed drugs. They discovered, for example, that 7 percent of prescriptions are never filled, 4 percent are never picked up, and 20 percent are never taken.[42] Some suggest that from 30 to 50 percent of prescribed drugs are either not taken or are taken improperly. Although health care consumers are guilty of forgetting and distorting facts, they continue to criticize lack of sufficient information more than any other aspect of medical care. Health care providers give important information constantly, so they must learn what causes loss, distortion, and failure to comply and how to transmit information more effectively.

Causes for Loss and Distortion of Information

Inaccurate or inadequate communication of health care information and failure to comply with this information is usually caused by attitudes of medical personnel, problems of patients, or ineffective transmission methods. Health care providers place much greater emphasis on eliciting information than on giving information and explanations. Although the strongest predictor of patient satisfaction is how much information is given on the condition and treatment, two-thirds of physicians in one study underestimated patient desire and overestimated how much information they had given. In a typical 20-minute interview, less than 2 minutes is devoted to information giving. And health care providers tend to give information selectively. For instance, they tend to give more information and elaborate explanations to educated, older, and female patients than to others.

Patients' illnesses, fears, anxieties, and suspicions often affect their ability to hear, listen, comprehend, and remember.[43] Some people protect themselves from unpleasant experiences by refusing to listen or understand. Many patients interpret information and instructions according to their personality types. For example, if a physician says, "You have six months to a year to live," a pessimist may tell friends, "I have less than six months to live," but an optimist may declare cheerfully, "The doctor says I might live for years." We tend to hear what we want to hear. Patients desire information but want the provider to make decisions so they can blame providers if something goes wrong. The physical and psychological condition of a patient may lead to extreme distortions in simple interactions. The patient in the following exchange was a 36-year-old chronic paranoid schizophrenic:[44]

1. **Nurse:** Oh, Elsie, you're having some difficulty, aren't you? Let me give you a hand . . . .

2. **Patient:** *(Elsie gazes downward rather blankly. She stares first at her own right hand and then at her left hand, and then looks at the nurse's hand.)*

3. **Nurse:** *(The nurse looks down to see what Elsie is staring at; there is a pause, then)* No, Elsie, I don't mean I can really give you a hand! Of course, I can't! *(pause)* I would just like to help you.

Patients, like Elsie, and many with fewer major medical problems, often take words quite literally. Metaphors, which by their nature require the receiver to complete the implied comparison, may confuse persons who are frightened and anxious. Also, older patients tend to have less knowledge and understanding of medical situations and greater difficulties in giving information.[45]

Patients often do not understand or comprehend information because they are untrained or inexperienced in medical situations. Few settings are as replete with communication-stifling gadgets, smells, noises, and goings-on. Patients are bombarded with unfamiliar abbreviations (IV, EKG, D & C, pre-op, chemo) and strange jargon (adhesions, contusions, nodules, cysts, benign and malignant tumors, steroids, chemotherapy, diuretic, metastases). The aura of authority may inhibit people from asking for clarification and explanation of information even though they must rely on the provider to evaluate and understand technical information. For instance, a woman who did not understand what nodule meant did not ask questions "because they all seem so busy, I really did not want to be a nuisance . . . and anyway she [the nurse] behaved as though she expected me to know and I did not want to upset her."[46] The strange setting combined with hope for a favorable prognosis may lead patients to oversimplify complex situations or to interpret information as not really aimed at *them*. Others are afraid they will appear stupid if they ask questions and reveal they do not understand words, explanations, problems, or procedures.

Some researchers have studied the influence of "lay theories" on communicating risk to patients. These include many theories you probably hold: All "natural" products and practices are healthful; if I do not feel bad, I do not need to take (or to continue to take) this medicine; if a little of this medicine helps, a lot of it will do more good; if this medication worked for me, it will work for you; and radiation and chemicals are bad for you. According to Rowan and Hoover, "Scientific notions that contradict these and other powerful lay theories are often difficult for patients to understand because patients' own lay alternatives seem irrefutably commonsensical."[47] Providers must be able to detect these theories and counteract them if their instructions are to be effective.

Health care providers contribute to information loss and distortion in a number of ways. Studies indicate that health care providers underestimate receivers' need for information and overestimate the amount of information they give. But on the other hand, they may assume patients understand all they just told them and take few steps to verify that *assumption.* The physician in the following example was trying to give a thorough briefing to a patient about what tests had revealed:[48]

> Well, Mrs. Jones, I expect you'd like to know exactly what is wrong with you. *(pause)* Well, we here at this hospital believe in telling you and all our patients the truth about their illnesses and their treatments. I promise you that we will tell you everything you want to know. Well, now, in your case, we have carried out all the investigations and tests, and sadly, we have found that you have a rather nasty tumor on your ovary . . . . I am sure you know what a tumor is . . . . Well, now, we have had some very good results from giving our patients a course of treatments which involves a series of injections of platinum.

The physician left the room convinced that he had informed his patient thoroughly and effectively. Unfortunately, this patient later exclaimed to family and friends, "Thank goodness I haven't got cancer. I only have a tumor." Five days later she learned that she had cancer from another patient, not from her physician or other medical personnel.

Research with health care providers reveals that many are reluctant to give information to patients because (1) they do not want to get involved, (2) they fear patients' reactions, (3) they fear they are not allowed to give information, or (4) they are afraid of giving incorrect information. Nurses, for instance, often have insufficient data about a patient's condition, may be uncertain about what the physician wants the patient to know, or may be unaware of what the patient already knows. Too often the result is an uninformed or misinformed patient or family.

Information is also lost or distorted because of ineffective transmission methods. Too often when patients are informed, they are overloaded with data, details, jargon, and explanations far beyond their abilities to comprehend. Ley discovered in a study that 82 percent of patients could recall two items, but the percentage dropped to 36 percent for three or four items, 12 percent for five or six items, and 3 percent for seven or more items.[49] Ley also discovered that health care providers tend to give diagnostic information before instructions. Not surprisingly, patients remember diagnostic information twice as often as instructions because diagnosis seems more important to them or they are still thinking about it (and paying little attention to the provider) during the instructions and information giving. Some providers, by habit or intent, deal in confusing and meaningless ambiguities: "Now, Mr. Brown, you will find that for some weeks you will tire easily, but you must get plenty of exercise."[50] How long is "some weeks"; what does "tire easily" mean; and how much is "plenty" of exercise, not to mention type of exercise? Simple repetitions of jargon, slang, abbreviations, or unknown procedures do not help. The patient learned nothing in this example:[51]

1. **Interviewer:** We need to get you ready for an EKG.

2. **Interviewee:** A what?

3. **Interviewer:** An EKG! *(vocal stress)*

4. **Interviewee:** Oh.

Medical personnel too often rely on a single medium such as a written note or a brief oral exchange with a patient. Davis and Cohen relate numerous problems caused by such efforts.[52] For example, a physician provided a poorly written abbreviation O. J. that was read as O. D., which means right eye. The patient received a solution in the right eye rather than orally in orange juice. A nurse coming on duty on a ward asked one patient if he was Mr. Thomas, and he said "Wright." Mr. Wright received Mr. Thomas's medication. Health care providers often respond to information requests with a simple "Here's a pamphlet that'll answer all of your questions."[53] There is little chance that a patient will either read or understand pamphlets provided with little or no comment or instruction.

Transmitting Information More Effectively

Jones and Phillips write that "the best doctor-patient relationship is one in which there is a maximum of information exchanged in a reasonable time."[54] How can this all-important exchange be brought about? First, establish a relationship of trust and confidence with each patient or consumer by being informative, helpful, understanding, and communicative. This means listening, touching, looking at the patient, and sounding confident, friendly, and sensitive. The information you give must seem authentic, a judgment patients often base upon effective presentation. A recent study revealed that adherence to medication and instructions is most likely when communication between parties is optimal.[55] If you detect a patient referring to or acting on one of the lay theories mentioned earlier, Rowan and Hoover recommend that you (1) help him or her recognize the theory, (2) recognize its reasonableness, (3) show its inadequacy, and (4) establish the greater adequacy of the medical/scientific theory or practice.[56]

Second, encourage patients to ask questions so they can make informed decisions. Too many health care providers believe erroneously that patients do not want much information and, if they do, they will ask for it. Providers must provide clear and adequate information and recognize that a silent interviewee is probably feeling intimidated or too hopelessly confused to follow instructions. And both parties must recognize their differences of opinions but work to understand one another and resolve these differences in an open and questioning manner.

Third, do not overload patients with information or professional language. Discover what they (including perhaps family and friends) know and proceed from that point, eliminating unnecessary or irrelevant facts. Relate new information to information the interviewee already understands. Reduce explanations and information to common and simple terms because patients indicate greater satisfaction with nontechnical and simple language and have more difficulty comprehending and recalling technical language. Define technical terms and procedures, or translate them into words and experiences patients understand. You might present information in two or more brief interviews instead of a single lengthy one. As a rule, provide only enough information to satisfy the patient and the situation. For medications, necessary information includes the name, benefits, and possible side effects in explicit statements. Do not assume the patient understands any of these. When possible, involve family members or friends so they can help retain and interpret information and aid in compliance with instructions.

Fourth, organize items of information systematically so they are easy to recall. Try presenting important instructions first so they do not get lost in reactions to the diagnosis. Repeat important items such as benefits and side effects two or more times during an interaction so they will stand out and be easier to recall.

Fifth, practice good communication skills. When giving information orally, emphasize important words, dates, figures, warnings, and instructions to aid patients' memories. Use your voice (pitch, loudness, speed, tone, pauses) to substitute for the underlining, bold lettering, highlighting, and italicizing used in printed materials. Be sure that important words and phrases stand out from less important words. And be aware of how your voice and manner might influence a patient. One researcher discovered that a physician emphasized the danger of swallowing medication for a canker sore in such a direct and dire manner that the patient did not get the prescription filled. Another physician employed self-deprecating humor and a lighter tone when prescribing an acne medication, and it was filled.[57] Listen and watch for nonverbal signs that the patient is confused, unsure, or overwhelmed. Common cues are gasps, moans, puzzled expressions, raised eyebrows, or looking down. Do not rush through information.

Sixth, use a variety of media to present information, including pamphlets, leaflets, charts, pictures, slides, videos, models, and audio recordings. Never use just a pamphlet. Dentists, for example, often use models of teeth to explain dental problems and videos to show the benefits of flossing and brushing frequently. Emergency medical technicians use mannequins to teach CPR. And knee surgeons use facsimiles of knee joints to explain injuries and treatment. Patients report that they find written materials included with prescriptions to be helpful but admit they do not always read them. And provide written records of conversations, prescriptions, and instructions.

Seventh, include a number of sources to reinforce and repeat important information and instructions. A common practice today is for the attending physician to fill out a prescription order but rely upon the pharmacist to explain its benefits and possible side effects. Research indicates that compliance, understanding, and proper use are enhanced when both the physician and the pharmacist provide the same information; however, patients prefer to get information from their physicians.[58] Other important sources of information include nurses, technicians, patient representatives, family members, and receptionists.

Eighth, involve patients in the information giving process. Encourage them to ask questions as you go along, not at the end of your presentation, and listen for misinterpretations. Ask the patient to repeat or recall what you have said so that you can listen for distortions, missing pieces, and misunderstandings. Ask for definitions or explanations of key terms, medications, diagnoses, or regimens. See if the person can apply what you have said or tell you why certain procedures must be followed.

Ninth, make sure that all staff in the organizational hierarchy are thoroughly informed about the status of all patients. Take the time to review available data, and know exactly what you can and cannot tell each patient. Do not *assume* you are informed, because if you are uninformed, the patient will not only be uninformed or misinformed but perhaps treated erroneously and fatally.

Counseling in the Health Care Interview

Most health care providers are trained to be task oriented. Not surprisingly, they perceive their tasks to be the care and treatment of physical ailments they were trained for in medical, dental, nursing, or technical school. They tend to rely more on verbal expertise to gain compliance rather than empathy to gain understanding of a nonphysical problem. But with ever greater emphasis on treating the whole person, the provider needs to become a counselor to help a patient understand and deal with a problem, whether it is physical or not. Unfortunately, many barriers inhibit counseling in the health care setting.

Barriers to Effective Counseling

Patients and their families often make counseling difficult by becoming silent, withdrawing, or complaining about a physical problem rather than admitting a psychological one. A student in the department of one of the authors told her instructor a few years ago that she had missed a test and several classes because she had cancer. Only later did the instructor learn through a third party that the student had long suffered from severe depression and suicidal tendencies; the student felt it was more acceptable to have a "physical" than a "mental" problem. Often when nothing is found wrong physically, a patient is dismissed with a diagnosis of stress, nerves, or an overactive imagination. The emotional or physical problem remains intact until its seriousness demands attention and proper treatment, if it is not too late. A patient may take days to get up the nerve to ask a nurse or physician about death, physical impairment, or cancer, and the patient is likely to hint at the concern rather than ask directly.

Health care professionals spend little time talking to patients because they have many tasks to perform and see talking as social activity rather than nursing or doctoring. The interviewer initiates most interactions and usually makes them short. Care and treatment are considered more important than getting acquainted with the patient. Predictably, interviewers often fail to detect subtle cues that a patient wants to talk about a serious topic. They find silence awkward. Many providers talk instead of listening and observing, often rarely looking at the patient during an entire interaction.

photo by Joe Doakes

Health care professionals may spend little time talking with patients because they are task oriented rather than people oriented.

Health care providers employ a variety of blocking tactics to avoid counseling or getting involved. Some make jokes or deny the seriousness of a problem; others pursue the least threatening line of conversation. One of our female friends was concerned about results of stress in her job, but when she mentioned this during a routine visit with her physician, he shut her off with, "Which women's magazine did you get that diagnosis out of?" Common tactics include ignoring the patient's comment or question, pretending not to hear, becoming engrossed in a physical task, changing the subject, pretending to have a lack of information, hiding behind hospital rules, passing the buck to the registered nurse on the floor or a specialist, using an empathic terminator discussed earlier, or simply running away. The nurse in the following exchange illustrates common blocking tactics:[59]

1. **Nurse:** There you are dear. OK? *(gives a tablet to the patient)*

2. **Patient:** Thank you. Do you know, I can't feel anything at all with my fingers nowadays.

3. **Nurse:** Can't you? *(minimal encouragement)*

4. **Patient:** No, I go to pick up a knife and take my hand away and it's not there anymore.

5. **Nurse:** Oh, I broke my pen! *(walks away)*

This patient desperately wanted to talk to the nurse about his disturbing and worsening condition, at least to get a little acknowledgment. She was determined not to get involved.

Health care providers must understand themselves, particularly their reactions to counseling situations and outside factors that might influence them. For example, when a patient started talking about his father's death, a resident physician switched to the less emotional topic of the patient's mother. The resident later explained that he thought the patient might cry, not exactly an emergency. Upon further questioning, however, it was discovered that the resident's own father had died eight months earlier. He was protecting himself rather than the patient.[60]

Guidelines for Effecting Counseling In Health Care

Review carefully the principles and guidelines presented in Chapter 11 on counseling interviewing. These are easily adapted to the health care situation. Approach each interview with the realization that five relational factors are critical: empathy, trust, honesty, validation (when a person feels others accept and respect what she or he has to say), and caring.

Set aside time to talk to each patient and work at establishing a close relationship. Even if only a few minutes, this time is likely to be a major event in the relationship and good therapy for both parties. You will become someone the patient can confide in and better able to detect subtle requests for help. Therefore, you should strive for collaboration in the interview by showing respect for the patient's agenda and encouraging mutual sensitivity. Health care counseling is likely to be effective when information about a person is gathered and evaluated, possible treatments are identified and weighed, and treatment decisions are implemented successfully.

Use directive, nondirective, and combinations of these approaches (see Chapters 2 and 11) to enhance communication and self-disclosure. Sharf and Poirier have used a theoretical framework developed by psychiatrists Szasz and Hollender to teach medical students how to select appropriate interviewing approaches.[61] An active (directive approach) is recommended when a patient is passive and unable to participate. An advisory (nondirective) approach is recommended when a patient is compliant because of acute illness and thus not at full capacity. A mutual participation (combination directive-nondirective) approach is recommended when gathering data, solving problems, and managing an illness of a patient who can participate fully.

Employ a number of tactics to encourage patients to talk. For instance, if you share your own experiences and feelings, the patient is more likely to confide in you, thus enhancing self-disclosure and getting beyond Level 1 and 2 interactions. Employ nonverbal communication (smiles, nods, touches, and eye contact) to show that you care about the patient. Listen with comprehension and empathy (not sympathy) so you can see the situation as the patient does. Avoid making judgments as you try to clarify and interpret a patient's problem. Use open-ended, reflective, and mirror questions to encourage patients to talk and clarify their meanings. Do not ask too many questions or seem overly curious. Use a range of responses and reactions (from highly nondirective to highly directive), and avoid giving advice unless the patient lacks information, is misinformed, or does not react to less directive means.

Employ positive and reinforcing techniques for past performance such as following prescribed regimens, taking prescribed medications, and showing up on time for treatments. Avoid fear appeals and threats because more often than not they lead to patient denial or avoidance of regimens, medications, and checkups.

Approach a solution to the problem when the patient is ready; do not push for a solution too soon. Present clear courses of action, not bland reassurances. Fully one-third of all patients fail to comply with medical advice, and the figure jumps to 50 percent "when treatment instructions are 'preventive,' when patients are without symptoms, and when the treatment regimen lasts for a long period of time."[62] Present specific instructions and demonstrate that they are easy to follow. You should also convince the patient that the remedy will work and that dire consequences may result if instructions are not followed (stroke brought on by high blood pressure, liver damage caused by drinking too much alcohol, gum disease due to not flossing). Remember, however, that you need not, and indeed cannot, solve the problem for the patient.

Summary

The health care interview is difficult and complex. Situations vary from routine to life threatening, and the relationship between health care provider and patient is affected by tradition, myths, professional and societal expectations, and the differing perceptions of both parties. Both providers and patients often feel threatened, and many take defensive measures ranging from reticence to hostility to escape. The provider may act as information giver, information getter, and counselor within a brief interview. Each role is fraught with difficulties, but the difficulties can be recognized and overcome. The provider (from receptionist to physician) must realize that good communication is essential for effective health care and that communication skills do not come naturally or merely with experience but require thorough training and practice.

A Health Care Interview for Review and Analysis

This interview is between a nurse practitioner and a 27-year-old woman who has fallen from a ladder while wallpapering her bathroom. A neighbor rushed her to an emergency medical center because her right arm appeared to be broken near the shoulder. The patient is in a great deal of pain. She has just been admitted to a treatment room.

Assess the relationship between patient and practitioner. How effectively does the practitioner get information and give information? How effectively does the practitioner counsel the patient? How appropriate is the blend of directive and nondirective reactions and responses? How effectively does the practitioner detect cues from the patient? How effectively does the practitioner use questions? How does the patient help and hinder the interview process?

1. **Practitioner:** Erica Vorhees?
2. **Patient:** Yes.
3. **Practitioner:** How are we doing?
4. **Patient:** Not very well, I'm afraid.
5. **Practitioner:** I'm sure that's true. What did you do?
6. **Patient:** I fell from a ladder while wallpapering my apartment.
7. **Practitioner:** That's not good. I see it's your right arm. Can you move it?
8. **Patient:** It's too painful.
9. **Practitioner:** Okay. Are you okay otherwise; any pain in your back or legs?
10. **Patient:** I've got a headache and my right hip is very sore.
11. **Practitioner:** Well, we'll need some x-rays. Let me get your blood pressure.
12. **Patient:** Can I have something for the pain?
13. **Practitioner:** Of course. *(takes the blood pressure reading)* Your blood pressure is a bit high, but that's to be expected. Now let me get your temperature.
14. **Patient:** It's really hurting.
15. **Practitioner:** I know. Broken arms can be very painful.
16. **Patient:** I don't know what I'm going to do with school starting in a week.
17. **Practitioner:** Yes, it's about the end of summer already. My kids can't believe vacation is almost over, but they've been getting bored the past few weeks.
18. **Patient:** It really hurts, and I'm getting nauseous.
19. **Practitioner:** That's a classic symptom. We'll give you something for that. Your temperature is fine.

20. **Patient:** I can't believe I did something so stupid. And with so many things happening in the next few weeks.

21. **Practitioner:** Would you like a painkiller now or after x-rays?

22. **Patient:** Now!

23. **Practitioner:** We need to give this in the hip.

24. **Patient:** Will I be in a cast or what?

25. **Practitioner:** I suspect you will simply be in a sling—unless you need surgery and perhaps a pin.

26. **Patient:** Surgery?

27. **Practitioner:** Usually a sling will do.

28. **Patient:** A broken arm in a sling?

29. **Practitioner:** Yes. The break may be too high for a cast, and besides, we like to avoid casts if possible.

30. **Patient:** It sure hurts.

31. **Practitioner:** They always do, but it will ease up with some painkillers.

32. **Patient:** I hope so. It's pretty bad right now. And I've got so much to do during the next few weeks.

33. **Practitioner:** You're not going to be able to do much for a few weeks. Here's Jacob. He'll take you down to x-ray, and Dr. Dearborn will be in to see you when you get back. *(leaves the room)*

Health Care Role-Playing Cases

An Emergency Room Patient

The patient was brought into the hospital by EMTs at 4:30 in the afternoon after suffering severe chest pains during high school football practice. He wants to go home and is insisting that the pains were caused by overexertion in the heat. The season opener is just a week away. The nurse must get a medical history from the patient. She knows he is impatient and may become hostile if the interview seems irrelevant or prolonged, but she must ask a series of questions. He keeps asking to see a doctor, but the emergency room doctor is unavailable at the moment because of a multiple-car accident on the interstate.

A Terminally Ill Patient

The patient is 62 years old and just retired from a sales manager position with a large company. She was admitted for exploratory surgery after suffering blurred vision and severe headaches. She retired early so she could do the traveling she had always dreamed about, including cruises to Hawaii and Alaska during the next year. The interviewer is the patient's surgeon, who has asked to speak with the patient and her family about the results of the surgery and tests on tissues taken from behind the right eye. The surgeon must explain that inoperable cancer has been found in brain tissues and that the patient is unlikely to live more than six to nine months.

A Young Child and His Family

The patient is eight years old and has experienced nausea and diarrhea on and off for several days. At first his parents did not think much of the problem and did not begin the usual treatment until two days ago. He seemed fine otherwise. Now they are afraid their lack of concern may have caused or prolonged a serious problem. They feel guilty for having been negligent. The interviewer is the child's pediatrician, who must try to get information about the condition and treatment from the child. The child's parents, however, are now overly anxious to be helpful and will attempt to answer most questions. The physician must be very tactful and, above all, must avoid giving any impression that the parents are to blame for their child's problems.

A Hostile and Disturbed Patient

The patient is a long-term resident at Fairview Nursing Home. He rarely has visitors or receives telephone calls and has become increasingly reticent. When staff members try to talk with him or cheer him up, he becomes hostile and withdraws even more. He views minor incidents as personal affronts and insults. The interviewer is a counselor at a local medical health facility who is often asked to counsel patients at Fairview. In this first conversation, the interviewer hopes to begin establishing trust and a cooperative relationship and to discover why the patient avoids visits and conversations with others.

Student Activities

1. Visit a friend at a long-term health care facility in your community. Observe how physicians, nurses, technicians, orderlies, and office staff interact with patients. How do their positions in the health care hierarchy affect their relationships with your friend? What are the strengths and weaknesses of their communication techniques?

2. Visit a pediatric ward of a local hospital. Observe how physicians, nurses, technicians, orderlies, and office staff address and interact with their young patients. Talk with some of the staff about how their communication training and interviewing techniques have been adapted to children. If they have worked with both adults and children, what communication problems have they encountered that are unique to different age levels?

3. Arrange to observe a medical counseling interview, perhaps for a friend or family member. Try not to be an obvious third party. Observe the opening, questions, responses, nonverbal behavior of both parties, self-disclosure, effect of interruptions, suggestions, directive and nondirective techniques, and the closing. Write a detailed report of the interview with suggestions for improvement.

4. Interview three different types of health care providers (nurse, nurse practitioner, physician, technician, pharmacist, dentist, physical therapist, chiropractor) about their information giving techniques. How do they present information so it will be understood, remembered, and followed? What problems do they experience most often with information giving? How do they try to avoid them?

Notes

1. Donald J. Cegala, Kelly S. McNeilis, Deborah Socha McGee, and A. Patrick Jonas, "A Study of Doctors' and Patients' Perceptions of Information Processing and Communication Competence During the Medical Interview," *Health Communication* 7 (1995), p. 179; and Dale E. Brashers and Austin S. Babrow, "Theorizing Communication and Health," *Communication Studies* 47 (1996), pp. 243–51.

2. Brent D. Rubin, "What Patients Remember: A Content Analysis of Critical Incidents in Health Care," *Health Communication* 5 (1993), p. 106.

3. Averial Stedeford, "Couples Facing Death II—Unsatisfactory Communication," *British Medical Journal* 24 (1981), pp. 1098–101.

4. D. Fasbinder, "Patient Perceptions of Nursing Care: An Emerging Theory of Interpersonal Competence," *Journal of Advanced Nursing* 20 (1994), p. 1085; and Judith Ann Spiers, "The Use of Face Work and Politeness Theory," *Qualitative Health Research* 8 (1998), p. 28.

5. Alan S. Robbins et al., "Teaching Interpersonal Skills in a Medical Residency Training Program," *Journal of Medical Education* 53 (1978), p. 998.

6. K. W. Moore and K. S. Schwartz, "Psychosocial Support of Trauma Patients in the Emergency Department by Nurses, as Indicated by Communication," *Journal of Emergency Nursing* 19 (1993), pp. 297–302.

7. Barry J. Edwards, Robb O. Stanley, and Graham D. Burrows, "Communication Skills Training and Patient's Satisfaction," *Health Communication* 4 (1992), pp. 155–70; R. A. Barbee and S. A. Feldman, "Three-Year Longitudinal Study of the Medical Interview and Its Relationship to Student Performance in Clinical Medicine," *Journal of Medical Education* 45 (1970), pp. 770–76; and Sonia L. Nazario, "Medical Science Seeks a Cure for Doctors Suffering from Boorish Bedside Manner," *The Wall Street Journal,* March 17, 1992, p. B1.

8. Teresa Thompson, "The Invisible Helping Hand: The Role of Communication in the Health and Social Service Professions," *Communication Quarterly* 32 (1984), pp. 150, 152, and 154.

9. Laura L. Cardello, Eileen Berlin Ray, and Gary R. Pettey, "The Relationship of Perceived Physician Communicator Style to Patient Satisfaction," *Communication Reports* 8 (1995), p. 27; see also Rubin, p. 107.

10. Steve Booth-Butterfield, Rebecca Chory, and William Beynon, "Communication Apprehension and Health Communication and Behaviors," *Communication Quarterly* 45 (1997), pp. 235–50.

11. Gary L. Kreps, "Relational Communication in Health Care," *Southern Speech Communication Journal* 53 (1988), pp. 344–59.

12. Barbara F. Sharf and Richard L. Street, Jr., "The Patient as a Central Construct: Shifting the Emphasis," *Health Communication* 9 (1997), p. 3.

13. Rubin, p. 109.

14. Patricia Geist and Jennifer Dreyer, "The Demise of Dialogue: A Critique of Medical Encounter Ideology," *Western Journal of Communication* 57 (1993), pp. 233–46; and Gary L. Kreps and Barbara C. Thornton, *Health Communication: Theory and Practice* (Prospect Heights, IL: Waveland Press, 1992), pp. 44–53.

15. Richard L. Street and John M. Wiemann, "Differences in How Physicians and Patients Perceive Physicians' Relational Communication," *Southern Speech Communication Journal* 53 (1988), p. 425.

16. Michael Balint, *The Doctor, His Patient, and the Illness* (New York: International Universities Press, 1975), pp. 4, 217, and 276–279.

17. Street and Wiemann, p. 425.

18. Dean C. Barnlund, "The Mystification of Meaning: Doctor-Patient Encounters," *Journal of Medical Education* 51 (1976), pp. 716–25.

19. Donald J. Cegala, Deborah Socha McGee, and Kelly S. McNeilis, "Components of Patients' and Doctors' Perceptions of Communication Competence during a Primary Care Medical Interview," *Health Communication* 8 (1996), pp. 23–24.

20. Denise Wigginton Cecil, "Relational Control Patterns in Physician-Patient Clinical Encounters: Continuing the Conversation," *Health Communication* 10 (1998), pp. 140–41.

21. Bruce L. Lambert, Richard L. Street, Donald J. Cegala, David H. Smith, Suzanne Kurtz, and Theo Schofield, "Provider-Patient Communication, Patient-Centered Care and the Mangle of Practice," *Health Communication* 9 (1997), pp. 27–43.

22. Marti Young and Renee Storm Klingle, "Silent Partners in Medical Care: A Cross-Cultural Study of Patient Participation," *Health Communication* 8 (1996), pp. 29–53; and Patricia Geist and Lisa Gates, "The Poetics and Politics of Re-Covering Identities in Health Communication," *Communication Studies* 47 (1996), pp. 218–28.

23. Sylvia E. Zakus et al., "Teaching Interviewing for Pediatrics," *Journal of Medical Education* 51 (1976), pp. 325–31; and Marie R. Haug, "The Effects of Physician/Elder Patient Characteristics on Health Communication," *Health Communication* 8 (1996), p. 256.

24. Haug, pp. 253–54; and Anne S. Gabbard-Alley, "Health Communication and Gender," *Health Communication* 7 (1995), pp. 35–54.

25. Connie J. Conlee, Jane Olvera, and Nancy N. Vagim, "The Relationships among Physician Nonverbal Immediacy and Measures of Patient Satisfaction with Physician Care," *Communication Reports* 6 (1993), p. 26.

26. Haug, pp. 251–52.

27. Karolynn Siegel and Victoria Raveis, "Perceptions of Access to HIV-Related Information, Care, and Services among Infected Minority Men," *Qualitative Health Care* 7 (1997), pp. 9–31.

28. Kreps and Thornton, pp. 157–78. See also Gary L. Kreps, *Effective Communication in Multicultural Health Care Settings* (Thousand Oaks, CA: Sage, 1994).

29. Allen J. Enelow and Scott N. Swisher, *Interviewing and the Patient* (New York: Oxford University Press, 1986), pp. 47–50; and A. D. Wright et al., "Patterns of Acquisition of Interview Skills by Medical Students," *The Lancet,* November 1, 1980, pp. 964–66.

30. Roger W. Shuy, "The Medical Interview: Problems in Communication," *Primary Care* 3 (1976), p. 376.

31. Shuy, pp. 376–77.

32. Carol Lynn Thompson and Linda M. Pledger, "Doctor-Patient Communication: Is Patient Knowledge of Medical Terminology Improving?" *Health Communication* 5 (1993), pp. 89–97.

33. Julie W. Scherz, Harold T. Edwards, and Ken J. Kallail, "Communicative Effectiveness of Doctor-Patient Interactions," *Health Communication* 7 (1995), p. 171.

34. Spiers, pp. 25–47.

35. Kreps and Thornton, p. 37.

36. Marlene von Friedericks-Fitzwater, Edward D. Callahan, and John Williams, "Relational Control in Physician-Patient Encounters," *Health Communication* 3 (1991), pp. 17–36.

37. Anthony L. Suchman, Mathryn Markakis, Howard B. Beckman, and Richard Frankel, "A Model of Empathic Communication in the Medical Interview," *Journal of the American Medical Association,* February 26, 1997, pp. 678–82.

38. G. P. Maguire and D. R. Rutter, "History-Taking for Medical Students," *The Lancet,* September 11, 1976, pp. 556–58.

39. Analee E. Beisecker, "Patient Power in Doctor-Patient Communication: What Do We Know?" *Health Communication* 2 (1990), pp. 105–22.

40. Annette Harres, "'But Basically You're Feeling Well, Are You?': Tag Questions in Medical Consultations," *Health Communication* 10 (1998), pp. 111–23.

41. P. Ley, "What the Patient Doesn't Remember," *Medical Opinion Review* 1 (1966), pp. 69–73; and Joshua Golden and George D. Johnson, "Problems of Doctor-Patient Communication," *Psychiatry in Medicine* 1 (1970), pp. 127–49.

42. L. J. Heyduck, "Medication Education: Increasing Patient Compliance," *Journal of Psychosocial Nursing* 29 (1991), pp. 32–35; and Sharon Lee Hammond and Bruce L. Lambert, "Communicating about Medication: Directions for Research," *Health Communication* 6 (1994), pp. 247–51.

43. Katherine E. Rowan and D. Michele Hoover, "Communicating Risk to Patients: Diagnosing and Overcoming Lay Theories," in *Communicating Risk to Patients* (Rockville, MD: The U.S. Pharmacopeial Convention, 1995), pp. 74–75.

44. "Talking Points No. 12," *Nursing Times,* April 16, 1981, p. 676.

45. S. Deborah Majerovitz, Michele G. Greene, Ronald D. Adelman, Gerald M. Brody, Kathleen Leber, and Susan W. Healy, "Older Patients' Understanding of Medical Information in the Emergency Department," *Health Communication* 9 (1997), pp. 237–51; and Thompson and Pledger, pp. 89–97.

46. Patricia MacMillan, "What's in a Word?" *Nursing Times,* February 26, 1981, p. 354.

47. Rowan and Hoover, p. 74.

48. MacMillan, p. 355.

49. Ley, pp. 69–73.

50. F. S. Hewitt, "Just Words: Talking Our Way through It," *Nursing Times,* February 26, 1981, pp. 5–8.

51. "Talking Points No. 9," *Nursing Times,* March 26, 1981, p. 556.

52. Michael Cohen and Neil Davis, *Medication Errors: Causes and Prevention* (Philadelphia: Stickley, 1981), pp. 46 and 71.

53. Rubin, p. 108.

54. A. Jones and G. Phillips, *Communicating with Your Doctor* (Carbondale: Southern Illinois University Press, 1988), p. 24.

55. M. Robin DiMatteo, Robert C. Reiter, and Joseph C. Gambone, "Enhancing Medicated Adherence through Communication and Informed Collaborative Choice," *Health Communication* 6 (1994), p. 261.

56. Rowan and Hoover, p. 76.

57. Roxanne Parrott, "Exploring Family Practitioners' and Patients' Information Exchange about Prescribed Medications: Implications for Practitioners' Interviewing and Patients' Understanding," *Health Communication* 6 (1994), pp. 267–80.

58. Parrott, p. 278; and David H. Smith, Karen Graham Cunningham, and William E. Hale, "Communication about Medicines: Perceptions of the Ambulatory Elderly," *Health Communication* 6 (1994), pp. 290–91.

59. Jill M. Clark, "Communication in Nursing," *Nursing Times,* January 1, 1981, p. 16.

60. Nicholas G. Ward and Leonard Stein, "Reducing Emotional Distance: A New Method to Teach Interviewing Skills," *Journal of Medical Education* 50 (1975), p. 612.

61. Barbara F. Sharf and Suzanne Poirier, "Exploring (Un)Common Ground: Communication and Literature in a Health Care Setting," *Communication Education* 37 (1988), pp. 227–29.

62. Shelley D. Lane, "Communication and Patient Compliance," in Loyd F. Pettegrew, ed., *Explorations in Provider and Patient Interaction* (Louisville, KY: Humana, 1982), pp. 59–69.

Resources

Beck, Christina S.; Sandra L. Ragan; and Athena du Pre. *Partnership for Health: Building Relationships between Women and Health Caregivers.* Mahwah, NJ: Lawrence Erlbaum, 1997.

Kreps, Gary L. *Effective Communication in Multicultural Health Care Settings.* Thousand Oaks, CA: Sage, 1994.

Montgomery, Carol Leppanen. *Healing through Communication: The Practice of Caring.* Newbury Park, CA: Sage, 1993.

Roter, Debra, and Judith A. Hall. *Doctors Talking with Patients, Patients Talking with Doctors: Improving Communication in Medical Visits.* Westport, CT: Auburn House, 1992.

Stewart, M.; J. B. Brown; W. W. Weston; I. R. McWhinney; C. L. McWilliam; and T. R. Freeman. *Patient-Centered Medicine: Transforming the Clinical Method.* Thousand Oaks, CA: Sage, 1995.

Thompson, Teresa L. *Communication for Health Professionals: A Relational Perspective.* Lanham, MD: University Press of America, 1988.